GAME DEVELOPMENT WITH UNITY

BY MICHELLE MENARD

Course Technology PTR
A part of Cengage Learning

COURSE TECHNOLOGY
CENGAGE Learning

Australia • Brazil • Japan • Korea • Mexico • Singapore • Spain • United Kingdom • United States

COURSE TECHNOLOGY
CENGAGE Learning

Game Development with Unity
By Michelle Menard

Publisher and General Manager,
Course Technology PTR: Stacy L. Hiquet

Associate Director of Marketing:
Sarah Panella

Manager of Editorial Services:
Heather Talbot

Marketing Manager: Jordan Castellani

Senior Editor: Emi Smith

Project/Copy Editor: Kezia Endsley

Technical Reviewer: Jonathan Tanner

Interior Layout Tech: MPS Limited, a Macmillan
Company

Cover Designer: Mike Tanamachi

Indexer: Larry Sweazy

Proofreader: Gene Redding

For product information and technology assistance, contact us at
Cengage Learning Customer & Sales Support, 1-800-354-9706

For permission to use material from this text or product,
submit all requests online at **www.cengage.com/permissions**
Further permissions questions can be emailed to
permissionrequest@cengage.com

All images © Course Technology unless otherwise noted.

All trademarks are the property of their respective owners.

Library of Congress Control Number: 2010942056

ISBN-13: 978-1-4354-5658-7

ISBN-10: 1-4354-5658-0

Course Technology, a part of Cengage Learning
20 Channel Center Street
Boston, MA 02210
USA

Cengage Learning is a leading provider of customized learning solutions with office locations around the globe, including Singapore, the United Kingdom, Australia, Mexico, Brazil, and Japan. Locate your local office at: **international.cengage.com/region**

Cengage Learning products are represented in Canada by Nelson Education, Ltd.

For your lifelong learning solutions, visit **courseptr.com**

Visit our corporate website at **cengage.com**

Printed in the United States of America
1 2 3 4 5 6 7 12 11 10

For James. While games aren't really his thing,
I'm pretty sure he'll at least flip through
the first couple of pages and see this.

About the Author

Michelle Menard is a writer and designer currently at Firaxis Games, based out of Hunt Valley, Maryland. Previously she has worked as a freelance writer, an editor, and associate producer, and also a brief stint as a UI programmer, contract artist, and museum kiosk programmer. When not attempting to finish her latest project, she procrastinates by breaking various body parts on her spinning wheel or by making Pokémon catch-rate charts in Excel.

Michelle holds an MFA in Game Design from the Savannah College of Art and Design, and a double BA from Brown University in Applied Mathematics and Music. On the side, she works as a masters-level course developer for SCAD.

Contents

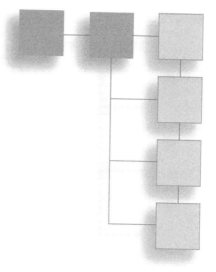

PART I   IN THE BEGINNING. **1**

Chapter 1   Preface **3**

Inboxes and Emails 3

Chapter 2   Introduction **7**

What Will Be Covered (and What Not) 7

Intended Audience 8

The Book's Structure 9

Installation Instructions 10

The Unity Engine 10

Using the DVD Contents 12

Optional Installs 12

Chapter 3   An Overview of the Unity Engine **15**

Getting Acquainted with the Interface 15

The Project View 16

The Hierarchy View 18

The Inspector 20

The Toolbar 22

The Scene View 23

The Game View 33

The Animation View 39

The Console and Status Bar 39

The Profiler and Asset Server 40

Customizing the Editor 40

Unity's Basic Concepts 42

Available Unity Licenses 43

Editor Summary 44

Chapter 4   Your First Game: Where to Start? **47**

Basic Design Theory 47

Finding the Core Idea 51

Brainstorming 51

Researching Other Games 53

Paper Prototyping: It's Not Just for Business Software 54

Planning It All Out 55

A Basic Outline 55

A Simple Level Document 56

Getting Started 60

PART II   ASSEMBLING THE GAME ASSETS **61**

Chapter 5   Setting the Stage with Terrain **63**

Unity's Terrain Engine 64

Customizing Terrain 66

Building Height Using a Heightmap 66

Painting Height Using Brushes 67

Painting Textures 73

Placing Trees 78

Cluttering It Up with Grasses and Detail Meshes 82

Terrain Settings 87

Lighting and Shadows 89

Adding a Skybox and Distance Fog 93

Adding Water to Your Terrain 95

Chapter 6   Building Your Environment: Importing Basic Custom Assets **97**

Design First, Then Build 97

Importing Textures 99

More on Importation 99

Supported Formats 103
Importing Textures for *Widget's* Terrain 104
Importing Basic Meshes 114
Setting Up Simple Shaders and Materials 119
Unity-Provided Shaders 121
Bumps, Spec, Cubes, and Details 124
Assigning Shaders and Materials 127
Making a Custom Skybox Material 132
Adding Water 134
Helpful Tips for Working with Assets 137
Prefabs, Prefabs, Prefabs! 137
Mass Selecting and Grouping Objects 138
Snapping to the Grid 139
Reworking the Terrain 139

Chapter 7   Creating Characters 141
Basic PC 101 141
Importing Characters and Other Nonstatic Meshes 142
Introducing *Widget* 142

PART III   BRINGING YOUR PROPS TO LIFE WITH INTERACTIVITY 153
Chapter 8   Scripting in Unity 155
One Editor, Three Languages, a Whole Lotta Choice 155
Picking a Script Editor, or, Do You Want Autocompletion
with That? 157
Fundamentals of Scripting in Unity 159
Variables 160
Operators and Comparisons 171
Operators 171
Comparisons 173
Conditionals 175
The if Statement 175
The if-else Statement 176
The switch Statement 177
The Conditional Operator 178
Loops 178
The for Loop 178
The while Loop 179

Functions 180
    Variable Scope 183
Naming Conventions 184

Chapter 9   Writing the Character and State Controller Scripts 185
Setting It Up and Laying It Out 185
A Simple Third-Person Controller 186
    Controller Variables 188
    Unity's MonoBehaviour Class 189
    FixedUpdate: Make *Widget* Move 191
Setting Up Unity's Input Manager 197
    A Redux of the Input Class 200
    Naming Conventions for the Axes 201
    Sample Xbox-Style Controller Setup 202
Hooking Up the Camera 203
Assembling the Status Controller 208
    Coroutines 210
    Updating the Character Controller 212
Completed Scripts 213
    Widget_Controller.js 213
    Widget_Status.js 216
    Widget_Camera.js 218

Chapter 10   Hooking Up the Animations 221
Animation in Unity 221
Animation API 222
    The Animation Class 222
Setting Up the PC's Animations 224
    Defining the Problem 225
    Updating the Controller 225
    Creating the Animation State Manager 227
Creating Animations Inside Unity 231
    Some Basic Concepts 232
    Animation View 232
Setting Up a New Animation Clip 233
    Creating the Custom Animation 234
    Hooking It Up 236
Adding Animation Events 239
Completed Scripts 242

Widget_Controller.js Update 242

Widget_Animation.js 246

Chapter 11 Using Triggers and Creating Environment Interactions . . . 251

Triggers and Collision 251

Setting Up a Basic Trigger Object 252

Gizmos for Sanity 256

Inventory Management 258

Setting Up Other Kinds of Triggers 261

Death Triggers 262

Checkpoints—The Anti-Death Trigger 263

Completed Scripts 267

PickupItems.js 268

Widget_Inventory.js 269

DamageTrigger.js 271

CheckPoint.js 271

Widget Status 273

Chapter 12 Building Adversaries and AI 277

Artificial Intelligence: Definitely Artificial, Not Much Intelligence . . . 277

Some Simple AI Guidelines 278

A Simple Workflow 280

Setting Up a Simple Enemy 281

The AI Controller 282

A Simple State Manager for a Simple Bunny 290

Hooking Up Widget's Attacks 292

Rewarding the Player for a Job Well Done 295

Spawning and Optimization 297

Completed Scripts 300

EBunny_AIController.js 300

EBunny_Status.js 304

Widget_AttackController.js 306

Enemy_RespawnPoint.js 307

Chapter 13 Designing the Game's GUI (Graphical User Interface) . . . 309

Basic Interface Theory 309

Steps of Interaction 310

Designing for Your Users 310

Unity's GUI System 312
   Buttons 313
   Sliders 314
   Labels and Boxes 314
   Text Entry 315
   Toggle 315
   Toolbars and Selection Grids 315
   Windows 316
A Custom Skin for Widget 318
   Creating the GUISkin 319
   Defining Custom Styles 320
   Importing New Fonts 321
Setting Up the HUD 323
   GUIContent 324
   Character Displays 329
   Resolution 336
A Sample Pop-up Screen 337
Adding Full-Screen Menus 341
Completed and Updated Scripts 345
   GUI_CustomControls.js 345
   GUI_HUD.js 347
   Widget_Attack_Controller.js 350
   EBunny_Status.js 352
   GUI_WaypointStore.js 354
   WaypointBehavior.js 355
   GUI_MainMenu.js 356

PART IV   POLISH AND THE FINISHING TOUCHES **359**

Chapter 14   Creating Lighting and Shadows **361**
Types of Lights 361
   Light Properties 363
   Basics of Lighting 365
Lighting the World 368
Creating Shadows 369
   Lightmaps 371
   Projector-Made Shadows 373
Other Light Effects 376
   Lens Flares 376
   Cookies 378

Chapter 15   Using Particle Systems **381**

Particles: from Smoke to Stardust 381

Setting Up a Simple System 382

Particle Emitter 383

Particle Animator 385

Particle Renderer and Materials. 387

Advanced Particle Components 390

World Particle Collider 390

Trail Renderer 391

Line Renderer 393

Particles for Widget 394

Pickup Items 394

Checkpoint Activation 397

Widget's Attack 399

Enemy Explosion 402

Updated Scripts 404

PickupItems.js 404

CheckPoint.js 405

Widget_AttackController.js 407

EBunny_Status 409

Chapter 16   Adding Audio and Music **413**

Feedback and Ambience 413

Setting Up a Simple Audio Clip 415

Ambient Sound Effects 417

Controlling Sounds Through Scripts 417

Adding Background Music. 420

Updated Scripts 421

PART V   PUBLISHING AND DISTRIBUTING BUILDS **425**

Chapter 17   Basic Unity Debugging and Optimization **427**

Debugging in Unity 427

The Console 428

The Log Files. 429

Optimization 431

The Profiler. 431

Basic Code Optimization 431

Emulation 433

Rendering Statistics Page. 435

Reducing File Size 437

Other Ways to Optimize Graphics 437

Chapter 18 Creating the Final Build. 439

Prepping for the Build 439

Setting Up the Player 439

Finally, the Application Class 441

Build Settings 443

Other Build Features 446

New Assets and DLC 446

Packing Up Assets for Later 446

The End of the Road? 448

Index **449**

Part I

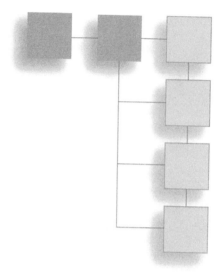

In the Beginning...

As with any new endeavor, it's usually best to start somewhere in the beginning. And before you even start, it's best to lay out your tools and get your ideas in order. You wouldn't attempt (I hope) to build a house without a blueprint, and games are no different. The best game ideas in the world won't get you very far unless you have the knowledge, skills, and discipline to see them fully realized and implemented.

Before Unity, making a game from scratch for the newbie game designer was a rather daunting process. Engines, especially free ones, weren't terribly easy to come across, and those that were often suffered from poor execution or lack of documentation. Now with Unity, you can quickly get your ideas in motion, even if you lack a strong art or programming background.

In this section, you'll learn the basics of the engine and its interface, as well as how to refine your game idea from the get-go, hopefully saving you some time and energy later in the process.

CHAPTER 1

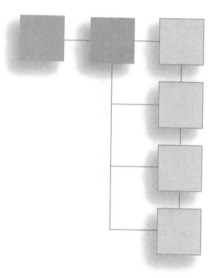

PREFACE

INBOXES AND EMAILS

Winston Churchill once remarked: "Writing a book is an adventure. To begin with, it is a toy and an amusement; then it becomes a mistress, and then it becomes a master, and then a tyrant. The last phase is that just as you are about to be reconciled to your servitude, you kill the monster, and fling him out to the public." My hat's off to the man; truer words on the subject have never been uttered.

Much like how the unbeknownst hero, sitting in his quiet home village, gets an unexpected call to journey forth and adventure, I received an email out of the blue from my former advisor, Brenda Brathwaite, asking if I wanted to write a book. Her publisher desired a new gaming text, and she didn't have the time currently to write one. Bright-eyed, bushy-tailed, and *incredibly* naïve and stupid, I readily agreed. Sure, I've written 100-plus page texts before, had some time on my hands, how bad could it be? Turning in my plowshare for a pen, I set off on what I thought would be a relatively easy, quick romp through the woods.

Well, I'm happy to admit I was quite, quite wrong.

Originally this book began life as a manuscript focused on beginning game design using Microsoft's Popfly Game Creator as a learning tool. Never heard of it? Well, you and the rest of the world, apparently. About three-quarters of the way through the manuscript's progress, I received an email from the Popfly dev team announcing that the site would be shut down later in the month, and all resources and references to the API would be removed. After snorting hot coffee through my nose and wailing at all my friends unlucky enough to be in the office that early, I contacted my acquisitions editor Emi Smith with the news. Book and Adventure Number One seemed to be over prematurely. Your princess is in another castle, but sorry folks, we don't know which one, and there isn't a handy little trail to follow or mushroom man to point you in the right direction. Game over. Put the controller down and walk away. Defeated.

Even though I was a wee bit discouraged (and admittedly useless in the matter), Emi wasn't to be stopped, and she immediately went back to the drawing board, coming up with no less than six new ideas the very next day. Running down the lines, nothing really seemed to catch my interest (or play to my skill set) until I reached the last line of the list—Unity. Hmm. I had heard of the engine before and read a brief article or two, so I figured it was at least worth a quick download and look-see.

And thus began my love affair with a little game engine, out to show the world how it could change its attitude towards development. Two years and 400 pages later the manuscript is finally done, test project finished, and the whole mess sent off to the printer with a silent fanfare. Pen laid down, I trek back to the village intent on working in the garden again, sitting around doing nothing productive, and maybe sleeping in for the first Saturday in months. Maybe I'll get a cat.

So why bother with all this? What's it to you, dear reader, whether the book took one year or two, changed focuses or not? On the surface, probably not too much. But writing a book is a hell of a lot like making a game, especially if it's your first endeavor in either field.

You've probably got tons of great game ideas up there floating in your head. Maybe you've even started working on one, the big one that'll net you that dream job or needed raise. Or perhaps you've started two games, or three, or...you get the picture. Working on making your snippets of ideas and musings into playable games is great—but how many have you actually *finished*?

Making a game is a huge commitment (like writing a book), fraught with tons of unforeseen setbacks, design changes, software explosions, and enormous amounts of overtime, all for a tiny little bundle of ideas that you hope others will love as much as you do. It's far too easy once the first dragon rears its head to stop working, take an extended break, and never return to the field to try again. It's not procrastination, you tell others, it's just a short time away to rest your eyes, to let your ideas simmer free of worry. The short break becomes a week, and then a month, and years roll by as your little unfinished game collects dust in the corner.

If you're going to lie to others about the state of your current game, at least be truthful to yourself. Tackling a lot of problems in design is hard, nasty work, and many times you need to be able to admit to yourself that your idea was wrong, it didn't work out as expected, or it's just plain un-fun. Don't walk away from the whole project and leave the game unfinished—try something else, even if you're unsure where this new path will take you. Maybe it won't work out, but maybe it'll be the solution to a whole host of problems. Try, make mistakes, learn, and try again. You can't really call yourself a designer until you finish a game, and you can't really finish a game until you're comfortable learning from your mistakes.

Finish that game, and then finish another. It doesn't matter if you think they're horrible, terrible piles of swill you'd be embarrassed to show your own mother. Show her anyway. They may suck, they may not, but analyze what you did that worked and didn't work. The process of designing is as much about learning as it is about creating, and no one ever excelled by stopping half way. If you get discouraged, it *is* okay to take a quick break (or snort some hot coffee), but always, always come back to it in the end. Support from friends can help greatly in this, and involve some of your buddies in rounds of routine play tests. Make a party of it. Celebrate in what you do and remember to have fun. If you're not having fun, you're probably not making fun.

In that same vein, this book would definitely have not been possible without the support and encouragement of a whole bunch of people whose names don't appear on the cover. I probably would have floundered forever at that first major setback a little over a year ago had it not been for the fine folks over at Cengage Learning. Emi's been a fantastic resource and editor, and her experience in the field shines through clearly in her decisions and help. Kezia Endsley, copy editor extraordinaire, has been a complete joy to work with. Despite all the foibled email addresses, countless formatting mistakes, and completely bogus outlines I provided her on my end, she's always been upbeat, cheerful, and quick to respond to anything I threw at her. The editing team was rounded out by Jonathan Tanner, friend and peer, who I shameless conscripted into tech editing my pile of ramblings a few months before going to print (there may have been beer involved). If any code functions as intended in here, you can thank him. He likes Scottish ales.

Realizing that I may have bitten off more than I could chew with the game test project, I contacted one of my artist friends from grad school, Sarah Tempas. She graciously accepted to help out on the art needs, despite becoming recently engaged, moving to a new state, and looking for a new job. All the expanded artwork for the City is hers.

Above all, I need to thank my husband James for his continued, god-like patience and support over the years that it took this book to reach fruition. He sacrificed time on many a night and most weekends for the past two years, allowing me to sit undisturbed for hours on end starring at a computer screen. He took care of the house and yard work, cooking, cleaning, and if we had cat, he would have taken care of him, too. His occasional pointed reminder towards the end: "Aren't you done *yet?*" would always make me put down the DS, knitting needles, or random deviation of the day and pick up the pen once more. I can be a dogged procrastinator, and he always knew when to let me take a break or kick me squarely in the butt. As thanks, which I know isn't nearly enough, I dedicate this book to him. I promise I'll also vacuum after I finish this page.

So, to wrap it all up (and risk this sounding like a closing paragraph to a self-help book), always be ready to accept the call to adventure, wherever that random email may take you. Yes dear, it's finally done.

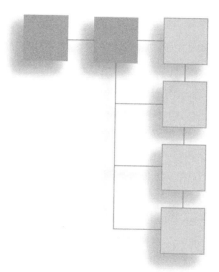

CHAPTER 2

INTRODUCTION

First things first, welcome to the Unity Engine! Whether you're new to game development or a seasoned pro looking into new technology, the Unity Engine has a lot to offer. Available for both Mac and PC development, the engine can create games that can be deployed on just about any platform available, from the web to the Wii and even on SmartPhones. Its easy interface, friendly development environment, and wide-ranging support of all popular gaming platforms make it a great choice for the student, indie, and larger developer team.

Unity's clients include such names as Ubisoft, Disney, and Electronic Arts, but the engine is also highly utilized by small independent studios, hobbyists, students, and even companies outside of the gaming industry (primarily for medical sims and architectural walkthroughs). Whatever the end goal, Unity allows anyone, regardless of background, to create fun, interesting, and interactive content. Let's get started.

WHAT WILL BE COVERED (AND WHAT NOT)

Primarily, this book is an introductory look into the engine. It explains what Unity has to offer and gives a few pointers on how to best utilize its capabilities for whatever it is you want to do. If you're a hobbyist or student, you'll probably want to start reading from the beginning and follow along with the example project. If you're using this book as a tool to evaluate whether the engine is right for you, you're probably best skipping around to the relevant chapters.

If you start from the beginning, you'll learn all the important interface commands, how to set up and organize your project, and all the basics of getting a 3D game up and running, from character importation to scripting to audio. After completing the example project, you'll have all the skills necessary to go out and make your own games.

What this book isn't, however, is a crash course in the Unified Theory of Game Development and Design. By that, I mean you won't be granted some mystical information or mad skills for everything there is to know in design, programming, art, or sound. Each topic covered (such as game design) does include some basic theory and information, enough to get you going on working vocabulary and introductory concepts. This book won't make you a star designer or a world-class programmer—that kind of scope coverage is simply not realistic or possible.

If, after reading, you do find yourself interested in a particular field, check out the "Resources" section of the DVD for pointers on where to get more information. Think of this as a sampler course stretching across multiple cuisines, and not an in-depth exploration of one particular food type.

More advanced and singular topics such as network integration and discussions on Unity's shader language are also not covered.

Intended Audience

So, who exactly is this book for then anyway? If you fall into any of the following categories, you've come to the right place:

- A solo developer or generalist looking for some well-rounded information on utilizing the engine.

- A developer looking to evaluate the engine for use in future projects.

- A hobbyist needing a how-to guide about some specific areas.

- A student (or prospective student) wanting to know whether game development is right for him or her.

- Anyone looking to build his or her game portfolio using an affordable (or in some cases free) professional engine.

As stated earlier, all the game development topics will cover some basic background knowledge and go over a few key terms. However, the text does assume some knowledge or skills in a few areas, if you plan on working away from the example project.

For example, creation of 3D art assets and how to use a 3D modeling package are not covered. All the required models used in the text (and then some) are included on the DVD, but their creation is not described. If you stick to the example project while reading through the book, you won't really need any outside knowledge or skills (although any game development information is a plus). If you plan to work on your own project from the start, using this book as a guide, you'll need to educate yourself in the other areas of development or find other places and people to provide art and code.

THE BOOK'S STRUCTURE

The information in the book is organized into six large parts, each covering a general aspect of game development. Within each part, a chapter is devoted to each single concept, such as one chapter for AI development and another for particle effects. If you need help on just a specific area of Unity, go to the corresponding chapter or use the handy index. The appendix part, found on the DVD, includes a list of common and helpful shortcut keys, a rundown of the most-used classes, and exercises for you to complete if you want a few pointers on what to do once you finish reading. A compiled glossary for all keywords introduced in the text is also contained there.

I've tried to make learning the engine a little more straightforward by using some general formatting guidelines. Steps for you to complete in the engine always appear in numbered lists, which are boxed off from the regular text. If you see such lists coming up on the page, you should open Unity to follow along.

Links between steps in a folder chain or nested menu are marked with an ▶ sign. So the line "My Documents▶My Unity Project" would mean to open the My Documents folder and then open the folder My Unity Project contained within it. Pretty straightforward.

Code to write in the engine is blocked off in its own formatting, as shown here:

```
//I'm a comment
Update()
{
    print("Hello World");
}
```

Finally, some extra information is included in the form of sidebars. These kinds of blocks mostly cover more advanced technical data or engine specs and aren't required knowledge for using the engine on a day-to-day basis. They do tend to be helpful, however. Also be mindful of tips, notes, and warnings scattered throughout the text. These little offset blocks are often important, contain information about common pitfalls, and help to stave off potential hard-to-fix disasters. If time was taken to graphically embellish something, it's probably worth a second look.

INSTALLATION INSTRUCTIONS

Installing Unity is quick and painless and technically requires a one-time Internet connection. Unity comes in two flavors, Free and Pro, and both are regularly updated by the developers. Although you won't need the Internet again after activation, it is advisable if only for the patch updates and fixes.

The Unity Engine

First up, install Unity. Unity can be downloaded from the Unity Technologies website: http://unity3d.com/. This is also available as a link in the "Resources" section of the DVD. From the Download menu, click on either the Mac or Windows version button, whichever is right for you. (This book uses the Windows version for all its examples.) You can choose to download the Free version directly or get a Pro license trial version free for 30 days. It doesn't really matter as far as the book is concerned, but it can be fun to see what goodies the Pro version does include. Unity is roughly 160MB in size and takes about five minutes to download on a typical cable connection. Make yourself a sandwich while you're waiting.

Once it's finished, run the UnitySetup-###.exe file, accept the terms of agreement, and follow the onscreen command prompts. When you get to the Choose

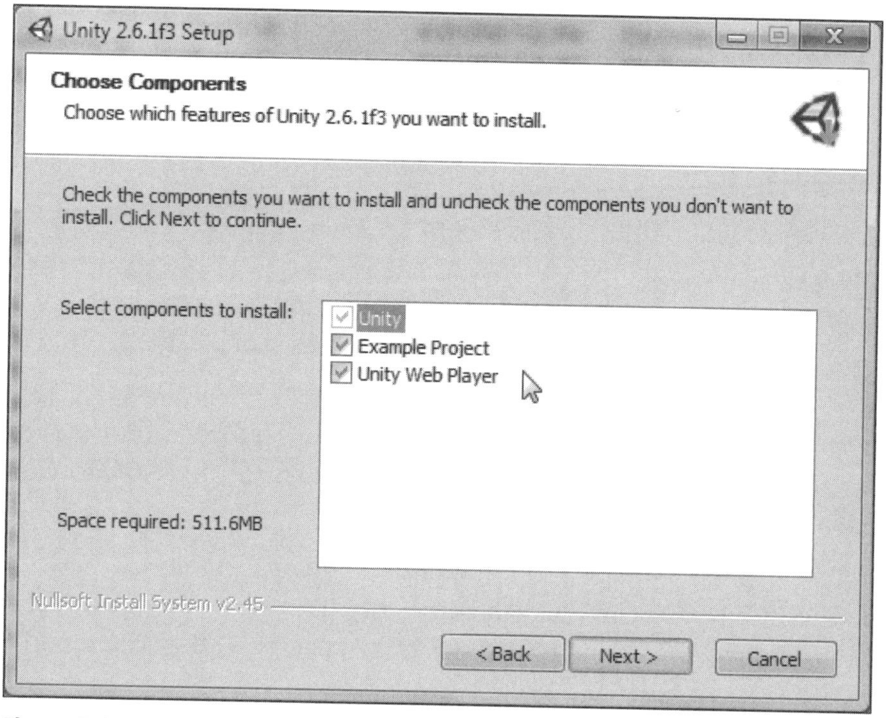

Figure 2.1
Check all the components on this screen.

Components screen, as shown in Figure 2.1, make sure that the Example Project is checked. You'll probably want to also check the Unity Web Player line as well, in case you ever want to publish your games to the Internet.

Use the default install path or select your own, and then click Install. Unity takes just a little more than 500MB of install space, so make sure that your selected destination can handle this plus any other add-ons or projects you want to use later. Follow the other onscreen instructions to complete the install.

After the basic install has finished, Unity will prompt you to register your copy. For the free version and trial Pro, this is easy. Select the Internet version (if available) and fill out the form on the website the engine takes you to—usually it's just your name and email address. After this, Unity is yours to use.

Once the engine has finished installing, it's time to move on to the DVD contents.

Using the DVD Contents

Locate the DVD at the back of the book and break the little paper cover, voiding the return and making the book safe from resale racks. The DVD is divided into a few main sections:

- **Chapters:** This folder contains subfolders for each chapter in the book, whenever they require the use of files or assets. You can either copy the entire Chapters folder to your hard drive now or just grab the individual files when you need them. The text always specifies when a file is needed and where to grab it.

- **Design Documents:** This folder houses all the basic information for the example project discussed in the text, *Widget*. When the text says to view the Design Docs, they're located in here.

- **Shader Test:** An example project detailing and comparing all the basic shaders side-by-side that are available in Unity. If you're not sure which shader to use or how some may interact in a specific lighting rig, modify and use this file as needed.

- **Final Project Files:** Unlike the Chapters folder, which houses all the individual files as they come up in the text, the Final Project Files folder is a complete Unity Project for the *Widget* game. If you ever get stuck or want to see how something fits together later, you can always check out the game here. Extra assets such as more models, textures, and UI elements are also included here, for any further expansion you may want to pursue.

The Resources file in the root of the DVD directory contains links to further reading, optional software downloads, and access to information on working with Unity and game development in general.

Optional Installs

Between Unity and the DVD contents, you can complete every exercise in the book and get the example project up and running. However, you may find yourself wanting to tweak a graphic or texture here or there, or maybe even sculpt a new model to import. Many free software packages are described both in the text where appropriate and in the Resources file on the DVD. If you don't already have something installed on your computer, check the file for information and a link.

Unity also installs a free code editor to use for scripting, but you can use your own favorite coding environment if desired. Chapter 9 covers compatible ones in more detail, and the Resources file also provides links where appropriate.

Now that your development environment is all set up and ready to go, open up Unity and start with Chapter 3.

CHAPTER 3

AN OVERVIEW OF THE UNITY ENGINE

Unity is a powerful integrated game engine and editor, allowing you to quickly and efficiently create objects, import external assets, and link them all together with code. The editor is visually driven and built around the principles that you can do everything with a simple drag-and-drop motion, even connect scripts, assign variables, or create complicated multi-part assets. Unity also boasts an integrated scripting environment, built-in networking capabilities, and the ability to build and deploy for multiple platforms. All of this is wrapped up in a simple, intuitive, and customizable workspace.

GETTING ACQUAINTED WITH THE INTERFACE

Before diving headfirst into making your first game with Unity, it's worth the time to first take a quick look at how to get around in the editor. Unity may look a bit daunting when you first open it, but you'll find that you can easily master its basics in a day.

If you haven't done so already, open Unity (Start menu ▶ Programs ▶ Unity (C:\Program Files\Unity\Editor\Unity.exe, or click the desktop icon if you created one) and load Ch3_TestFile.unity located on the DVD to follow along. Alternatively, you can browse to the location on your computer where you saved all the DVD files and double-click on Ch3_TestFile.unity to launch it in the editor.

Note

If you installed the island or shooter demo with the engine, the base "Islands" scene will load by default until you either load a different scene or create a new one.

The editor's default layout is broken into a series of different panes and tabbed windows called *views*. Each view details a specific aspect of the editor and allows you to perform different functions when working on your game. If you've used a 3D modeling program or other game editor in the past, you may find some of this familiar.

The Project View

All of a game's files—scripts, objects, scenes, anything and everything—are organized into a Project folder, each of which contains an Assets folder. The Assets folder houses *everything* you've created or imported to include in your game— meshes, textures, scripts, cameras, levels ... everything. See Figure 3.1. The Project View panel displays this Project folder and the incorporated Assets folder.

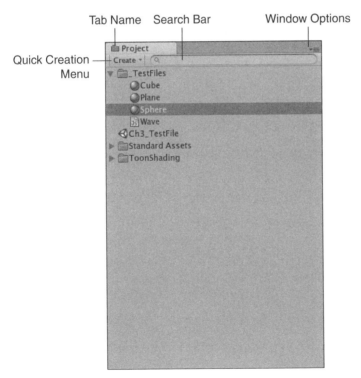

Figure 3.1
A sample collection of assets.

The Project view displays everything that is included in the game's Assets directly, exactly how they are organized and arranged on your computer's hard drive. If you are unsure, however, of where these files are located (or ever forget), you can simply right-click on any selected asset in the Project view and select Show in Explorer. Arrows next to folders indicate nested layers, and clicking on any one will expand that folder's contents. You can also Shift+left-click on an arrow to fully expand or contract its contents. Moving and organizing files into different folders can be achieved in the Project view with a simple click and drag.

Caution

Be careful about moving your asset files around outside of the Unity Editor—in fact, you should probably avoid it at all costs. If you need to reorganize or move an asset, do it from within the Project view. Not doing so could break or remove any metadata or links associated with that asset, possibly breaking your game in the process.

Files can also be opened and edited directly from within the Project view. If you find you need to tweak or correct something in any file (like a Photoshop file), simply double-click on the file to open it in its default editor. Save the file normally to have Unity import it back into your project.

Each type of object listed also has its own descriptive icon or thumbnail, making it easy to quickly scan the contents. If your project contains hundreds or thousands of files, you may find visually scanning for a specific file to be cumbersome or downright impossible. Happily, you can type any part of the name of your file into the Search Bar to search through all levels of your project. The Project view's list will dynamically update after each letter you type, allowing for easier browsing if you don't quite remember the exact name.

Sometimes you'll find it necessary to make new assets or objects that aren't contained already in your Project view. Unity makes this easy from within the view—simply left-click on the Quick Creation menu to bring up the available options. This shortcut menu is located right beneath the Project tab, directly next to the Search Bar. From here you can make new folders, empty script files, or other game specific objects without having to leave the editor. Right-clicking in the Project view itself will also give you a link to the Quick Creation menu and its options, placing the new file at your current location in the file tree.

Tip

To rename any file or folder, you can left-click twice slowly on the name (*not* a normal fast double-click) or select the desired file and press the F2 key. Press Enter when you are done renaming your file.

Right-clicking in the Project view will bring up a few advanced options, including asset importation, syncing with external project controllers, and asset package manipulation. See Figure 3.2. These are covered in more depth in later chapters.

All tabbed windows have a Windows Options drop-down box, allowing you to maximize the selected view, close the viewed tab, or add another tab view to the window. Click the icon to bring up the available options.

The Hierarchy View

Whereas the Project view lists *all* the objects and files available in your game, the Hierarchy view lists just the ones you're actually using in the current scene. The objects in the scene are simply listed alphabetically, and as you add or remove objects from your game, the Hierarchy view will update with each change.

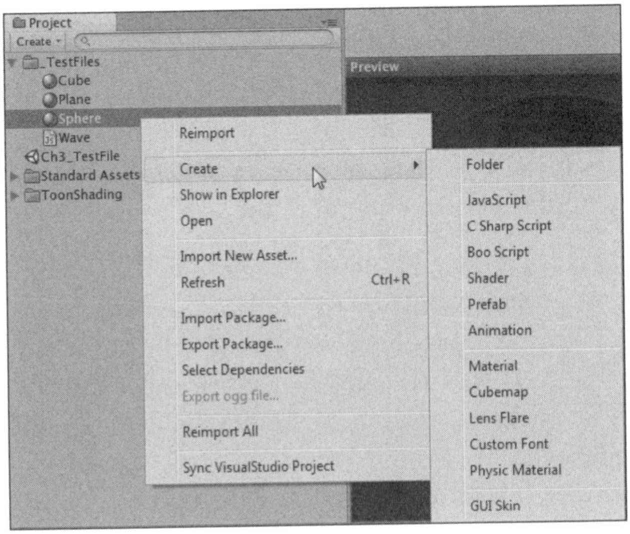

Figure 3.2
The right-click menu and Create menu options.

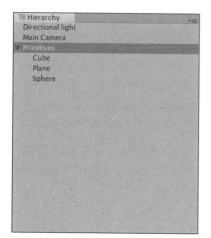

Figure 3.3
The game scene's current contents.

Selecting an object in the Hierarchy and pressing the Delete key (or right-clicking and selecting Delete) will remove the object from your current scene in the game, but not from the project's Assets folder. Figure 3.3 shows the game's current contents as an example.

Each *instance* (a copy or occurrence) of an asset will be listed individually, making good naming conventions especially important. If you have 30 instances of an object all named Cube, you may have trouble finding the one you want later. Thankfully, you can rename any object in the Hierarchy independently of its actual filename in the Project view. A simple mesh named Cube in your Project view can then be instanced and renamed in the Hierarchy to anything you want, like Crate, Box, or Mystery Pickup23, making it easier to find and use later. This will not update the filename of the actual object in the Project view or on your computer. To do that, you must change the name from within the Project view.

Parenting objects together in the Hierarchy view can also help with organization and make editing your game easier. When you parent objects together, you are basically taking a collection of unrelated objects together and linking them in a group under a single object, the parent. All the other objects under this parent are called its children, or child objects. See Figure 3.4.

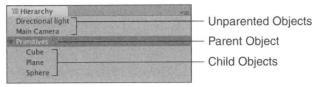

Figure 3.4
Parented and unparented objects.

In the example, the parent object is an asset called Primitives, under which three child objects are located: Sphere, Cube, and Plane. Clicking on the arrow next to Primitives will expand or collapse the group, much like with the folders in Project view. However, parenting gives you one other important benefit besides a speedy way to group like objects together—moving or manipulating the parent object will in turn do the same to all the children underneath it. They are said to *inherit* the parent's data. The child objects can still be edited independently of each other and the parent object, giving you more control.

If you're still uncertain about parenting, think of a normal person's body. An arm is parented to the torso, and a hand is parented to the end of the arm. Moving the torso forward (the parent) will move the arm with it, which will in turn move the hand (the two children). However, you can move and rotate the hand around without moving the torso or the arm.

Using parented objects can make moving large numbers of objects around much easier and more precise and should be used whenever possible. A few more advanced concepts of parenting will be covered in Chapters 6 and 7.

The Inspector

The Inspector, as its name suggests, displays the detailed information contained in each object in your game (see Figure 3.5). Click on the Sphere object (you may need to expand Primitives to see it) to bring up its details in the Inspector view.

On first glance this may seem overwhelming, but all Inspector views follow the same basic principle for each object. At the top of the Inspector is the object's name, followed by a list of the different aspects of the object, such as Transform and Sphere Collider. Each of these different kinds of properties will be discussed in greater detail later, but for now know that this is where you come to edit any piece of information about your object.

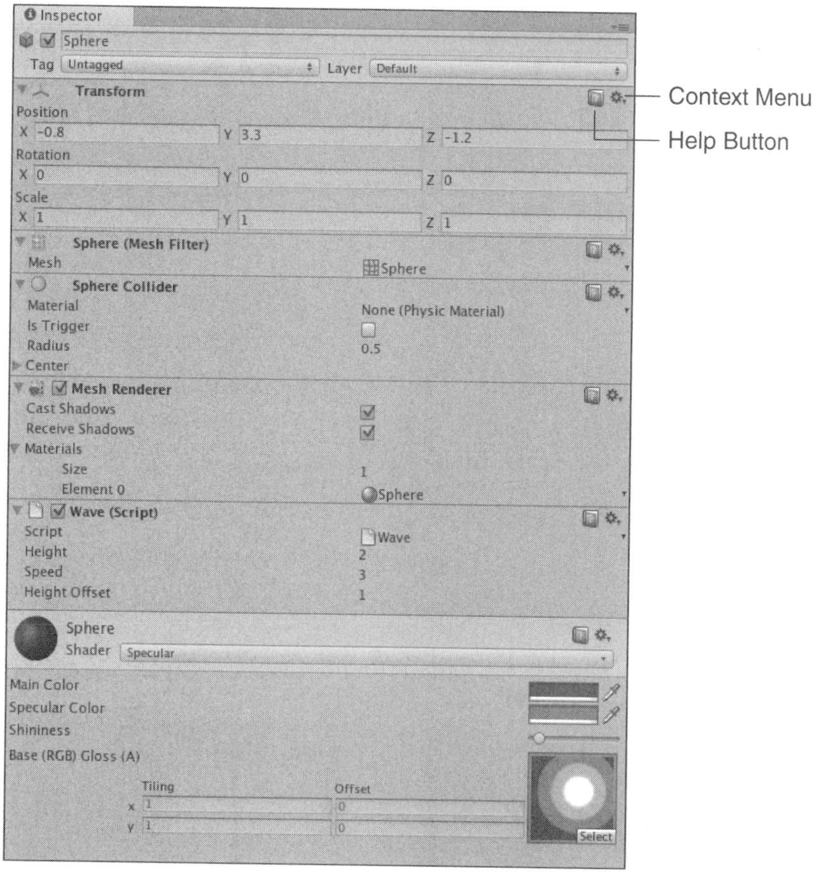

Figure 3.5
The Inspector view for the Sphere object.

Each property in the Inspector has a Help button and Context menu attached to it. Clicking on the Help button will bring up the related document for the property in the reference manual—try it with any one of the properties. Clicking on the Context menu will give you specific options related to just that property, as well as a way to reset the property back to its default values.

N o t e

You will need an active Internet connection to view the reference manual when you click the Help button, which is hosted online at Unity's website.

Figure 3.6
The Toolbar.

The Toolbar

The Toolbar, shown in Figure 3.6, consists of the available menu lists and five basic control groups for your game. The drop-down menus along the top of the editor contain the basic generic options available to you and are grouped by function.

- **File menu:** Open and save scenes and projects and create builds of your game.

- **Edit menu:** The normal copy and paste functions, as well as selection setups and settings.

- **Assets menu:** Everything having to do with creating, importing, exporting, and syncing assets.

- **GameObject menu:** Creating, viewing, and parenting GameObjects.

- **Component menu:** Creating new components or properties for GameObjects.

- **Terrain menu:** Creating and editing a terrain for your game scene.

- **Window menu:** Brings up specific views (such as the Project or Hierarchy view).

- **Help menu:** Links to the manuals, community forums, and where to activate your license.

For now, just be aware of the general functionality contained in each menu—the individual aspects will be discussed in detail as they're needed.

The control tools are also grouped by function and serve primarily to assist with editing and movement in the Scene and Game views, discussed more fully next.

- **Transform tools:** Used in the Scene view to control and manipulate objects. In order from left to right, they activate the Hand tool, Translate tool, Rotate tool, and Scale tool.

- **Transform Gizmo toggles:** Change how the Transform tools work in the Scene view.

- **Play controls:** Used to start and stop testing a game from within the editor.

- **Layers drop-down:** Controls which specific objects are displayed in the Scene view at any given time.

- **Layout drop-down:** Changes the layout of your windows and views, and saves any custom layouts you create.

The Scene View

One of the most important windows in the editor is the Scene view—a visual representation of your game world or level (see Figure 3.7). This is where you'll maneuver, manipulate, and position all your objects and assets listed in the Hierarchy, creating the physical space that your players will explore and interact with.

As you can see, the objects listed within the Hierarchy are displayed in all their brilliance in the Scene view. You can click on the object's name in the Hierarchy to select it or just manually click on it in the Scene view. Clicking on the different objects in the Scene view or Hierarchy will update the Inspector with the object's appropriate data.

Note

If you see lists of items populating your Hierarchy, but the Scene view appears to be empty, your view may be zoomed out too much to view the individual assets. To fix this, select an item in the Hierarchy, move and hover your mouse over the Scene view, and press the F key to zoom in.

Note that by clicking on the Primitives object in the Hierarchy, you actually select all the child objects in Scene view. There isn't a separate "Primitives" object displayed in the Scene view, so if you want to select an entire parented group of objects, you must do so through the Hierarchy.

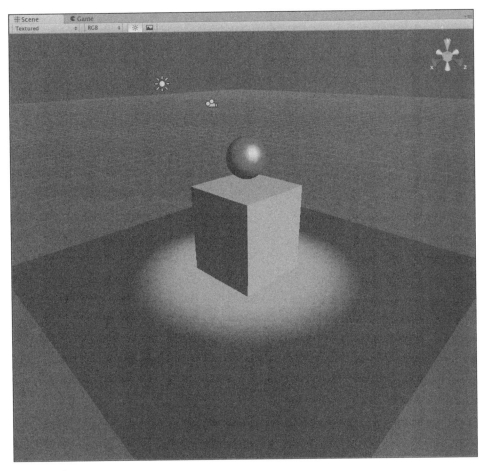

Figure 3.7
A simple Scene view.

Camera Navigation

Learning to move around quickly in the Scene view is one of the most important aspects of the editor to master. (If you're an Autodesk Maya user, you'll be right at home with these controls.) You can think of the Scene view as the output or focus of a virtual camera. To move around the scene, you move your camera's view around as you look at different objects.

- **Tumble** (Alt+left mouse button): The camera will pivot around all axes, thus "tumbling" the view.

- **Track** (Alt+middle mouse button): Moves the camera left, right, up, and down in the scene.

- **Zoom** (Alt+right mouse button or mouse scroll wheel): Zooms the camera in and out of the scene.

- **Flythrough mode** (right mouse button+WASD keys): The camera will enter a "first-person" mode, allowing you to quickly move and zoom around the scene.

- **Center** (selected GameObject+F key): The camera will zoom in and center on the selected object in the view. Your mouse cursor must be located in the Scene view, not over the object in the Hierarchy.

- **Full Screen Mode** (spacebar): Press the spacebar to make the active view take up all available space in the editor. Press it again to return to your previous layout. The active view is whichever one your mouse is hovering over.

If your mouse has only one button (or if you only want to use your left mouse button), you're not at a complete loss; don't worry. Select the Hand tool from the Toolbar to put your mouse in Move mode (or press the Q key on your keyboard).

- **Tumble** (Alt+mouse button): The camera will pivot around all axes, thus "tumbling" the view.

- **Track** (mouse button): Click and drag to move the camera left, right, up, and down in the scene.

- **Zoom** (Ctrl+mouse button): Zoom the camera in and out of the scene.

Try the different movement controls until they become comfortable and second nature. Being able to quickly move around your game scene with precision will make your development time much faster and more enjoyable.

The Scene view also contains a special tool called the Scene gizmo, as shown in Figure 3.8. This special tool gives you fast access to the scene camera's orientation, allowing you to quickly change the view to premade selections.

Figure 3.8
The Scene gizmo.

Buzzword

A *gizmo* is an icon or symbol often used for something that doesn't have a visual representation in the real world. In 3D programs (like Unity), gizmos are often used to represent movement and camera controls.

Try clicking on the different arrows on the Scene gizmo and watch how the Scene view updates. Each arrow changes the camera's view to one of the different orthogonal, or 2D, directions, like Top, Back, Front, or Right (see Figure 3.9). Sometimes you'll need to change to one of these views to properly line up an object in the scene. Click the center cube icon on the gizmo to return to the default Perspective (3D) view.

Note

The Plane object seems to disappear in some of the side views because it is a 2D object—planes are defined only along two axes and don't have height. If ever your 2D objects seem to disappear, switch to a different orthogonal view.

If you Shift+click on the center cube, you'll enter a similar mode called *Isometric view*. Perspective view emulates a real-world 3D space, where objects get smaller as they become farther away. Notice, however, that in Isometric view the objects do *not* change size or shape as they become farther away and remain the same uniform size; this camera view lacks the emulation of perspective. You may recognize this look from many older games. See Figure 3.10.

Also note that each of the arrows is color coordinated to match one of the axes of the game world: red for the X axis, green for the Y axis, and blue for the Z axis. Unity's worldspace is set up in a *Cartesian* coordinate system—the X and Z axes form the ground plane, and the Y axis defines the height and depth of the world. The center of the world is located where these three axes intersect at the *origin*, the point (0,0,0). This is common *vector* notation for x = 0, y = 0, z = 0, or more generally, (x, y, z).

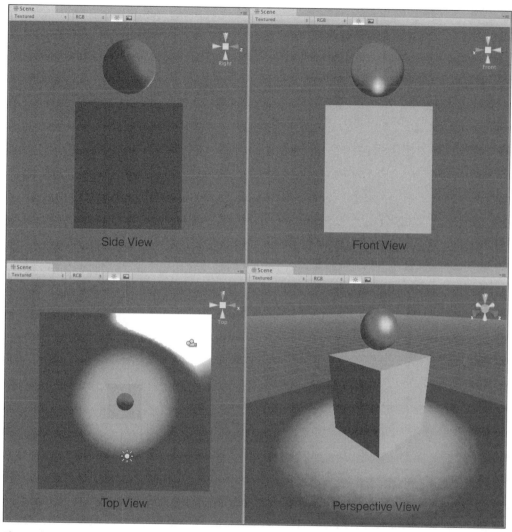

Figure 3.9
The four main orientation views.

Note

If you're more comfortable using different colors than the defaults to denote the world axes, you can change them to anything you like by going to the Edit menu▶Preferences▶Colors.

The Scene view's Control Bar, shown in Figure 3.11, changes the way the camera views the scene. The default values give a good approximation of what your

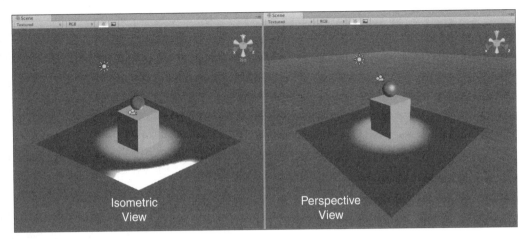

Figure 3.10
Isometric versus Perspective view.

Figure 3.11
The Scene view's Control Bar.

scene would look like rendered in game, as well as displaying a handy grid to help position and move objects.

The first drop-down list, Draw Modes, controls how the objects are drawn in your scene. The default value is Textured—the objects are drawn using the colors and texture maps assigned to them. Click on the menu to change the draw mode to Wireframe—this shows the objects' physical meshes without textures attached. The final selection, Tex–Wire, shows the objects' textures with their wireframes overlaid. None of these selections change the way your game will display, only how the Scene view's camera views the objects.

Advanced Viewing Options

The Render Modes drop-down is useful for optimizing your game scene by fine-tuning your objects. The default value of RGB shows all the objects colored as normal.

Selecting Alpha from the drop-down will show all the objects in the scene by their alpha values—fully opaque objects will render as white, fully transparent objects will render as black, and objects that are partly translucent will render in different shades of gray. Overdraw shows how much of the screen is consuming overdraw time, or how many objects are being drawn behind others. The final selection, Mipmaps, attempts to show ideal texture sizes for your objects. Objects drawn in blue have textures that are too small, and objects drawn in red have ones that are too large. Of course, this might not be completely correct, based upon the resolution of your game.

The Scene Lighting button toggles whether the Scene view uses the default built-in lighting or your own implemented lighting. If you haven't placed a light source in the scene yet, using the built-in lighting setup can be useful. The final toggle button, Scene Overlay, updates the camera to show the scene as it would appear in game—the grid is hidden, and other effects like fog, GUI (graphical user interface) elements, or the Skybox are rendered.

Play with the different selections to see their effects.

Manipulating Objects

Besides moving your camera view around, you'll also need to reposition and move objects within the scene. These manipulations are called object *transforms*, which handle the position, rotation, and scale (relative size) of any selected object. Object transforms can be performed in one of two ways, either by typing in new values for the transforms in the Inspector or by manually moving and manipulating the object with gizmos.

Click on the Sphere object in the Hierarchy or Scene view to bring up its information in the Inspector, shown in Figure 3.12. The first property listed for each object is Transform, which stores the object's current position, rotation, and scale. Click and type in any of the boxes to change the numbers. Unity's base units are in meters, so making $y = 2$ will move the sphere two meters into the air. Making $y = -2$ will move the sphere beneath the plane.

Besides typing discrete values, you can also *scrub* the value in any of the boxes. Click on any one of the axis labels in the Transform Component box (X, Y, or Z) and drag your mouse left and right. The object will move or deform with your changes. This isn't a very precise way to position or manipulate your objects, but

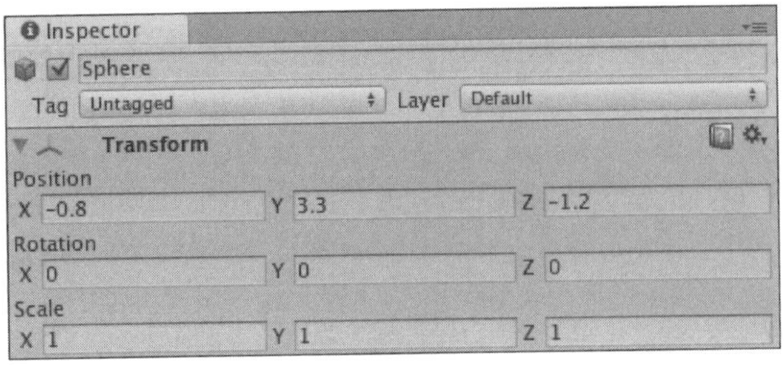

Figure 3.12
The Transform Component property.

it can be a quick and dirty way to get your objects basically where you want them before fine-tuning.

Your other option for transforming objects is by using the Transform tools. You can either manually select a tool from the Toolbar or use the hotkeys provided in the following sections to switch between them faster (definitely recommended).

The Translate tool, shown in Figure 3.13, moves the selected object's position around the scene, either along one of the three axes or freely in space. Click on the Sphere object in the Hierarchy and press the W key to activate the Translate tool.

Grab one of the handles, or arrows, to move the object along that axis in the game world (again, red for along the X axis, green for along the Y axis, and blue for along the Z axis). Notice that the values in the Inspector will update based upon your changes. You can also scrub using the Translate tool—simply select a handle with the mouse and then click and drag the middle mouse button to move the asset along the chosen axis.

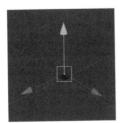

Figure 3.13
The Translate tool.

Figure 3.14
The Rotate tool.

You can also click in the center of the tool (or on the object itself) and drag around the scene to freely move the object along all three axes. This usually isn't the best method, however, as you don't have the finest of control over place-ment. You'll find that switching between the *orthographic* views (like Front and Right) via the Scene gizmo can help greatly in the precise placement of objects.

The Rotate tool, shown in Figure 3.14, rotates the object around any one of the given axes. Click on the Cube object and press the E key to activate the tool. The handles for this tool resemble three colored rings wrapped around a center sphere. Drag the handles or scrub around to rotate the object. Note that the colors for these rings don't line up with the world axes colors—they instead indicate around which axis the object will rotate. If you grab the blue handle, for instance, the cube will rotate around the Z axis. The tool also has a simple yellow ring encompassing the other three. You can click and drag this ring to rotate the object in all three axes.

The final Transform tool is the Scale tool, accessible by pressing the R key on your keyboard. This tool, shown in Figure 3.15, works similarly to the Translate tool—you grab one of the handles to scale the object only in that axis, or use the

Figure 3.15
The Scale tool.

center yellow square to scale the object uniformly in all three dimensions. Try this out with any of the three objects in the scene.

Scaling your mesh using this tool comes with its own risks. While it does seem like a great quick way to resize any of your assets, you may slow down performance of your game if you use too many scaled objects or stretch your textures completely out of whack. The best way to adjust scale is to ensure that the mesh in your 3D application is the right size to begin with.

N o t e

You can change the default keys for any of these tools from Edit▶Preferences▶Keys.

Moving Multiple and Parented Objects

Up to this point you've only been moving single objects around, the child objects of the Primitives object. Try now selecting the Primitives object in the Hierarchy view and moving it to the point (0,–3.5,0). The entire Primitives group, including all its children, will move to the new location. Now click on any one of the child objects and look at its information in the Inspector. Notice anything? The individual position transforms of the children did not update or change when you moved the Primitives object to its new location, even though you can clearly see they have changed. This is because child objects inherit *all* transform data from their parent object; the transform values of the children are actually relative values to the parent object, not world values.

For example, examine the Cube's position data in the Inspector. The Y coordinate doesn't mean that it's located at position $y = 1.5$ meters, it instead means that it's located 1.5 meters above the location of the parent object. Changing the parent's objects location in the world won't change the fact that the Cube will remain one and a half meters above it. The child's position is referred to as *local coordinates,* and the parent object houses the *global coordinates.*

For this reason, it's often good practice to manually place an object you plan to make a parent at the origin before applying its child. This will make it easier in the long run once you need to start placing hundreds of assets relative to each other.

You can also select multiple objects in a scene by holding down the Shift key while you select different items with the left mouse button. If you accidentally select an item you didn't mean to, hold down the Control key and left-click to remove it from the selection.

Transform Gizmo Toggles

Remember the Transform gizmo toggles from the Control Bar? These dictate how the Transform tools behave and function. The first toggle button, Pivot/Center, changes where in space the tool is located. Select the Primitives object in the Hierarchy and then activate the Rotate tool. The default value, Pivot, places the tool at the object's *pivot point,* the point in space around which the object transforms. (Pivot points are generally predefined at the object's creation and can be easily moved from within your chosen 3D application.) Change the Scene view to an orthographic view like Front or Back and rotate the object around one of the axes. Note that the object always rotates the same relative distance from the pivot point.

Now press the Pivot Toggle to change it to Center—the Rotate tool now jumps to the local center of the selected object. Try rotating the object again. This time the object rotates around its center, instead of around the imaginary pivot point in space. Using both Pivot and Center to your advantage can greatly reduce headaches when trying to move assets into position.

Return to the Perspective view, and this time select the Plane object and rotate it 45 degrees around its Y axis. Activate the Translate tool. With the Local Toggle active, the Translate tool's axes stay relative and local to the object's position. Press the Local Toggle to change it to Global, and watch how the tool updates to realign itself with the world coordinate system. Being able to move an object in either its local space or global space is hugely beneficial, especially once objects become rotated at haywire angles. Figures 3.16 through 3.19 show the location and visualization of the various toggles on an object when selected.

The Game View

In the default Tall layout, the Game view is located on a tab next to the Scene tab. Here, your game is rendered out exactly as it would be when you finalize your build and publish it. You can test and play your game at any time from within the editor using this view, never having to stop to build or cook anything.

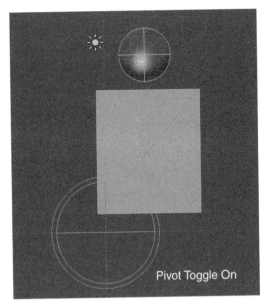

Figure 3.16
The Pivot Toggle active.

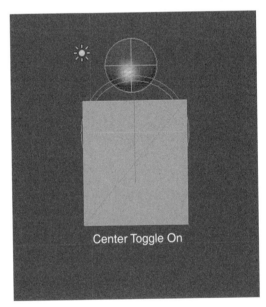

Figure 3.17
The Center Toggle active.

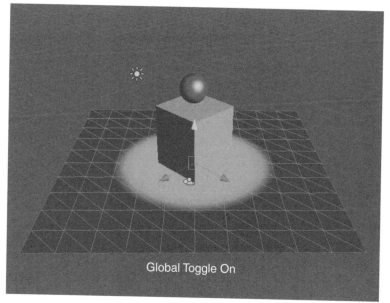

Figure 3.18
The Global Toggle active.

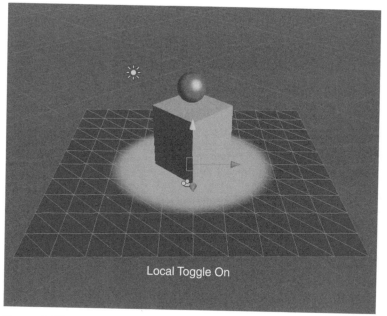

Figure 3.19
The Local Toggle active.

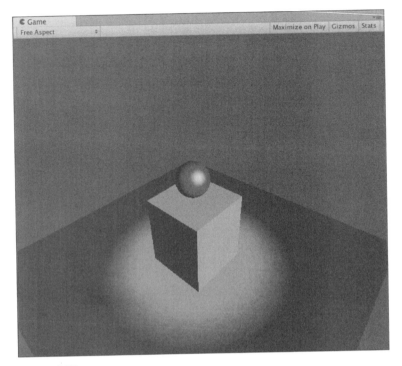

Figure 3.20
The rendered Game view.

While this may not seem like the biggest deal to you right now, when you start to tweak and balance hundreds of little details, having the flexibility to switch between the editor and the game on the fly is priceless. See Figure 3.20.

To test the game, press the Play button in the Play Control groups on the Toolbar (the one that looks like a right-facing arrow). The editor will make the Game view active, slightly darken all the UI (user interface), and start your game. Test this now.

There is a small script attached to the Sphere object that is causing it to slowly move up and down. See Figure 3.21. While this isn't anything revolutionary (or even in the neighborhood of fun), it does serve to illustrate one very important feature of the Game view.

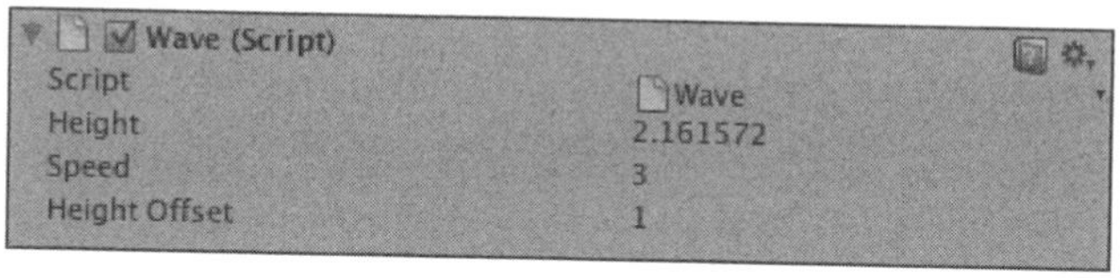

Figure 3.21
The Wave script component on the Sphere object.

While your game is playing, click on the Sphere object in the Hierarchy and take a look at the Wave script component on the Inspector. There are three *variables* defined in the script, values that dictate how the script behaves and affects the sphere—Height, Speed, and Height Offset. Notice that as the sphere moves, the Height variable updates on the fly to reflect the sphere's current position.

Now here's the fun part: Click on the number next to Speed and change it to anything else, like 1 or 10. The script and sphere both update in real time with your new change! Try playing with the Height Offset number too to see how it affects the game.

Note

If you want to see the smidgen of lines used in the code script to make the sphere move, you can either click on the Wave file in the Project view (under _TestFiles) or double-click on the Wave script in the Component field in the Inspector (the actual icon to the right of the Script field, not the title).

Being able to change any variable or value of any asset while you actively test your game will become your new best friend. Think your character is moving too slow? Try a faster speed value. Too fast? Scale it down a bit. Not having to rebuild your game after every small change is one of the highlights of Unity.

Caution

Do take note, however, that any change you make while your game is playing *won't be* saved once you stop the Play button. You can easily click the Play button to stop the game, update the value field with your new permanent change, and click the Play button again to jump back in. This is worth repeating—*any change* made while playing won't be saved.

The other two buttons on the Play Controls group of the Toolbar help with debugging and testing your game. The middle button, Pause, obviously pauses

Figure 3.22
The Game view Control Bar.

the game. Press the Pause button again to start play back up from where you left off. The last button is the Step button, and it allows you to move frame by frame through your game. This is especially useful when you need to debug a particularly bad patch of code and need to see where something starts to go wrong.

Like the Scene view, the Game view also has its own Control Bar, as shown in Figure 3.22. The first area, the Aspect drop-down menu, lets you change the aspect ratio of the Game view on the fly, even while it is currently playing. Free Aspect will allow the Game view to fill up all the available space of the current window size, whereas the other selections will emulate the resolutions and rations of most common monitors. This is really handy when you need to start making your GUI conform to different size screens.

Clicking the Maximize on Play toggle button will expand your Game view to take up the entire editor view when you start playing. Note that you can't change this toggle when the game is currently playing; you need to stop first and restart to update with the change.

If press the Gizmos button, you'll toggle all gizmos to be drawn and rendered in your game. Currently, you don't have any gizmos in the scene, so this doesn't do much right now. Later, though, you could have something like a custom gizmo denoting a special area of your game, and you may want to always see exactly where its boundaries are, even when playing.

Lastly, the final button on the Control Bar will bring up the Render Statistics page. This is extremely useful when you start optimizing your game. This may look mostly like garbage and gibberish to you right now, but it will all be covered in greater detail in Chapter 17. Know for now that this is a quick way to view your game's *FPS*, or Frames Per Second, a general indicator for how smooth or choppy your game is running. Click the Stats button again to hide the page.

The Animation View

Unity now includes an Animation view, where you can view and tweak animation curves. This window isn't open by default, but you can view it by either going to Window▶Animation or by pressing Ctrl+6. The Animation view will pop up in a separate floating window, which you can drag around or resize. Right now this window will be empty, as the scene doesn't contain any animations. Later in Chapter 10 you'll see how you can use this view to view clips and update data outside of a 3D animation application.

The Console and Status Bar

Two other useful debugging tools are the Console and the Status Bar, shown in Figure 3.23. The Status Bar is always visible along the bottom of the editor (usually it's a blank gray line), and the Console can be brought up by navigating

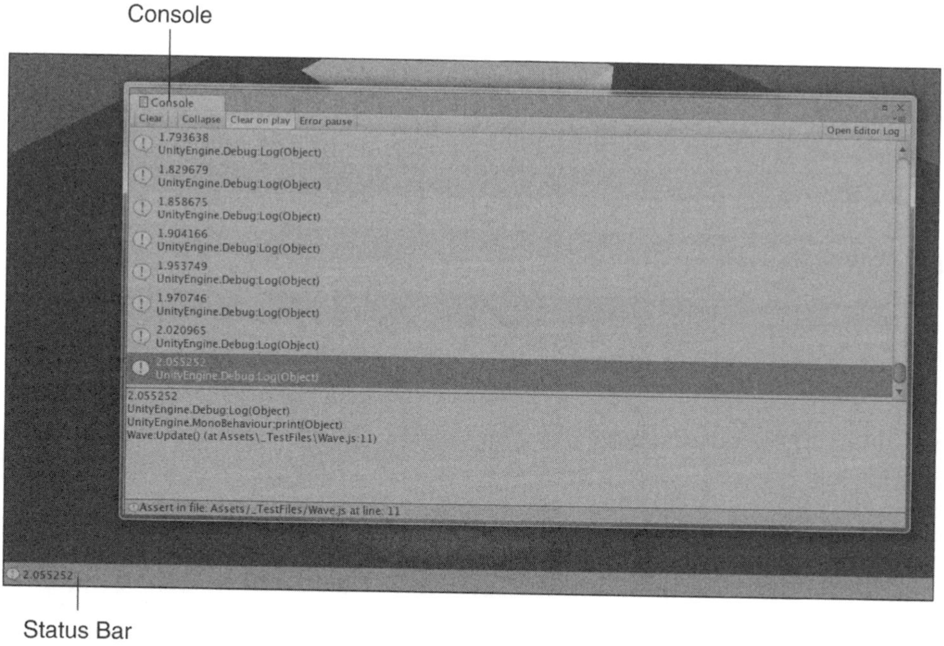

Console

Status Bar

Figure 3.23
The Console and the Status Bar in action.

to Window▶Console or by pressing Ctrl+Shift+C. You can also click on the Status Bar to open the Console.

Press the Play button to begin testing the game and watch how the Console and the Status Bar both update with the sphere's height data. It's possible in your scripts to have the game spit out pieces of information to the Console and the Status Bar, which can help with debugging and fixing errors. Any errors, messages, or warnings your game comes across will also be displayed here, along with any details about the specific bug.

The Profiler and Asset Server

You may have noticed two other options available under the Windows menu— Profiler and Asset Server. If you are using the free, basic version of Unity, these two options will be grayed out and inaccessible. If you have a Pro license, you can open the Profiler by clicking here or by pressing Ctrl+7 on your keyboard. The Profiler is a very powerful integrated debugging and optimization tool that's covered more fully in Chapter 17. If you have purchased the optional Asset Server add-on, you can access it here from within the Windows menu or by pressing Ctrl+0.

Customizing the Editor

While the default layout of the editor is pretty good, you may find it either not to your liking or that you require a specific layout of windows for a task at hand. The Layout drop-down menu on the Toolbar has a few saved common layouts available for you, as well as the ability to save custom layouts, delete layouts, or return to the default "factory" layout. You can also view the available saved layouts by going to Window▶Layouts.

Customizing your editor's layout is as simple as dragging and dropping. Any window can be moved by clicking and dragging on its tab (you'll know you did it right when a small gray box attaches itself to your cursor). You can dock tabs to any edge of the editor's window by dragging the tab to any of the edges. You can also make any tab a floating window by dragging it into the middle of the editor and releasing the mouse button. If you want to layer windows behind each other, drag a tab next to another to dock it to that same window.

Play around with the layout options until you find something that works for you. There isn't any right layout, and you probably have a personal workflow you like to follow. See Figure 3.24. When you find a layout that works for you, click on the Layout drop-down and click Save Layout. A small pop-up will open, allowing you to type a custom name for your new layout. Click the Save button when you're done.

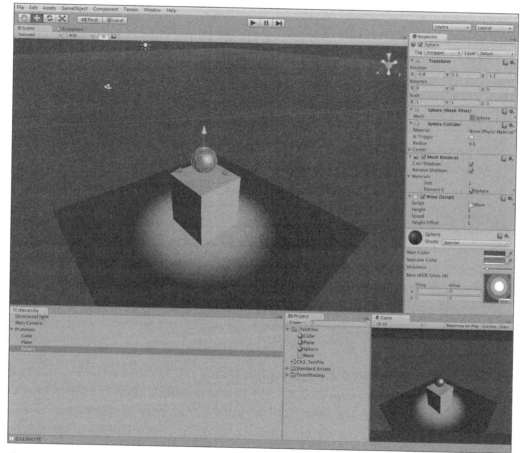

Figure 3.24
A completely custom editor layout.

UNITY'S BASIC CONCEPTS

Unity is a unique development tool, one that is very much different from other editors and engines on the market. As such, there are a few basic concepts to familiarize yourself with in order to make full use of its capabilities.

As mentioned earlier, each game you create is organized into its own project. The project contains all the scenes, levels, assets, sounds, scripts, and anything else your game uses. Projects can be created, saved, and opened from the File menu.

Your game is made up of a series of connected Scene files. Oftentimes, each level in your game will be contained within its own Scene file. Scene files can also be used for full-screen GUI elements (like a Main Menu or Game Over Screen), cut scenes, or anything else you want to load separately.

Buzzword

The basic building blocks within your Scene files are *GameObjects (GO)*. At its most basic form, a GameObject is a simple container for pieces called *components*. All GameObjects have at least one component (the Transform component) and often contain many more. In the test scene, the Sphere, Plane, and Cube objects are all GameObjects. (As are Main Camera, Directional Light, and Primitives, as well as imported 3D models or texture files.) GameObjects can also be nested within other GameObjects by parenting, as with the Primitives object. This is known as a GameObject hierarchy.

Note

If you use the menu option GameObject▶Create Empty to create a new GameObject in the scene and select it, you'll notice that it's still not actually empty. Even this so-called "empty" object still contains a Transform component.

Click on any one of the GameObjects in the Hierarchy view and look at the Inspector. Each division in the Inspector window is a component. For example, the Cube object has Transform, Cube (Mesh Filter), Box Collider, Mesh Renderer, and Shader components. You can think of each component being a different defining aspect or characteristic, and when combined, they create the object you see in the game. There are no limits to the numbers of components you can place in a GameObject, and many kinds of components can be placed multiple times upon the same GO (like scripts). If you browse through the Component menu, you can see different kinds of components available for use, all organized by base function.

Note

Components *cannot* be found or placed alone in your scene; they must be connected to a GameObject.

This helps to describe the major difference between Unity and other development tools: It is asset-centric at its core, not code-centric. Everything in your game has a visual representation and physical presence in the editor—even intangible things like scripts, cameras, and light sources. In this way, you'll find that working in Unity is more similar to working in a 3D modeling application, rather than in something like a strict coding environment.

AVAILABLE UNITY LICENSES

Unity comes in a variety of different flavors and natively supports multiple platforms. Depending on your needs or desires, you'll have five basic licenses to pick from: Unity, Unity Pro, Unity iPhone Basic, Unity iPhone Advanced, and Unity Wii. While all of these offer the same basic package with the integrated editor, there are a few major differences between Unity and Unity Pro if you are going to be developing for a PC or Mac. Both versions of Unity will give you the tools required to make and publish a game, but Unity Pro offers a few more perks and polished bits that might make it more appealing to a small development team or studio. Some of the major benefits offered in the Pro package include:

- **C/C++/Objective-C Plugins Support:** Build and deploy any custom plug-in or integrate a custom native library.
- **External Version Control Support:** Add integrated support for popular version control software, such as Perforce or Subversion.
- **Full-Screen Post-Processing Effects:** Comes with premade effects such as glow and motion blur, as well as the support to make your own.

- **Low-Level Rendering Access:** Allows custom rendering techniques and the ability to bypass Unity's built-in rendering pipeline.

- **Profiler:** An integrated visual tool for game optimization and code instrumentation.

- **Realtime Shadows:** Adds self-shadowing support for soft and hard cast shadows.

- **Script Access to Asset Pipeline:** Allows direct access to Unity's asset pipeline.

A complete side-by-side comparison of all the licenses is kept up to date on Unity's website.

Although all these optional features will make your game shinier and your development pipeline more customizable, it does come with a price tag attached. If you're a solo or new developer, you may want to start with the basic free Unity license before determining if you need, or want, to upgrade to the Pro license.

Note

Be aware when shopping around that there are two license restrictions currently in place for Unity. If your company (or incorporated entity) made a profit of over US$100,000 in its last fiscal year, you must license Unity Pro (or iPhone Advanced) over the other licenses. Also, a development team cannot mix licenses of Unity Pro and Unity or iPhone Basic and Advanced—the team must use the same type of license together.

Besides these basic licenses, Unity also offers license upgrades, an optional integrated asset server, a license for the editor's source code, as well as educational licenses.

EDITOR SUMMARY

Unity is a powerful, yet elegantly simple integrated editor and engine giving you all the tools necessary to create and publish a game, from 3D first-person shooters to casual 2D puzzle games.

All of its functions are organized into different tabbed window views, each providing different editing and manipulation capabilities for the task at hand.

The editor is completely asset-centric, creating physical links and references for all of its types of objects, even for things like code.

Unity's licensing schema and optional add-ons also allow just the right amount of power and customization when and where you need it, giving it the flexibility to be used by either the one-person hobbyist or the large-scale development team.

CHAPTER 4

YOUR FIRST GAME: WHERE TO START?

Designing and building your own game from the ground up may seem like a daunting or even impossible task, but it doesn't have to be. Much like any other large or lengthy undertaking, it can help to break your game up into manageable-sized chunks and approach the design one area at a time. A good place to start is learning the basics behind game design theory and its terminology, which can help organize your ideas first on paper before bringing them to life on the computer. Planning some of your high-level ideas first can help make the first time you sit down at the computer to build your game a little less intimidating and a little more fun.

BASIC DESIGN THEORY

If this is your first foray into making a game, you may find yourself lost for ideas or perhaps uncertain where to begin. Some fledgling designers have the uncanny ability to start making a game at a moment's notice, without any thought paid to structure or planning, and create something imaginative and fun on the first go round. Lucky them. For the rest of us, learning basic design theory can help organize a random collection of ideas into something that can later be turned into a playable and fun game.

The video game industry is a relatively young one, having only come into being in the latter half of the 20th century. The academic study and classification of video games is even more new, and it's only fairly recently that a standardized set of theories and terminology has come into somewhat standard use.

The most basic building block of the game is a *mechanic*, a rule or description that governs a specific, single aspect of play. In a video game, pressing a specific sequence of buttons to make your character jump is a simple mechanic. Defeating an enemy onscreen when you hit him with a fireball is also a mechanic. Collecting colored bubbles for points is another mechanic. All games are built on a collection of mechanics that, when put together in a meaningful way, create a fun and interactive experience. Think of your favorite game and make a list of all the different things you as a player can do in the game world. Each item on this list is a mechanic of the game.

Similar and interrelated mechanics can be grouped into a larger set of rules known as a *system*. Well-designed and imaginative systems are at the heart of any fun game, and this is often where the bulk of a designer's time can be spent polishing, balancing, and tweaking. You can identify systems in any given game by thinking of the high-level descriptions of what you can do as a player. For example, a sample game allows you to move a character around by tilting a joystick, jump into the air with the push of a button, and have your character take flight by holding down two buttons at once. Each of these three mechanics can be grouped into a larger movement system—they all relate to how you as the player control your character. While many games have similar kinds of systems in place—movement, combat, leveling-up—it is the individual mechanics in each system that make a game unique.

When you start designing a game, one of the first things you should identify is the *core* of your game. The core is basically one defining and unifying statement that describes your game. You can think of the core as a thesis statement for a research paper—every paragraph in the paper relates to and supports the thesis, much like every part of the game supports and strengthens the core idea. Taking the time to define and develop a strong core statement can make your design process much easier and more efficient as your game begins to take shape.

Core statements are often composed as a "who-what-where" style of statement, describing who the players are, where they are, and in very general terms what they'll be doing in the game. Pretend a friend asks you about your game.

How can you quickly strip down the game to its bare essence and answer in just one sentence? Your answer is your core game idea.

Tip

Besides defining your game's main idea, the core statement can also be used later to help solve dilemmas while designing. For example, you have two fun vehicle ideas for your game, and you don't know which one to use. You only have time to implement one, so testing both isn't an option. Look at both objectively and determine which one relates more strongly to the core idea, in everything from gameplay functions to physical form. If you have to go with just one, pick the one that more strongly supports your core idea.

If the core is a thesis statement of a paper, the *feature set* is the collection of main ideas from each supporting paragraph. Each element in the feature set describes a main part of the play in your game, and each should definitively relate back to the core idea. Let's say you're making a game about pirates. A possible core idea for a pirate game could be: *Work, duel, and beguile your way up from a deck scrubber to the captain of your own ship as you become the most feared pirate on the Seven Seas.* As it stands, this core idea could describe any number of pirate games, so you'll need to create a more defined list of features that will help develop your idea into something more complex and unique. One feature set for this game could be the following:

- Completely customize your own pirate ship with over 100 unique parts
- Sail around the game's open world and visit more than 50 different port towns, each with its own characters and culture
- Find hidden treasure and bury your own goods with a detailed mapping system
- Fight one-on-one sword and saber duels with other members of the ship to work your way up the pirate ranks
- Defend your ship in epic sea battles against rival pirates and enemy vessels with upgradable cannons and over 20 kinds of ammunition

Note

A game that's said to be "open world" has no defined levels that the player must progress through in a set order. Players can roam around the world and visit any place whenever they want.

This isn't the only possible feature list you could make from this core idea. A second game could be as follows:

- Swindle your deck mates out of cash and treasure by mastering the in-game collectable card game

- Promote your character through the pirate ranks by performing quests for the captain, combating other pirates in pirate competitions, or finding the most unique treasure in city raids

- Purchase unique and randomly generated islands to build your pirate fortress and store your most valuable finds

- Seduce governors' daughters and ransom pompous politicians for fame or fortune

- Assemble a pirate fleet from more than 30 kinds of ships

- Unlock special ships, treasure, and upgrades as you play

Both of these feature sets describe and support the core statement, but each details a completely different game experience. Neither of them is better than the other; they both equally describe a game about pirates. If you find yourself stuck when trying to make a feature list, think of yourself as a new player placed into your world. What is it that you want to do? What would be fun or cool to you? Do you like collecting things? Racing? Customizing characters or vehicles? Researching and developing new items? Make a list of tasks that would interest you in the world, and then ask yourself how you could go about actually performing these actions. Each of these is a possible feature for you to use.

Tip

Never throw away an unused game or feature idea, even if you think it's the silliest idea in the world. Keep a notebook or file with all your ideas and add any new ones you have to it. Even if an idea doesn't work for you at the current moment, later on you may find it's the perfect solution to a different design problem.

From the feature set, you can now begin to develop your systems and mechanics. Let's say you decided to go with your first pirate feature set. Just from quickly reading the entries, you know you'll need some sort of sailing system, a character customization system, a dueling system, a treasure hunting and burying system, a combat system, and a research system to develop new cannons and ship parts. Now pick one of your systems and begin to flesh out the individual mechanics. For the ship combat system, you know you'll need a cannon firing mechanic, a loading and mixing ammunition mechanic, a mechanic to control how damage is applied to the ship, and perhaps a dodge or evasive maneuvers mechanic.

At this stage you don't need to know how every little mechanic works, and in fact, sometimes it's better if you don't. Most of the best games are built upon an iterative process—trying one idea, testing it, and tweaking it a few times until you're happy with the result. Oftentimes you may not be sure if a mechanic is working well when you first implement it, and it isn't until you begin to get more pieces into the game that certain flaws or merits in your mechanics become apparent. Don't be discouraged if things don't seem to work out right in the beginning. A game constantly evolves and grows throughout the design process and will invariably face a few hurdles along the way before it meshes into something fun and playable.

FINDING THE CORE IDEA

Ideas for new games can come from anything, anytime, anywhere. There's no one definitive or magical way a designer comes up with a game idea, and each designer has a process that works uniquely for himself and sometimes no one else. Ideas can come from watching movies or television shows, reading a book, playing other games, flipping through the newspaper, daydreaming, shopping, or taking a walk. Some lucky designers actually find they have too many ideas to ever have time to fully develop and make and have to instead pick only one idea from a collection of hundreds. Others can wrestle with one idea for weeks or months at a time before they work out something they're happy to continue with.

Brainstorming

Designing is a different process for each person, but there are basic methods of brainstorming that can help if you find yourself staring at a blank screen.

- **Free writing:** Get out a blank sheet of paper (or open a new computer file), set a timer for five minutes, and begin to list topics or ideas as they come to you. Simple, single nouns are fine at this point. Don't worry about whether the idea makes sense or if the noun is silly or doesn't mean anything. Just write down words as they pop into your head. Look around the room, glance out a window, or flip through a magazine and write down things that interest you. Don't think about what you're writing down—just write. At the end of five minutes, look back through your list and see if one item or a collection of different listings catches your attention.

▪ **Random searches:** Go online to your favorite search engine, encyclopedia, or database and request a random page (*Wikipedia* works well for this). Keep refreshing and looking up random pages until something catches your eye—write it down. Just as with free writing, don't think about what the idea could mean or what you could do with it; just write it down if it interests you. When you've compiled a sizable list, look it over and see if anything stands out. You can also open a volume of a physical encyclopedia to a random page or browse around the local library and pick up random books and jot down the title or subject matter.

▪ **Matching items:** Make a list of subjects or hobbies that interest you, such as "Coffee," "Cats," "Murder Mysteries," "The 100 Years War," "Irish History," "Barcelona," or "Hiking." Place each of these subjects onto a small slip of paper or index card and place into a box. Now make a second list of kinds of games you like to play, such as "Puzzles," "Platformer," "Adventure," "Card Collecting," "Flight Simulator," or "Racing." Put each of these game types onto its own card and put it in a separate box. Now mix up the cards and pick one card from the subject box and one card from the game type box. Make a list of the combinations you draw. Does anything look interesting to you? You can also try drawing two or more subject cards for each game type card to make a more detailed list.

▪ **Browse a bookstore:** Go to either a physical store or online store front and read the descriptions and summaries of books and movies that interest you. Find one that sounds like fun to you—would it be fun for you to play a game with this or a similar description? Make a list of the basic descriptions and formulate a core idea from each summary. Do keep in mind however that you shouldn't blatantly copy an idea from an existing product, but rather you should use it as a springboard for your own ideas.

- **Consult your notebook:** If you've been keeping a design notebook with all your various ideas, take a moment to read it over. Does anything in it strike your fancy? Could a few of the items you wrote down be used for the basis of another brainstorming method, like creating a matched list? You should probably make it a habit to read through it on a regular basis—you never know when a random idea will come in handy.

Brainstorming shouldn't be a painful process, and if you find you're getting frustrated, take a break and come back to it later—there's no rush to create that first game idea. Forcing an idea will pretty much guarantee it won't be something all that fun for you to work on. Remember, you'll be spending a large amount of time on your game (weeks or months, and maybe years for larger projects), so make sure it's an idea that can interest you for that long.

Researching Other Games

Besides other methods of brainstorming, you should also actively research and document games that you enjoy playing. If it's a game you like to play for hours on end, it stands to reason that that particular style of game could also be fun for you to make. You don't have to write a lengthy, in-depth analysis of every game you play, but begin to notice certain features or kinds of gameplay that stand out as fun to you.

First, write down the basic core statement of the game you like. What's it about? What about it draws you to it? Is it the subject or theme material or the actual gameplay itself? Create a list of the features that appeal to you. Do you like driving different kinds of cars, picking out new armor for your warrior, or matching up colored stones into a defined pattern? What is it about the feature that makes it fun for you?

After you've broken down the game a bit, begin to question what you would do differently, or what added features you'd want to see. Change the theme, modify one feature, delete another, or add a new gameplay element. Again, the object isn't to copy another game already out on the market but to identify common features and elements you think are fun and to use that as a starting point for your own game.

Also, rent or borrow games in other genres you don't usually play. If you've never tried a first-person shooter, pick one up from a friend, get a quick tutorial, and see how it works and what makes it fun for others. Even if it's a game that you end up really disliking, there might be an idea floating around in it you could use and incorporate into your own design. Constantly expand your game horizons and try new genres and kinds of games. Not only may you find something new to play, but you'll also expand your design repertoire into a fuller and richer body of ideas.

Paper Prototyping: It's Not Just for Business Software

Another method for brainstorming video game ideas is to try similar ones in the non-digital realm first—make a board or card game using similar mechanics. *Paper prototyping* is a term used in interactive markets, often in a business setting, when a new piece of software or website is being developed. It can be very expensive to hire a team of programmers to make a custom program, and businesses want to capitalize on the time they have without forgoing quality.

Designers work out the software or website on paper first, creating sheet after sheet of the different screens a user would see. They then run tests with focus groups, using these sheets to determine if their basic ideas make sense. Even though it's not on a computer screen, users can still point out if a button placement doesn't make sense, if the wording is too vague, or if the layout of the program's interface is too hard to understand. This way, the designers can work out the kinks in their design and iterate as much as they want before spending thousands on actual implementation. It's a lot cheaper and faster to change something on paper than it is to recode a program.

Games aren't any different. While it takes time to create the art and code up the game systems, it's a lot faster to write some quick notes on some cards and draw up a basic game board on a sheet of paper. Although not all video games can be easily turned into a board game, many of the underlying mechanics can. If you're unsure of an idea, try it on paper first and invite some friends over to play. You'll have the chance to quickly change rules to see how it affects play and discover new aspects of play you may not have thought of before. Perhaps a side mechanic that didn't mean much to you is an absolute hit with the play group— you now know that it's something you could focus more on. Or maybe that movement system you had made it way to easy to get across the world—you can probably scale it back some and make it more competitive.

You don't need to create fancy artwork or get specialized pieces for testing— blank paper, pencils, and random bits found around the house all work to get a point across. There are, however, many stores that sell random game parts and pieces if you find it useful to have those on hand. While browsing around parts or craft stores, you may also come across pieces or items that intrigue you by their shape, color, texture, or other physical aspect. Just because it's physical doesn't mean it won't translate well to the digital realm. Is it something you could add into your video game? What about it do you find fun and interesting, and is it something you can incorporate into your larger design?

PLANNING IT ALL OUT

Once you have a basic core idea and feature set, it's time to begin to really plan your game design. Some designers can simply sit down at the computer at this point and begin to knock out their game piece by piece, but especially for first time designers, it may be easier to take a more systematic approach. This way, you'll know you won't forget to add something and can set out a better schedule to get your game finished. Haphazardly designing and implementing features in your game can make the process more unwieldy and introduce problems or inconsistencies where none originally existed.

A Basic Outline

The first thing you might find useful is to flesh out a simple gameplay-oriented outline of your game. A sample blank template for you to use if you want is included on the DVD (see DVD▶Design Documents▶ Blank_Outline_Template). This can help form a preliminary basis for you to get all your ideas in order. You can either use the provided template or think about the following questions as you compose your outline: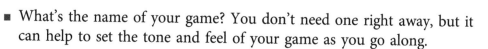

- What's the name of your game? You don't need one right away, but it can help to set the tone and feel of your game as you go along.

- What's your game's core statement? Is it something that interests you?
- Describe the feature set. Is it a unique list and does it fully describe and support the core statement?
- Provide a basic description of the game world. When and where does it take place? Are there any special features of note? Is it an open world or is it comprised of many individual levels?
- What's the overall victory condition or goal in the game? Is the player trying to reach a certain space or collect a set number of a specific item? How does the player win? Does the game actually ever end?
- Where does the game start? What options are available to the players when they start the game?
- Who are the characters in the game? What do they look like? What do they do in the game? Do they provide any services to the player? Does the player control any of the characters?
- What are the main systems in your game? Which features do they support?
- What are the main gameplay mechanics in the game and to which system do they belong?

Figure 4.1 shows a sample outline page using the pirate game described earlier in the chapter.

If you can answer most of these questions, you're at a great place to begin. Don't feel that your answers must be set in stone once you write them down—you may have a better idea later or need to tweak something if it's not turning out to be that fun. If you can't answer all these questions at the moment, that's also fine. Not everyone designs in the same manner or at the same pace, so don't feel the need to compare your process to someone else's. If what you're doing works for you, stick with it. If you're having problems keeping everything in order and coming up with new ideas, try a new approach.

A Simple Level Document

Creating a simple level design document can also help you get your game information in order. Levels documents are compiled for many games and generally detail one individual level or section of the world.

Game Name:	High Seas

Core Theme/ Idea: In High Seas you work, duel, and beguile your way up from a lowly deck scrubber to the captain of your own ship as you become the most feared pirate on the seven seas.

Feature Set

1 Completely customize your own pirate ship with over 100 unique parts

2 Sail around the world and visit more than 50 different port towns, each with its own characters and culture

3 Find hidden treasure and bury your own with a detailed mapping system

4 Fight one-on-one sword and saber duels with other members of the ship to work your way up the pirate ranks

5 Defend your ships in epic sea battles against rival pirates and enemy vessels with upgradable cannons and over 20 kinds of ammunition

6 Seduce governor's daughters and ransom pompous politicians for fame or fortune.

7

8

9

10

World Description

High Seas takes place across the Atlantic, from the New World to the western coasts of Africa and Europe. Hundreds of islands dot the waves and players can freely navigate around the open world. Coastal port towns offer opportunity for looting and purchasing of goods, and each town is uniquely decorated with specific cultural items and flair.

Victory or Goals

Players attempt to promote their way up to the rank of pirate captain, and then have the option to complete online against other players for the top score. The game ends ten in-game years after the status of Captain is reached. A special New Game+ mode may be unlocked along the way.

Player Start

The player starts out in a random city with the rank of Deck Scrubber, no funds, and only the clothes on his back. He must find a crew in port to join to begin his journey.

Figure 4.1
High Seas' first outline page, based on the provided template.

If your game is small enough, it could even cover the entire game world. The concept behind the level doc is simple—you provide a map of your game world and add specific notes and map points detailing all the important aspects of your game. Important gameplay notes and descriptions accompany the map. The idea behind the document is that any person who saw it would have enough information to build your game exactly as you envisioned, down to each individual detail.

A sample blank template is provided on the DVD (see DVD▶Design Documents▶Blank_Level_Template), or you can think about the following questions and lines of direction to compile your own level document:

- What does your game map look like? Where and what are the important features?

- Where does the player start and finish? Are these places obvious in the game world?

- Who are the characters in the world and where are they located? Does the player need to do anything special to reach them? Do they do something for the player or say anything?

- Are there items located around the world to pick up or hidden items to find? What do they look like? What do they do?

- Are there enemies or obstacles in the world? Where and what are they? Do they have special abilities, or does the player need special items to overcome them?

- Do all the listed and mapped elements relate back to your core and feature set?

- Is there a specific path the player must follow through the world or a set sequence of actions he must take? Are there side paths with special rewards to find?

- Are there special abilities the player needs to acquire to reach certain areas of the map? Are there specific items he needs to complete the journey?

Figure 4.2 shows a sample level document page and map using the pirate game described earlier in the chapter.

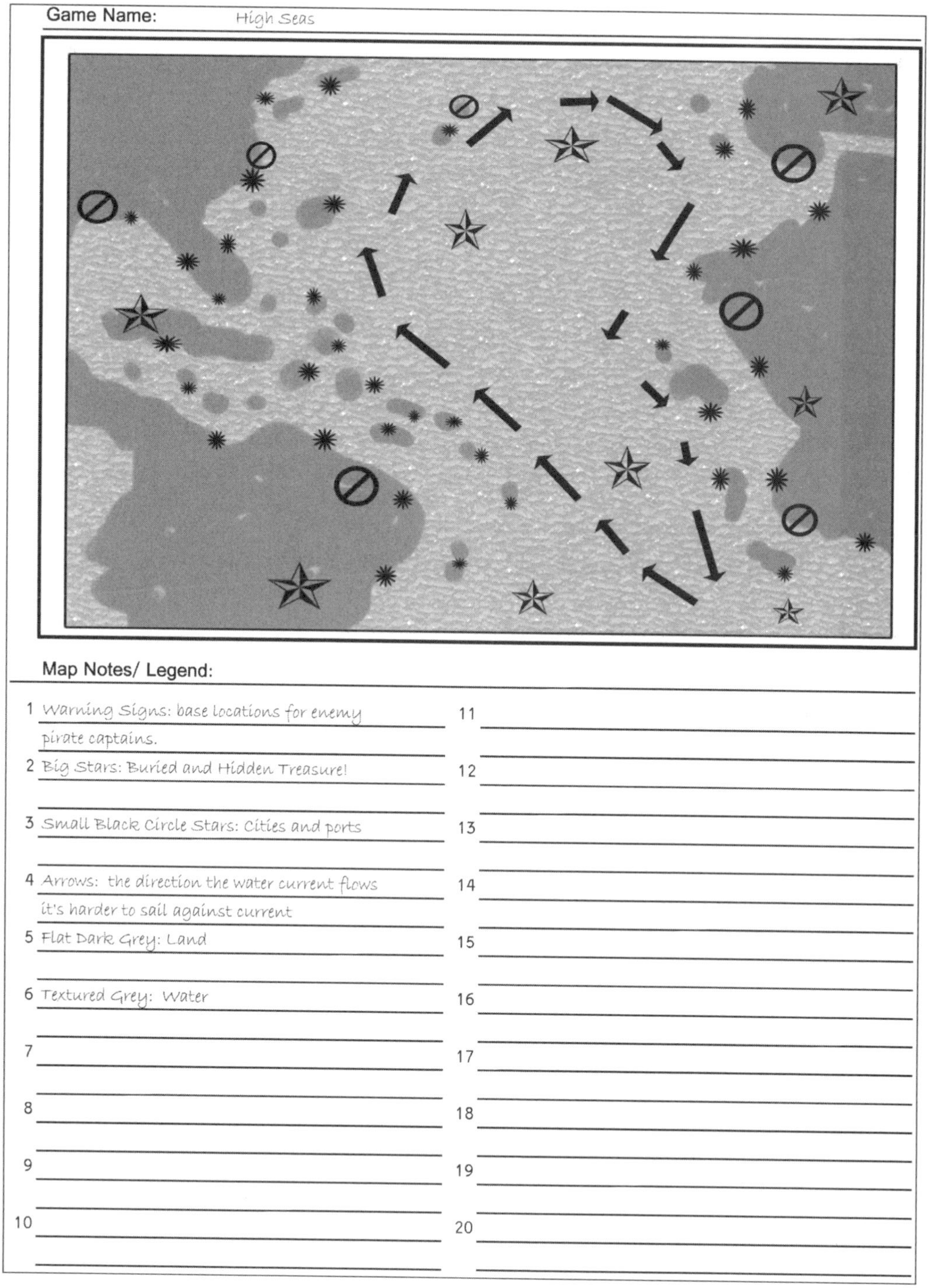

Game Name: High Seas

Map Notes/ Legend:

1 Warning Signs: base locations for enemy pirate captains.
2 Big Stars: Buried and Hidden Treasure!
3 Small Black Circle Stars: Cities and ports
4 Arrows: the direction the water current flows it's harder to sail against current
5 Flat Dark Grey: Land
6 Textured Grey: Water
7
8
9
10
11
12
13
14
15
16
17
18
19
20

Figure 4.2
High Seas' map with points of interest marked.

Even if you decide not to write a full-level document, you should at least draw up a simple map of your game world. Besides a sheet of paper or a computer drawing program, a good material to use for level designing is a plain whiteboard and set of markers. The whiteboard makes it easy to erase and redraw areas of your level as you see fit and to quickly use different colors to denote different areas of your map. You can also get color-coded or uniquely shaped magnets to place on your whiteboard—these can be used for specific gameplay notes, enemy positions, item pick-up locations, or anything you want.

Have fun with your map and don't hesitate to draw up a few different iterations of it. Look at other game maps you enjoyed playing and try to pick out specific features you thought were fun or interesting. Observe real-world maps of cities and land masses to get an idea of how real maps flow. If your game map is more 3D in nature, try physically building it out of wooden blocks or other children's toys.

Much like your design ideas, save your map ideas even if you're not using them for this specific game. You never know when you might want to use one in the future.

GETTING STARTED

Spend some time thinking up and planning what you'd like to make in Unity. At this point, shoot for the proverbial moon and just concentrate on what's fun, not about actual logistics of making it—that'll come in time. From this point forward, each chapter of the book will focus on implementing specific features using the tools within Unity to create a simple, sample game. All of the files and resources referenced are available for use on the DVD, split up by chapter as well as compiled into a final build. You of course also have the option of making your own idea from scratch and just following along for the process or using the provided assets as a springboard for your own unique creation.

The design files for the sample game, *Widget*, can be found on the DVD under "Design Documents," and you should familiarize yourself with the basic idea if you plan on using the sample as a learning aid. Each chapter folder on the DVD contains the base files referenced in the text, and you can pull them down to your own computer as you need them. A final compiled project folder is also included, and this can be pulled down and viewed if you run into trouble.

Part II

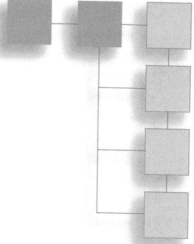

Assembling the Game Assets

You now have a working knowledge of Unity's interface and at least the beginnings of a new idea to work with. In Part II, you'll look at compiling and importing the different art assets the *Widget* game will require, from terrain sculpting to character setups. Unity has one of the slickest asset importers around, and with it you'll be creating your game worlds in no time.

CHAPTER 5

SETTING THE STAGE WITH TERRAIN

Now that you have a basic idea of what you want to make, you need to start compiling the various pieces and parts needed to bring the game to life. Some of these items, like terrain and simple primitive objects, can be created directly within Unity. Others, like a main character and special pick-up items, will need to be imported from other 3D modeling packages, such as Autodesk's Maya or Blender. One of the flashier and more rewarding parts to start with is fleshing out the world's environment—the physical space around which your character will run, jump, defeat enemies, and save the proverbial princess. Getting this laid out first will make placing your characters and items a bit easier and straightforward.

In Unity, game environments can be made, in effect, in three ways: using only terrain generated from within the engine, importing a complete 3D mesh of the world, or using a combination of terrain and meshes to carve out the world's space. *Widget* will use the latter, but you may especially find it useful to make your entire game's environment in a 3D package and just import it in at once—you'll know that everything fits together and is exactly where you want it, without having to reposition. Unity's free "3D Platformer" tutorial, available for download from their site, uses this method. If you find that you want something organic or want to simulate real-world landmasses, you should consider using terrain.

UNITY'S TERRAIN ENGINE

At this point you should set up your project space on your computer. With Unity open, choose File▶New Project and click on the Create New Project tab. Browse to where you'd like to save your files and decide whether to import the Standard Assets and Toon Shading packages. If you're following along with *Widget*, select both and click Create. This new project will be loaded by default until you open or create a new one.

Open your project in Unity and create a new scene, if it isn't already. Add a directional light (GameObject▶Create Other▶Directional Light) and rotate it so it doesn't point directly down. This will act as the "sun."

Creating a terrain is as simple as creating a base primitive GameObject; just navigate to the menu option Terrain▶Create Terrain. You'll be greeted with a large, gray, plane-like object, as shown in Figure 5.1.

As it stands, you could run this in the engine and have a little character run around it, but it isn't terribly interesting to look at. This default terrain may not be exactly what you were looking for, so to change its settings, make sure it is selected in the Hierarchy, return to the Terrain menu, and select Set Resolution. This dialog box will allow you to change the basic features of your terrain's size and resolution:

- **Terrain Width:** The total width of the terrain in units.
- **Terrain Height**: The total *possible* max height of the terrain in units. This does not set the height of your terrain to match.
- **Terrain Length:** The total length of the terrain in units.
- **Heightmap Resolution:** The resolution of the terrain's generated *heightmap*.
- **Detail Resolution**: The resolution of the terrain's generated detail map. Low numbers here are good for performance, but depending on what you need, you may need to raise it.
- **Control Texture Resolution:** The resolution of the splat map used when painting the different terrain textures onto the terrain.
- **Base Texture Resolution:** The resolution of the generated texture that is used for the terrain at far distances.

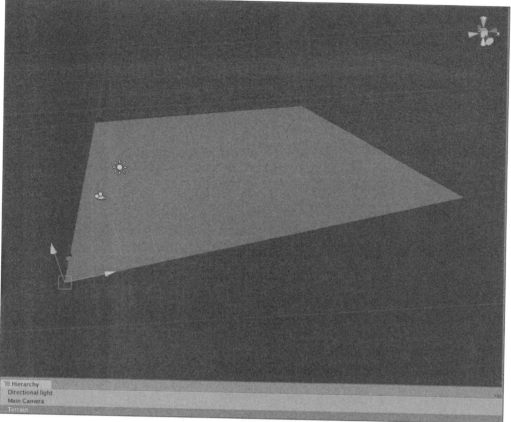

Figure 5.1
A default terrain.

An important piece of information to keep in mind is that by default, Unity's units equal 1 meter. If you know how big you need your map to be, set it up front. Also, change any of your external applications to match this scale, and you'll have an easier time placing all your assets.

The major decisions you should consider making now are described in the first four settings of the terrain's size and resolution—you'll have time later to change the detail and texture resolutions after you edit the terrain's height, but modifying these settings after you start can cause massive headaches. In particular, if you change any of the resolution features, you will delete all dependent detail information—that's not fun for anyone. Unity's defaults are a good place to start if you don't have a plan in place, but if you designed your environment first, most of this shouldn't be an issue.

Note

You can have more than one terrain in your scene, and in fact, some techniques require you to do so. If you find that you seriously misjudged your terrain's size early on, you may be able to fix the error by using a second terrain.

When using terrain, Unity also gives you some unique movement controls to make editing your game easier. Terrains can get pretty massive, and it can take a while to scroll around or find the one tiny detail you want to tweak. With the terrain selected in the Hierarchy, move your mouse cursor over an area of the terrain in the Scene view you'd like to see and press the F Key. The camera will zoom in to that spot. If you want to see the entire terrain again, move the mouse off the terrain in the Scene view and press F again—this will zoom out far enough to fit the whole terrain into the Scene view.

Note that you cannot rotate or scale your terrain and that you can only change its dimensions by using the Set Resolution menu option—it does not act as any other normal GameObject. You can still move the terrain around the world using either the Translate gizmo or by changing its position values in the Inspector.

CUSTOMIZING TERRAIN

A terrain in Unity can be edited in one of two ways: by importing a prerendered grayscale image (a *heightmap*) or by dynamically painting peaks and valleys onto the terrain's surface using the provided brush tools. Both offer unique advantages and their own associated issues, but you can always switch between the two if you find what you're doing isn't working.

Building Height Using a Heightmap

If you know exactly what you want (and have the tools to make it), using a heightmap can be the fastest way to get the best results. Basically, a heightmap is a grayscale image used to represent 3D height changes on a 2D image. Lower elevations are depicted with darker shades of gray going towards black, and higher elevations are shown with lighter shades of gray running towards white. Truly professional-looking heightmaps can be made in external programs such as Terragen or Bryce, but a quick (albeit lower-quality) one can be painted in a 2D graphics editor such as Photoshop or GIMP. Be sure to always keep your image sizes square or in powers of two if you decide to make your own. You can use any program to make your heightmap, so long as it exports to a .RAW format—this is the only file format Unity will read in for your maps.

Once you have your heightmap, highlight your Terrain asset in the Hierarchy and navigate to the Terrain menu: Terrain▶Import Heightmap – Raw. If you don't have a heightmap available, you can use any of the ones provided on the DVD, found in the Chapter 5▶Heightmaps folder. Once you select the file you want to use, a dialog box will display the import choices available for heightmaps:

- **Depth:** Set per your file specifications: either 8-bit or 16-bit. Import using the quality at which you created the file. Use the default for the provided maps.

- **Width:** The width of your heightmap image, which should be grabbed automatically from the image size.

- **Height:** The height of your heightmap image, which should be grabbed automatically from the image size.

- **Byte Order:** Set per your file specifications: Mac or Windows. Use the one that encoded the file (Windows if you're using the provided files on the DVD).

- **Terrain Size:** This links back to the Terrain Set Resolution options and lets you change the size if you find your heightmap image size differs wildly (see Figure 5.2).

In general, a good estimate to use when setting your terrain size to match your heightmap is one square pixel equals two meters square. In this case, a 1000×1000 pixel image maps to a 2000×2000 unit terrain. You can change these if your map requires a finer resolution, but you'll find that performance will take a noticeable hit (see Figures 5.3 and 5.4).

Painting Height Using Brushes

Creating a heightmap may not be your style or even feasible without the proper tools, which is where the included brush tools come in. Either create a new terrain or return your current one to its default flat level: navigate to the Terrain menu and select Terrain▶Flatten Heightmap.

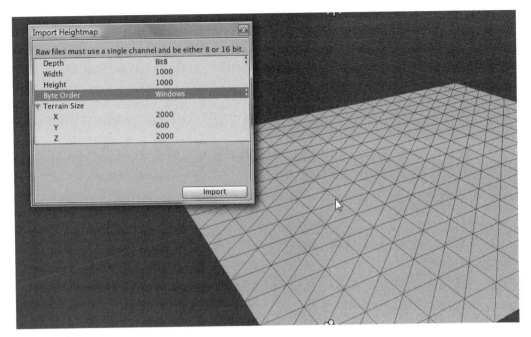

Figure 5.2
Importing a heightmap.

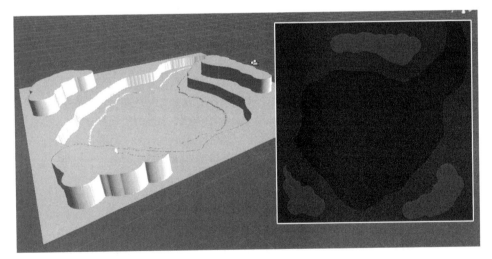

Figure 5.3
A sample terrain and the heightmap used to create it.

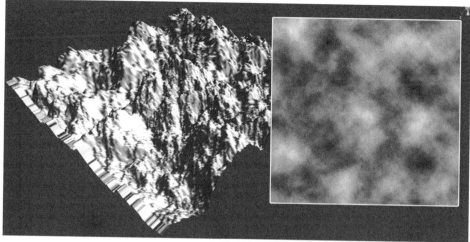

Figure 5.4
A more complicated heightmap and its associated terrain.

Type a **0** into the Height box to return the terrain to its default starting height.

Tip

You can use the Flatten Heightmap tool to bring the entire level of the terrain up by any number of units, such as 50 or 100, which can be useful if you need to push it down later to create valleys or canyons.

With the terrain selected in the Hierarchy, examine its information in the Inspector, as shown in Figure 5.5.

The Terrain component is where the majority of the action happens. Across the top of the component are seven buttons making up the Terrain toolbar, each activating a different submenu for manipulating and editing the terrain. The first three buttons—Raise and Lower Height, Paint Target Height, and Smooth Height—manipulate the general shape of the terrain.

Click on the first button in the list to activate the tool to raise and lower the terrain's height. Your mouse cursor will have a blue circle attached to it if you hover over the terrain in the Scene view—this is your selected brush's area of effect. By default, the first brush in the Inspector will be selected, but you can

Paint Terrain

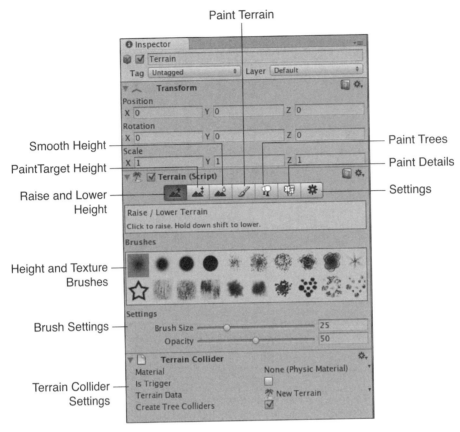

Smooth Height

PaintTarget Height

Raise and Lower
Height

Paint Trees

Paint Details

Settings

Height and Texture
Brushes

Brush Settings

Terrain Collider
Settings

Figure 5.5
The terrain's default Inspector properties.

change it to any of the other brushes by clicking on them (see Figure 5.6). As in other graphics programs, the brush you select dictates how your painted strokes will look.

Most brushes come with two available settings: Size and Opacity. Size, obviously, dictates how large an area the brush will cover. Small numbers will paint over smaller amounts of terrain, and larger numbers (up to 100) will paint a larger block. Opacity also works the same as in other painting programs; it describes how transparent, or how much, your brush will paint at once. Low values will move the terrain just a tiny bit, and high numbers (again up to 100—it's a percentage) will drastically raise or lower the terrain.

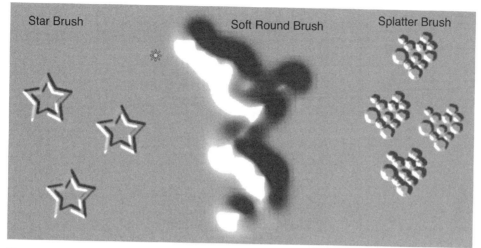

Figure 5.6
Some of the available brushes.

Pick one of the brushes and click and drag anywhere on the terrain in the Scene view. The terrain will begin to deform and push up where you painted your stroke. You can change the brush's size and opacity in the Inspector to paint more or less of the terrain in soft gentle strokes or with harsh hard lines.

Experiment with the different brush offerings and their settings to get a feel for painting on the terrain. You can also hold down the Shift button while painting to lower the terrain instead of raising it. The terrain will not go below a height of zero, so if you want to create canyons or valleys, you should move your entire terrain's height to a higher level and then lower specific parts down to zero. Your terrain is also limited by the overall height you set in the Set Resolution dialog box, and your brushes will plateau once you reach that height.

Using these brushes, you can easily create soft hills, mountain peaks, and streambeds, limited only by the resolution of your terrain (see Figure 5.7).

While these terrains can be quite natural and beautiful, they're not the most conducive to moving a character across. The second button in the Terrain toolbar will let you paint up to a set height, thereby allowing you to create nice flat walkways and plateaus for your characters. The Brush Size and Opacity settings work just the same as for the Raise and Lower Height tool, the only difference being the inclusion of the Height slider and text field. Choose any

Figure 5.7
Like any 3D mesh, a terrain's possible deformation is limited only by the resolution available.

Select Target Height

Figure 5.8
By setting the target height to different values, you can create tiered landscapes for your characters to explore.

target height (within the limits of your set maximum height) to paint the terrain and have it plateau at that new height (see Figure 5.8).

Holding down Shift while painting works a little bit differently when using this tool—instead of slowly lowering the terrain based on your opacity settings, it samples the height data at the brush's location, making it easy to turn any area of your map into a flat walkway. If you want to actually lower a part of the terrain, just type in or sample a lower height value and paint normally.

The last tool available to paint the height of terrains is the Smooth Height tool. This works just like the other two tools in that you paint with a chosen brush

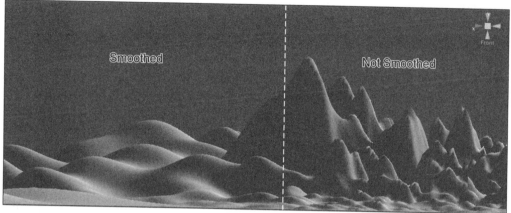

Figure 5.9
Both sides of this mountain range were created with a splatter brush, the left side then being smoothed afterwards with a soft round brush.

directly onto the terrain in the Scene view. As you might expect, this brush smooths out sharp changes in height and makes the terrain look a bit more eroded and natural (see Figure 5.9).

You can of course also mix and match the two approaches; there's nothing saying that once you've decided to import a heightmap you're stuck only with that. You can always use a heightmap to get the base structures in place and then clean up specific areas using the brushes, or you can paint the terrain using the brushes and then export the generated heightmap to edit in an external program.

When you paint with the brushes on your terrain, you're basically creating your own grayscale heightmap image within the engine, which is being applied to the terrain dynamically as you paint. You can export this 2D image by going to Terrain▶Export Heightmap – Raw, which allows you to tweak or edit it on another external package. Unity will export these images only as .RAW files, but you can set the resolution and bit depth of the file when you export.

Painting Textures

Once you get the general feel for the terrain's height, it's time to start adding color and detail. Painting color onto the terrain works the same way as painting height—tileable textures are uploaded to the tool, and you use the same brushes and controls to paint the textures directly onto the terrain in the Scene view. The quickest way to get into terrain painting is to use the textures provided in the Standard Assets package.

Note

This book will not cover how to create your own tileable textures, but there are plenty of free online tutorials that do. Check Appendix D, "Resources and References," found on the DVD, for links to these and other helpful tutorials.

Expand the Standard Assets folder in your Project view and open the folder Terrain Textures. The Standard Assets package comes complete with four available textures: two grass variations, a dirt texture, and a decent rocky cliff face texture. When Unity creates the texture pages for the terrain, it does so in blocks of four—no surprise then that the standard textures come in a set of four. When you make and upload your own terrain textures, it makes more sense for performance reasons to upload textures only in multiples of four. If, for example, you have five textures, Unity will still have to create a second texture page for the terrain to fit the fifth texture and will leave three extra slots open, so you should either try to remake your textures so that you only need four, or you could create three more textures to make use of the available space. Once these textures are painted onto the terrain, they are commonly referred to as *splat maps*.

To begin painting textures onto your terrain, make sure it is selected in the Hierarchy view and select the Paint Terrain Textures button in the Inspector (the one that looks like a paint brush). See Figure 5.10.

The main noticeable difference between this mode and the painting height modes is the inclusion of a Textures field and its associated Options button. Click on the Terrain Options button to add, edit, and remove available textures to paint on the terrain (labeled with the text "Edit Textures"). Click on this button and select Add Texture from the drop-down to bring up the Add Terrain Texture dialog box, shown in Figure 5.11.

The first thing you'll need to do is pick a texture to turn into a terrain splat, which you can do by either selecting a texture from the drop-down box or dragging a texture over from the Project view into the (Texture 2D) slot. These kinds of dialog boxes are common in Unity, and all will attempt to give you

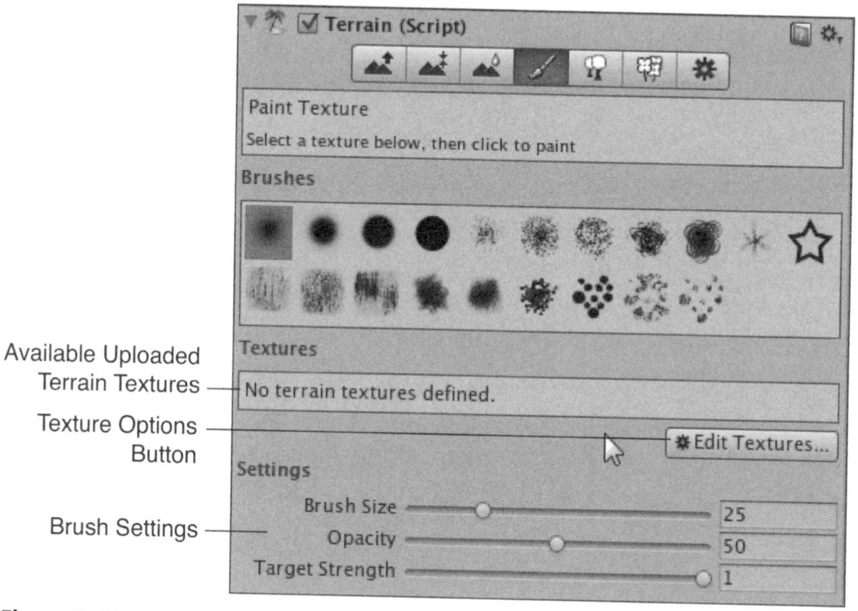

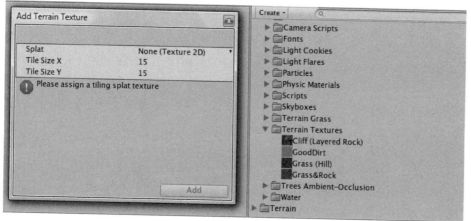

Available Uploaded
Terrain Textures

Texture Options
Button

Brush Settings

Figure 5.10
The Paint Terrain Texture component toolbox.

Figure 5.11
The Add Terrain Texture dialog box.

some sort of helper text explaining what kind of GameObject it expects, like a 2D texture. Unity won't let you assign a type of asset that won't work with the Options box. If you choose to select a texture instead from the drop-down box, all the available textures in your Assets folder will be listed, giving new meaning to the importance of proper naming conventions. You may find it faster just to find the file in the Project view and drag it over manually, rather than scrolling through the list.

You should be a bit savvy about the first texture you upload to the terrain—Unity will tile this one texture for you across the terrain upon upload, so make sure it's something that you want to cover the majority of the terrain. Otherwise you may find yourself doing a lot of unnecessary painting. Pick one—Grass (Hill) is a good first choice—and set the tile size for the texture in units. Smaller numbers will make the texture smaller and tile it more times across the terrain, while larger numbers will create a larger splat that tiles less often. Depending on your texture, these numbers could be as small as 4 units or as large as 4,096 units. The default of 15 × 15 works well for this case. Click Add when you're done.

Note

If you find you don't like the tile size you picked once you see it on the terrain, either click the Terrain Edit Options buttons and select Edit Texture or double-click on the texture's swatch in the Inspector to bring up the dialog box again. You can keep changing the tile sizes until you find something you like.

Now that your terrain is all nice and green, add some variation by uploading the extra three textures from the Standard Assets▶Terrain Textures folder with the same method as the first. Click on one of the none-grass textures in the Inspector to select it, pick a brush, and start painting in the Scene view. See Figure 5.12.

A good rule of thumb is to start with a low opacity and low target strength and apply the color in thin layers until you get the effect you're after. You can always undo a stroke if you don't like it, but the best terrains feature well-blended and varied textures, which you can only get using thin layers. Play around also with the different brush shapes to make painting different shapes easier.

In reality, you're not painting textures, but painting their *alpha channels* as they map to the terrain's surface. When you upload a new texture to the terrain, Unity basically creates a grayscale texture swatch in the background, much like the heightmap. Instead of painting lights and darks to raise the height, you're painting lights and darks to signify where that color should be placed. This is why the first texture you upload covers the entire terrain at once—Unity makes

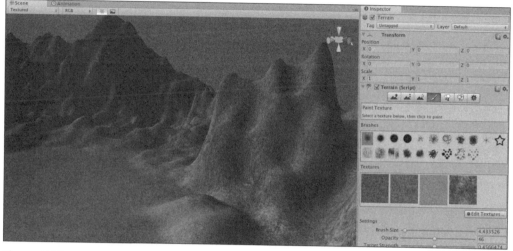

Figure 5.12
The terrain painted with the four available textures.

its default alpha value all white, meaning it covers the entire space. Every other uploaded texture's alpha is defaulted to all black (or completely transparent), and then you have to slowly paint in the areas you want to show.

Tip

An interesting technique to help paint the heightmap of a terrain is to use an imported texture (like a screen capture of Google Maps) as a guide. Import the texture as a terrain splat and make sure the tile size is the exact size of your terrain. You can now use the color information as a guide for your own hand-painting of the terrain's height and detail information, and the base color is already done for you.

If you find that you don't have the control you'd like with your textures, check the Control Texture Resolution setting under Terrain▶Set Resolution. A smaller texture resolution size (such as 512px) will save on memory, but you may not be getting the precision you need to paint small details or paths. You can also look at the Base Texture Resolution setting, right below it, if you feel your textures lose fidelity at far distances. Again, be aware of the possible memory hits that large numbers can mean for your game.

Note

If you're feeling particularly snazzy, you can run your game now and walk around it using a pre-made first person camera. Grab the First Person Controller asset from Standard Assets▶Prefabs and drop it into your Scene view. Make sure that it is placed above the terrain and press the Play button to start your game. Movement controls use the WASD keys and the spacebar for movement and the mouse to look around.

Placing Trees

Your terrain is probably looking pretty spiffy now all painted, but there still is more you can do to bring it to life, specifically with adding plant life. Unity's Terrain Engine places trees using a special *billboard* treatment, rendering any trees close-up to the camera in full 3D, but transitioning other trees automatically to 2D billboards when they reach a certain distance. This allows you to create full, lush scenery without taking the massive memory hit that full 3D trees would produce.

With the terrain still selected in the Hierarchy, select the Paint Trees option from the Terrain toolbar. Much like with the textures, you'll need to add some trees to your available library of paintable assets. Terrain trees are special assets (more on this later) and are made and uploaded a little differently than other assets. The Standard Assets does happily come with one tree prepackaged, a palm tree, which you'll use now.

Click on the Edit Trees button to add a tree to the available library, just like with the Terrain textures. You can find the palm tree under Standard Assets▶Trees Ambient-Occlusion▶Palm. Drag the Palm asset (not the Palm folder) into the Tree field of the dialog box or select the Palm asset from the drop-down list. This dialog box also offers one other option that's new: Bend Factor. Besides transitioning trees to billboards, Unity also offers the ability to have your plant life sway and bend in the wind, making them seem more natural. You can set this number to anything you'd like, but try small numbers first unless you're trying to simulate gale-force winds (even a smallish number like 2 will result in large amounts of bending). Also keep in mind that larger numbers will start to affect your game's performance, as the engine needs to calculate all this swaying and bending. See Figure 5.13.

To place trees, you paint them onto the terrain just like you did with textures, but this time your brush settings are different. Instead of using a selection of

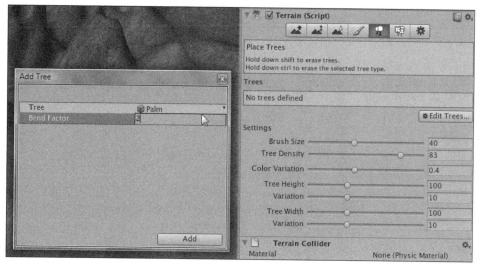

Figure 5.13
Adding a tree GameObject.

different possible brushes, trees only use one round brush that offers seven unique settings:

- **Brush Size:** The brush's radius in units. Larger sizes mean more trees placed at once.

- **Tree Density:** Percentage of each brush stroke that is covered in trees.

- **Color Variation:** Amount of randomness to apply to each tree's color.

- **Tree Height:** Allows adjustment of the asset's base height.

- **Height Variation:** Amount of randomness to apply to each tree's height.

- **Tree Width:** Allows adjustment of the asset's base width.

- **Width Variation:** Amount of randomness to apply to each tree's width.

As you can see from the options, even though there's only one base tree loaded into the engine, each painted tree will be unique, just like in nature. Using these options effectively can really cut back on modeling time if you want a unique-looking landscape. See Figure 5.14.

To erase trees, simply hold down Shift as you paint. Another option available for tree placement can be found from the Terrain▶Mass Place Trees menu option. If you know you need a dense forest, this may be the easier route to take. Type a

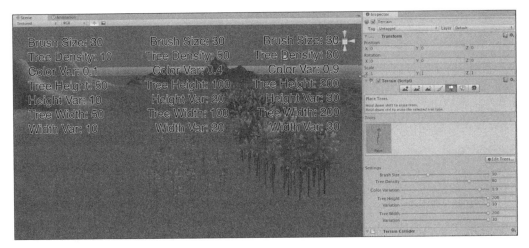
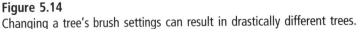

Figure 5.14
Changing a tree's brush settings can result in drastically different trees.

number, and your terrain will be blanketed with that many trees. This will randomly sample from all the trees you've loaded into your library, so if you only want the engine to use one or two, remove any others you may have added. See Figure 5.15.

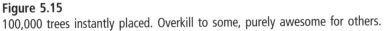

Figure 5.15
100,000 trees instantly placed. Overkill to some, purely awesome for others.

You can also use the Mass Place Trees function to "mass delete" all trees by typing **0** into the dialog box.

It's also possible to create your own trees for use in the Terrain Engine, and you only have to follow a few simple steps to do so. In short, to make your own custom trees to use with the Terrain Engine, you must:

1. Place your assets into a folder whose name includes the words "Ambient-Occlusion." The trees will not work otherwise. Note that you can nest folders inside of this folder if you want to keep your trees separate and organized.

2. The tree needs to use the Nature/Soft Occlusion Leaves and Nature/Soft Occlusion Bark shaders. Placing the trees in the aforementioned folder will allow these shaders to work.

3. Ensure that your tree mesh is one combined mesh but with two unique materials on it—one material for the leaves and another for the trunk for the two aforementioned shaders. If your tree is not a single mesh, it will not render.

4. The pivot point of the tree needs to be at the base of the trunk. Otherwise you could end up with floating trees.

5. The tree model should be on average around 2,000 tris (triangles) or fewer. The example palm tree only uses 220 tris.

6. Make the tree a *prefab* if you want to generate collisions for it (see the sidebar, "Generating Tree Collision," for more information).

After you've created your own tree, you may find you need to make updates to it. Unlike other assets, all tree files must be manually reimported after you save them by choosing Terrain▶Refresh Tree and Detail Prototypes. This will update all the trees in the scene to display your changes.

Unity also offers a free package of trees available for download from their website (you can find the link in Appendix D on the DVD). Although you may not want to necessarily use these in your game, they're helpful for reference when making your own.

Generating Tree Collision

You may also want to add *collision* to your trees at some point, as right now a character could walk right through them. Adding collision and creating prefabs will be covered more fully in later chapters, but the basic steps to add collision are simple:

1. Create a normal instance of your tree by dragging it from the Project view to the Hierarchy or Scene view, don't paint it on.

2. Add a *capsule collider* to the tree—this will break any previous prefab links or data. You should use this kind of collider only for trees; the others may not function correctly. Resize this collider to fit the trunk.

3. Make a new prefab using this tree, and use this one to populate your Terrain tree library.

4. Ensure that the checkbox Create Tree Colliders is checked (it is by default) on the Terrain's Collider component in the Inspector.

Depending on your scene file, however, adding collision may make it too hard to move around and navigate, especially if your trees are close together. With some trees, the capsule collider doesn't fit all that well around the mesh, and you may find that the collision makes your game less fun even if it is more "realistic."

Cluttering It Up with Grasses and Detail Meshes

Trees aren't the only things you can paint onto the terrain—you can also add grasses and detail meshes. The Terrain Engine also treats these items differently, drawing and rendering them only when they are near the camera to save on memory and help boost performance.

To paint these objects, click on the Paint Details button on the Terrain toolbar, the button that looks like a clump of little flowers. Just as with the other paintable features, you'll need to populate your library of available assets for the engine to use. However, unlike with trees and textures, you can choose to add your asset as either a grass or a detail mesh, each of which offers unique advantages. Refer to Table 5.1 for help in selecting which one to use.

Grasses are like trees in that they will bend in the wind, but unlike trees and other detail meshes, they are built only from 2D textures and have no depth. Detail meshes on the other hand are displayed as 3D objects, but don't billboard into the distance or bend in the wind like a tree does—these are useful for things

Table 5.1 Basic Differences when Using Trees, Grasses, and Detail Meshes

Variables	Trees	Grasses	Detail Mesh
Wind	Supported	Supported	Not supported
Asset	3D mesh	2D texture	3D mesh
Collision	Supported	Not supported	Not supported
Lighting	Ambient or direct occlusion	Grass only	Vertex or grass
Shadows	Real-time or baked	Not supported	Not supported
Rendering options	3D and 2D billboarding	2D or 2D billboarding*	3D only*

Viewable only at close distances—objects are not rendered farther away.

like small rocks or other pieces of random clutter you want to through around the world. Both use the same brushes and options to paint.

The Standard Assets package comes with one grass texture already ready for use, located from Standard Assets▶Terrain Grass. Click the Edit Details button and choose Add Grass Texture to bring up the dialog box (see Figure 5.16). Select the asset Grass from the drop-down box or drag the Grass asset onto the Detail Texture field from the Project view.

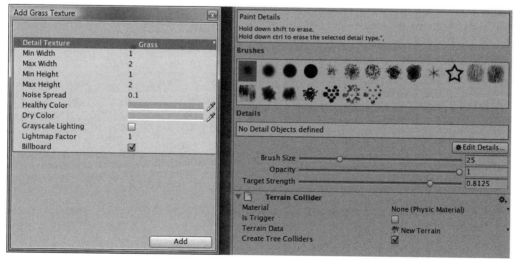

Figure 5.16
The Add Grass Texture options box.

The basic options for adding grass are as follows:

- **Detail Texture:** The texture to be used for the grass. The texture file should have an alpha channel to define the individual blades of grass.

- **Min Width:** Minimum width of each individually placed grass texture.

- **Max Width:** Maximum width of each individually placed grass texture.

- **Min Height:** Minimum height of each individually placed grass texture.

- **Max Height:** Maximum height of each individually placed grass texture.

- **Noise Spread:** The size of the clusters of grass.

- **Healthy Color:** Tints the color in the center of the grass clusters.

- **Dry Color:** Tints the color along the outer edges of the grass clusters.

- **Grayscale Lighting:** Makes grasses only accept grayscale lighting—any colored lights affecting the terrain are converted to grayscale.

- **Lightmap Factor:** How much, if at all, the grass should be affected by the lightmap lighting.

- **Billboard:** Makes the texture always rotate to face the camera.

Change any of these if you like and click Add to finish. Select a brush and try painting a few strokes in the Scene view. Remember that you can change the brush settings as well when you paint to vary the look of your grass. At any time you can also click the Play button to see your grasses and trees bend in the wind. See Figure 5.17.

You add a detail mesh the same way, but instead of choosing Add Grass Texture, you pick Add Detail Mesh. These meshes should be created from prefabs, just like the trees, and will show up in the same library as the grasses. See Figure 5.18.

- **Detail:** The mesh to be used for the detail painting.

- **Noise Spread:** The size of the generated mesh clusters.

- **Random Width:** Maximum amount of width randomness allowed for each individually placed mesh.

- **Random Height:** Maximum amount of height randomness allowed for each individually placed mesh.

Figure 5.17
Grass and trees reacting to wind upon the landscape.

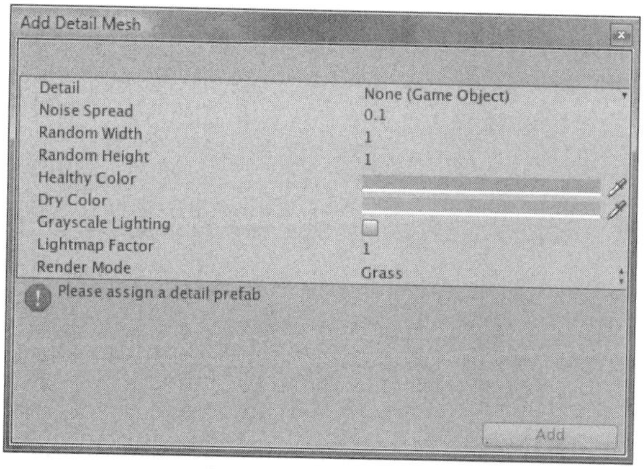

Figure 5.18
Adding a detail mesh is very similar to adding a grass texture.

- **Healthy Color:** Tints the color in the center of the mesh clusters.
- **Dry Color:** Tints the color along the outer edges of the mesh clusters.
- **Grayscale Lighting:** Makes the detail only accept grayscale lighting—any colored lights affecting the terrain are converted to grayscale.
- **Lightmap Factor:** How much, if at all, the detail should be affected by the lightmap lighting.
- **Render Mode:** Select whether this mesh should use the special grass lighting or be vertex lit. For foliage, choose the grass lighting, but for objects like rocks you must choose vertex lighting for the object to render correctly.

Once you add a detail mesh, you paint onto the terrain exactly as you would with the grass textures.

Grasses and detail meshes can be edited after import by clicking the Edit Details button while the asset is selected in your Terrain library, and choosing Edit. You can then change any of the options you selected upon import. As with the trees, if you changed your mesh or texture after placing it on the terrain, you'll need to manually update them by navigating to the Terrain menu and selecting Refresh Tree and Detail Prototypes.

If you find you're having trouble placing grasses or meshes in tight clumps, check the setting for your Detail Resolution under Terrain▶Set Resolution. As with the terrain textures, you're not really painting these features onto the terrain, but rather you're painting a generated alpha map that tells the engine how and where to display your assets. If your resolution for this detail texture is too low, you won't have enough resolution to paint fine groupings of objects.

Remember that all these textures and meshes are unlike trees in that they only appear close up to the camera—they do not billboard into the distance and are only meant to be details, not permanent fixtures of the terrain. You don't need to be limited by the words given to each kind of Terrain asset: Tree, Grass, and Detail Mesh. If you want your grass to be visible in the distance, consider building it as a mesh and adding it as a tree. Want some flags or poles to blow in the wind? Maybe that could be a tree or grass, depending on whether it needs to be 3D. Import your assets for what you want the end result to be, not based on the naming convention alone.

Troubleshooting Steep Terrains

You may have noticed another distinct difference between placing grass and trees—grasses will tend to nicely follow the shape of the landscape if viewed from head on, but if you try to paint a tree onto a steep cliffside, you'll probably end up with a tree partly floating in midair. This is due to the location of the tree's pivot point and how trees are painted onto the terrain. Depending on the size of your trees and how close they'll be to the camera, this may not be an issue, but there are a few steps you can try to make your trees stay firmly rooted to the ground.

- You can try taking your tree into a 3D modeling program and moving the pivot point up a little bit. This will definitely help with the close-up trees, but your 2D billboards may end up floating above the landscape. Depending on your terrain, this could work, and the floating billboards may not be visible.

- You can individually mold the terrain around the most problematic trees, if they are few and far between. This could take too long if you have many trees to individually tweak and can be frustrating to get right.

- If you really need a tree on a slope and don't want to futz around with molding or re-importing, place the trees individually as GameObjects and not as terrain features. These trees won't bend in the wind (unless you add a custom script to make them) or have some of the available features of other terrain items, but you can individually drop and rotate them into place.

- If you have the memory to spare, you can try adding an exact copy of your terrain directly below the primary one. To do this, export your terrain as a heightmap, create a new terrain and lower it by about half a meter, and then import the heightmap onto it. This gives you an exact copy. Paint your trees onto this secondary lower terrain, and any floating bits will be hidden under the primary terrain, making it look like your trees are naturally growing from the surface. You do need to be aware of and look for any performance hits using this method.

- Or the simplest and most memory friendly—avoid trees on steep slopes. They probably wouldn't grow there anyway.

Terrain Settings

The terrain has a few other general options you can tweak by clicking on the final Settings button in the Terrain toolbar. See Figure 5.19.

Base Terrain settings:

- **Pixel Error:** How many errors are allowed when drawing the terrain. A higher number will render quicker, but it won't be as precise.

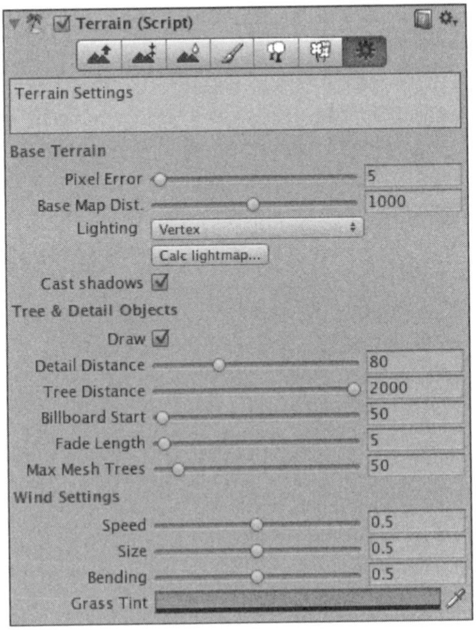

Figure 5.19
The settings for the terrain in the Inspector.

- **Base Map Dist:** The distance from the camera before the terrain textures are displayed in low resolution.

- **Lighting:** Choose whether the terrain is lit in Vertex mode, with a lightmap, or with pixel-based lighting. See the following section for lighting tips.

- **Cast Shadows:** Makes the terrain cast shadows.

Tree and Detail Object settings:

- **Draw:** Draws all painted Terrain objects. When unchecked, Terrain objects are unrendered. This is useful when you need to optimize or tweak a specific section of the terrain and don't want the view cluttered with detail meshes.

- **Detail Distance:** The distance from the camera where detail meshes will stop being displayed.

- **Tree Distance:** The distance from the camera where trees will stop being displayed—this includes billboards, too.

- **Billboard Start:** The distance from the camera at which tree meshes will start being displayed as billboards instead.

- **Fade Length:** The total distance at which the trees transition from meshes to billboards. Set this high enough so the change isn't too abrupt.

- **Max Mesh Trees:** The maximum number of trees to be displayed as meshes—this will override the fading distances if too many trees are in view.

Wind settings:

- **Speed:** The speed of the wind as it blows through the grass. This does not affect trees.

- **Size:** The amount of the grass affected all at once by the wind.

- **Bending:** How much the grass will bend due to the wind. If you want to change the amount of wind bending for the trees, edit their Bend field.

- **Grass Tint:** Overall tint color for all the grasses *and* detail meshes loaded into the terrain.

For most of these settings, it's helpful to tweak them while the game is playing, as they are heavily dependent on motion and camera location. Just remember to record your changes before you stop playing, as these won't be saved while the game is running.

LIGHTING AND SHADOWS

When faced with the three choices on how to light your terrain, you may not be sure exactly where to start. Right now the terrain is lit using vertex lighting provided by one direction light, which is only as good as the terrain's resolution. This lighting is calculated only per vertex, so while it is generally the fastest option to render, it can also look blocky and shaky, depending on how many vertices are actually available.

For the terrain, you should consider building a *lightmap*, which is a texture that bakes in the lighting data provided by your scene. Terrains lit with lightmaps not only look nicer than vertex-lit ones, they also render faster than pixel lighting! For once, performance and prettiness line up. Creating one is easy:

1. Make sure you have at least one directional light in your scene—which you should have added earlier. You can also add more directional lights and position them if you think you need more lighting and better shadows.

2. Navigate to the Terrain menu and select Terrain▸Create Lightmap or click the Calc lightmap button if you're still viewing the terrain settings in the Inspector. Pick a high enough resolution for the generated map and verify that all the lights you want are included in the drop-down Lights list. You can edit this list by changing the size and dragging or deleting any lights you want. Only directional lights are used to calculate the lightmaps; any other kinds of lights such as point or spot lights won't be taken into account.

3. Check if you want to generate shadows and at what resolution they should be made (Shadow Sampling). Click Create when you're done.

Now that your lightmap is generated, select the terrain and go back to its settings in the Inspector. Cycle between the three available lighting solutions: Vertex, Lightmap, and Pixel (see Figure 5.20). The vertex lighting is decidedly harsher and darker, whereas the lightmap and pixel lighting solutions are more natural and fluid. The main difference between the latter two can be seen in the foreground slopes—the pixel lighting is a bit special. Up close to the camera, it lights every individual pixel, taking more rendering time but producing a more realistic shadow. As the terrain gets farther away from the camera, it switches to displaying the information from the lightmap.

For almost all cases, using the Lightmap setting will work quicker and better. While the pixel lighting is nice, the increased processing required may not be justifiable for the minimum beauty benefit.

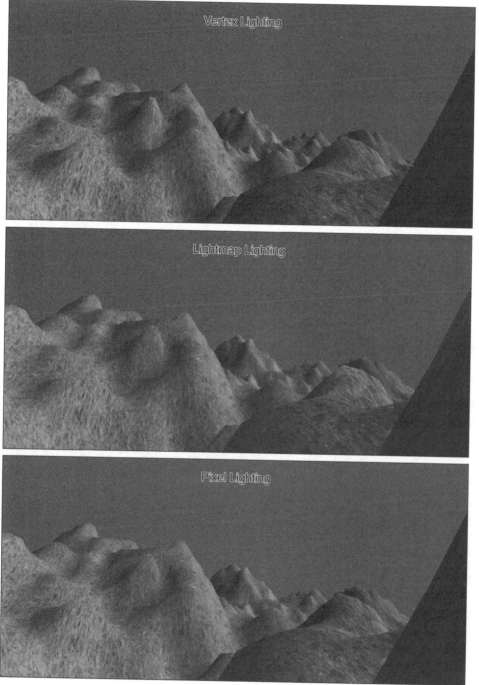

Figure 5.20
The three available terrain lighting solutions.

Shadows are the last piece to look at when lighting your terrain. While the terrain does self-shadow based upon the lights, notice that the trees and details cast no shadows upon the terrain, making them seem almost to float across the top of the landscape. You have basically two options to fix this: either bake the tree shadows into the lightmap using a custom script if you have Unity Pro or hand-paint in the shadows. The former probably sounds like the obvious best choice, and while it is quicker, hand-painting does give you finer control and a better end product.

You can hand-paint the shadows either by painting directly onto an exported lightmap or by creating darker terrain textures to paint directly onto the terrain. Creating different terrain textures is as easy as opening a texture in your graphics editor, darkening it a bit, and saving it with a different name. Exporting and painting the lightmap is a bit trickier and more involved, but it does give you even finer control and doesn't affect your performance like adding more terrain textures does.

Follow these steps:

1. Locate the Island Demo included in your Unity install or download it again from the Unity website.

2. Navigate to the folder Assets▶Editor and copy the LightmapExport.cs file.

3. In your own Project Assets folder, create an Editor folder, and drop the copied script file into it. This Editor folder is special in that it allows custom scripts to be run directly from within the editor. Failure to place the script in the properly named folder will result in it not working.

4. Once you do this, a new menu option will appear between Terrain and Window: CUSTOM. If you look in here, the custom script called "Duplicate Texture" is now available. This is exactly what you need to export your lightmap for edits. You might need to manually refresh the Project view if the new menu item doesn't quickly appear (press the Ctrl+R key to do so).

5. In your Project view, find your Terrain asset (probably called New Terrain unless you changed it earlier). Expand its hierarchy to see its lightmap texture. Select this texture and then run the Duplicate Texture option from the menu.

6. Your new texture file, called "LightmapDuplicate," will be placed into the root of your Assets folder. It may not show up in the Project view until you manually refresh (press the Ctrl+R key to do so).

Now you can take this file into your graphics editor of choice and paint onto it—make your adjustments on new layers to save yourself headaches later. If you decide to paint custom shadows for all your details, you should consider putting trees, grasses, and detail meshes all onto their own unique layers. The only problem now is that this new file isn't assigned to your terrain, the old one still is. Thankfully, this is a much easier fix:

1. Click on your new Lightmap file in the Project view and in the Inspector, change its Texture Format setting to RGB 24-bit. Your lightmap will not work if you forget to do this.

2. Click on your base Terrain asset in the Project view (not the Hierarchy view).

3. Its Inspector view will show only one option: Lightmap! Drag your new lightmap texture file onto this slot (or select it from the drop-down menu).

And there you have it; your lightmap will be applied to your terrain. You can now go back and forth between your graphics program and Unity and tweak your own custom lightmap to your heart's content.

ADDING A SKYBOX AND DISTANCE FOG

If you play your game now, your terrain will be looking good and ready to walk on, but there will be one glaring omission in your scene—the sky. Sure, the default blue is okay for prototyping, but it's kind of "blah" against the lit and painted ground beneath it. Adding a skybox will fix all that right up.

In Unity, a *skybox* is a special virtual "box" wrapped around your scene; there isn't any real piece of geometry there, it doesn't accept lights or shadows, and it's rendered in the background before anything else in the scene, helping give it the illusion that it's far away.

Skyboxes can be applied to your scene in one of two ways: either to the entire scene at once using Render settings, or to individual cameras, allowing it to change during a scene. The Standard Assets package comes with two premade skyboxes: Sunset and Blue Sky. You'll use one of these for now. Later, you'll create your own skybox from scratch.

To find and use a premade skybox, follow these steps:

1. Navigate to the Edit menu and select Render Settings. The available options will show up in the Inspector view, not in a dialog box.

2. Under Skybox Material, select Blue Sky from the drop-down menu. This is one of the special skybox materials already preassembled. You can also drag it into the slot by finding it under Standard Assets▶Skyboxes in the Project view.

3. Your skybox will automatically work now when you play the game, but to see it in the Scene view, click the Scene Overlay toggle button on the Scene view's Control Bar.

While you're in the Render settings, you may also want to enable Fog (click the box to check it) and adjust the Fog Color and Fog Density settings (see Figure 5.21). Right now your terrain abruptly ends and doesn't appear to fade off into the distance as it would in real life. Adding appropriate fog can help simulate this illusion. Change the fog color to something that matches your sky color and the density to a very low number. You'll definitely want to tweak this while playing the game, as it can be a finicky one to get right. If you haven't yet, add the First Person Controller prefab from the Standard Assets package to your scene in order to walk around.

Figure 5.21
The scene with fog and skybox in place. This fog density is set at 0.005.

ADDING WATER TO YOUR TERRAIN

The last terrain-related feature you can add to your scene is water. Writing believable and beautiful water shaders is often left to senior graphics programs, but Unity's Standard Assets comes packaged with Daylight and Nighttime water examples. If you have Unity Pro, your default water will have real-time reflections and refractions (no such luck, Unity Basic programmers).

To access the water prefabs in Unity, follow these steps:

1. From the Standard Assets package in the Project view, find the Water folder and expand it.

2. Drag the Daylight Simple Water prefab into either the Scene or Hierarchy view to add it to your scene. The Simple Water prefab uses a round mesh (this can be changed if you like, but it's not necessary for this example). See Figure 5.22.

> 3. Use the Transform tools or Inspector properties to place the mesh slightly above your lowest terrain level, and scale it so that it covers the terrain.

It's not perfect, but it's quick enough to throw in to get a point across. You'll also probably want to go back and clean up some of the painted details to make sure you don't have swimming trees. You can also create your own water from scratch, but the Standard Assets are there if you want them.

You're now an expert on using the Terrain Engine and Standard Assets package, so it's time to start thinking about importing your own custom assets. In the next chapter, you'll learn to import assets for the *Widget* game and combine them with your new terrain skills to build a simple environment to explore.

Figure 5.22
Even the basic Simple Water prefab turns the drab landscape into an island paradise.

CHAPTER 6

BUILDING YOUR ENVIRONMENT: IMPORTING BASIC CUSTOM ASSETS

Now that you're familiar with the Standard Assets package and using the Terrain Engine, it's time to start looking at creating your own custom environment for your game. The Standard Assets package has some helpful premade pieces, but to make your game your own you'll need to import some custom GameObjects.

Starting with this chapter and moving forward, all examples will use the provided assets on the DVD and will revolve around creating the game *Widget*. Individual assets referenced in the chapter can be found in each chapter's folder on the DVD, and the compiled final project is contained in the Final Project Files folder. If you get stuck, individual scene files for each chapter are also included in this folder.

DESIGN FIRST, THEN BUILD

Before you jump in and start building your environment, it's helpful to first mock it up either on paper or within the engine using primitive objects, called *greyboxing*. This may seem like a waste of time if you know exactly it is what you want to do, but getting distances and proportions down first can make working in the engine faster and more fluid.

Drawings of *Widget's* maps and environments can be found on the DVD under Design Documents▶Maps and Concept Art. There's no right or wrong way to draw your game's maps, so do what works for you. Some find it easy to work with blobby shapes and just get a general feeling for the game's flow down, while others like working with graph paper and getting everything "just so" before starting on the computer. Odds are you'll be changing and iterating upon your environments as you work through the game, so nothing's going to be perfect the first time through anyway.

While you're drawing your maps, begin to make notes of the various items you'll need to create: In effect, you need to create your asset list. Creating a list up front like this will help ensure you don't forget something later down the road. This book won't cover the basics on how to model or texture your own assets (some suggested sources are listed in Appendix D, "Resources and References," which is on the DVD), but everything you need to create the *Widget* game is included on the DVD—you'll just need to learn how to import them.

It's now a good time to also start arranging your project's Asset folder with sensible subfolders. You can create your own directory and organization system, or you can use the sample one provided with the final game. In general, you may want to consider adding the following folders within your Assets folder:

- Audio
- Characters
- GUI
- Editor
- Particles
- Props
- Scenes
- Scripts
- Skybox
- Terrain

These folders will be referenced throughout the examples to follow, but you can place your imported objects anywhere so long as they are within the Assets folder of your project space. The choice is yours.

IMPORTING TEXTURES

To start building the first scene in *Widget,* you'll use an imported texture as a design guide to make sure the terrain is built in the proper place and shape. You could always freehand the map design or sketch something out on a slip of paper, but this way it's sure to fit the dimensions specified on the master map plans.

If you haven't yet, open Unity and start a new scene file. If you need to, set up a new project by going to File▶New Project and saving it to a location that's easy for you to access. Make sure to check the boxes to import both the Standard Assets package and the Toon Shader package, as you will need both of these.

Importing custom assets into Unity is extremely easy—if you can save a file, you can import a file. Find the TerrainMap1.jpg file in the Chapter 6 folder on the DVD and drag it into your project's Assets folder on your computer. (If you can't remember where you saved your project, right-click on anything in the Project view and select Show in Explorer. This will open a window in your Assets folder.) After dragging the file into the folder, switch back to Unity. Voila, instant file importation: You can now use TerrainMap1.jpg in your Unity project! Simple, right?

Note

> I placed my file in a nested folder hierarchy: Assets▶Terrain▶Textures. This way I can keep all the terrain pieces in one easy-to-find area and all the associated textures grouped together as well.

Make a habit to start saving your work directly into Unity's Assets folder—your file will automatically be imported into your project, and you can always continue to edit it later without having to worry about copying or moving old versions around. This is a major hassle saver, and you should take full advantage of it.

More on Importation

Okay, while Unity does perform the bulk of the operation for you, there are a few importation settings you should check whenever you import a new file into your project. Select the new file in the Project view to bring up its import settings

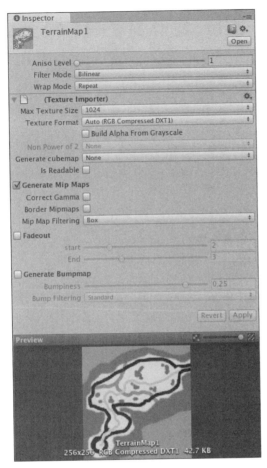

Figure 6.1
The sample terrain map's import settings.

and preview in the Inspector (this brings up the import settings for *any* custom asset). See Figure 6.1.

■ **Aniso Level:** Sets the level for anisotropic filtering—this is mostly a big word for how well the texture is displayed when viewed from a steep angle. For textures applied to grounds or floors, you'll probably want to bump this up a level or two, but for everything else the default setting is fine. Increased levels of filtering will use some rendering memory on your graphics card, but it can make a huge difference if your ground is looking blurry.

- **Filter Mode:** Filters how the texture looks when stretched. Choose Point from the drop-down menu to allow your texture to look a little blocky when viewed from very close. You can change it to Bilinear to have the texture blur some up close, or to Trilinear to have it also blur between its mip map switches (more on those later).

- **Wrap Mode:** Determines whether your texture will tile indefinitely or be displayed only once. Choose Repeat to tile or Clamp to have the texture's edges stretch to fill any gaps in sizing.

- **Max Texture Size:** Available sizes range from 32 to 4,096, with all powers of two represented. This tells Unity at what size it should import your texture, allowing you or an artist to work at any desired resolution.

- **Texture Format:** The compression format or representation used for the texture on import. See Tables 6.1 and 6.2 for exact specs for each format.

- **Build Alpha from Grayscale:** Check this box if you want Unity to build an *alpha channel* from your texture, using its converted grayscale values to render transparency. By default, it's unchecked.

- **Non Power of 2:** If the texture you're importing has dimensions not represented by a power of two, this option will become available. You can have Unity keep your texture its original size (Keep Original), Scale to Nearest power of two for each side (a 33×247 texture would be scaled

Table 6.1 Native Texture Formats

Format	File Extension	Notes
PSD	.psd	Native Photoshop file
TIFF	.tif	Adobe format, "Tagged Image File Format"
JPG	.jpg	Common compression format, can contain artifacts
TGA	.tga	Up to 32 bits of precision per pixel
PNG	.png	Lossless data compression, designed to replace GIFs
GIF	.gif	Popular Internet format, limited color space
BMP	.bmp	Can be quite large uncompressed
IFF	.iff	Typically used for storing animation frames
PICT	.pict or .pct	Standard Apple Macintosh format

Table 6.2 Texture Compression Formats

Format	Colors	Alpha	Memory Usage (Bytes/Pixel)
RGB DXT1	16 bit	No	0.5 bpp
RGBA DXT5	64 bit	Yes	1 bpp
RGB 16 bit	65K colors	No	2 bpp
RGB 24 bit	Truecolor	No	3 bpp
Alpha 8 bit	none	Yes	1 bpp
RGBA 16 bit	65K colors	Yes	2 bpp
RGBA 32 bit	Truecolor	Yes	4 bpp

to 32×256), Scale to Larger to have both sides move to the next larger power value, or Scale to Smaller to do the opposite. For most cases, you'll want to just make your textures a power of 2 in your graphics program, *except* for textures you plan on using for GUIs—these can be any size and shouldn't be scaled.

■ **Generate Cubemap:** Unity builds a cube map from your texture (more on these later as well). The texture file must be square for this option to be available.

■ **Is Readable:** Allows scripts to access texture data directly, specifically functions from the Texture2D class. This will create a second copy of the texture for this purpose, so use wisely and sparingly.

■ **Generate Mip Maps:** Unity generates *mip maps* of your texture. Mip maps are smaller and smaller versions of your texture that are displaced based upon where the object is in relation to the camera. When an object is very far away, a tiny version of the texture is displayed (saving some processing power), and as the object moves closer, more detailed and larger versions of the texture are displayed. This is checked by default and should always be used for textures meant for GameObjects.

■ **Correct Gamma:** Enables per-mip-level correction of the gamma.

■ **Border Mip Maps:** Clamps the borders of smaller mip maps and stops colors from seeping into edge spaces. This is particularly useful for light cookies.

- **Mip Map Filtering:** Chooses which kind of filtering you'd like Unity to use when fading between the different mip levels. Select Box for a simple blurring and smoothing algorithm, or Kaiser if your textures are looking too blurred.

- **Fadeout:** Your mip textures slowly fade to gray as they get smaller. This is useful for detail maps. Set the start and end mip level using the two sliders.

- **Generate Bump Map:** Unity converts the color channels of your texture into a real-time *bump map*. See the "Bump Maps" section later in this chapter for more info. Change the Bumpiness slider to alter the depth of your bumps (higher numbers equal more depth). The Filtering drop-down menu controls how the bump map is created—Standard creates a generic, smooth-looking map and Sobel creates a sharper map.

This may seem like a lot of information at first, but you don't need to deal with most of these selections for the majority of textures you import. The most important ones to check (in general) are the max texture size, format, mip map generation, and your wrap mode. You'll probably use the others on a more case-by-case scenario.

Supported Formats

Unity natively reads a bevy of different file formats and supports most of the more common texture compression formats. Importing your textures at a smaller size is helpful, but most textures are compressed as well to help save on space and memory. A good chunk of a game's available memory space can be eaten up by textures alone, so it's important to use the best compression possible to still get the look you want.

If you work with Photoshop files or TIFFs, you can continue to use layers as normal. Unity will flatten the image when it imports it into the project (making it much smaller), but your original file will not be changed, and all your layers will be preserved, allowing you to continue layer edits as often as you want. No more having to save multiple files and flatten images manually now, or worrying about accidently flattening the wrong file. Refer to Tables 6.1 and 6.2.

Tip

To determine how much memory your texture page will take up, multiply the height by its width, by bpp (bits per pixel). If your texture contains mip maps, multiply this number by 1.33 to get the final usage.

In most cases, you'll probably want to work with PSDs, TIFFs, and TGAs primarily for texture work, for the superior color quality and layer abilities. There's nothing wrong with the other images, but you may find yourself working around artifacts or bad compression when a different file format could have saved you the trouble.

When it comes to compression, you've really got a few options. DXT1 is a common compression for textures that just need to act as a diffuse, or just a flat color with no special effects. If your texture has an alpha channel or needs to support a specular map, DXT5 is usually the way to go. Some specific texture instances will require you to use one of the truecolor formats, but for almost *everything* else you should stick with the DXT compressions.

Importing Textures for *Widget*'s Terrain

Now that you can import textures, you can start building *Widget*'s terrain with custom assets. The terrain map is already loaded up and ready to go, but you'll need to import the splat map textures for painting and the other custom pieces for things like the skybox. If you look at the Design Documents on the DVD, you'll see that this terrain map only encompasses the bottom-left of the entire map—the rest of the pieces will be built later. Otherwise, the map could become a bit unwieldy to navigate and take too long to load. No one likes to wait.

To start *Widget*'s map:

1. In your new scene, create a directional light and rotate it so that it's not pointing straight down (choose GameObject▶Create Other▶Directional Light). It doesn't matter where it's placed, as long as the rotation is to your liking.

2. Expand the Standard Assets folder in the Project view and open the Prefabs folder. Drag the First Person Controller prefab into either your

Scene or Hierarchy view. You'll use this for testing your terrain for now, until a different character is imported. This controller allows you to walk around using the WASD keys and use the spacebar to jump. If you examine its settings in the Inspector, you can change the Walk and Jump Speed to your liking. Delete the default Main Camera by selecting it in the Hierarchy and either by pressing Delete on the keyboard or by right-clicking and selecting Delete from the menu. The controller prefab comes with a game camera attached.

3. Create a new terrain (choose Terrain▶Create Terrain) and set its resolution to 200 meters long by 200 meters wide (in the Terrain▶Set Resolution dialog box). Remember, one unit in Unity is equal to one meter. Change the terrain's max height to 50 meters and the heightmap resolution to 1,025. The other resolution settings are fine for now.

4. Rename your terrain to something more meaningful than "New Terrain." (I chose "Terrain—Entry and Villa," since that's what it is.) You can also move your terrain into the Project's Terrain folder, if you didn't create it there to begin with. You can rearrange any files from within the Project view by clicking and dragging, and any moving should actually be done here within Unity. If you move files outside of the editor, sometimes metadata will be lost, and links will be broken. It's repairable, but not a good time.

5. Use the Terrain tools in the Inspector to add Terrainmap1.jpg as a terrain texture splat map. This will automatically apply the map to the terrain, and you can use it to paint more precisely where the height is to go. Change the X and Y tile size to 200 × 200, the size of the terrain's resolution. This will center it squarely on the terrain.

6. Begin to paint the area's height using the map and following pictures as a guide. Feel free to use your creativity if you want to move some things around. Also see the TerrainMap1 legend shown in Figure 6.2 for tips and hints on how to paint out the map. Start by lying in all the surrounding plateaus, to box in the playable space.

7. Make the playable space (the light green area) about two meters high—that way you can cut in the path and river and have them at a lower depth.

8. Remember to use all the tools at your disposal—use different brush shapes to get different effects, paint gentle gradated plateaus using the Target Height tool, and work up areas in thin layers with a low opacity setting.

As a general guideline, keep these points in mind:

- The green areas are low-lying plateaus covered in trees and vegetation, with a height equal to about five meters.

- The light brown areas are higher plateaus, with heights ranging between 10 and 20 meters.

- The heavy black border denotes the playable space—everything within it should be about two meters high.

- The light orange line is a path, cut into the terrain at about a depth of one meter.

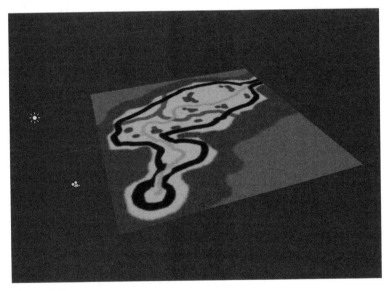

Figure 6.2
The terrain map applied to the terrain.

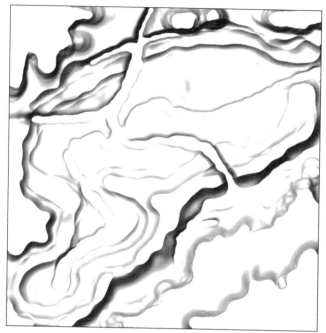

Figure 6.3
An overhead view of the painted heightmap.

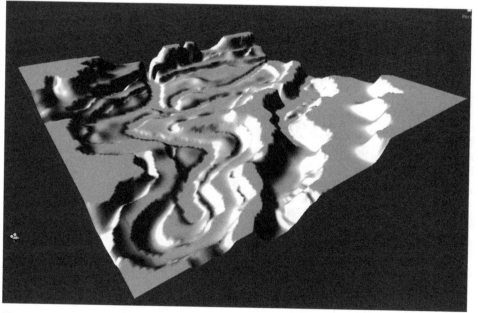

Figure 6.4
A side view of the heightmap, the texture removed for clarity.

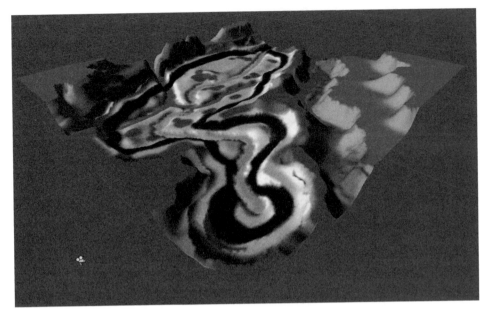

Figure 6.5
The terrain with the texture in place.

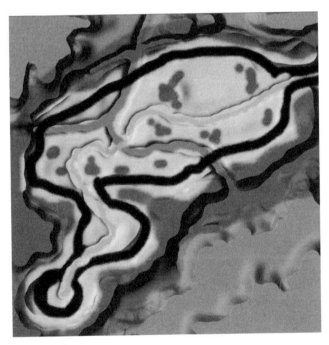

Figure 6.6
An overhead view of the terrain and texture.

- The light blue line is a river snaking through the map, with its height set to zero. This will make it easier to place the water plane later.

Note

At this time you can also create your lightmap and export it to handpaint if you desire, as described in the previous chapter. However, final lighting passes aren't covered until Chapter 14, "Creating Lighting and Shadows."

You've now got a pretty respectable custom map, well done! It's looking a little sad and bland, though, and could really use some real color. The Standard Asset terrain textures are definitely an option, but you can always create your own to match whatever art direction you choose for your game.

The Design Documents for *Widget* outline the art direction to be cartoon-like and bright, using toon shaders to look more like hand-drawn items. The textures provided in the Standard Assets are nice, but they don't match the selected style. In the Chapter 6 folder on the DVD, grab these Terrain files and import them into your project:

- Dirt_Dark_DIFF.tif
- Dirt_Light_DIFF.tif
- Grass_Dark_Blotch_DIFF.tif
- Grass_Dark_DIFF.tif
- Grass_Flowers_DIFF.tif
- Grass_Light_DIFF.tif
- Stone_Path_DIFF.tif
- Water_DIFF.tif

Tip

All of these textures end in the suffix _DIFF for "diffuse." When you start working with a large number of textures, it's helpful to also have a consistent and meaningful naming convention to help find and sort your files faster.

Import these textures into the Terrain tool and start painting the terrain. If Unity ever misses a file in your folder or doesn't import something for any reason, you can always force a reimport by right-clicking in the Project view and selecting Import New Asset.

1. You can either continue to use the terrain map texture as a guide or delete it when you start your imports.

2. Import the textures into the Terrain tool with a tiling size of 10×10. Set the terrain's detail resolution to 1,024 and the control texture resolution to 512.

3. Check each file's individual import settings in the Inspector and verify that they each have DXT1 compression and are no larger than 1,024 in size. Depending on your computer, you may want to make them all 512 in size or smaller. Play with the aniso levels until you arrive at settings you like—you'll have to come back to these once you have the textures down on the ground.

4. Begin painting just like the height—get a base color down and then start with low opacities and work your detail color in slowly in layers.

5. Paint the plateaus with the dirt colors, using some grass sparingly along edges where plant life could grow. Paint some darker browns to define some rocky areas more clearly. Use the different grass textures together to create interesting patterns. All the grasses use the same green detail as a base, allowing them to tile together seamlessly.

6. You can paint the path using the stone path texture, dirt texture, or a combination of both. Add some dirt along the edges of the stream bank.

7. Paint the bottom of the stream bed with the water texture or dirt texture. A water plane will be placed in later to simulate the surface of the water, but the base can be painted in whichever you like.

8. Feel free to take any of these textures into your own graphics editor and customize them—for example, you can change the texture of the tile stones or the color of the flowers. Remember, however, that Unity organizes its terrain textures into blocks of four, so overwrite one,

delete one, or add textures in multiples of four to best use the memory space.

9. Save your file often, in case of unexpected crashes. Create a new folder in your Project view called **Scenes** if you haven't already and save your file there. If you need to move your file, do so from only within the Project view—don't move it outside of Unity.

You can now grab the grass detail texture to give the landscape some life. In the Chapter 6 Terrain Textures folder, import Grass_Terrain_DIFF.tif as a grass detail for the terrain. When importing, make sure that it has a DXT5 compression (not DXT1 like the others) to preserve its alpha channel. Paint this item around the terrain. Play with the wind setting and vary its height, width, and noise patterns until you get something you like.

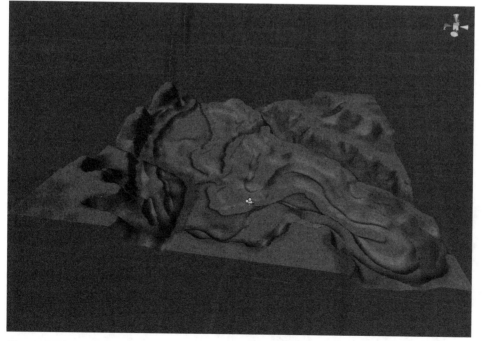

Figure 6.7
Laying down the dirt textures, contouring the ridges with the darker dirt texture.

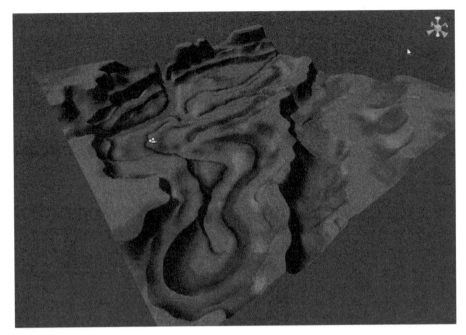

Figure 6.8
Blocking in the grass textures.

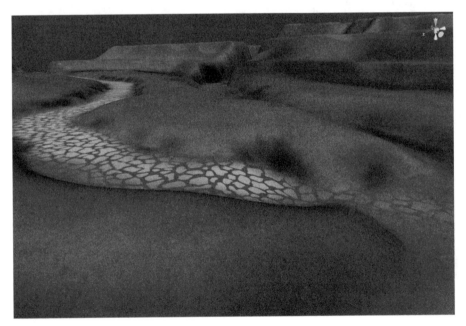

Figure 6.9
Cutting in the path and starting to detail the small dirt ridges.

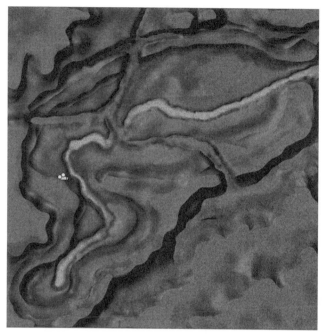

Figure 6.10
An overhead shot of the finished texture.

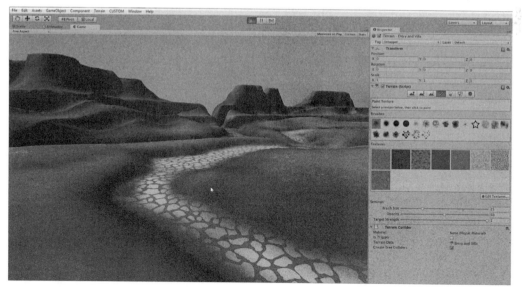

Figure 6.11
An in-game render of the painted terrain.

Figure 6.12
Some grass blowing in the wind.

My settings were a minimum height and width of 0.3, a maximum of 1.2, and a noise spread of 0.67. The result of these settings is shown in Figure 6.12.

IMPORTING BASIC MESHES

Importing basic *static meshes* is no harder than importing textures. Unity can natively read scene files from Maya, Cinema 4D, 3ds Max, Cheetah3D, and Blender when the files are saved in the Assets folder. Unity also supports other popular export formats, like .fbx and .obj, so if your 3D package can export to one of the available formats, you're home free. Here are the supported formats:

- **Maya 8.0 or later:** Native .ma, .mb. Save your Maya file into the Assets folder to have Unity import all nodes, transforms, pivot points, names, meshes (up to two UV sets per), vertex colors, normals, materials, textures, and animations (FK, IK, and all bone-based). Unity will support multiple materials per mesh on imported Maya files, but does *not* import blend shapes. If you are using IK animations, you'll have to bake these upon importation.

- **Cinema 4D 8.5 or later:** Native *.c4d.* Save your Cinema file into the Assets folder to have Unity import all transforms, pivot points, names, meshes, UV sets, normals, materials, textures (multiple materials per mesh supported), and animations (FK, IK, and all bone-based). Unity will not import point-level animations at this time. As with Maya, if you use IK animations, you'll have to bake them prior to importation.

- **3D Studio Max:** Native *.max.* Save your .max file to the Assets folder to have Unity import all transforms, pivot points, names, meshes (up to two UV sets), vertex colors, normals, materials (multiple materials supported), textures, and animations. If you use bone-based animations, you should collapse the motion trajectories before importation and export the file as an .fbx.

- **Cheetah3D 2.6 or later:** Native *.jas.* Save your Cheetah file to the Assets folder to have Unity import all transforms, pivot points, names, meshes, UVs, normals, materials, textures, and animations.

- **Lightwave 8.0 or later:** No native file formats—must be exported to an .fbx file format. See the Unity site for .fbx exporter plug-ins for Lightwave. When converted, Unity will import all transforms, pivot points, names, meshes, UVs, normals, materials (multiple per mesh supported), textures, and animations.

- **Blender 2.45 or later:** Native *.blend.* Save your Blender file into the Assets folder to have Unity import all transforms, pivot points, names, meshes, UVs, and animations. Textures and materials will not be automatically imported and assigned and must be done manually.

- **Modo:** No native file formats—must be saved from within Modo to an .fbx file format. After saving, Unity will import all nodes, transforms, pivot points, names, meshes, normals, UVs, materials, and textures. Unity will support multiple materials per mesh.

- **Other Applications:** Unity will natively read in .fbx, .dae, .3DS, .dxf, and .obj files as well, so if your application can save or export to one of these formats, you can import your files without any hassle.

To use any of the native file formats, you must have that program installed on the computer you want to run Unity on, as the engine runs the 3D application in the background to import your files. If you don't have access to these programs all the time, you can always export your assets into an .fbx file format, allowing Unity to read it natively without your application. Visit the Autodesk site (http://autodesk.com/fbx) for available .fbx plug-ins and converters. Some 3D applications can also export to Collada files (.dae), so if you're having trouble finding an FBX exporter, try Collada.

The terrain could use some trees and other objects to throw around, so grab the Chapter 6▶Terrain▶Meshes folder on the DVD and copy that into your Assets folder. Also copy the remainder of the files located within the Terrain▶Textures folder; the meshes will need these to work. Save all of these into your Terrain subfolder in the Assets folder.

Switch back to Unity and allow it to finish importing the files—this could take a few seconds or a few minutes, depending on your computer's speed, but it only happens the first time the file is imported. In the Project view, open the Meshes subfolder in the Terrain folder and find the file called "tree2" (the file extensions are left off of all assets in the Project view). Clicking on a mesh asset in the Project view brings up its import settings in the Inspector, as shown in Figure 6.13.

This is similar in nature to the texture importer—all your available options are laid out by function, and a preview of the object is shown at the bottom of the Inspector (you can tumble this around using the mouse). The first field, Animation, is grayed out and unavailable as this is a static mesh, meaning it has no bones, skinned mesh data, or animation driving it. It just sits there, static—for a tree that's just fine. In Animation, importation and splitting are covered in Chapter 7. The last animation section is also covered there.

The other settings are as follows:

- **Scale Factor:** If you didn't model your asset using Unity's one meter equals one unit paradigm, you can use this field to resize the asset upon importation. Set the factor to 1 if the model was created correctly.

- **Mesh Compression:** Select Off, Low, Medium, or High to dictate whether your mesh will be compressed upon importation and how much. As with texture compression, this can help save a lot of memory, but you need to be careful that you don't introduce artifacts or other irregularities by setting the compression too high. Test your asset in the game and select the highest compression that still gives you the best look.

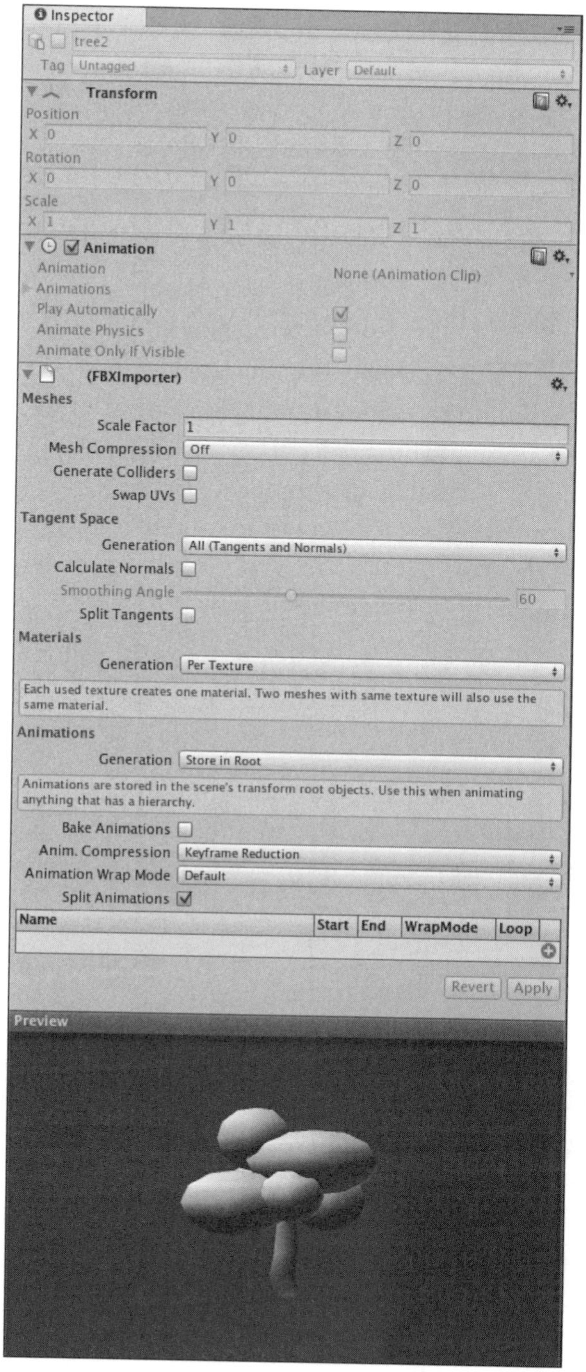

Figure 6.13
Tree2's import settings.

- **Generate Colliders:** Check this box to have Unity automatically generate a mesh collider for your object. If the object is to be static, like this one, check this box. This will make your object "solid" in the game world. If your object will move or be animated, a different kind of collider will need to be created, discussed later.

- **Swap UVs:** Sometimes when you import a mesh, the wrong UV channels get picked up by the shaders. If you notice your asset isn't behaving as it should (with lightmaps in particular), check this box.

- **Tangent Space Generation:** Use this drop-down box to determine which auxiliary parts of the vertex data should be generated during importation. Selecting All will generate all tangents and normals, allowing real-time lighting and bump mapping. Select Normals Only to allow for the lighting (but no bump shaders) or None to disable both the normals and tangents. If you know you don't need either of these, you can attempt to save some space by selecting None.

- **Calculate Normals**: Check this to have Unity recalculate the normals of your mesh on importation. Usually you'll want to make sure this is correct in your 3D application.

- **Smoothing Angle:** If you checked the Calculate Normals box, this slider allows you to tell Unity at what point you want the engine to start treating edges as hard edges. If your asset has a normal map applied to it, set this to 180 degrees.

- **Split Tangents:** If you notice that UV seams on your model are showing up in the engine, check this box.

- **Materials Generation:** Select how you want Unity to handle importing materials, if at all. If you select Off, Unity will not import material data with your mesh or generate a new material for it in the engine. Select Per Texture to have Unity create a new material each time it encounters a new texture file (this is the default). These materials are project wide and can be shared throughout multiple scenes. If you don't want materials shared between scenes, use the Per Material selection. Materials are covered next in this chapter.

For the meshes in the Terrain folder, set up all the import settings as follows:

1. Set Mesh Scale Factor to 1 if it is not already.

2. Set Mesh Compression to High and check the box to have Unity generate colliders. None of these assets will be moving around.

3. Change Tangent Space Generation to Normals Only and Materials Generation to Off. For now, you'll set up the materials manually.

4. Ignore the Animation data (as it has none) and click the Apply button to save your changes.

Select Apply to finalize any changes you make to the asset and have Unity reimport it, or select Revert to undo any changes. You can change any of these settings at any time while working on your game—nothing you select here is set in stone, and any changes you make will propagate to all instances of the asset you've placed in your game. Import the Props folder from the Chapter 6 folder in the same way. Keep these in their own separate Props folder, and not in Terrain.

When you import a mesh, Unity will attempt to import all your textures and materials along with it, saving you the trouble of having to relink them after importation. Granted, this isn't always perfect, or you may want to use a pre-configured material you already made in Unity, but it can help speed some importations along. If you want Unity to do this, save your texture files into a folder called Textures, located either at the same level as your mesh in the hierarchy or at any level above it. Unity will look *only* through these folders to find your textures.

SETTING UP SIMPLE SHADERS AND MATERIALS

Creating materials and assigning shaders to them in Unity is not a complicated process and can be done in a few quick clicks. A *shader* is basically a coded set of instructions describing how to calculate rendering effects on a given object, like lighting. You'll typically run across shaders that either calculate instructions per vertex (vertex shaders) or ones that take up a bit more computational overhead but calculate per pixel (pixel shaders). You don't apply shaders directly to an object, but rather hook them up to individual materials, which are then applied to the mesh. Materials take the shader instructions and link them to a texture file, which is then applied to the asset. Assets can share the same material if they share the same texture file, and many materials and assets can share the same shader.

Without shaders in Unity, your objects would be white, sad, and lifeless, only being colored by the lights around them. Shaders help create the illusion that your objects have depth, are made from a specific kind of real-world material (such as wood, feather, furs, skin, and so on), and drive the artistic direction of your game.

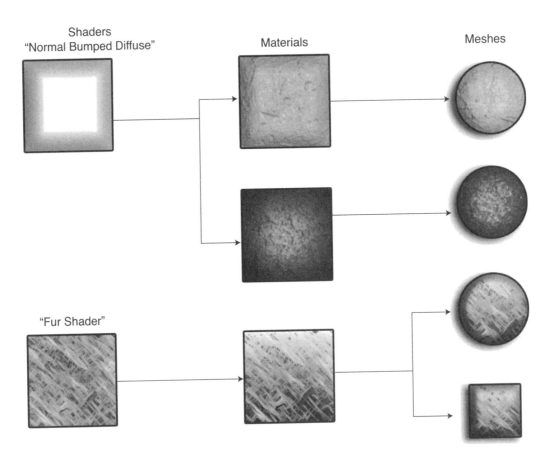

Figure 6.14
A simple diagram showing the relationship between meshes, materials, and shaders.

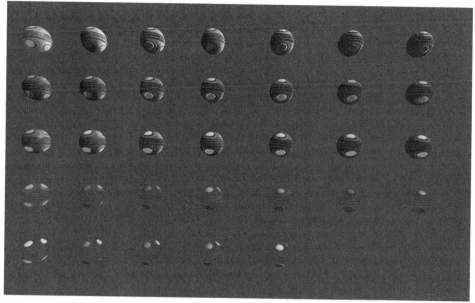

Figure 6.15
Some of the different shaders available for use, all displaying the same textures in their materials for reference.

Unity-Provided Shaders

Unity comes packaged with a large library of prebuilt shaders, most of them divided into categories or families: Normal, Transparent, Nature, Self-Illuminated, Reflective, and Lightmapped to name a few. There are also special shaders such as the skybox shader and other unique shaders for displaying particles and text. Some of the more prominently used ones are shown in Figure 6.15.

The scene file used to generate this image is included on the DVD in the Shader Test project folder; go to DVD▶ShaderTest▶Chapter6_shadertest.unity. Browse through the file and tumble around to see how the light affects the different objects. You can see which shader is applied to which object by clicking on one of the spheres in the Scene view and viewing its information in the Inspector.

- **Normal Family:** These are the most basic shaders, good for opaque objects like wood, cloth, or plastic—things that generally don't have a reflection.

- **Reflective Family:** As the name suggests, these shaders reflect the surrounding environment onto itself, accomplished through the use of a cube map. These are great for objects like shiny, waxed floors or grease.

- **Self-Illuminated Family:** These shaders appear to emit their own light and are great choices for objects like lamps or displays. They won't actually emit light onto other objects, just on themselves.

- **Transparent Family:** For objects that need to be fully or partly transparent, you'd use one of these shaders. Transparent shaders can be used for water, glass, ice, or anything else that is not totally opaque.

- **Transparent Cutout Family:** These are very similar to the Transparent shaders and are grouped together under the same drop-down menu. Instead of allowing for smooth, gradual shifts from opacity to transparency, the Cutout shaders create hard lines between what is drawn and what isn't. This is good for complicated objects such as wire meshes or fences, where you don't want accidental bleed into an area that's supposed to be transparent.

- **Lightmap Family:** These are a bit more special in that they use a secondary texture to define lights and shadows on an object, even in the absence of a Scene light. They are like self-illuminated shaders in this regard, but much more powerful. You've played around with lightmaps already on the terrain in Chapter 5. Lightmaps, however, can be used for any object in the game and are often baked with substitute lighting in a 3D modeling application.

The other shaders are used for specific features and effects, like the Nature Soft-Occlusion shaders used for trees. Most of the Particle and FX shaders are used only for specific cases, and you wouldn't use them for an ordinary mesh. Many other kinds of shaders can be either downloaded from the Unity site or written from scratch.

There's one other kind of shader available for download with Unity—the Toon shader. These allow for handdrawn and cartoony effects, displaying the body of the object in a cel-shaded manner and drawing an outline around the general shape. The Toon Shader package is not automatically installed with every Unity project and must be selected during creation. The *Widget* project will make heavy use of the Toon shader, so if you didn't include it in the project's creation, it must be added.

All the families of Pixel shaders share similar properties, in that they can have a Diffuse channel or a Specular channel or create the illusion of height with bump and normal maps. Once you pick which family of shaders you need to work with for your item, you need to decide which properties that shader will have. The main properties shared are as follows:

- **Diffuse:** Defines your object's basic color. Diffuse can be controlled with a texture or simple color selector. All shaders have some kind of diffuse property.

- **Bump and Parallax Bump:** Shaders with Bump or Parrallax in their name have a property that allows the simulation of height and depth on the object. Modeling every tiny scratch or detail on an object is pricey and a bit silly, so bump maps are used to simulate these small details. Parallax Bump shaders are similar but use a different algorithm to calculate the depth of each detail.

- **Specular:** Shaders with Specular properties allow the object to have a nice shine or gloss feature when light hits it, like along the rim of a polished stoneware vase. This is not the same as reflection, which actually reflects objects around it back onto itself using a texture.

Out of the Pixel shaders, the Normal Diffuse shaders are going to be your cheapest to render, followed by shaders with bumps maps, and then Specular Maps, Bumped Specular, and finally Parallax shaders being the most expensive. All the vertex-lit shaders are cheaper than the Pixel shaders, but they're a little more limited in use.

Shaders in Unity are written in a custom language called ShaderLab, similar in nature to nVidia's CgFX. Although it's not too hard to learn the syntax for the shader language, the art of writing optimized, effective, and beautiful shaders is not a trivial one, and a veritable mountain of books has been written on the subject. Detailing how to write a complex shader is beyond the scope of this book, but if you're interested, see Appendix D on the DVD for good places to start.

Bumps, Spec, Cubes, and Details

When choosing your shaders, some will require more input than others to do their job. Besides providing color to an object, textures are used to describe height, transparency, reflection, details, and many other auxiliary properties. Sometimes a singular texture can be used to provide multiple details at once, but often you'll need to create multiple textures to shade a single object.

Bump Maps

Bump maps are grayscale images that define height or depth on an object. Areas of the texture that are darker seem to recede into the object, and lighter areas on the texture mark spots on the object that should be raised or project out.

The object here is only a simple sphere, but by applying a shader with a bump channel, it makes it look as if the sphere has been sculpted with crevices and raised patches. In this case, the bump map is just a grayscale version of the diffuse color map, as shown in the middle image in Figure 6.16.

When you import a texture to use as a bump map, check the Generate BumpMap box on the import settings to actually have Unity produce a *normal map* of your texture. Normal maps are RGB-encoded images, not grayscale ones, that use color data to define the bumps and creases on an object. (They tend to look kind of blue or purple.) Normal maps, depending on their creation method, can often lead to better-looking results than a normal grayscale bump map. When generating a normal map, play with the Bumpiness slider to increase its effectiveness.

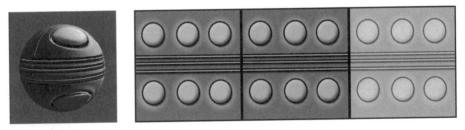

Figure 6.16
The diffuse, bump, and normal textures that lead to the finished Sphere object.

Specular and Illumination Maps

Specular maps define which parts of the object are shiny and which parts aren't. Instead of being a separate texture like bump maps, specular information is often stored in the texture's alpha channel as a grayscale image. Parts that are painted white are glossy, and parts that are black are not. Using a map to define individual parts of an object can make your asset more interesting, instead of just applying a wholesale specular value to the entire thing. While a person's finger nails and hair may be shiny and glossy, giving them shiny and glossy skin to match would be a little odd. The skin part of the texture can easily be painted black to avoid any gloss highlights.

Illumination maps for self-illuminating shaders work the same way. Instead of having the entire object emit light, only select parts can be chosen to do so.

The self-illuminated, bumped, Specular shader shown in Figure 6.17 shows it all in one package using only two textures. The base diffuse color (Base RGB) is defined using one texture, and the gloss pattern for the specular highlights is stored in its alpha channel (Gloss A). The bump information for the normal

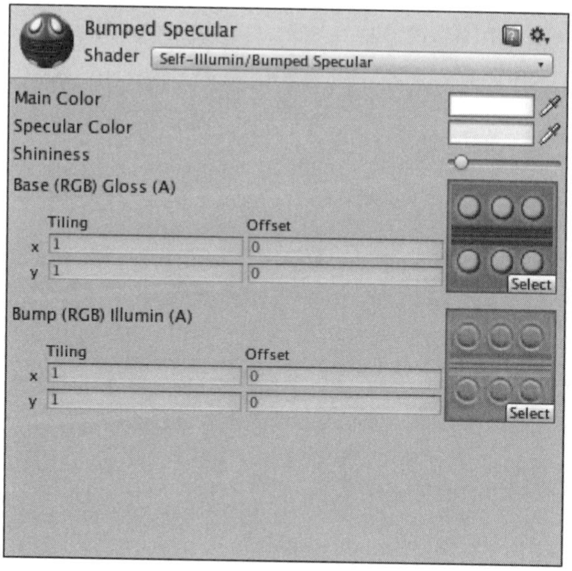

Figure 6.17
Unity clearly marks in the Inspector where you need to store your data.

map is a separate texture (Bump RGB), whose own alpha channel houses the illumination data.

A color for the specular color can be chosen as well (if you don't want the glossy highlight to be stark white), and the overall shininess of the glossy patches can be adjusted with the slider.

Cube Maps

A cube map is another special kind of texture, which in reality is actually made up of six separate textures that map to the faces of a virtual cube. Sound familiar? Skyboxes are in fact a kind of special cube map. Some shaders, like Reflective shaders, use cube maps to simulate the world around them. Instead of actually calculating reflections around an object (which is expensive), a cube map basically serves as a snapshot of each cardinal direction around the object, which is then overlaid on top of it. See Figure 6.18.

Cube maps fake reflections pretty well and can be made by hand from six square images, or Unity can generate one from a square image. If you'd like Unity to create a cube map, choose a kind of cube map from the Generate Cubemap drop-down box in the texture's import options. This option will be grayed out if your image isn't square. Sphere maps are more common than the other selections, but play around with them until you find something you like. The generated cube map is stored underneath the original texture in a hierarchy in the Project view.

Figure 6.18
This applied cube map makes it look like the sphere is reflecting its neighbors.

Detail Maps

Detail maps are another kind of special texture and are used only by the Diffuse Detail shader. They act kind of like a reverse mip map, in that as you get closer to an object, the special shader begins to take over. Detail textures are used to apply small, fine details to an object, like individual blades of grass on a terrain or bricks on a wall. If the camera is far away from the object, the normal diffuse texture is shown. As the camera gets close, however, the detail texture is slowly overlaid on top of the original, adding additional interest at a fairly cheap cost.

Detail images are often grayscale and must be completely tileable in all directions, or you will see seams. Darker values in the texture will make the diffuse texture darker, and lighter values will make the object lighter. When you import a detail texture, be sure to enable the Fade Out property and set the mip maps levels you want it to function at.

Assigning Shaders and Materials

Linking a material and shader to an object is very simple and follows Unity's drag and drop principles. Close the Shadertest project (if open) and reopen the Widget project. The tree2 object looks like it could use some color, so right-click in Project view and select Create▶Material. This will place a new material object in the active folder in the Project Hierarchy. Just to keep things tidy, create a new folder in the Terrain subfolder and name it **Materials**. Drag your new material in here and select it to see its properties in the Inspector. See Figure 6.19.

New materials are empty by default and are assigned the basic Normal Diffuse shader. At this point, you could just pick a color for the material, like a nice green for the leaves, and call it a day, or you can assign a texture to a material, one that fits the UV map of the object. First, in the Inspector, click on the Material component to expand its options. To assign a texture, use the Select button over the dark gray Texture thumbnail, or drag and drop one from the Project view to the square where it says "None (Texture 2D)." From your Terrain Texture folder, drag the Tree2_DIFF texture into this space to assign it to the material. The Preview sphere will update to show a green and brown texture wrapping around it, as shown in Figure 6.20.

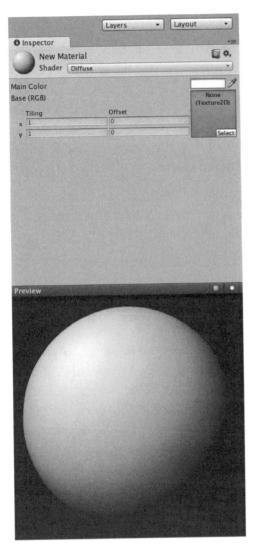

Figure 6.19
The default Material object.

Note

If your sphere instead disappears and turns into a latticework-looking object, it's not the end of the world. Look at the import settings for the Tree2_DIFF file and make sure that its compression setting uses DXT1, not DXT5—these kinds of errors pop up from rogue alpha channels being displayed.

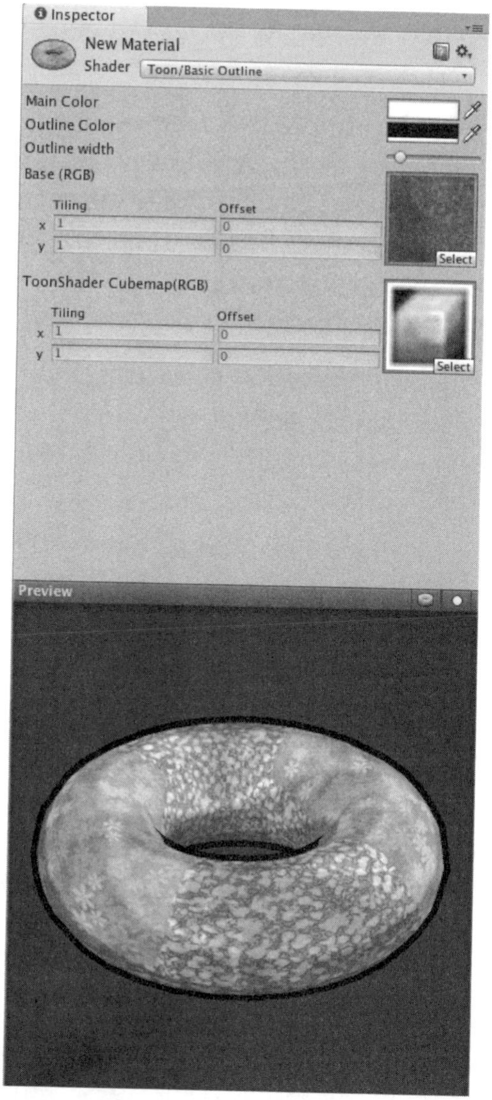

Figure 6.20
The finished Toon shader, applied to a torus.

Besides assigning a texture and color, you can also change the tiling of a texture or its offset values through a material. Leave the default values if your texture has been painted to the UV map of the object; otherwise it won't match. These properties can be useful for creating animating textures on objects, as they can be referenced by scripts to create moving water, fluctuating energy beams, or anything else you can think up.

At the top of the Material Inspector is the Shader drop-down menu—change this to Toon▶Basic Outline. This will help give your tree a handdrawn cartoon look and make it match the terrain better. The material now has some different options available, namely an Outline Color, Outline Width, and a Toon Shader cube map. The default outline values are fine (although you can change them if you want), but you need to get a cube map for the object to display properly.

Luckily, the Toon Shader package comes with a pregenerated cube map. From the Select drop-down menu, pick "toony lighting—generated cube map" or navigate to Toon Shading▶Sources▶toonylighting▶generatedCubemap in the Project view and drag that on.

The Preview will update with these changes, but the sphere doesn't display the shader all that well, due to its shape. At the top-right corner of the Preview window is a small blue sphere—click this to cycle through the basic primitive shapes to see how your shaders behave on different objects.

Now you're ready to apply the material to the asset. To assign new materials to objects, start by dragging the tree2 GameObject from the Project view into the Scene or Hierarchy to add it to the game. This creates an instance of the object. Notice that the tree2 object has a hierarchy of its own—it's made up of two unique meshes: one for the leaves, and one for the trunk. When assets are made up of multiple meshes, each mesh can take a separate material and shader. Right now you're only going to be hand placing a few trees, so you can keep the Toon shader in place.

Click and drag your new material from the Project view onto both of tree2's parts: Leaves and Trunk. Look at your tree in the Scene view to see the new material in effect. Don't forget to name your new material something more meaningful than "New Material." Green Tree or Tree2 are some possibilities.

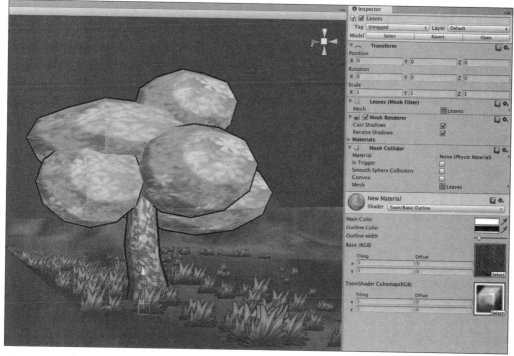

Figure 6.21
The shaded tree and its Inspector properties.

Now the rest of the assets need shaders and materials, too:

1. Make seven new materials and place them in your Terrain▶Materials folder. Rename them **CherryBranches**, **GreenBranches**, **LooseRock**, **Poppy**, **SunFlower**, **Greens**, and **Trunk**. These will be the materials for the meshes you imported earlier.

2. All but the CherryBranches and SunFlower materials need to have the Toon▶Basic Outline Shader attached to them. These two will be a little different.

3. The CherryBranches and SunFlower assets need to use one of the Transparency Cutout shaders, as both of them use alpha channels to define flower parts. Assign the CherryBranches and SunFlower materials the Transparent▶Cutout▶Diffuse shader.

4. Now assign the textures and cube maps to these new materials. Cherry-Branches will receive the Tree1_DIFF file, GreenBranches the Tree2_DIFF file, the LooseRock Material is assigned the LooseRock_DIFF file, Poppy, Greens, and SunFlowers are assigned the Flowers_DIFF file, and the Trunk material can use either one of the Tree files. All the Toon shaders use the same toony lighting cube map.

5. Drag the two rock, two tree, and two flower meshes into the scene (they should be located under Terrain▶Meshes if you imported them earlier) and assign the materials to the objects as follows:

   ▪ Flower1: Flowers receive the SunFlower material, and Leaves_and_Stalk receives the Greens material.

   ▪ Flower2: Assign the Poppy material.

   ▪ Rock1 and Rock2: Assign the LooseRock material.

   ▪ Tree1: Leaves gets the CherryBranches material and Trunk gets the Trunk material.

   ▪ Tree2: Leaves gets the GreenBranches material and Trunk gets the Trunk material.

You can use the Main Color property of each material to adjust the overall tints of the objects, if you think the colors aren't gong together so well. The color's alpha channel will determine how much of your tinting shows through.

Before populating the entire space with these objects, there're a few more things to do.

Making a Custom Skybox Material

The Standard Assets package's skyboxes don't fit the artistic direction for the game, so you need to create a custom one.

Skyboxes are created from six separate textures, each corresponding to one of the six sides of a cube. This virtual cube is rendered around and behind your game scene, giving it the illusion that there's a big 'ol sky up there far, far way. To use a skybox, you'll need to create six seamless, interlocking textures, which can be a bit more complicated than it looks. Or you can find a nice square tiling

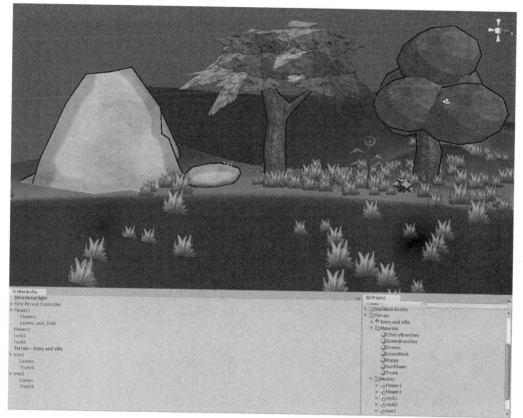

Figure 6.22
The added plant life with materials in place.

sky texture and have Unity make one for you. Lucky for you, there's a skybox texture premade for use on the DVD.

Copy the Skybox folder from Chapter 6 on the DVD over to your Assets folder to import the skybox textures—all these textures *must* have their Wrap mode set to Clamp. If the textures are left at their default Repeat mode, there will be seams. Make a new material in this folder and name it **BlueSunnyDay.** Skyboxes use one of the special shaders, found under RenderFX. In your new material, select RenderFX▶Skybox to create the proper fields. Now assign each of the six sides one of the matching textures—each has been named to correspond with the correct skybox slot it fits into (left, right, top, and so on).

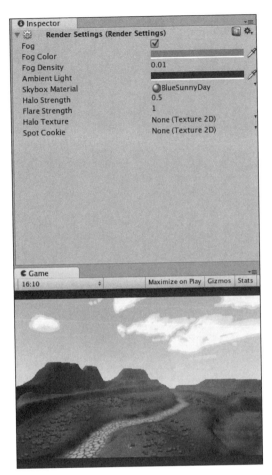

Figure 6.23
Skybox and fog in place, viewable in the game.

Once your material is set up, you need to hook it up to the scene. As the entire scene will use the same skybox, you can just hook it up to the General properties. Navigate to the Edit menu and select Render Settings to bring up the scene's properties in the Inspector. Drag your new skybox material into the Skybox property, or select it from the drop-down menu. You can also take this time now to fiddle with the fog, fog color, and ambient light.

Adding Water

The last major addition needed for the map's landscape is water. Right now the riverbeds are a little dry and don't pose much of a challenge to the player wandering around. In Chapter 5, you just used one of the prefab water objects from the Standard Assets package, so this time you'll make a more custom water plane to fit in better with the rest of the game.

To create a custom water plane, follow these steps:

1. Create a new GameObject plane (GameObject▶Create Other▶Plane) and position it at (100,0.2,100) to center it on the map and place it just a hair above the ground. Scale it about 21 times along each axis to make it fit around the entire map.

2. Make a new material, name it **Water**, and assign it the Water shader by selecting FX▶Water(simple) from the Shader drop-down menu. Put this new material in your Terrain▶Materials folder and assign it to the Plane object.

3. Now locate the water script to run the shader. The water material uses a script to animate the different texture fields, giving the water an illusion of movement. Grab the WaterSimple script from the Standard Assets▶Water▶Sources folder and drag this onto the Plane object as well. The plane is now covered with a very simple, very plain water shader. Spruce up the material by adding some textures.

4. Select the Plane object in the Hierarchy to view its properties in the Inspector. The Wave Shader wants four different textures to function: three normal textures and one cube map. You already have one custom water texture imported: Water_DIFF. Place this texture into both the Waves Bumpmap and Wave Speed texture slots.

5. Select the Water_DIFF texture in the Project view and change its import setting of Generate Cubemap to Spheremap. Click Apply to have Unity reimport this texture and create a cube map from it.

6. Apply this new cube map to your water's Reflective color map. The last file you need can be found in the Chapter 6 folder on the DVD—rivergradient.tif. Import this file into your Terrain Texture folder and add it to the Reflective Color slot. Change the Horizon and Wave scale sliders until you get an effect you like.

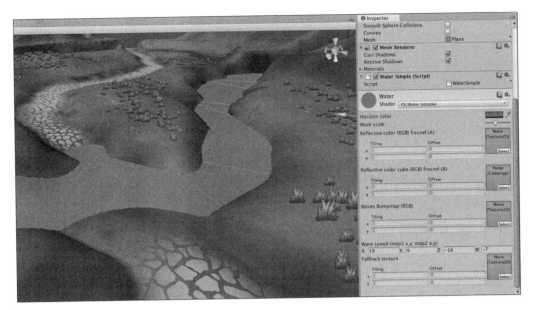

Figure 6.24
The simple water plane in place and its empty Inspector properties.

Figure 6.25
The finished water material, all hooked up.

Helpful Tips for Working with Assets

Now that you can import textures and meshes, you can begin to populate your map with a wide range of fantastic items. While this is definitely fun to start, the allure can begin to wear off after you've placed your 100th fence post. Thankfully, there are a few available tricks you can employ to make your life easier when working with large arrays of assets.

Prefabs, Prefabs, Prefabs!

Unity has another trick up its sleeve for when it comes to working with assets more effectively: prefabs. *Prefabs* are a special kind of GameObject that can only be created from within Unity. Making a normal asset into a prefab creates a template from which all other copies of that can be instanced. If you need to make a change to the prefab—like update a material, edit a mesh, or attach new scripts—all instances of the prefab are updated as well, making it *extremely* useful.

Making a prefab is pretty simple. In the Project view, right-click and select Create▶Prefab. A new Prefab object will be placed into the active folder hierarchy. These new prefabs are empty at first, but they can be easily populated and templated with any object currently in the game. Drag one of the assets currently in the Hierarchy, like tree2, onto the prefab in the Project view, as shown in Figure 6.26. Rename the new prefab **Green Tree** or something similar. That's it. Any asset that's currently in the Hierarchy can be made into a prefab.

Now if you want to put more of the green trees around the map, use the prefab tree2 instead of the base asset. Then if you ever need to change anything, you only have to do it once instead of for each instance of the tree.

Sometimes you may want to change an individual instance of the prefab, and these changes are shown in bold in the Inspector. For the most part you can override any prefab setting and still keep the link back to the parent object, except if you want to add or remove a component or child GameObject. When you override a setting, Unity will ask if you want to propagate the changes to all the other prefabs or just the current one.

Make all the other assets you imported earlier into prefabs, especially if you know you'll be using them more than once. You can always spot a prefab in the Project view by its icon of a little blue box. These are similar to imported assets,

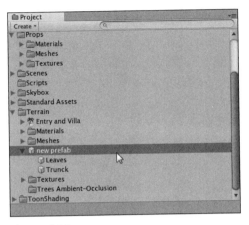

Figure 6.26
A new prefab in the Project view, based off the Tree2 asset.

but they lack the small file picture attached to those. Make sure you grab these and not the base assets when populating your scene.

Mass Selecting and Grouping Objects

Place some of your new prefab items around, 10 to 20 all together. Now if you wanted to move them all one meter to the right, you'd have to go around individually moving every single one. Instead of doing this, you can use one of two techniques to group your objects to make edits and selection easier.

The first way is to create an empty GameObject, place it at (0,0,0), and then make all your objects a child of this GameObject. You can then select the parent object to manipulate all the children at once. Using empty GameObjects can also be a handy way to clean up your Hierarchy view if it's getting unwieldy.

The other option is to use Smart Selection Groups. To try this, place a few of the different trees around and then select them all. Navigate to the Edit menu and go to Save Selection▶Save Selection 1. Now deselect everything and go back to the Edit menu. This time pick Load Selection▶Load Selection 1. All the items you had previously saved are now selected again. This can be useful for saving large sets of like objects that you may want to reference later, like all enemies, all item pickups, or all plant life.

Figure 6.27
Snap Settings dialog box.

Snapping to the Grid

Depending on the type of game you're making, you may need to snap assets together or align them perfectly with the grid. With the items in question selected, navigate to the Edit menu and choose Snap Settings. The Snap Settings dialog box, shown in Figure 6.27, opens.

You can now enter the exact measurements for how you want the item to move and whether you want it to snap along all axes or just one in particular.

Reworking the Terrain

Once you begin to place items and assets into the map, don't forget to go back and rework the terrain. Oftentimes things will look better if they seem to organically fit into the map and not look like they were placed right on top without any thought. Using a smaller brush size, work the edges of the terrain up around the edges of trees, fences, houses, or any other feature that would naturally have dirt start to pile up around it.

This doesn't just extend to height, but also to the splat painting. Paint in darker areas around assets and put some dirt around well-traveled areas. Darkening the map around the bases of assets can help with shadowing and make it look like the asset "fits" rather than "floats."

Figure 6.28
The landscape now populated with trees, grasses, textures, and atmospheric effects.

Now that you've got all the basics down on working with assets, go back to that Props folder you imported at the beginning of the chapter and fix those with materials and prefabs. The Fence asset has two textures for use: a white variation and a brown variation. Set up two materials so you can use fences in either color.

Once you have all these prop pieces and terrain pieces set up with prefabs, place some trees down around the borders to keep the player in and hide the world's end. Make some flower beds, line the pathway with fences, or do whatever you want. The final scene file can be found in the Final Projects folder▸Scenes▸Chapter6.unity if you want ideas for how to place things (see Figure 6.28 as well). You can also check the Design Documentation for maps and level guides on individual item placement.

Special trees are also included that can be placed into an Ambient-Occlusion folder if you want to use the Terrain Tree painting feature, prefaced with the term "terrain." Also don't forget to change the terrain settings from the toolbar to calculate your lightmap, reconfigure the draw distances, and perfect the wind speed. Name your scene file something like **GameStart** and save often.

CHAPTER 7

CREATING CHARACTERS

It's all well and good if you have an immaculately designed space for your game to take place in, but most settings need some sort of populace to inhabit them for the illusion of complexity to really come alive. Your players would also probably like to control an actual real character, and not the simple controller thrown in right now.

BASIC PC 101

Designing and building unique characters to populate your world will help give your players something to focus their interest on and empathize with. Creating believable characters has been a goal of oral and written literature for thousands of years. With video games, the problem of creating a believable character is only enhanced, as characters are expected to interact with players at some acceptable level. This chapter will not cover how to model, skin, or rig a character, but links to resources are provided in Appendix D, "Resources and References," on the DVD.

Player characters, or PCs as they are often called, are simply the avatars players actively use to interact with the game. Games can handle the PC very differently, from prewritten characters that develop in accordance to a story, to completely player-generated characters that evolve as the players see fit. Some games don't even have PCs in the traditional sense, and yours doesn't have to, either.

In general, the PC will fall into one of three categories: first-person, third-person, and implied/non-existent. Unity will allow all these variations, as the PC is primarily defined by a scripted custom *character controller*, and not by something predefined and hardcoded in the engine. Right now the *Widget* scene is using a crude approximation of a first-person PC controller that is lacking a mesh altogether, which is primarily for ease of use when testing the game. The actual game will utilize a third-person approach common in platformer type games. To do that, though, you'll need to import some new assets.

IMPORTING CHARACTERS AND OTHER NONSTATIC MESHES

Beyond creating just the physical mesh for the character, you'll also need to account for its animation data. Most meshes you'll import will be static (not mobile), but characters will need to move around on their own, react to scripted commands, or be controlled by a player. For most characters, you won't be able to get away with using Unity's built-in Animation Editor, but you will need instead to import and link animations created in an outside application.

Introducing *Widget*

Back in Chapter 5, you learned the basics of how to import meshes, but I skipped over the animation properties in the Inspector—you'll return to that now. From the DVD, drag the contents of the Chapter 7 Widget folder into your project's Asset folder to begin the importation process. This is *Widget*, the star of the game and the character that the player will control. Arrange these files into a folder called **Characters** to keep everything organized.

Widget has a much more complex hierarchy than any of the previous static meshes: His body is broken into two skinned mesh components, called "Body" and "Wheels" (which correspond to the simple meshes "Body" and "Wheels" below them), a separate node called "root" housing his *character rig* data, and a Take001 animation clip (the one layer of animation his file contains). The animation clip has a separate property displaying the sample rate (how many frames per second the animation was created at) and whether the file has been compressed already. The skinned mesh components (the ones with a box and file icon) show the default material that was created for each piece, along with a textured preview of the piece. If you click on just the Mesh component (the icon that looks like a mesh box), the particular part will be displayed just showing the wireframe. The number of vertices and triangles that make up the particular mesh (tris) will also be overlaid on the preview.

Note

Unity automatically triangulates all meshes being imported, so this isn't something you must take care of on your own.

Select the root of the hierarchy "Widget" to bring up all his importation properties in the Inspector, shown in Figure 7.1.

Set up the base importation features, like ensuring the Scale Factor is set to 1, Generate Colliders is enabled, and allow Unity to generate a Material Per Texture. Continue down to the Animations submenu.

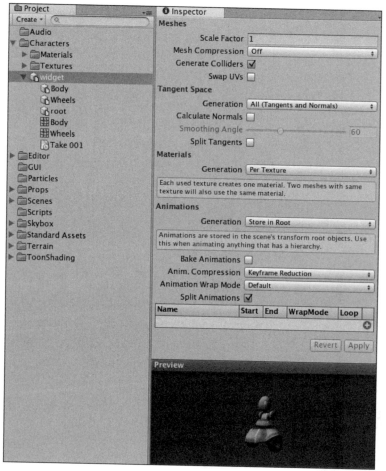

Figure 7.1
Widget and his animation importation settings.

- **Animation Generation:** This setting controls how any animations stored within the file are imported. Only certain kinds of files can wrap animation data along with the mesh data, like .fbx files or .mb files. (Other file types like .obj cannot house animation data.) The default selection is Store in Root, the root node of the file's hierarchy. You can also have Unity not import any animations (Don't Import), have it "Store in Nodes" or "Store in Original Roots." Storing animation in the nodes is good for complex animations that you may want to keep separate, such as if *Widget* had some crazy animation data particularly for his wheels. Storing in the original roots will keep the animation stored as it was in your external application where you created the animation, but this won't always work correctly for all tasks. For most cases, stay with the default selection.

- **Bake Animations:** If you used IK, blend shapes, or any other forms of non-bone–based or FK animation in the file, the animation data must be baked upon import. Check this box to do so. *Widget* doesn't need any of his animations baked, so leave this unchecked in this case.

- **Animation Compression:** Animations can be hefty memory users, and you can set the type of compression you want to apply to the file here. You can select "Off" to have no compression applied, "Keyframe Reduction" or "Keyframe Reduction and Compression." The last option will make a smaller file size but will sometimes introduce artifacts or jittering. Play with different selections and pick the one that looks most like the original file.

- **Animation Wrap Mode:** This sets the default wrap mode for all the animations stored within the file: Default, Once, Loop, ClampForever, and PingPong. Any of these settings can be individually overridden through scripting for any one-animation sequence, so pick the one used for the most cases. The Default selection can be set and described from scripting as well. Choose Default for *Widget*—you'll specify specific cases for the individual animations as they're set up.

- **Split Animations:** Check this box to enable splitting a single animation layer into multiple sequences. The empty table under this selection is where the individual sequences will be set up.

Figure 7.2
The setup if *Widget* used multiple animation files.

Usually you'll find animations created for characters stored in one of two ways: Either all the animations will be created in one file and just have buffer *keyframes* between each unique animation, or each animation will have its own unique file storing only one piece of data, like walk, run, or fire. *Widget* has all his animations stored within his one file, so you'll use the Split Animations feature to process the different animation sets.

If you wanted to store the information in unique files (if you had multiple animators working on one model, for instance), Unity allows a simple naming mechanic to relink all the files. See Figure 7.2.

Name your animation files with the name of the base model file, followed by an @ sign, followed by the name of the animation sequence. The sequence name will be the one you use when you reference particular animations in scripts. Using this naming convention, Unity will link all these animations to the base model file.

Since *Widget* does have all his animations stored together, go back to the Inspector and enable Split Animations. *Widget* has nine animations stored within his .fbx file, each spanning a set length of specific keyframes in the animation layer. These are listed in Table 7.1.

In the Split Animations table, click on the gray + sign to create a new clip. By default, Unity populates the fields with a sample "idle" clip and random number data.

- **Name:** The given name of the clip and the one you will reference from scripts, so give it something more meaningful than "clip1" and be mindful of spaces.

Table 7.1 *Widget's* Animation Data

Name	WrapMode	Frames	Loop
Slow Roll	Loop	1–23	No
Fast Roll	Loop	30–53	No
Taser	Once	60–83	No
Got Hit	Once	90–101	No
Duck	Once	105–128	No
Jump	Once	135–147	No
Fall Down	Once	150–162	No
Idle	Once	170–242	No
Die	Once	250–322	No

- **Start:** The first frame of your animation.

- **End:** The last frame of your animation.

- **WrapMode:** How the animation is to be played. The same selections are available from the Animation WrapMode drop-down menu.

- **Loop:** This *isn't* a selection box to make the clip loop—you set that in WrapMode. Checking this box will create a duplicate of the first frame specified and tack it onto the end of the clip. If you find your looping animations look a little jittery, try enabling this option to create the buffer frame.

- **Plus and Minus buttons:** Add a new clip to the sequence or delete the selected clip.

To rename the clip or alter any of the information, simply click on the desired cell in the table and retype. Enter all of *Widget's* animation data as shown in the table and click the Apply button to save. The new clips you create are added to *Widget's* hierarchy in the Project view—see Figure 7.3.

To test the new animations, add an instance of *Widget* to the scene and give him a large plane to stand on. Select the *Widget* object in the Hierarchy view to bring

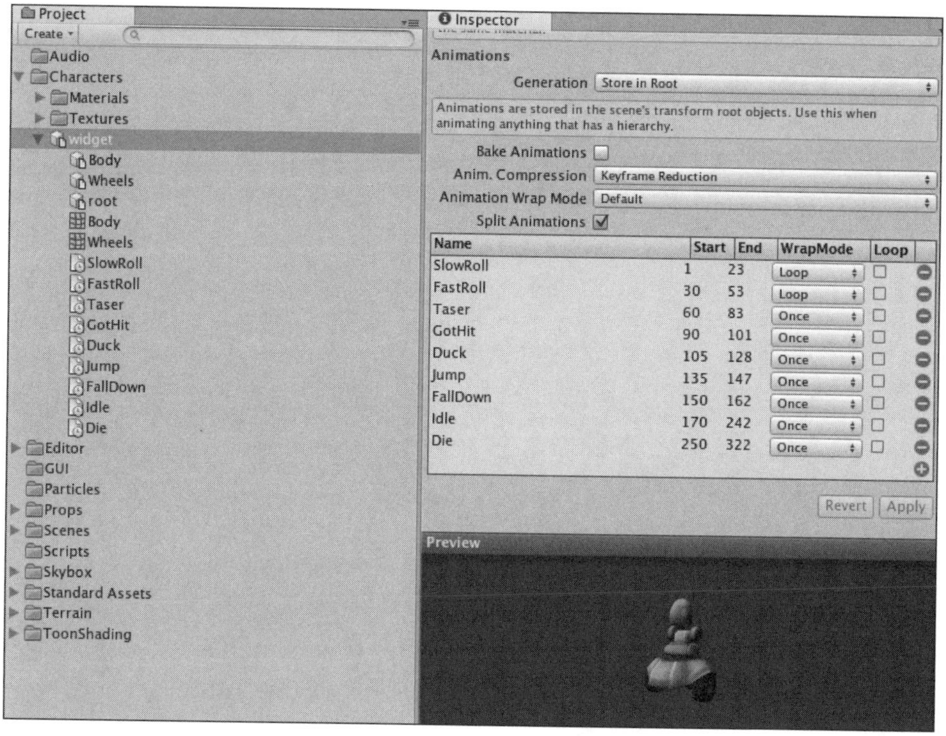

Figure 7.3
Widget's newly created clips.

up his information in the Inspector. The animation component describes his basic data and default behavior, as shown in Figure 7.4.

The first Animation field houses *Widget's* start animation (picked by default from the first clip entered into the sequence), and the Animations array lists all the animations that have been either clipped or linked to the model. Play Automatically will do just that when the game is started (using the selected clip in the Animation field above), and Animate Physics will allow the animation to interact with physics bodies. Animate Only if Visible will play the selected model's animations only if it currently is within the view of the active camera, saving on memory by not moving things off screen. By default this and Play Automatically are checked.

Drag one of *Widget's* animation clips from the Project view into the Animation slot or select one of his animations from the drop-down menu to change his default.

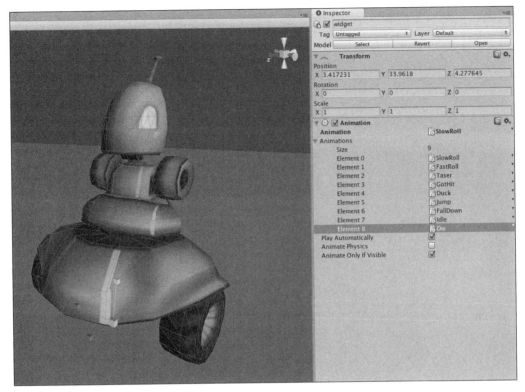

Figure 7.4
Widget's Animation component.

Center the view on *Widget* in the Scene view and press the Play button to view his animation. Remember that you can use the Pause and Step buttons to refine how you view each animation. See Figure 7.5.

Widget's almost ready to be dropped into the game's populated scene file, but he needs a few more tweaks first. First up, his materials need to be set up so that he matches the rest of the game world. The default diffuse material applied during importation is all right for testing, but he'll need a Toon shader to match the rest of the game. *Widget* should also be made a prefab immediately so that all future updates to him will be easily produced and changed when needed. Many more parts will be added to him through the course of the book (like a character controller and other scripts), and this will be much easier if you work with a prefab from the beginning.

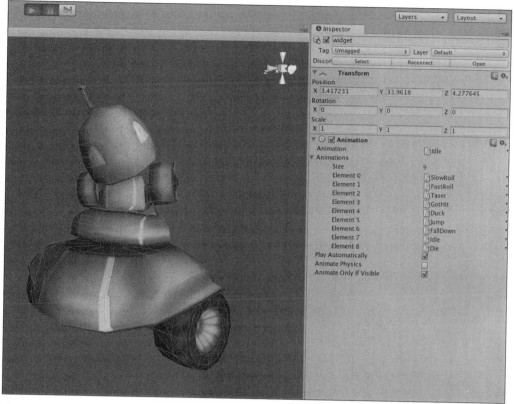

Figure 7.5
Widget's Idle animation in action.

Follow these steps to set up *Widget*:

1. Assign *Widget* a material (if you didn't have Unity generate one on import) and give it the Toon▶Basic Outline shader. The base RGB file uses the widget_diff texture, and the ToonShader cube map needs the toonylighting - generatedCubemap texture.

2. Change the main color to a darker gray, to avoid him being washed out by the lights. (R, G, and B = 145 works fairly well.)

3. Create a Capsule Collider component for *Widget*'s body piece by selecting the Body part in the Hierarchy view and going to Component▶ Physics▶Capsule Collider (see Figure 7.6). This will allow him to interact with other physics bodies in the world. Change the radius, height, and center of the collider so that it fits snuggly around him. Don't try to include the antenna or all the wheels in the collider bounds—just get most of him in.

4. Create a new *Widget* prefab and populate it with the current *Widget* asset.

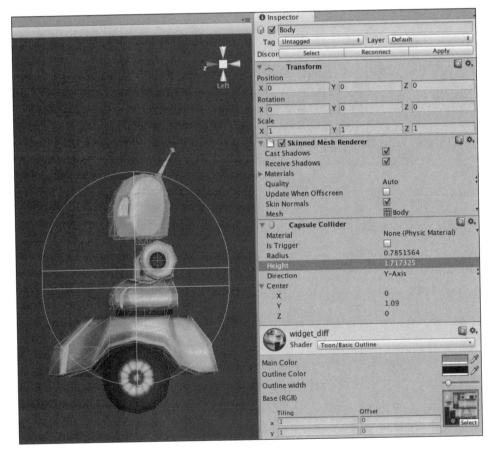

Figure 7.6
Fitting *Widget's* Capsule Collider.

Figure 7.7
Widget overseeing his new environment.

Your character is now ready to go and can be imported into any scene file in the game (see Figure 7.7). The major thing he lacks now is a *controller,* some means to move him based upon the player's input. He'll also need an animation *state machine,* a piece of code to drive which animations should be played how and when. In the next chapter, you'll look at the basics of scripting in Unity, followed by creating a simple controller to drive *Widget* around.

PART III

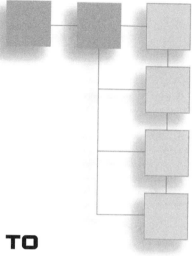

BRINGING YOUR PROPS TO LIFE WITH INTERACTIVITY

Interactivity is what makes games actually playable—it turns a collection of static artwork and pictures into a living system that responds to your commands. In Unity, most interactivity is achieved through scripting, pieces of instructions that are attached to individual GameObjects that describe how they should behave in a given circumstance. Part III explores some of the different ways scripts can be used to enhance your game, from animation control to crafting AI.

CHAPTER 8

SCRIPTING IN UNITY

If models, textures, and the like give your game environment a physical description and setting, then scripts and code chunks give your game and its contents *life*. Scripts define the basic interactions, behaviors, and rules of all the pieces in your game—without them you'd be hard pressed to call your scene file a game at all. One of Unity's most powerful aspects is the way it incorporates scripts and their member pieces directly into the editor, allowing for fast, intuitive linking and manipulation of any GameObject in the scene.

This book does not assume any prior knowledge of working with a scripting language and will cover some basic fundamentals at the end of the chapter, enough to explain the workings of all the scripts needed for the *Widget* game. However, this is no substitution for a more formal approach of learning how to program efficiently and effectively—a selection of further reading and learning resources is included in Appendix D, "Resources and References," on the DVD.

ONE EDITOR, THREE LANGUAGES, A WHOLE LOTTA CHOICE

A brief warning to the new scripting initiates in the room: The first half of this chapter may seem a bit technical in nature, as it details some of the fundamental aspects of working in Unity. Don't be discouraged if you don't understand all of it on the first go—you can always return to it later once you've gotten your feet wet.

In line with the engine's dedication to usability and flexibility, Unity natively supports three scripting languages: C#, Boo (a dialect of Python), and JavaScript, also sometimes referred to as UnityScript. Unity allows the programmers to pick their language on a per-script basis, meaning that a single project can contain scripts in all three languages, running in tandem peacefully and quickly. There is no need to choose one particular language at the start of a project and only stick to it; each user on the team can work in a different language based upon personal preferences. It's even possible (although not necessarily recommended) that scripts can access functions in other files written in other languages, and a single GameObject can have scripts in all three languages attached to it running at the same time. It's all thumbs up for Unity.

All of Unity's game logic is based on *Mono*, an open source .NET platform based around creating cross-platform applications. All three languages have access to the underlying .NET libraries, providing support for common desirable features like file access, networking, and reading XML files. More information on Mono and the .NET framework can be found on the website: http://mono-project.com/.

To top that off, each language is equally fast at runtime. Yes, equally fast. "How can that be," scoffs the long-time C# programmer. "Everyone knows that JavaScript is an interpreted language and can't possibly be as fast as any compiled language." Well, this is where perhaps officially naming the scripting language "UnityScript" rather than "JavaScript" would have saved on the confusion. Unity's implementation of JavaScript *is* in fact JIT (Just in Time) compiled to native machine code, thanks to Mono. It runs up to two orders of magnitude faster than any other implementation of JavaScript on the market, giving rise to Unity's claim as to having created the "world's fastest JavaScript." This claim is quite possibly (and happily) completely justified.

So in summary, you can use C#, Boo, or JavaScript, based purely on personal preference. Each language does have its own individual quirks and strengths, perhaps making one better suited to a particular task than another, but as far as Unity is concerned they're all equally valid.

Scripting in C# and Boo: A Few Caveats

Despite the three languages being equally supported by the engine, there are a few non-syntax related issues to look out for if you want to use C# or Boo.

■ Neither C# nor Boo behavior scripts automatically inherit from MonoBehaviour, unless you created them from within the editor directly. If you created your script file in an outside editor, you must provide the definition yourself:

```
//C#
using UnityEngine;
using System.Collections;
public class MyNewBehaviorScript : MonoBehaviour {/*your code here*/}

#Boo
import UnityEngine
class MyNewBehaviourScript(MonoBehaviour): #your code here
```

■ Use the Awake and Start functions to do any initialization, and do not use the constructor—Unity automatically invokes this, and using the constructor elsewhere could create errors.

■ The class name you provide in your script must match the file's name, because each behavior script file is treated as its own class implementation. So in the previous example snippet, "MyNewBehaviourScript" is also the name of the C# and Boo files.

■ Only member variables of the class are shown in the Inspector; properties are not.

PICKING A SCRIPT EDITOR, OR, DO YOU WANT AUTOCOMPLETION WITH THAT?

Besides picking which language to use, you'll also need to decide which *scripting environment* you'll actually do your coding in. Unity comes prepacked with a scripting environment right out of the box: UniSciTE for Windows licenses and Unitron for Mac. Unfortunately, this does exclude Linux. UniSciTE and Unitron are simple in nature, but they get the job done. Both provide a few options for customizing the workspace and the ability to change the selected language for syntax highlighting, but they lack any robust autocompletion functionality.

If UniSciTE/Unitron isn't to your liking, you can use a third-party solution, a few of which are listed here:

- **Visual Studio C#:** Unity now supports syncing to a Visual Studio C# project, either with the free Express or licensed Professional edition. Setting it up is easy: From within Unity, navigate to Assets▶Sync Visual Studio Project. From within Visual Studio, open the newly created .snl file in the root of your Project directory, one level up from the Assets directory. VS will provide you with much more sophisticated highlighting and autocompletion, but it may give you access to new C# features not currently supported by Unity. VS 2008 is officially supported.

- **MonoDevelop:** This open source IDE supports C# on Windows, Mac, and Linux. Since versions of MonoDevelop 2.2 or greater are compatible with Visual Studio solution and project files, you can follow the same setup as for Visual Studio C#. Sync the project and open the created solution file with MonoDevelop instead.

- **UnityDevelop:** Modified from the open source FlashDevelop editor, UnityDevelop creates a nicer coding environment for JavaScript users; however, it's only Windows. Setup is a bit more involved than VS or MonoDevelop, and detailed instructions can be found on UnityDevelop's download page.

- **SubEthaEdit:** A lean text editor available for Mac users, supporting JavaScript and C#. Two Unity-specific modes for the editor are available for download from SubEthaEdit's site.

Links to all these download and development sites are provided in Appendix D. If you're still unsure as to which language to write your projects in, knowing which scripting environment you prefer to work in can help you narrow the field down.

All examples and code moving forward are created in UniSciTE using Unity's JavaScript. You'll find that all of Unity's online documentation is also written in JavaScript—perhaps that's why it is the "recommended" programming language for the engine by some users—but you can use whichever language you feel most comfortable working in.

Scripting in JavaScript: A Few Caveats

Not to be left out, Unity's implementation of JavaScript does change some functionality that may seem strange or downright upsetting to longtime "traditional" JavaScript users. Some particularly important ones include:

- To initialize a string variable, you need to use Mono's String class, not JavaScript's string class. Strings also must be designated with double quotation marks, not single ones.

```
var myString : String;
var myOtherString = "Using Double Quotation Marks";
```

- You need to formally declare a variable before using it, and should try to explicitly declare its type whenever possible if not assigning a value straight away.

```
var myName : String;      //myName is a string variable with no assigned value.
var myAge = 35;           //myAge is an int variable containing the value '35'.
myAge = "TreeBranch";     //This will raise and error - myAge is an int.

var myJob;                //Type is not declared
myJob = "Engineer";       // myJob contains a string type value...
myJob = 7.5;              //...but now it's a float.
```

Unity will dynamically type a variable for you if you don't implicitly set one, but this could lead to undesired effects or errors, as shown here.

- Switch statements require that you insert a break for each listed case, you cannot declare anonymous functions, and semicolons at the end of statements are not optional.

- Each .js file actually implements its own class, and while incredibly handy, this does need to be taken into account when organizing your code.

FUNDAMENTALS OF SCRIPTING IN UNITY

Anyone familiar with working in a scripting environment for a game engine will have no trouble picking up Unity's API (Application Programming Interface), but there are some aspects worth mentioning up front. Also, if you're completely new to scripting, make sure that you understand the basic concepts presented here, or the next few chapters may be a little rough.

If you want to try some of the following examples for yourself, go to Assets▶Create▶JavaScript, either from the top menu or by right-clicking in the Project view, and create a new NewBehaviorScript. Double-click on this script in the Project view to open it for editing in UniSciTE.

To run your script, attach it to any GameObject in the Hierarchy by dragging the script from the Project view onto the object in the Hierarchy. Press the Play button to start the game and run the script. For simplicity's sake, you can just drag the script onto the default Main Camera. You can also find all the script examples in this chapter in the Chapter 8 folder on the DVD.

If you find that your scripts don't seem to update with changes even if you click the Play button, try clicking on the Options button of the script's component Inspector field and choosing Reset.

Note

Unity is case sensitive, so make sure you follow syntax exactly if you choose to type the examples. WORD is not the same thing as word or Word.

Variables

Variables are the means by which your script can store data—you can think of them as an empty box waiting to be filled. Like boxes (if you extend the analogy a bit further), variables come in different "shapes and sizes" that can fit different kinds of data. Not all data can be stored in every kind of variable, much like how you wouldn't expect to fit a refrigerator inside a shoebox. All variables also have a name, a unique identifier helping to remind you what the data inside is, like writing the contents of a box on its outside face. So simply, variables are comprised of two parts: a symbolic name and a container for data.

Once you create a variable in your script (known as "declaring" it), you can assign a value to it—in effect putting something in the box—perform tasks with it, change its value, swap the item in the box with another, or destroy it. Variables allow you to store large quantities of data and then quickly and easily find them again.

To make a new variable, you do so in a simple statement:

```
var myBox;
```

This line creates a new variable of the name myBox, with the keyword *var* declaring that the element myBox is a variable. Right now myBox is empty and is waiting to be filled with some type of data.

Buzzword

A *keyword* is any word in a programming language that is reserved to mean something special in that particular language. For example, in Unity, var is a keyword that defines the following word as a variable. A list of important Unity keywords is included in Appendix B, "Common Classes," on the DVD.

Common Variable Types

Unity's JavaScript has many kinds of variables available for use, but you'll find that you'll run across some kinds more than others. In general, you can break down the available variables into a few categories: Numbers, Strings, Booleans, Arrays, Enums, and Component-Specific. To declare any variable as having a certain type you can use one of two formulas:

```
var myVariable : myType;                    //ex. var myNumber : int;
var myVariable = "some assignment value"; //ex. var myNumber = 5;

//You can also use a combination of the two:
var myVariable : myType = "some assignment value";

//But this is a little redundant and not necessary.
```

Also note that you cannot use spaces in your variable names, even if it's a multi-word phrase like "my variable."

Number Variables   Number variables themselves are available in a few types, allowing you to pick one that fits the case at hand. Two of the more common ones are listed here, with a more complete list available in Appendix B.

- *Integers* are whole numbers that lack any fractional data, numbers like 0, 3, –5, and 1,024. Integers are useful for counting, incrementing data, and representing data for which fractional data doesn't make sense, like how many players are actively in a game. If you try to assign a number that has fractional data, say 3.5, the decimal part of the number will be lost and discarded. Keyword is int.

- *Floating point* numbers, in contrast, can have fractional data, such as 3.5, –20, or 3.14159. Notice that you can in fact assign the value –20 to a float variable, even though it may appear to look like an int. –20 can always be written as –20.0, but the decimal 0 is unnecessary. Floats are useful for any calculation that will result in the variable data having non-integer data, such as through division or when multiplying a number by something like a fraction of a second. Keyword is float.

Example:

```
var myFirstInt : int;     //declare the variable as type int
var mySecondInt = 10;
/* print is a special function that prints out
anything between the () to the Console. */
print(mySecondInt);

mySecondInt = 7;
myFirstInt = -30;
print(mySecondInt + myFirstInt);

var myFirstFloat = 3.14159;   //declare a variable as type Float
print(myFirstFloat);

myFirstFloat = myFirstFloat * 7;
print(myFirstFloat);
```

print( ) is a special function that will print anything between the parentheses to the Console view. The last printed line will always be displayed on the status line, but you can open the Console at any time to see all the print statements in order. Inserting print statements makes it easy to see what's going on at any point in your code.

The double slash mark notation // is a sign for a one line or inline comment—something in normal speech that you may want to say about your code. Anything on the line after the double slashes isn't compiled or read by the engine, allowing you to make notes or explain something in more detail. If you need more than one line to make a note, you can use what's known as a block comment, denoted by a matched pair of /* symbols, as shown:

```
//I'm a one line comment
/* Anything after the slash-star is a comment.
```

```
Including this.
To end a block comment, use :    */
```

String Variables   Besides numbers, a variable can also hold data that takes the form of text, giving rise to the ubiquitous and much loved "Hello World" example. Variables of this type, called *strings*, can be a word, a letter, a phrase, or even an entire novel (provided of course you have the memory space to do something like that). Strings allow you to store useful data like overlay text for buttons, players' names, or NPC messages.

Example:

```
var myString : String;
var myOtherString = " ";

myString = "Hello";
myOtherString = "World!";

print(myString + " " + myOtherString);
```

This example takes the two strings and prints them out together, using the moniker " " to denote a single empty whitespace (like a single spacebar tap). To assign a text value to a string variable, you must always enclose it in double quotation marks.

Booleans   *Booleans* are a special kind of variable, and you have run across them before, even if the name is unfamiliar at the moment. Booleans can only have one of two possible types: True or False. That's it. Booleans are incredibly useful for when you need to start performing tests on your data, determining if it fulfills some criteria you set. The data either does, True, or doesn't, False. Yes or no.

```
var aTrueVariable : boolean;
var anotherBoolVariable = false;
aTrueVariable = true;

print(anotherBoolVariable);
print(anotherBoolVariable + " doesn't equal " + aTrueVariable);
```

Notice that even though you *must* set the value of the Boolean variable using a lowercase true or false, the results will print out capitalized in the Console. Unlike in many other programming languages, False does not equate to 0 nor True to 1, and you cannot use these to test for equality or assignment.

Arrays   You should now have a good handle on the basic types of variables you can use. With even this small amount of knowledge you'd be surprised at how much you can get done. Let's suppose that you want to create some variables that are a bit more interesting.

You may find yourself at some point creating hundreds upon hundreds of integer values, storing your player character's inventory piece by piece. One variable may store how many health potions he has, another how many iron ingots. This, however, can get tediously unwieldy, especially if you have to do something involving the entire inventory at once. Arrays to the rescue!

An *array* is a special kind of object that allows you to store multiple values and objects together in a single variable. Think of it like a numbered list: In slot number 1 you have health potions, in slot number 2 you have manna potions, in slot number 3 you have repair kits, and so on, but all these slots belong to one variable—your item list. All these variables are then stored in one object, the array, making reference and manipulation much easier than had they been their own unique variables.

Not to make this more confusing than it needs to possibly be, but Unity gives JavaScript users their choice of two different kinds of arrays—ones that can be resized and ones that have a fixed size (or number of slots to fill).

A *bulitin array* is created with a fixed size (statically sized, so to speak) and is extremely fast to run. Arrays can take the type of any other kind of variable, like float, int, or string and house *only* values of that type. To access a value in an array, you specify its slot number using a special [ ] notation, as shown next.

Example:

```
//makes an empty array that could store float values
//an empty array has 0 slots
var myArray: float[];
//makes an empty array that could store string values
var myOtherArray: String[];

//makes an array with 10 slots in it for integer values
//note that to make a non-empty array you use the "new" keyword
var myInventory = new int[10];
var myInventoryLookup = 9;
```

```
myInventory[0] = 1;
myInventory[1] = 5;
myInventory[2] = 0;
myInventory[9] = 20;

print(myInventory[0]);     //prints 1
print(myInventory[1]);     //prints 5
print(myInventory[2]);     //prints 0
print(myInventory[7]);     //prints 0

print(myInventory[myInventoryLookup]);     //prints 20
```

There are a few other special bits about arrays: Slot numbers don't start counting at 1, they instead start at 0. So saying an array has 10 possible slots, or *indexes*, really means that you can use an index reference number from 0 to 9. Also, as shown in the last line, you can use another int variable, like myInventory-Lookup, to reference a specific index number. Since myInventoryLookup stores the value of 9, the line of code prints out what value lives in the ninth slot of myInventory.

Any builtin array you build will have all its default values start at 0, as with myInventory[7]. You didn't explicitly assign a value to it, like with myInventory [1], but it still has a value.

The only thing you must be careful of is not referencing a slot number that doesn't exist in the array, like in this example, myInventory[10]. This hasn't been allocated to the array and will result in an error.

The other kind of array can be resized on the fly, and it's called a *JavaScript array*. These are a bit slower to use than the builtins, but do provide some extra nice functionality.

Example:

```
var myInventory = new Array();

myInventory.length = 1;
myInventory[0] = 1;

//Oops!  We need to add another item, so increase the size of the array
myInventory.length = 10;
```

```
var myInventoryLookup = 9;

myInventory[0] = 1;
myInventory[1] = 5;
myInventory[2] = 0;
myInventory[9] = 20;

print(myInventory[0]);    //prints 1
print(myInventory[1]);    //prints 5
print(myInventory[2]);    //prints 0
print(myInventory[7]);    //prints Null
print(myInventory[myInventoryLookup]);    //prints 20
```

Besides the obvious resizing allowance, there is one more important difference to note—observe the result of the print statement for myInventory[7]. What's going on here? Unlike builtin arrays, which initialize all values to 0, JavaScript arrays initialize all values to *null*, a fancy way of saying. . .nothing. It's extremely important to remember that null does not mean zero; it's its own separate thing. If you don't assign a value to a JavaScript array index, it doesn't know what value it should point to, so it points to nothing in memory. The value of zero is a defined value in programming, and you shouldn't be interchanging it with "nothing" as we do in colloquial speech. Be very mindful of this or you may find yourself with some errors and bugs down the road.

You can happily convert between the two kinds of arrays if you ever find you need to change your mind. More information on arrays is included Appendix E, "Glossary," on the DVD.

Note

The JavaScript array class is, surprise, only available in JavaScript. For C# or Boo, you'll have to use an ArrayList, Dictionary, or Hashtable for the same basic functionality.

So in these examples, you could say myInventory[0] holds the number of health potions your character has, whereas myInventory[1] holds the number of fish scales he's picked up. However, there's still one small issue with these—it could be painful or downright impossible to remember what myInventory[0] means a couple of hundred lines of code later. What to do?

Enum Enter the enum. An *enum* (or enumerated type) is similar to an array, but instead of consisting of a list of index (or slot) numbers and value pairs, an enum contains a list of named identifiers paired with values. So now you really can say in code "healthPotions = 1" and not just "slot[0] = 1," making it a lot easier to read and understand. The syntax for declaring and using an enum is similar to using arrays.

Example:

```
//Here's a list, or enumeration, of all possible inventory items in the game
//Inventory has now been declared as a new variable Type
enum Inventory
{
    HEALTHPOTIONS,
    MANAPOTIONS,
    SWORDS,
    FISHSCALES,
    BESTSHIELDEVER
};

//To use this enum, you need to first make an array Inventory to hold the items
var myInventory: int[] ;
myInventory = new int[5] ;

//Assignments can now be made using the enum values instead of integers
myInventory[Inventory.HEALTHPOTIONS] = 1;
myInventory[Inventory.MANAPOTIONS] = 5;
myInventory[Inventory.BESTSHIELDEVER] = 1;

print(myInventory[0]);                        //prints 1
print(myInventory[Inventory.MANAPOTIONS]);    //prints 5
print(myInventory[Inventory.FISHSCALES]);     //prints 0
```

It's a bit easier now to see exactly what inventory slot you're updating. You can of course always use numbers (or variables) to reference the same slots, as seen in the first print statement, because you can think of the enum declaration as actually saying this:

```
HEALTHPOTIONS = 0,
MANAPOTIONS = 1,
SWORDS = 2,
FISHSCALES = 3,
BESTSHIELDEVER = 4
```

You can also use enums to assign the value of a variable, or anywhere a named list just makes more sense.

```
enum GameState
{
    START,
    LOADING,
    PAUSED,
    VICTORY,
    GAMEOVER
};

//Initialize the new GameState Variable. MyGame is now of type GameState
var myGame : GameState;

//Now we can change the state of the game using the named enum.
myGame = GameState.START;
print(myGame);

myGame = GameState.VICTORY;
print(myGame);
```

In this example, you declare myGame to be a variable of the new enum type—GameState—thus allowing it to hold the value of any of our predefined states. This is much easier to read and work with than something like myGame = 0. Do note however that you must use the dot notation to reference the enum value. Typing "myGame = VICTORY" will give you an error.

Component-Specific So beyond these more normal variable types, you can also declare a variable as having a specific component type—any component that can be found attached to a Unity GameObject. This basically tells Unity that the variable in question must contain a value (or reference an object) that has this component attached to it. Any object that doesn't have this component can't be assigned to the variable. This is especially important for debugging later on if you start to dynamically assign objects in your world to variables. You'll immediately get an error telling you if the assigned object was missing the requested component type.

```
//CocmponentTest.js
//This creates a variable that must be assigned to
```

```
//an object with a Controller attached.
var myController : CharacterController;

//This variable must take a GameObject with a Transform
//component - almost anything could go here
var myGenericObject : Transform;

//This variable looks for an object with an instance of
//a script attached - this one to be precise.
var myTestObject : ComponentTest;
```

Explicitly typing your variables like this, especially once you start to work with GameObjects and not just script variables, can make reading and working with your code a much more enjoyable experience. Also, it's faster for the engine to run, so it's really a win-win situation.

Options for Declaring Variables

When declaring a variable to use, you have a few more options besides just the plain keyword var, which itself does mean something very specific. In Unity, you have three different kinds of variable keywords to use.

A variable defined only with the keyword var is defined as a *member variable* of the script class if defined outside of a function (more on that later). However, variables defined in this way have a very special feature associated with them— they can be directly assigned and edited from within the Inspector.

To try this, open a new scene in Unity, create a new JavaScript script file, and create an empty GameObject. Type this small script into your NewBehaviour-Script file and then drag it onto the empty GameObject. (Remember to save it first.)

```
var myCamera : Transform;
```

Yes, it doesn't do anything at the moment; just wait. Select the GameObject element in the Hierarchy and look at its components in the Inspector. Under the New Behavior Script (Script) component (yes, this is your script), you'll see the variable listed: My Camera. Setting myCamera's type as Transform tells Unity that myCamera can store any kind of data that has a Transform component attached to it, which is a very broad type indeed. You can now drag any GameObject you want into the None(Transform) slot (for instance, the Main

Camera object) to assign that object to myCamera. Try it. myCamera can reference and interact with the scene's Main Camera. Unity will also allow you to choose from the pull-down menu attached to the script any available GameObject in the scene that fits this declaration, if you don't want to drag and drop.

You should be starting to see the power of this one tiny variable declaration. With it, you can easily find and assign any kind of GameObject in your game to a variable in a script *and* even update numbers and objects on the fly while playing and debugging the game. Just remember that any changes you make to a variable assignment or value while the game is running won't be saved once you stop.

Go back and look at the sample scripts in the Inspector if you haven't already. Booleans will give you a smart little checkbox to toggle them as True or False, strings will allow you to type a phrase of your choosing, and the GameState enum will give you a drop-down box to choose items from. Almost all types of variables can be exposed to the Inspector in this way (JavaScript arrays are one exception—they won't work).

Another option you have is to declare a variable as a *private variable*, appending the keyword "private" to the front of your variable declaration. Private variables are not visible to the Inspector, nor to any other script at all—they are "private" and only viewable and editable from the script in which they were declared. This is particularly useful if you have important data that you don't want accidentally overwritten, like a character's maximum health amount or the value of your world's gravity constant.

```
private var mySecretData : Transform;
```

If you replace your previous code line with this one, you will no longer be able to see the variable in the Inspector.

In contrast, you can also create a *global variable*, in effect making it a super-editable and readable variable. To define a variable as global, append the keyword *static* to the beginning of the declaration. Global variables are shared between all instances of a script in the game world. For example, let's say you have 10 GameObjects in your scene, each of which has the same enemy team script attached to it. In the script, a global variable is declared:

```
teamColor = someColor
```

The minute you assign one of the enemies a teamColor, say blue, all the other enemy GameObjects will also share that teamColor, as they share the global variable.

```
static var enemyTeamColor = "blue";
```

Like private variables, static variables are also not accessible from the Inspector. However, there's nothing stopping you from declaring a normal member variable, setting that variable's value in the Inspector, and then assigning the value of the member variable to the global one. It's a bit silly, but it works.

Note

This isn't quite the same as global variables in other languages you may be familiar with. If you want to access it from another script, you will still need to reference it as if it were a normal member variable:

```
someScript.myGlobalvariable = 42;
```

OPERATORS AND COMPARISONS

Now that you have all these different kinds and types of variables defined, what can you do with them, you may ask? Plenty.

Operators

You've already seen operators at work in the first integer script example: print (mySecondInt + myFirstInt). The plus sign is the operator for addition, just as it is in classroom math. JavaScript has many such operators that allow you to manipulate and map your data from one form or space to another.

```
//Operators you can use in JavaScript
var x = 1.0;

//Addition
print(x+1);         //prints 2
//Subtraction
print(x-3);         //prints -2
//Multiplication
print(x*5);         //prints 5
```

```
//Division
print(x/2);        //prints 0.5
//Equate or assign to
y = 32.0;
print(y);          //prints 32
//Modulus (the remainder after division)
print(x%2);        //prints 1
```

The first five should be familiar to you, but the last may not be. The modulus operator (%), or mod for short, returns the remainder after division has occurred. So x%2 is just a compact way of saying "give me the remainder of x divided by 2."

As seen in the string example earlier, you can also use the addition operator to join (or *concatenate*) strings together to form an even longer string:

```
//This....
print("Hello"+ " " + "World!");
//....is the same as this:
print("Hello World!");
```

You may be wondering now if it would be possible to concatenate a string and number variable together using the addition operator, since it seems to work on both equally. Yes, with one small warning. Just remember that while the number (or number variable) is being concatenated with the string, it will also be considered a string itself.

```
print("Hello" + " " + x);  //prints "Hello 1"
```

x may be defined as a float, but in the phrase "Hello 1" it is treated as a string with the value of 1.

There are also two other special operators: increment (++) and decrement (--). Sometimes you may find that you just want to quickly increase or decrease the value of a number by 1, and it can get pretty tedious writing "x=x+1" over and over again. An easier way to do this in JavaScript, as well as in many other languages, is to write "x++." This simple phrase tells Unity to take the value of x, increase it by one, and save x with this new number.

```
x=1;
print(x);    //x = 1
x++;
print(x);    //x = 2
x++;
```

```
x++;
print(x);    //x = 4
```

On the exact opposite side is the decrement operator, allowing you to system-atically decrease the value of your number by one.

```
x=1.5;
print(x);    //x = 1.5
x--;
print(x);    //x = 0.5
x--;
x--;
print(x);    //x = -1.5
```

Notice that the operators work with both float and integer numbers.

Comparisons

Besides adding and subtracting variables, you can also compare them with each other. Many of these will also be familiar to you from elementary math classes.

The first comparison you can make between two variables is to ask if they are equal in value; does x in fact equal y? Note that the equality comparison operator uses two equal signs, and that the assignment operator only uses one equal sign. This can be easy to mix up at first, and you don't want to be assigning random values instead of comparing them. (x ==y) is not the same as (x=y).

```
var x = 1;
var y = 7;
var z = 1.0;

//is equal to?
print(x == y);         //prints False
print(x == z);         //prints True, even though type doesn't match
//is greater than?
print(x>y);            //prints False
//is less than?
print(x<y);            //prints True
//is greater than OR equal to?
print(x>=z);           //prints True
//is less than OR equal to?
print(x<=y);           //prints True
```

These comparisons work with all variable types, not just numbers, allowing you to compare if two strings are equal, if a random GameObject matches the one you're looking for, or if one array's value is bigger than another one's.

It is also possible to string and combine comparisons together using logical comparison operators: AND, OR, and NOT. This will allow you to do useful things like query if an object is, say, both round and blue in one statement, or ask the game engine if your player is not moving. To ask a statement involving AND, you use two ampersands together between the statements: &&. To ask a statement involving an OR question, you use two pipe symbols also between the different statements: ||. Finally, to query if something is NOT another thing, you use an exclamation point in front of the conditional question.

Examples:

```
var x = 1;
var y = 7;
var z = 1.0;

print( (x == z) && (x < y) );      //prints True
print( (x == 3) || (y == 2) );     //prints False
print( (x == 3) || (y == 7) );     //prints True
print( !(x == z) );                //prints False
print(x!=y);                       //prints True
```

The first line is asking Unity if x is equal to z AND if x is also less than y. This happens to be a true statement, so the engine prints True. Both statements on either side of the double ampersands (&&) need to be true for the entire statement to return True.

For an OR comparison, only one of the two statements needs to return True, as in the third comparison: x is equal to 3 OR y is equal to 7. x isn't equal to 3, but y is equal to 7, so the entire line returns True. If both statements return False, then the entire line will as well.

The NOT comparison is shown in the last two lines. It's very important to correctly place the ! symbol exactly where you mean to create the negative query—one space off can lead to a completely different result. The first comparison is asking Unity what the result is for NOT x equal to z. First Unity needs to ask if x is equal to z and finds that it is, so Unity returns True.

This simplifies the comparison to: ! (True) or Not True. Another way of saying something is not true would be to label it False, which is what Unity prints.

The second comparison asks if x is not equal to y, using the handy unequal operator !=. It is a correct statement that 1 is not equal to 7, so Unity returns True. Out of the two, you'll find that != is a much more common way of phrasing the same question.

It's all well and good to see if some comparison of values is True or False, but wouldn't it be handier if you could also ask that IF this were the case, Unity then do something else afterward? Thankfully, there is.

CONDITIONALS

Conditional statements allow you to execute different actions based upon different current criteria. For example, you could play a different background music theme in your game based on the current level. Or you could have your character jump if a certain key were pressed. Anything of the form "if this question is true, then do something" is a conditional.

The if Statement

The simplest form of a conditional is the *if* statement: "If a given comparison is true, then do something." Any one of the former comparisons (or combinations of) can be used for queries in if statements.

```
var myGame = "Loading";

if (myGame == "Loading")          // <-If Statement and Comparison
{                                 // <-Open body bracket
    print("Game is Loading...");  // <-Code to execute if True
}                                 // <-Closing body bracket.
//. . .Script continues after this. . .
```

This example defines a variable to store the state of the game: myGame. The following if statement asks Unity to check the current value of myGame and see if it is equal to the string "Loading." If this statement returns True, Unity will execute the code in the body of the if statement—the block of code in between the curly brackets. If statements execute their body code only if all the comparisons they test return True. If the comparison returns False, no code inside the body will be executed, and your script will continue.

The if-else Statement

The if statement is definitely handy, but what if you wanted to do something else when a condition tested False and not just continue on as if the condition didn't matter? In these cases you can use an *if-else* statement: "If a given condition is true, do A. If False, then do B."

```
myGame = "Running";

if (myGame == "Loading")
{
    print("Game is Loading...");
}
else
{
    print("Game has finished Loading");
    print("Game is now running!");
}
```

This example again tests for the value of the variable myGame. If myGame is equal to the string "Loading," the first print statement will be executed. If myGame is equal to anything else, any code in the body of the else statement will be executed instead. As you can see, you can put any number of lines of code inside the body of the statements.

You can also string if and else statements together for more complicated queries:

```
if (myGame == "Loading")
{
    print("Game is Loading...");
}
else if (myGame == "Running")
{
    print("Game is now Running!");
}
else
{
    print("Game is over!");
}
```

Unity will go down the line of if statements until either one of them returns True or until it gets to the else statement, at which point it will execute that code.

For these kinds of linked conditionals, you need to be mindful of the order in which you place your statements.

The switch Statement

Similar to the if-else statement is the *switch* statement. This performs the same action as the if-else-if statement, but can be easier to read.

```
myGame = "Game Over";

switch (myGame)
{
    case "Loading":
        print("Game is Loading...");
        break;
    case "Running":
        print("Game is now running!");
        break;
    case "Game Over":
        print("Game is over. Thanks for playing!");
        break;
    default:
        print("Game is in an unknown state");

}
```

In the switch statement, you first tell Unity which variable you want to check for in the parentheses, in this case "myGame." Each case statement is then an equality comparison looking to see if myGame is equal to either Loading, Running, or Game Over. Any code then between the current case and the *break* statement is executed, just like the body of the if statement. The break statement is necessary after each case test, as it tells Unity to exit out of the switch statement and no longer look for comparisons. You must have a break statement for each case comparison.

The default keyword is just what it sounds like—Unity will default to this if none of the case statements return True. The default keyword should always be placed last in your list and generally serves as an error catch-all. myGame should always match True to one of the three case statements in the example, but just in case it doesn't, the default is there to keep the game from crashing or malfunctioning in unexpected ways. Unlike the case statements, default doesn't need a break statement, as it's the final step of the switch statement.

The Conditional Operator

One final conditional is the *conditional operator*, a short and sweet way to write a simple if-else statement. In this form of conditional, you don't have a body to write a set of statements in, so it's particularly useful if you just want to change the value of one specific variable. The conditional operator takes the form of:

```
(comparison test) ? TrueStatement : FalseStatement ;
myGame = " ";                //myGame equals only an empty space character
var x = 1;
var y = 5;


myGame =  (x > y) ? "Loading" : "Running" ;
print(myGame);               //prints "Running"
```

In this example, myGame starts out as an empty string variable, only holding a single whitespace character. You'd like to store a value for its current state based upon a given comparison; in this case, is x greater than y? If the comparison is true, myGame will be given the value of Loading. If false, it will be assigned the value of Running. This shorthand is nice to use for small assignments like this, but it won't be fitting for every case.

LOOPS

Loops allow you to perform an action multiple times, either indefinitely or until a certain criterion has been met. There are a few different kinds of loops in JavaScript you could use, but for simplicity's sake you can make do with two basic ones: the for and while loops.

The for Loop

for loops execute a given body of code while a given condition is True, and you generally know how many times the loop should execute. They take the basic form of:

```
for ( startValue; Condition; stepCounter)
{
       ...code to run every time the loop restarts
}
```

The for loop needs some sort of counting value, which keeps track of how many times the loop has executed. At the start of the loop, the counter is compared against some condition. If it's True, the body of the loop executes and the counter is increased by the specified amount. The loop then starts over and again looks at the comparison statement. The loop continues to run until the condition returns False.

```
for (i = 0; i < 5; i++)
{
    print("i is now equal to " + i);
}
```

This example asks Unity to print out the value of i for as long as it is less than 5. After that, the loop will cease to run. Incrementing step count values is one place where the increment operator gets a lot of use.

Be careful that you don't set up an infinite loop! If there's no way your condition can ever be False, the loop will never end, and your script will be stuck there forever, like this: (Don't actually run this example, unless you want to crash Unity.)

```
for (i = 0; i >= 0; i++)
{
    print("i is now equal to " + i);
}
```

i will always be either greater than or equal to 0, and the loop will continue to run ad infinitum. Be nice to Unity and your computer—don't write infinite loops.

The while Loop

The *while loop* is similar to the for loop and runs a given piece of code *while* a specific condition is True.

```
while (some given condition is true)
{
[...]code to run every time the loop restarts
}
```

Example:

```
var myCounter = 0;
```

```
var loopNumber = 1;

while (myCounter <= 20)
{
    print(loopNumber);
    loopNumber++;
    myCounter = myCounter + 2;
}
```

The loop starts looking at the given comparison and executes the body of code as long as it remains True. Since no ending condition is built into the loop definition (like in the for loop), you need to be especially mindful of setting up some way for your loop to finish.

FUNCTIONS

You've already seen some functions in action even if you're not aware of it. That little print statement you've been using to show data in the Console? That's a function. When you create a new JavaScript file in Unity, it opens with a default line of code:

```
function Update ()
```

This is also a function. Up until now, you've just been typing code into your script files directly in order, and Unity diligently runs through them line by line. What if you wanted to execute a prewritten block of code only at a specific time, or only when needed? Functions allow this to happen. Anything you don't want Unity to run by default when it starts playing should be placed inside a function.

Functions are simply defined by the keyword *function* and follow this syntax:

```
function   FunctionName ( optional arguments )
{
[...]some code here
}
```

Unity will not run anything inside a function at startup. To use one, you must *call* the function from elsewhere in your code, which gives you complete control over when and where it runs.

```
//This loop executes at startup
for(var i = 0; i <11; i++)
```

```
{
    if(i%2 == 0)
    {
        SayHi();
    }
    else
    {
        SayBye();
    }
}
//These only execute once they're called from within the for loop
function SayHi() {
    print("Hello World!");
}
function SayBye(){
    print("Goodbye Unity!");
}
```

This example defines two functions, SayHi and SayBye. SayHi will print out a greeting phrase when called, and SayBye will print "Goodbye Unity." Neither of these two functions will run when you press Play and will only execute once they're called from within the for loop. In the loop, when the counter i is even, SayHi will be called. When i is odd, SayBye will be called instead.

Functions can also be defined to have optional *arguments* (or variables) passed to them when called and *return* other pieces of data after they've finished running, allowing you to do something more profound than printing out silly messages. An argument is any piece of data you place inside the parentheses of a function—like the bits of code you've been placing inside the print statement parentheses. These are the arguments that give print( ) the data it needs to execute.

```
var myGame = " ";

myGame = ChangeGameState(myGame);
print(myGame);          //prints out "Loading"

myGame = ChangeGameState(myGame);
print(myGame);          //prints out "Running"

//Change the name of any string given
function ChangeGameState ( someGame : String )
```

```
{
    if (someGame == "Loading")
    {
        return "Running";
    }
    else return "Loading";
}
```

This example defines a ChangeGameState function that takes one argument. When defining arguments you need to give them some kind of variable nickname, allowing you work with them in the body of the function. When you run the function, any variable you place in the parentheses will replace the given argument, so basically in this case, anywhere you see someGame in the function will be replaced with the value of myGame, since that was the passed argument.

In this case the variable someGame is also defined to be of type string. You don't need to explicitly type your arguments, but it makes debugging big functions a lot easier if you do. Any variable now that is passed to ChangeGameState that isn't a string will spit back a detailed error.

ChangeGameState will take in any string variable and compare it to the phrase "Loading." If the string value is equal to Loading, then it will *return* a value as well, in this case, Running. If the comparison is False, then the function returns Loading as its value. If you return a value from a function, you must store it in a variable, or else the value is lost. You do this by setting the myGame variable equal to the function call, basically saying: "Change the value of myGame to the one returned by ChangeGameState when it runs."

Return statements can also effectively exit a function prematurely—they can act like a break from a switch statement. You can have them exit with a value, like with Running, or you can use them singularly to just exit the code without returning a value:

```
function DoNothing()
{
    return;
    print("This never runs");
}

DoNothing();   //function exits before the print statement is reached.
```

Unity will attempt to give you a warning if ever it finds code in a function, like the previous example, that will never, ever run.

VARIABLE SCOPE

An important concept to understand at this point is variable *scope*. Up until now you've been declaring all your variables as member variables outside of all functions. But what happens if you declare a variable from *within* the body of a function?

```
var myNumber = 0;

SetNumber();

print (myNewNumber);

//Function to change the value of the number?
function SetNumber()
{
    var myNewNumber = 10;
    myNewNumber = myNumber;
}
```

In this example, you define a function SetNumber ( ), in which a new variable myNewNumber is declared. SetNumber then attempts to take this new variable and give it the value of the old variable, myNumber. After calling the function, a print statement is made, asking for the value of myNewNumber. What do you expect to happen: myNewNumber to get the value of myNumber and print out "0"?

Well...no, it isn't that simple.

Any variables defined inside a function are *local* to that function—they only exist *inside* that function and while the function is currently being run. A local variable only comes into being when its enclosing body of code begins to run. The minute the SetNumber function finishes executing and exits, myNewNumber ceases to exist, and the print statement can no longer find the variable called myNewNumber. This code will result in an error.

Any variables defined outside the body of a function or other closed body (like inside an if statement) can be referenced anywhere else in the script, like with the case of myNumber. A variable's scope is defined by its closest container—myNumber is a member of the ScopeTest.js object and can be accessed anywhere within the file. myNewNumber is only defined inside the function body of SetNumber() and can only be accessed in that one tiny space in the file.

NAMING CONVENTIONS

Before moving forward with some actual scripting for the *Widget* game, it's good to be aware of some of Unity's naming conventions. You are free to name your variables and functions anything you like, but you and anyone else you work with will have an easier time of it if there's some sort of systematic approach to it.

- **Most variables:** Variable names in Unity follow the convention of camelCase and do not use dashes or underscores between separate words. One example is *deltaTime*.

- **Keywords:** Keywords are always lowercase, including the inherited Unity keyword variables like *audio* or *transform.position*.

- **Enums:** Enumerated types generally are all capitalized, such as CAMELCASE.

- **Functions:** Functions defined in Unity's API always follow the convention of CamelCase, making it easy to identify them from other variables.

- **Classes:** As with functions, Unity class names also follow the naming convention of CamelCase.

Remember that while this chapter gives you the basics you need to understand and use the scripts presented for the game, it is no substitute for a more formal approach to learning to program. Learning the syntax for a language is one thing, but learning how to build beautiful, maintainable code is a whole 'nother story.

Now it's time to actually start giving some functionality to little *Widget* and his world.

CHAPTER 9

WRITING THE CHARACTER AND STATE CONTROLLER SCRIPTS

To get *Widget* up and running, he needs both a character controller and a state controller script. The former will define exactly how he moves and behaves while parsing the input from the player to direct him. The state controller holds all his necessary vitals and information, such as his current health and energy points and which functions can directly affect these stats. The state controller could also define more broad aspects of the character, such as whether he is controllable, dead, or alive. To get started, load your last save from Chapter 7 with the newly imported *Widget* character. All the scripts for this chapter are included on the DVD and can be simply imported into the scene by putting them in the Assets folder, or you can build your own as you go along.

SETTING IT UP AND LAYING IT OUT

Before jumping in and scripting, you need some idea of what it is you're setting out to do. You know at the moment that *Widget* needs some sort of controller script, but what exactly does that mean? How is *Widget* going to be controlled? Is it going to be first person or third person perspective? How should the camera follow him? The list of questions can go on and on, and they all need answers before you can effectively write his controller.

Although you won't always have the luxury of knowing all the answers up front or working with a finished, immutable design, it still helps to develop some kind of plan of action before sitting down to code. Writing code without any clear plan of attack and organization will quickly lead to code management hell, and it's not a fun place to be. A simple game like *Widget* will require only a couple hundred lines of code, which is a pittance to the hundreds of thousands of lines a commercial title may use, so it's a good, small place to start practicing.

To get started, lay out a plan for what you'll need in *Widget*'s controller. The Design Documents on the DVD have a basic rundown of the needs of *Widget* and are a good place to start for gathering information. If you haven't checked them out yet, now could be a good time to do so. As described in the game's details, *Widget*'s controller will need to handle these basic functions in some way:

- WASD key movement controls. The character should rotate with the D and A keys and move forward and backward with the W and S keys.

- *Widget* needs to be able to jump, "boost roll" (roll faster with energy consumption), and duck down. Ducking down should make his physics collider smaller.

- The controller should have editable variables for his movement and rotate speeds and some variable to keep track of whether he's controllable or not (such as if he died during his adventure—the player shouldn't be able to control him during the ripsaw).

- The script should also make sure that he's on the ground when accepting move input, so he doesn't end up accidentally floating or flying—this robot is definitely earthbound.

- Some kind of camera hookup to follow *Widget* smoothly.

With even this simple plan in mind, you can begin putting together the first scripts to get *Widget* rolling.

A SIMPLE THIRD-PERSON CONTROLLER

To make *Widget* move, you're going to need to take the previous list and turn that into usable code. To get started, create a new JavaScript file in the Scripts directory of your Assets folder and name it **Widget Controller**. You'll be doing all your work for the controller in here. Load your final scene file from Chapter 7 and ensure that *Widget* is imported in the scene as a prefab. Create an instance of the *Widget* prefab in the game world if needed and position him somewhere in a nice open spot.

First you should do a little bit of cleanup on the scene to get it ready for *Widget*'s big debut.

Follow these steps to do so:

1. Unparent the Main Camera from the first-person controller and make sure you don't parent it to something else by accident. Just leave it as its own free GameObject in the Hierarchy. Remove the Mouse Look script component from the Main Camera.

2. Delete the first-person controller—this was added only as a convenience to view the scene while you were building the environment, and it won't be needed any longer.

3. Select the *Widget* prefab in the Project view and go to Component▶Physics▶Character Collider. Agree to and click Replace if a pop-up box asks you if you're sure you want to do this.

4. Resize the new collider so that it fits around him. A base setting of Height = 2, Radius = 0.7, and Center Y = 1 works fairly well.

The old capsule collider works fine if *Widget* needed to interact only with other physics bodies in the environment, but it doesn't always perform as expected if used on a moving, controlled character. The character controller, on the other hand, gives you the abilities and responsiveness you want for player-controlled movement. Unfortunately, character controller colliders will not react with rigid bodies or other physics objects by default, but it's always possible to add custom code to allow them to do so.

Most of the properties of the character collider are self-explanatory, like Height, Radius, and Center. Some of the others could use some description:

■ **Slope Limit:** The character cannot climb slopes greater than the specified number. The controller won't be able to climb up vertical walls due to its shape, so that's not a concern by default. The default value of 90 usually works for most cases.

- **Step Offset:** This limits how tall a step or stair can be—the character won't climb anything taller than the specified value. For a normal 2 meter humanoid-size character, a value smaller than 0.4 works nicely.

- **Skin Width:** This can be a finicky value. Basically, two different colliders (like your character and the ground) can overlap each other a little bit, up to the depth of the specified skin width. A larger value will reduce movement jitters, but it can make it look like your character is walking into the ground. A small number may look nicer visually but could cause your character to get stuck on tiny little bits of geometry. A good rule of thumb to try is making the initial value 10% of your collider's radius and then fine-tuning it from there.

- **Min Move Distance:** The minimum distance the character must cover if he is to actually move—if the attempted movement value is below this number, the character won't move. For most cases, the default of 0 will be fine.

Widget's now ready to start moving.

Controller Variables

It's best to begin by defining the variables you know you'll need in the script file and assigning some base values. Open Widget Controller in your editor of choice, delete any helper text that Unity added at creation (like the Update function call), and add the following to the first couple of empty lines:

```
var roll Speed = 6.0;
var fastRollSpeed = 2.0;
var jumpSpeed = 8.0;
var gravity = 20.0;
var rotateSpeed = 4.0;
var duckSpeed = 0.5;
```

These are all defined as member variables and can be edited from within the Inspector. These variables will control how fast *Widget* is moving during any one of his actions and can be easily changed during playtesting so that they're just right. You need the gravity variable to apply to *Widget* every frame in order to keep him on the ground—20 gives a relatively good approximation of Earth-like gravity, but it can be changed to anything you find suitable for your game. The other variables directly control how fast he rolls, moves, and pivots around the world.

You'll also need a few private variables to keep track of *Widget's* current movement direction, whether he's on the ground or not, and his current height if ducking. Although you could get away with making all these variables normal member ones, you don't want to accidentally edit something like the direction *Widget* is moving—only the player through his controls should be able to do that.

```
private var moveDirection = Vector3.zero;
private var grounded : boolean = false;
private var moveHorz = 0.0;
private var normalHeight = 2.0;
private var duckHeight = 1.0;
private var rotateDirection = Vector3.zero;
```

The rotate and move directions are defined as 3D vectors, allowing movement to be calculated in all three planes simultaneously if need be. Writing Vector3.zero is a quick way of saying that the x, y, and z values all equal zero: (0, 0, 0). The moveHorz variable determines which direction the player is turning, and the grounded Boolean stores whether *Widget* is currently on the ground.

Widget will need one last variable to control whether he's actually currently controllable by the player:

```
var isControllable : boolean = true;
```

If, for example, *Widget* is dead, the player shouldn't be able to still input commands and move him around.

Now that you have your variables defined, you'll need to start making the loop to read in the player's input every frame and direct his movements.

Unity's MonoBehaviour Class

Whenever you create a new JavaScript script in Unity, it automatically derives itself from the MonoBehaviour class, giving the script access to all its built-in functions and inherited members, like special variables. MonoBehaviour controls most of the functions that involve collision detections, mouse events, camera events, component fetching and comparing, and functions that are called every frame or at fixed timestamps. This is exactly what you need in order to implement the game's behavior.

Tip

The MonoBehaviour class is discussed more fully in Appendix B, "Common Classes," (on the DVD) and on Unity's online documentation. Being familiar with this class and all its offerings will prove a worthwhile investment in time.

There are five MonoBehaviour functions that control when code is executed in the game, whether it be once per frame or only at startup. Placing custom code inside these functions will allow you to do things like move a box a little per frame or initialize a player's inventory only when the game starts up. Unity will run these time- and frame-related functions automatically—you don't need to call them somewhere else yourself in order to use them.

- **Update:** Code placed inside this function is called once every frame. You've probably noticed that Unity places an empty Update function in every script file you create.

- **LateUpdate:** Like the Update function, LateUpdate is also called every frame, but only right after Update finishes.

- **FixedUpdate:** FixedUpdate is called every physics time-step and is not the same as and should not be confused with Update. FixedUpdate should be used for objects dealing with rigidbodies or anything requiring physics calculations and a set, dependable calculation speed (like player movement).

- **Awake:** Code placed in the Awake function is called when the script is loaded at runtime. This can be a good place for some initializations.

- **Start:** Start is called after Awake and before the very first Update function is called. Start is another handy place to put any initializations, caches, or checks you want to make only once.

You should also at this point *cache* your new character controller component for use later in the script. The script will act directly on the character controller component you've placed on *Widget* in order to move him, so it makes good sense to cache the link to the component. Otherwise, you have to find the link to the component every frame again and again, which is a silly waste of computing power.

```
var controller : CharacterController ;
controller = GetComponent(CharacterController);
```

The GetComponent( ) function call is also inherited from the MonoBehaviour class and can be used in all your JavaScript files. It allows you to look for any component currently part of the GameObject your script is attached to and save a reference to it for later. Now when you move the controller every frame, you don't need to look up the link to the component every frame as well, a good time saver and scripting practice to remember. If you know you're going to need a component or variable frequently, cache a reference to it outside of any update functions.

FixedUpdate: Make *Widget* Move

Your character controller is set and ready, as are the needed variables and references. *Widget* is just moments away from being completely player controllable.

The simple third-person controller script will follow the basic logic outlined here:

- If the character is controllable, allow movement input from the player.
- If the character is on the ground, allow normal ground movement input from the player.
- Get the player's input and transform it so that it's applicable to the world space coordinates.
- Apply any special player controls to the movement, like jumping, ducking, or boosted speed.
- Factor in the world's gravity so that *Widget* can fall and jump naturally.
- With all the movement possibilities now taken into account, actually move the character and make note of whether his new position keeps him on the ground.

Laying out your thoughts like this before you start coding can help you spot any flaws in your logic or conditions you didn't think of, without wasting any implementation time or effort. Writing *pseudocode* (even small and loose examples like this) is a good practice to get into when dealing with new systems or large projects.

First off, you know that because you'll be moving a GameObject based on input and calculations, you should place your code in the FixedUpdate function call, and not just the default Update. The first block of code to go in, according to the outline you created, is to determine whether *Widget* is controllable by the player:

```
function FixedUpdate() {
    if(!isControllable)
        Input.ResetInputAxes();
    else{}
}
```

This tests for controllability every fixed update frame—if the character is not controllable (recognize the ! operator?), reset any controls the player may have input and continue. The Input class will be discussed a little later in this chapter. The else block will contain all the code for when your character is controllable.

Moving down the outline, you now need to test for whether the character is grounded. Inside the else statement, add:

```
    if (grounded) { }
```

Simple. If grounded is True, *Widget* is on the ground, and the code will continue.

Moving forward, now that you've established that the character is grounded for this frame, you need to collect the player's input and translate that into a direction in the world. Inside this grounded if statement's brackets, add this block of code:

```
moveDirection = new Vector3(Input.GetAxis
        ("Horizontal"), 0, Input.GetAxis("Vertical"));
moveDirection = transform.TransformDirection(moveDirection);
moveDirection *= rollSpeed;
```

Tip

In the previous code, moveDirection makes use of the compound assignment operator, *=. If you're new to scripting, this may seem a little enigmatic, but it's pretty straightforward. Basically, this is shorthand for writing moveDirection = moveDirection * rollSpeed; you're multiplying the original variable by a new value and then saving this new result over the original variable. Other commonly used compound assignment operators include +=, −=, and /=.

All right, now things are getting a little more complicated. The moveDirection variable gets populated with a new vector of the player's input, although only along the x and z planes of movement—leave the y part of the vector at 0 since that'll be controlled by jumping or gravity. The moveDirection vector is then transformed using the TransformDirection function, which takes a given direction and transforms its coordinates from local to world space—just what you need to translate the player's controls into movement. The vector's length isn't affected by this transformation. You then take the modified moveDirection vector and multiply it by the set rollSpeed variable, giving it a base speed to go with its direction.

This works to give the base direction you want *Widget* to face and roll, but what if you want the controller to pivot and turn based upon the input as well? Right now the mesh would just translate around the screen, always facing one direction—not very believable for a working robot. Time to factor in some rotation values. Continuing directly afterward, add:

```
moveHorz = Input.GetAxis("Horizontal");
if (moveHorz > 0)                            //right turn
    rotateDirection = new Vector3(0, 1, 0);
else if (moveHorz < 0)                       //left turn
    rotateDirection = new Vector3(0, -1, 0);
else                                         //not turning
    rotateDirection = new Vector3 (0, 0, 0);
```

You'll find the rotation of the character based upon the player's Horizontal input, for example, the left and right arrows on the keyboard. The Horizontal (and Vertical for that matter) input axis is mapped from positive to negative, with any positive value mapping to the right and any negative value mapping to the left. To find *Widget*'s movement rotation, you just query to see which direction the player is currently pressing. If no Horizontal axis key is pressed, then the character must be moving forward or backward only along the Vertical axis.

Now that *Widget's* base movement is decided, you need to get the player's input for special commands. Below the text for the rotation, add these lines:

```
if (Input.GetButton ("Jump")) {
      moveDirection.y = jumpSpeed;
}
if(Input.GetButton("Boost")){
        moveDirection *= fastRollSpeed;
}
if(Input.GetButton("Duck")){
    controller.height = duckHeight;
    controller.center.y = controller.height/2 + .25;
    moveDirection *= duckSpeed;
}
```

These three if statements look for specific button presses from the user, which you define using the key phrases Jump, Boost, and Duck (the keys themselves will be set up shortly). If the player presses Jump, you make the character move upwards by his jumpSpeed variable value. If boosted, *Widget's* speed is multiplied again to make it even faster. Finally, if the player ducks, *Widget's* speed is reduced, and his controller is made tinier so it's harder to hit. Controller is the reference to *Widget's* character controller that you set earlier, allowing you access to its Height and Center variables. Any of the component's variables and settings can be accessed in this same fashion.

Since you're changing the height and placement of the character controller on a duck move, you should also make sure you're resetting the default values at some point, or else *Widget* will duck forever! Return to the moveDirection *= rollSpeed line, and add this directly following:

```
controller.height = normalHeight;
controller.center.y = controller.height/2;
```

This will make sure the character controller is back to the normal default values at the start of every movement frame.

Almost done with the outline—the only tasks remaining being the gravity and actual controller movement. Outside of the grounded if statement (but still inside the else statement for the controllable query), add the following:

```
moveDirection.y -= gravity * Time.deltaTime;
```

This will make sure that *Widget* constantly remains on the ground or will fall down towards the ground if he ever jumps up. Just like on Earth, you want gravity to constantly act as a downward force.

This line also introduces another important class for scripting in Unity—time. The Time class gives you access to some nice read-only data, like how long the game has been running or how much time has passed since the level was loaded. deltaTime is another piece of read-only data, detailing how much time in seconds it took the last frame to complete. By multiplying the gravity constant by how much time it takes for the frames to complete, you are effectively calculating how much gravity should affect your characters per second.

Tip

Anytime you want to do something per second, multiply it by Time.deltaTime.

Finally, all you have left to do is move the controller. The character controller class comes with its own predefined Move function, which you can use to do most of the work for you. Under the last line, add:

```
var flags = controller.Move(moveDirection * Time.deltaTime);
controller.transform.Rotate(rotateDirection * Time.deltaTime, rotateSpeed);
grounded = ((flags & CollisionFlags.CollidedBelow) != 0 );
```

Move takes any direction vector and moves the attached GameObject by that amount—multiplying it by Time.deltaTime ensures that you get a nice even movement at all times. The Move function also does something else: It has a return value that marks any colliders it came into contact with during its move, so you can store that in the variable flags. These CollisionFlags will store whether the controller collided above, below, along the sides, or with nothing during its movement.

The Rotate function is another predefined one that all character controllers have access to. It uses a rotation vector and speed variable to rotate the controller along its center axis. Multiplying the rotation vector by Time.deltaTime ensures a nice, even pivot.

After rotating the controller, you test to see if the character's new position keeps it grounded for the next frame of movement. A handy check to see if the character collided with anything below it will work for this. If the Move function returns any CollisionFlags from below the controller, grounded will be set to True and the character can be controlled in the following frame. The & is a logical operator that acts like the word AND. So grounded is set to True only if both flags AND CollisionFlags.CollidedBelow are both not equal to zero. & may also be written as &&.

Now that you have something workable, you'll want to attach it to *Widget* and see it in action. However, there's just one small problem—*Widget* is currently a prefab. If you try to attach the script to the instance of *Widget* in the Hierarchy by the normal dragging and dropping method, you'll lose the link to the prefab. To attach the script, you need to select the *Widget* prefab in the Project view and add the script manually by going to Component▶Scripts and selecting it from the list. Right now this isn't so bad, but what if your game has hundreds or thousands of scripts? Finding it this way could be tedious.

Luckily, Unity has an answer to this in the form of a special command line:

```
@script AddComponentMenu("SomeFolder/SomeScriptName")
```

By adding this line to your scripts (outside of any function), you can have Unity index it in the Component menu in the subfolder of your choice. For the controller script, add this line to the bottom:

```
@script AddComponentMenu("Player/Widget'sController")
```

Now you can easily find the script by going to Component▶Player▶Widget's Controller and clicking there. Attach the controller script to the prefab and save.

N o t e

The completed Widget_Controller.js file is located on the DVD in the Chapter 9 folder for easy attachment.

If you can't wait and want to take *Widget* out for a test drive now, comment out the Boost and Duck if statements using block comments (you'll hook up these keywords next). Make sure that the camera is focused on *Widget* and then press the Play button. You should now be able to drive *Widget* around using either the arrow keys or the WASD keys for basic movement. Victory, your first controller class! Just remember to delete the comment blocks later if you did this.

But what about those special buttons, like Boost and Duck, which were defined earlier?

SETTING UP UNITY'S INPUT MANAGER

Setting up custom control schemes in Unity requires only a few simple button clicks and is easily accomplished from within the editor. Unity supports input from keyboards, mice, gamepads, and joysticks, and you can mix and match any number of these input devices for a single game, giving your players the choice to use their preferred control method. Every new project has 17 input axes defined by default, encompassing both standard keyboard and mouse controls. An *axis* is any defined movement or button press, like Jump, Run, Strafe, or Left Mouse Click.

To view or edit Unity's Input Manager, go to Edit▶Project Settings▶Input. The Input Manager will be displayed in the Inspector, as shown in Figure 9.1.

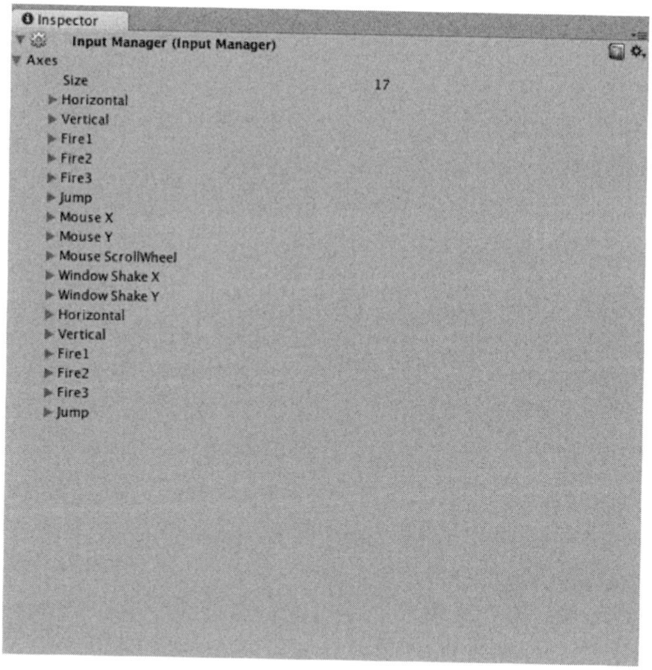

Figure 9.1
Unity's default input axes.

Each axis defines one type of control command, such as horizontal movement, jumping, or an attack called Fire1. Each of these axes has 15 settings that describe how the control works. You can set up the control axes in advance, and players can also customize these controls later through a provided configuration dialog box in the game. You may also notice that some axes look to be listed twice, like horizontal and vertical. It's possible in the Input Manager to define completely different control schemes that share a name, allowing two separate control devices to share the same role for the player—one could define keyboard presses, and another one could define joystick controls. Unity will handle the input choice for you, allowing you to only have to reference one value in your scripts. Horizontal movement would in the end be the same to Unity, whether it came from a keyboard press or a gamepad control stick.

To see and edit the settings, click on the arrow next to the axis' name.

- **Name:** This is the axis' name and reference for scripting. As written in the character controller class script, you use names to access the controls directly, like Input.GetButton ("Jump"). Any control can be accessed in this way by using its given name.

- **Descriptive Name:** The name displayed for the positive control value in the configuration dialog box in the game's standalone, finished build. This by default is blank, but you can type n a descriptive name if you like.

- **Negative Descriptive Name:** The name displayed for the negative control value in the configuration dialog box in the game's standalone build. So, for example, if your game used the arrow keys for control, the descriptive name for the right arrow could be Right Turn, and the negative descriptive name for the left arrow could be Left Turn. This can make it easier for players to know which control they're overwriting.

- **Negative Button:** The button the player presses to move the axis in the negative direction. For something like horizontal movement, this corresponds to the left direction.

- **Positive Button:** The button the player presses to move the axis in the positive direction. Again for the horizontal axis, this would correspond to the right direction.

- **Alt Negative Button:** An alternative button that the players can use. Assigning values to both the normal buttons and alternative buttons allows you to define two separate control schemes under one label in one go, like allowing the players to use, for example, either the arrow keys or WASD keys for movement.

- **Alt Positive Button:** An alternative button that the players can use.

- **Gravity:** The speed in units per second that the axis will return to neutral or zero if the player stops providing input. A larger number will return faster.

- **Dead:** For use with analog controls. Any values within this range from the analog controller will map to neutral and not provide any input.

- **Sensitivity:** For use with digital controls. The speed in units per second that the axis will move toward the given value, positive or negative. Some digital controllers require a quite high value here, such as 1,000, to respond quickly and smoothly.

- **Snap:** This makes sure the axis value is neutral if you press both the positive and negative control button at once, if checked. For example, if you press both the left and right arrows together, enabling this option will keep the controller moving forward in a straight line, not wobbling between the two directions.

- **Invert:** Swaps the positive and negative controls quickly.

- **Type:** The type of input device that the axis corresponds to. You can select Key or Mouse Button, Mouse Movement, Joystick Axis, or Window Movement. Make sure the correct selection is made here for the controls defined.

- **Axis:** Which axis of the input device directs this control schema (such as a gamepad control stick). Choices include X axis, Y axis, and then options for the third through eighth axes, only available on some kinds of gamepads and joysticks.

- **Joy Num:** If multiple joysticks are connected to the machine, determines which one will control this given axis. You can choose to get motion from all joysticks or assign a specific joystick, from 1 to 4.

You don't need to use these default axes and can overwrite or delete them as you see fit. The number of possible control axes can be changed by typing a new number in the Size field.

Unity provides you with a few default axes to describe the most common, basic controls. The Horizontal and Vertical axes are premapped to the WASD and arrow keys. Fire1, Fire2, and Fire3 are respectively mapped to Ctrl, Alt, and Command. Mouse X and Mouse Y read in the delta of the mouse movement, and Window Shake X and Window Shake Y map to the movement of the game window.

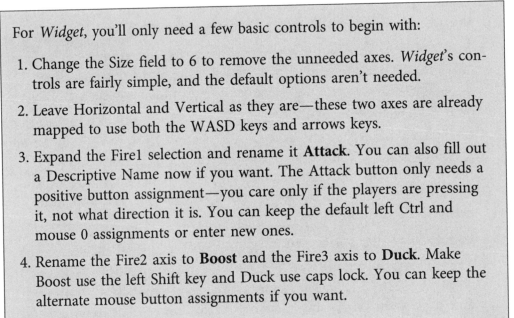

For *Widget*, you'll only need a few basic controls to begin with:

1. Change the Size field to 6 to remove the unneeded axes. *Widget*'s controls are fairly simple, and the default options aren't needed.

2. Leave Horizontal and Vertical as they are—these two axes are already mapped to use both the WASD keys and arrows keys.

3. Expand the Fire1 selection and rename it **Attack**. You can also fill out a Descriptive Name now if you want. The Attack button only needs a positive button assignment—you care only if the players are pressing it, not what direction it is. You can keep the default left Ctrl and mouse 0 assignments or enter new ones.

4. Rename the Fire2 axis to **Boost** and the Fire3 axis to **Duck**. Make Boost use the left Shift key and Duck use caps lock. You can keep the alternate mouse button assignments if you want.

5. Leave the Jump axis as is.

And there you have it. Now if you play your game again, you can use the Duck, Boost, and Jump buttons to control *Widget*.

A Redux of the Input Class

The *Widget* example used Input.GetAxis and Input.GetButton to read in the player's commands. The Input class has a few other useful functions to be familiar with, especially if you plan on using other control devices like joysticks or mice.

- **GetAxis:** Returns the value of the specified axis, such as Horizontal or Vertical. These are mapped from –1 to 1, with neutral sitting at 0.

- **GetButton:** Returns True if the specified named button is pressed. You need to use this function to reference joystick and gamepad buttons. This can also work on keyboard keys.

- **GetKey:** Returns True if the specified key is pressed. This will not return joystick button commands.

- **GetMouseButton:** As suggested, it returns True if the specified mouse button is pressed.

- **ResetInputAxes:** This doesn't take a named axis, like the other functions. Instead, use this function to reset all input and return it to neutral or 0, overriding any input from the players.

The Input class also has a few useful variables giving you access to some important read-only data. Two of the more commonly used ones are listed here:

- **anyKey:** Access this variable by typing **Input.anyKey**. Its value will be set to True if the player presses any key, button, or mouse button. "Press any key to continue" never looked so easy.

- **mousePosition:** Stores the current position of the mouse on the screen as a vector. For reference, the bottom-left corner of the screen maps to the coordinate (0,0).

Naming Conventions for the Axes

Any key or button can be used to map controls, and Unity's naming scheme is pretty straightforward and easy to remember—no need for lookup tables or pesky ASCII codes.

- **Main keyboard keys:** Simply type the full English name of the key as it appears, such as **a**, **w**, **3**, **enter**, **page up**, or **f1**. For keys that appear more than once on the keyboard (such as Ctrl and Alt), you need to specify which one you mean, "left ctrl" or "right shift."

- **Arrow keys:** Just type the direction of the arrow, such as **right**, **left**, **up**, and **down**.

- **Keypad keys:** To reference the keys on the keypad, enclose the key in brackets: [1], [3], [+], or [**equals**]. (The keypad is the small attached number pad located on the right side of full-sized keyboards.)

- **Mouse:** Mouse buttons all use the moniker "mouse" followed by a number: **mouse 0**, **mouse 1**, and so on.

- **Joysticks:** Joysticks follow the same convention as mice: **joystick button 0**, **joystick button 1**, and so on. If you want to reference a specific joystick, and not just any one attached to the computer, simply add a reference to the joystick number: **joystick 0 button 1**, **joystick 2 button 1**, and so on.

Sample Xbox-Style Controller Setup

Using the available named axes and buttons, it's possible to set up a USB-powered game controller to work with Unity. Just make sure first that your controller is set up correctly with your computer, calibrated, and turned on before starting Unity.

The basic settings are as follows:

- **Left Control Stick:** Horizontal movement maps to the X axis, and vertical movement to the Y axis.

- **Right Control Stick:** Horizontal movement maps to the fifth axis, and vertical to the fourth.

- **Left D-Pad:** Horizontal movement maps to the sixth axis, and vertical to the seventh.

- **Shoulder Triggers:** These map to the third axis. Left maps to –1 and right to 1.

- **Shoulder Buttons:** The right shoulder button maps to joystick button 5, and the left to joystick button 4.

- **Back or Select Button:** Joystick button 6.

- **Start Button:** Joystick button 7.

- **A Button (bottom):** Joystick button 0.
- **B Button (right):** Joystick button 1.
- **X Button (left):** Joystick button 2.
- **Y Button (top):** Joystick button 3.

Any controller in this style should map similarly, but you may need to fiddle with an axis name or two. Just remember that when using joysticks or gamepads, you need to use the proper Input function call to read in the controls.

HOOKING UP THE CAMERA

Now that *Widget* is fully functional and controllable, you need some way to keep the camera always locked on him or else it will be really easy for the player to roll outside the camera's field of view. To do that, you'll make a smooth follow script to control the camera's movement and rotation. There are some free available camera scripts in the Standard Assets▶Camera Scripts folder, and you can always use those if you want.

For the custom camera here, you'll want it to do a few basic things:

- Follow *Widget* from a set, specified distance at all times.
- Put a slight delay in the follow speed so that the camera's movement isn't jerky or jittery—you want it to smoothly change course and update its position as the player moves around.
- Always update its current rotation angle so that it's looking at *Widget*. Otherwise a jump action may send him flying out of view.

Create a new JavaScript file in the Scripts directory and name it **Widget_ Camera**. Delete the default Update function in the new file.

To start off, you know you'll need a few basic variables to define the following distance and the speed at which the camera catches up to *Widget*. You'll also need to create a variable to hold the reference to the *Widget* GameObject, or else the camera won't know what to look at. At the beginning of the file, add the following:

```
var target : Transform;
// The distance for X and Z for the camera to stay from the target
```

```
var distance = 5.0;
// the distance in Y for the camera to stay from the target
var height = 4.0;

// Speed controls for the camera - how fast it catches up to the moving object
var heightDamping = 2.0;
var rotationDamping = 3.0;
var distanceDampingX = 1;
var distanceDampingZ = 1;
```

The previous damping variables are going to define how much delay your camera uses before following *Widget*. These can be rather finicky to get right (and you may want to change some of them as you go along), but luckily you can change them on the fly in the Inspector.

On the next line, add the following:

```
function LateUpdate () {
    // Check to make sure a target has been assigned in Inspector
    if (!target)
        return;
}
```

This code uses the LateUpdate function instead of Update for one specific reason: *Widget*'s controller is based within the FixedUpdate loop, and you want to make sure that the player has finished inputting commands and that the controller has finished moving. If the camera script were to run before *Widget* had finished moving, it wouldn't necessarily know where to look or go.

The if statement is a safety check—if for whatever reason you forgot to assign a target for the camera to follow and look at, or if something happens to *Widget* during the game, the camera script will now stop working gracefully, instead of crashing and generating errors. These kinds of statements help your game stay stable in the case of any unforeseen errors or bugs.

After the if statement, you now need to grab references for the target's current position and the camera's current position. This will allow you to compute the distance and angle between the two.

```
// Calculate the current rotation angles, positions,
// and where we want the camera to end up
wantedRotationAngle = target.eulerAngles.y;
wantedHeight = target.position.y + height;
```

```
wantedDistanceZ = target.position.z - distance;
wantedDistanceX = target.position.x - distance;

currentRotationAngle = transform.eulerAngles.y;
currentHeight = transform.position.y;
currentDistanceZ = transform.position.z;
currentDistanceX = transform.position.x;
```

The wanted variables record the target's current angle and position and then factor in the desired distance and height specified earlier. The current variables grab the camera's data with the shorthand transform reference. Since the script will be attached as a component to the camera, the transform keyword references the camera's position and rotation automatically.

Now that you know where the camera currently is and where it's pointing, as well as where the target currently is located, you can start to update the camera and move it if necessary.

```
// Damp the rotation around the y-axis
currentRotationAngle = Mathf.LerpAngle
    (currentRotationAngle, wantedRotationAngle,
    rotationDamping * Time.deltaTime);
```

First let's start with fixing the camera's rotation. Mathf is Unity's built-in math library and contains a list of common math functions and constants, like the value of PI, trigonometry functions, exponentials, and rounding. It also has a few *interpolation* functions, one being LerpAngle. LerpAngle takes three arguments—a beginning value, end value, and time step—and interpolates the starting value towards the end one. This is exactly what you want the camera to do. By multiplying Time.deltaTime by the rotationDamping variable, you can change and vary the speed by which it interpolates.

After interpolating the rotation, you need to do the same for the distance of the camera to the target in all three axes.

```
// Damp the distance
currentHeight = Mathf.Lerp (currentHeight, wantedHeight,
                heightDamping * Time.deltaTime);
currentDistanceZ = Mathf.Lerp(currentDistanceZ,
                wantedDistanceZ, distanceDampingZ * Time.deltaTime);
currentDistanceX = Mathf.Lerp(currentDistanceX, wantedDistanceX,
                distanceDampingX * Time.deltaTime);
```

Now that you have these new positions and rotation angles, it's only a few simple steps to assign these back to the camera's current position. You'll also add in a line to index the script in the Component menu:

```
// Convert the angle into a rotation
currentRotation = Quaternion.Euler (0, currentRotationAngle, 0);

// Set the new position of the camera
transform.position -= currentRotation * Vector3.forward * distance ;
transform.position.x = currentDistanceX;
transform.position.z = currentDistanceZ;
transform.position.y = currentHeight;


}
@script AddComponentMenu("Player/Smooth Follow Camera")
```

Attach this script to the Main Camera object and drag the instance of *Widget* onto the target variable, or select it from the drop-down menu. Even without looking at functionality implemented yet, you can get a good sense of how the camera's looking. Play with the distance and damping variables until you arrive at a feeling you like. Getting the camera to feel "right" can be a lengthy, tedious process, but it's well worth it, and your players will thank you.

Now you'll build the function to make the camera look at *Widget* at all times. Outside of and below the LateUpdate function, add the following:

```
function LookAtMe(){    }
```

As suggested, this function will make the camera look at a specified target. To do this, you'll need to add two more variables. Up at the top of the file by the other variable declarations, add this:

```
//The camera controls for looking at the target
var camSpeed = 2.0;
var smoothed = true;
```

This will let you control how fast the camera rotates and whether you want the look at functionality to be smooth. Personal preference. Inside the LookAtMe function brackets, add the following:

```
if(smoothed)
{
// Find the new rotation value based upon the target and camera's
```

```
// current position. Then interpolate smoothly between the two
// using the specified speed setting.
    var camRotation = Quaternion.LookRotation
        (target.position - transform.position);
    transform.rotation = Quaternion.Slerp(transform.rotation,
        camRotation, Time.deltaTime * camSpeed);
    }
// This default will flatly move with the targeted object
    else{
        transform.LookAt(target);
    }
```

If smoothed is set to True in the Inspector, the camera will use a smooth interpolation to rotate to look at *Widget*. If not, it will use the default LookAt() function, which is a part of all transform components. Back in the LateUpdate function, add a call to LookAtMe( ) as the last action to perform.

```
// Make sure the camera is always looking at the target
LookAtMe();
```

Quaternions

The LookAtMe function uses functionality from the Quaternion library. *A quaternion* is a four-dimensional vector (x,y,z,w) used extensively for the calculation of rotations in three dimensions. Unity uses quaternions to represent all its internal rotation values, as they don't have problems with gimbal lock and can be easily interpolated between.

However, quaternions extend the complex number system; they're defined with an imaginary number component—$i^2 = j^2 = k^2 = ijk = -1$. As such, they may not be innately intuitive to every individual, and the thought of working extensively with them can be off putting if you're completely unfamiliar with them.

Thankfully, you don't need to edit the direct components of quaternions (and you shouldn't, unless you really know what you're doing) and can instead use the included class functions and identities. The two functions used in the camera example are two of the most commonly used—LookRotation creates a rotation along the forward direction, and Slerp spherically interpolates one value to another.

There are still a few other things you could add to the camera at this point (like collision detection so it doesn't run through geometry), but for basic functionality it gets the point across. Try *Widget* with his completed camera script in action.

ASSEMBLING THE STATUS CONTROLLER

Now that *Widget* is mobile, he needs to be able to store his states and vitals so that they can be updated when he encounters things like items and enemies. He'll need:

- Variables to keep track of his health, such as energy, max health, and max energy, as well as any other variables to determine how much energy is used to boost roll.

- At some point, he'll need audio variables for being hit and dying.

- Functions to add health and energy and to apply damage and remove health.

- Some kind of death function to handle an unfortunate early end and his respawning back into the game.

You'll add the audio cues later on down the road, but you currently have the skills and knowledge to start putting together the basics of his state controller. To start, create a new JavaScript file in the Scripts directory and name it **Widget_Status**. You can also delete the Update function created here since this script won't need to do anything frame to frame. As with his controller, he'll need some basic variables to store his pertinent data.

```
//vitals------------------------------------------------
var health: float = 10.0;
var maxHealth: float = 10.0;
var energy: float = 10.0;
var maxEnergy: float = 10.0;
var energyUsageForTransform: float = 3.0;
var WidgetBoostUsage :float = 5.0;
```

Widget has two main stats: health and energy. Besides defining what the starting values will be for each of these, you also need to record the maximum amount for each stat, so that they can be easily reset in case of death. You also need to define some base usage amounts for energy, specifically when he transforms, and boost rolls. All of these values can be updated or changed during play via the Inspector.

The script will also need to access data in the Widget_Controller.js script, specifically some of the variables stored within. To do that, you'll cache a link to that component to allow easy reference:

```
//Cache Controller--------------------------------
var playerController: Widget_Controller;
playerController = GetComponent(Widget_Controller) ;
```

As this script will also be attached to the *Widget* object, the GetComponent function is the easiest way to create the link. With *Widget*'s base stats now in place, all you need according to the outline is a few functions to help change and manage these variables.

The first function to create is an Add Health function, something you can use later to give extra health points to *Widget*. To do this, all you need to do is take a given number of health points and add it to his current health. You should then check to make sure the new amount isn't more than his maximum health, and if it is, reset his health to the allowed maximum.

```
function AddHealth(boost: float){
    //add health and set to min of (current health+boost) or health max
    health += boost;
    if(health >= maxHealth){
        health = maxHealth;
    }
    print("added health: " + health);
}
```

Pretty straightforward. Now you can call this function later at any time to add any number of health points to *Widget*. *Widget* will also need a similar function, but for energy:

```
function AddEnergy(boost: float){
    //add energy and set to min of (current en + boost) or en max
    energy += boost;
    if(energy >= maxEnergy){
        energy = maxEnergy;
    }
    print("added energy: " + energy);
}
```

With the two positive functions out of the way, *Widget* will also need some sort of function to subtract points from his health, in case he is damaged by something out in the world. Make a new function called ApplyDamage and have it take a single float argument:

```
function ApplyDamage(damage: float){    }
```

This is also pretty straightforward. First you just simply subtract the given damage amount from *Widget*'s current health. Then if this dips his health below zero, you need to call some sort of function that sadly kills *Widget* and removes him from the scene. Add to the ApplyDamage function the following:

```
health -= damage;
//check health and call Die if need to
if(health <= 0){
        health = 0; //keep it from ever displaying negative
    Die();
}
```

Now let's make this Die( ) function. The design for the *Widget* game allows him to be respawned at passed waypoints if ever killed, so you need to be able to remove him from the game and then place him back at a given location. You won't learn about the respawn or waypoint scripts until Chapter 11, but you can get the rest of it written now. Create a new function called Die( ):

```
function Die(){
    print("dead!");
    HideCharacter();
    yield WaitForSeconds(1);
    ShowCharacter();
    health = maxHealth;
}
```

This function uses two more helper functions, HideCharacter and ShowCharacter, both of which will take care of removing him from the scene and then having him reappear later. The center statement, however, is the most important part to take away—the yield keyword.

Coroutines

As you've seen a bit of now, when writing code for games, you often want things to occur in a set sequence: Event A has to occur and finish before the start of event B, and then only after those two finish can event C begin. For example, you can't update the camera controls until the character finishes moving for the frame. Using the yield keyword tells Unity to stop executing the current function, wait a frame, and then continue where it left off the next subsequent frame.

Chaining together a collection of yield statements in this manner allows you to write *coroutines*, or special functions that can basically start up and pause without losing their place and then continue where they last stopped with a certain command.

The yield statement will also stack with a few other instructions, specifically WaitForSeconds, WaitForFixedUpdate, and any named coroutine. For example, in the Die() function, yield is paired with WaitForSeonds (1), telling Unity to stop the execution of the Die() function, wait one second, and then continue where it left off. Without this yield statement, the function would continue on without pausing, which wouldn't give the player any time to recollect himself after dying.

Yield statements cannot be used in any of the various Update function calls.

Note

If you're using C#, you need to use MonoBehaviour's StartCoroutine to begin any coroutine. For example, if you had a coroutine named MyCoroutine, you would need to invoke it using:

```
yield return StartCoroutine( MyCoroutine() );
```

The HideCharacter and ShowCharacter helper functions are also pretty straight-forward. The first needs to hide the *Widget* object and take away the player's input controls, and the latter needs to restore the controls and object to view. Add to the script:

```
function HideCharacter(){
    GameObject.Find("Body").GetComponent(SkinnedMeshRenderer).
                        enabled = false;
    GameObject.Find("Wheels").GetComponent(SkinnedMeshRenderer).
                        enabled = false;
    playerController.isControllable = false;

}


function ShowCharacter(){
```

```
        GameObject.Find("Body").GetComponent(SkinnedMeshRenderer).enabled=true;
        GameObject.Find("Wheels").GetComponent(SkinnedMeshRenderer).enabled = true;
        playerController.isControllable = true;
}
```

Here is where you need to reference the controller. In the Controller script you wrote, the isControllable variable defines whether *Widget* currently accepts input from the player. In order to take that control away, you just need to set it to False. The GetComponent(SkinnedMeshRenderer) statement finds *Widget's* renderer and turns it off, thereby making him invisible. He's still on the screen, but the player won't be able to see or interact with him. Later in Chapter 11, you'll add some more functionality to the Die() function and make *Widget* reappear at a different spot and not just stay in his current location when he returns to the scene.

Add the indexing line to the bottom of the script and attach the state controller to *Widget*.

```
@script AddComponentMenu("Player/Widget'sStateManager")
```

Updating the Character Controller

Now that *Widget* has stats defined and working, you can make an update to his controller script. Currently, *Widget* can boost roll without using any energy, but this isn't in line with the design. Changing this is a simple rewrite of the Input. GetButton("Boost") conditional.

Open the Widget_Controller script and create a link to *Widget's* status manager. Underneath the cache to the CharacterController, add the following:

```
var WidgetStatus : Widget_Status;
WidgetStatus = GetComponent(Widget_Status);
```

This will allow easy access to how much energy *Widget* currently has. Now to rewrite the boost conditional:

```
//Apply any Boosted Speed
if(Input.GetButton("Boost")){
    if(WidgetStatus){
        if(WidgetStatus.energy > 0)
        {
            moveDirection *= fastRollSpeed;
```

```
            WidgetStatus.energy -=
                WidgetStatus.WidgetBoostUsage *Time.deltaTime;
        }
    }
}
```

First you make a safety check to make sure that there is a status controller script attached to *Widget*—you don't want to try and access the energy stat if the Widget_Status script doesn't exist. Then after a simple check to make sure that *Widget* has energy, you subtract from *Widget*'s current energy amount the amount of energy it takes to boost roll every second. Now when *Widget* rolls quickly, he will continually consume energy until he has none left. If *Widget* has no energy, the player cannot boost roll.

You'll find that, despite any best-laid plans, you'll be working between scripts constantly, updating one once you make a significant change in another. This is completely normal, but it does highlight the importance of clean writing and good naming conventions—if you can't figure out what you wrote a few months down the road, you can't really expect anyone else to be able to, either.

In Chapter 10, you'll start to hook up *Widget*'s animation state machine. It's all wonderful news that he can be controlled and can move, but it won't look right until he starts to use his animations in conjunction with the movement.

COMPLETED SCRIPTS

These can be found on the DVD in the Chapter 9 folder, but are included here for reference.

Widget_Controller.js

```
//Widget_Controller: Handles Widget's movement and player input

//Widget's Movement Variables---------------------------------
//These can be changed in the Inspector
var rollSpeed = 6.0;
var fastRollSpeed = 2.0;
var jumpSpeed = 8.0;
var gravity = 20.0;
```

```
var rotateSpeed = 4.0;
var duckSpeed = .5;

//private, helper variables-------------------------------------
private var moveDirection = Vector3.zero;
private var grounded : boolean = false;
private var moveHorz = 0.0;
private var normalHeight = 2.0;
private var duckHeight = 1.0;
private var rotateDirection = Vector3.zero;

var isControllable :boolean = true;

//cache controller so we only have to find it once--------------
var controller : CharacterController ;
controller = GetComponent(CharacterController);
var WidgetStatus : Widget_Status;
WidgetStatus = GetComponent(Widget_Status);

//Move the controller during the fixed frame updates------------
function FixedUpdate() {

    //check to make sure the character is controllable and not dead
    if(!isControllable)
        Input.ResetInputAxes();

    else{
        if (grounded) {
            // Since we're touching something solid,
            // like the ground, allow movement
            //Calculate movement directly from Input Axes
            moveDirection = new Vector3(Input.GetAxis("Horizontal"),
                        0, Input.GetAxis("Vertical"));
            moveDirection = transform.TransformDirection(moveDirection);
            moveDirection *= rollSpeed;
            controller.height = normalHeight; //reset for after ducks
            controller.center.y = controller.height/2;
                            //recenter for after ducks

            //Find rotation based upon axes if need to turn
```

```
    moveHorz = Input.GetAxis("Horizontal");
    if (moveHorz > 0)                    //right turn
        rotateDirection = new Vector3(0, 1, 0);
    else if (moveHorz < 0)               //left turn
        rotateDirection = new Vector3(0, -1, 0);
    else                                 //not turning
        rotateDirection = new Vector3 (0, 0, 0);

    //Jump Controls
    if (Input.GetButton ("Jump")) {
        moveDirection.y = jumpSpeed;
    }

    //Apply any Boosted Speed
    if(Input.GetButton("Boost")){
        if(WidgetStatus){
            if(WidgetStatus.energy > 0)
            {
                moveDirection *= fastRollSpeed;
                WidgetStatus.energy -= WidgetStatus.
                    WidgetBoostUsage *Time.deltaTime;
            }
        }
    }

    //Duck the controller
    if(Input.GetButton("Duck")){
        controller.height = duckHeight;
        controller.center.y = controller.height/2 + .25;
        moveDirection *= duckSpeed;
    }
}

// Apply gravity to end Jump, enable falling, and make sure
// he's touching the ground
moveDirection.y -= gravity * Time.deltaTime;

// Move and rotate the controller
var flags = controller.Move(moveDirection * Time.deltaTime);
```

```
            controller.transform.Rotate(rotateDirection * Time.deltaTime,
                    rotateSpeed);
            grounded = ((flags & CollisionFlags.CollidedBelow) != 0 );
        }
    }
```

```
//Make the script easy to find
@script AddComponentMenu("Player/Widget'sController")
```

Widget_Status.js

```
//Widget_Status: Handles Widget's state machine.
//Keep track of health, energy, and all the chunky stuff
//vitals-----------------------------------------------------------
var health: float = 10.0;
var maxHealth: float= 10.0;
var energy: float = 10.0;
var maxEnergy: float = 10.0;
var energyUsageForTransform: float = 3.0;
var WidgetBoostUsage :float = 5.0;

//Cache Controllers-----------------------------------------------
var playerController: Widget_Controller;
playerController = GetComponent(Widget_Controller) ;
var controller : CharacterController;
controller = GetComponent(CharacterController);

//Helper Functions------------------------------------------------
function ApplyDamage(damage: float){

    health -= damage;

    //check health and call Die if need to
    if(health <= 0){
        health = 0; //no negative health here
        Die();
    }

}

function AddHealth(boost: float){
    //add health and set to min of (current health+boost) or health max
```

```
    health += boost;
    if(health >= maxHealth){
        health = maxHealth;
    }
    print("added health: " + health);
}

function AddEnergy(boost: float){
    //add energy and set to min of (current en + boost) or en max
    energy += boost;
    if(energy >= maxEnergy){
        energy = maxEnergy;
    }
    print("added energy: " + energy);
}

function Die(){

    print("dead!");
    HideCharacter();

    yield WaitForSeconds(1);
    //Respawn work will go here later

    ShowCharacter();
    health = maxHealth;
}

function HideCharacter(){
    GameObject.Find("Body").GetComponent(SkinnedMeshRenderer).
                          enabled = false;
    GameObject.Find("Wheels").GetComponent(SkinnedMeshRenderer).
                           enabled = false;
    playerController.isControllable = false;

}

function ShowCharacter(){
    GameObject.Find("Body").GetComponent(SkinnedMeshRenderer).
                          enabled = true;
```

```
      GameObject.Find("Wheels").GetComponent(SkinnedMeshRenderer).
                              enabled = true;
      playerController.isControllable = true;


}
@script AddComponentMenu("Player/Widget'sStateManager")
```

Widget_Camera.js

```
//Widget_Camera.js: A script to control the camera and make it
//smoothly follow Widget.
// The object we want to follow and look at.
var target : Transform;

// The distance for X and Z for the camera to stay from the target
var distance = 10.0;
// the distance in Y for the camera to stay from the target
var height = 5.0;

// Speed controls for the camera - how fast it catches up to the moving object
var heightDamping = 2.0;
var rotationDamping = 3.0;
var distanceDampingX = 0.5;
var distanceDampingZ = 0.2;

//The camera controls for looking at the target
var camSpeed = 2.0;
var smoothed = true;


function LateUpdate () {
    // Check to make sure a target has been assigned in Inspector
    if (!target)
        return;

    // Calculate the current rotation angles, positions, and
    // where we want the camera to end up
    wantedRotationAngle = target.eulerAngles.y;
    wantedHeight = target.position.y + height;
    wantedDistanceZ = target.position.z - distance;
    wantedDistanceX = target.position.x - distance;
```

```
        currentRotationAngle = transform.eulerAngles.y;
        currentHeight = transform.position.y;
        currentDistanceZ = transform.position.z;
        currentDistanceX = transform.position.x;


        // Damp the rotation around the y-axis
        currentRotationAngle = Mathf.LerpAngle (currentRotationAngle,
                    wantedRotationAngle, rotationDamping * Time.deltaTime);

        // Damp the distance
        currentHeight = Mathf.Lerp (currentHeight, wantedHeight,
                    heightDamping * Time.deltaTime);
        currentDistanceZ = Mathf.Lerp(currentDistanceZ, wantedDistanceZ,
                    distanceDampingZ * Time.deltaTime);
        currentDistanceX = Mathf.Lerp(currentDistanceX, wantedDistanceX,
                    distanceDampingX * Time.deltaTime);

        // Convert the angle into a rotation
        currentRotation = Quaternion.Euler (0, currentRotationAngle, 0);

        // Set the new position of the camera
        transform.position -= currentRotation * Vector3.forward * distance ;

        transform.position.x = currentDistanceX;
        transform.position.z = currentDistanceZ;
        transform.position.y = currentHeight;

        // Make sure the camera is always looking at the target
        LookAtMe();
}


function LookAtMe(){
        //check whether we want the camera to be smoothed or not
        // - can be changed in the Inspector
        if(smoothed)
         {
            //Find the new rotation value based upon the target
            //and camera's current position. Then interpolate
```

```
            //smoothly between the two using the specified speed setting
            var camRotation = Quaternion.LookRotation(target.position
                            - transform.position);
            transform.rotation = Quaternion.Slerp(transform.rotation,
                            camRotation, Time.deltaTime * camSpeed);
        }
        //This default will flatly move with the targeted object
        else{
            transform.LookAt(target);
        }
    }
}

@script AddComponentMenu("Player/Smooth Follow Camera")
```

CHAPTER 10

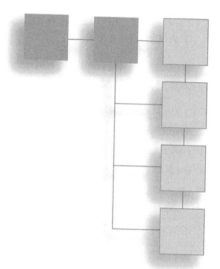

HOOKING UP THE ANIMATIONS

Animations are an important part of the visual structure of the game—they help breathe life and character into an otherwise static collection of objects. Besides this, they also can help provide important bits of information for the player: Am I running or walking? Jumping or falling? Did that enemy actually just hit me or did I dodge? Without clear and constant visual feedback, playing a game can be much harder and more frustrating than ever intended, and animations can help with this.

ANIMATION IN UNITY

Animations in Unity can be handled in a few ways: They can be created in an alternate editor and imported, procedurally generated using scripts, or created directly from within Unity in the Animation view. Each of these methods has its own pros and cons, with some befitting a certain task more than others. A complex, multipart character can be animated from within the Animation view, but the character artist may find he's more at home with a separate editor like Maya. A health or ammo pickup can be animated in an outside package, but some simple animation effects can be created more efficiently with a simple script. On the other hand, if you don't have access to an alternate Animation editor, you can with do everything you need from within Unity itself.

Analyze the task at hand and try to pick the best method for it. Work smarter, not faster.

ANIMATION API

Unity's Animation API is extremely powerful and comprehensive, with the inclusion of the integrated Animation editor. Often when one thinks of animations, it's dominated with visions of multiboned, carefully weighted character antics. However, it extends far beyond that, and in Unity it's possible to animate materials, light intensities, audio cues, procedurally created objects, and even variables inside your custom scripts. Some of this is easily handled through the Animation view, whereas other tasks can be quickly and deftly scripted using the API.

The Animation Class

The Animation class handles all the functionality to play, mix, blend, and fade animation clips. It can also change a few import settings, like whether an animation is to play automatically or what an individual clip's WrapMode is set to. With just a few simple function calls, you can set up a working, dynamic system.

The class derives from the Behaviour class, so it contains some of the functions and variables you're getting used to seeing, like GetComponent and Transform. The unique members of the class are relatively small in number and are easy enough to become familiar with.

One of the most critical aspects of the API to grasp is the concept of *animation layers*. In Unity, all the available animation clips on a given GameObject are assigned a layer, 0 by default. Depending on the layer number, a clip will be given a higher priority when the blending weights are assigned. Animations in lower layers can then be easily overwritten by one in a higher layer that needs to take precedence.

For example, many characters will often have an idle or a fidget animation that plays when the player isn't doing anything. At the same time, the character will also have animations for movement like running and then special unique animations like attacking. A good layer order would be to put the idle in layer 0, the fidget in layer 1, the run in layer 5, and then the attack in layer 10. This way, if the player attacks, it will receive precedence over the basic run, which will also override any attempts by the system to fidget or idle.

To set up a layer, initialize the clip when your animation script starts:

```
animation["myClipName1"].layer = -1;
animation["myClipName2"].layer = 10;
```

Yes, negative layer numbers are totally okay.

Putting clips on different layers also allows Unity the ability to *crossfade* and *blend* the weights to create more beautiful animations. Continuing the previous example, if a player would attempt to attack while also running, the system could blend the two animation clips together and create a running attack animation on the fly, since the two exist on different layers.

Additive animation mixing also allows for the same, but in a much more controlled and sophisticated manner. Using an additive mixing state instead of a blending mixing state would allow for more complex custom animations, like procedural facial animations or animations clips influenced by player input. A character's default run cycle could have a dynamic lean applied to it, based on whether the player was pushing the analog stick left or right. This kind of planned mixing can help to save on animation time and resources.

To set up a clip to use additive blending, simply reset its default blend mode when you initialize the clip:

```
myAnimationClip.blendmode = AnimationBlendMode.Additive;
```

Important Member Variables

A few member variables allow you to change the import settings of any clip, as well as query if any animation is currently playing.

- **wrapMode**: While a clip's Wrap mode may be set up during import, you can change it during your script's initialization. You can also easily loop through all the given animation clips on a GameObject (sometimes abbreviated as GO) and set their Wrap mode at once, which is especially handy if your character has hundreds of possible animations.

- **isPlaying**: This will return True if *any* animations are currently playing on the GameObject.

- **clip:** An easy way to reference the default animation clip of the GO. Usually this will be the first slip in the split list, unless a different one was specified in the import settings.

Often-Used Functions

The Animation class functions give you the abilities to Play, Stop, Blend, and Fade clips at a moment's notice.

- **Play:** A simple and fast way to play the named clip animation. This will not apply any blends or mixing.

- **IsPlaying:** Not to be confused with the variable isPlaying (note the capitalization difference). This function takes a single string argument, the name of any animation clip, and returns True if that particular one is playing.

- **Blend:** This blends a named clip towards a target weight over a given amount of time, mixing with any other weighted animations on the same layer.

- **CrossFade:** Similar to Blend, this function fades in an animation over a given amount of time, but will fade out and stop any other animations on the same layer.

- **SyncLayer:** Call this during initialization to sync all the playback speeds of any animation clips in the specified layer. Useful for when you have multiple kinds of runs or walks living in the same layer.

- **CrossFadeQueued, PlayQueued:** Crossfades or plays the named clip after any other previous animations have finished playing. This is particularly useful for setting up scripted sequences and cutscenes.

There are a few other variables and functions available in the class, but these are the most commonly used and referenced.

SETTING UP THE PC'S ANIMATIONS

For *Widget*, you imported a selection of different animations back in Chapter 7—nine clips were split up, named, and stored in the root of *Widget's* base mesh. Now it's time to actually hook these up to the character movement and player's input.

Defining the Problem

Much like with the other systems, it helps to first define what it is exactly you want to do. Now you not only need to figure out how you want the system to run, but also what order the clips need to be in.

- The system will need to hook up to the controller class in order to get access to the player's input and determine what *Widget* is currently doing.

- The script will need to account for the player when she isn't doing anything and play an idle-fidget animation after a set amount of time.

- The controller class will need to be updated with a few helper functions, to allow the animation manager access to the pertinent information.

- *Widget*'s animation clips will need to be set up in an appropriate layer order, with idle being the lowest and the death clip taking top priority.

With that together, it's time to give *Widget* some animations.

Updating the Controller

First up, you should update the controller with the few basic needs of the Animation Manager. Open the Widget_Controller file and add these member variables to the top of the file:

```
private var isDucking : boolean = false;
private var isBoosting : boolean = false;
```

These will help tell the Animation Manager what *Widget* is currently doing. In the Input.GetButton("Boost") conditional, add this line beneath the energy management statements:

```
isBoosting = true;
```

The same now for the Duck conditional. Add beneath the update to the moveDirection speed:

```
isDucking = true;
```

Now two new small conditional statements need to be added. Right below the Input.GetButton("Duck") statement body, add these two new conditionals:

```
if(Input.GetButtonUp("Duck")){
    controller.height = normalHeight; //reset for after ducks
```

```
    controller.center.y = controller.height/2;   //recenter for after ducks
    isDucking = false;
}

if(Input.GetButtonUp("Boost")){
    isBoosting = false;
}
```

These will help the Animation know when to stop playing, as the GetButtonUp event will be triggered whenever the player lets go of one of the keys. Finally, the controller needs these quick helper functions to return the private data so other scripts can access it. Add these to the bottom of the file, outside of the Update function.

```
function IsMoving(){

    return moveDirection.magnitude > 0.5;
}

function IsDucking(){

    return isDucking;
}

function IsBoosting(){

    return isBoosting;
}

function IsGrounded(){

    return grounded;
}
```

Now the Animation Manager will be able to tell if the player is currently pressing any special buttons or if *Widget* is in the air or grounded. Using functions like this is any easy way to get read-only access to a private variable from another script. An updated version of the controller script is available on the DVD in the Chapter 10 folder.

Creating the Animation State Manager

Now for the Animation Manager itself. Create a new JavaScript file in the Scripts directory and name it **Widget_Animation**. You can keep the Update function that's provided, as that's where all the animation calls will be made.

You'll need very few variables for this one, as the majority of the information will be driven from the controller script itself. In fact, the only ones you need are the ones to manage the idle time wait and the variable link to the player controller. At the top of the file outside of the Update function, add the following:

```
private var nextPlayIdle = 0.0;
var waitTime = 8.0;

var playerController: Widget_Controller;
playerController = GetComponent(Widget_Controller) ;
```

nextPlayIdle will be updated based on the system time, but you can also change the amount of buffer time between idle animation calls from the Inspector with the waitTime variable. Next up is to initialize all the clips into their respective layers and make any necessary updates to their individual Wrap modes. Make a new Start function:

```
function Start(){
//set up layers - high numbers receive priority when blending
    animation["Idle"].layer = 0;

    //we want to make sure that the rolls are synced together
    animation["SlowRoll"].layer = 1;
    animation["FastRoll"].layer = 1;
    animation["Duck"].layer = 1;
    animation.SyncLayer(1);

    animation["Taser"].layer = 3;
    animation["Jump"].layer = 5;

    //these should take priority over all others
    animation["FallDown"].layer = 7;
    animation["GotHit"].layer = 8;
    animation["Die"].layer = 10;
```

```
animation["Duck"].wrapMode = WrapMode.Loop;
animation["Jump"].wrapMode = WrapMode.ClampForever;
animation["FallDown"].wrapMode = WrapMode.ClampForever;

//Make sure nothing is playing by accident,
//then start with a default idle.
animation.Stop();
animation.Play("Idle");
}
```

This may look a little long and complicated, but it's all pretty straightforward. Remember the clips you imported back in Chapter 7? The clip names need to be entered here exactly as they were in the animation importer, or Unity won't be able to find them. The idle clip is set at the bottom of the layer stack on layer 0, followed by the various movement animations, and then by the unique one-off animations at the highest layers. Changing the Duck Wrap mode to loop will make it look like the character is actively ducking while the button is pressed, and the Clamp Forever Wrap modes will help the jump and fall down animation clips last for however long they need to, based purely on input.

Now that the clips are organized correctly for proper blending and weighting, it's time to start hooking them up. First up is the basic walk, or in this case, roll cycle for *Widget*. In the Update function, make the conditional statement to control *Widget*'s roll:

```
if(playerController.IsGrounded()){

    animation.Blend("FallDown", 0, 0.2);
    animation.Blend("Jump", 0, 0.2);

    //if boosting
    if (playerController.IsBoosting())
    {
        animation.CrossFade("FastRoll", 0.5);
        nextPlayIdle = Time.time + waitTime;
    }
    else if(playerController.IsDucking()){

        animation.CrossFade("Duck", 0.2);
            nextPlayIdle = Time.time + waitTime;
    }
```

```
    // Fade in normal roll
    else if (playerController.IsMoving())
    {
        animation.CrossFade("SlowRoll", 0.5);
        nextPlayIdle = Time.time + waitTime;
    }
    // Fade out roll and fast roll
    else
    {
        animation.Blend("FastRoll", 0.0, 0.3);
        animation.Blend("SlowRoll", 0.0, 0.3);
        animation.Blend("Duck", 0.0, 0.3);
        if(Time.time > nextPlayIdle){
            nextPlayIdle= Time.time + waitTime;
            PlayIdle();
        }
    }
}
```

First off, you check to make sure *Widget* is in fact on the ground by querying the controller with the new helper function. Then if that is the case, you quickly blend out any falling or jumping animations that might be lingering—otherwise there could be some degenerate cases where *Widget* has landed but the falling animation hasn't stopped playing. Blend takes three arguments: the animation clip in question, the weight you want it to receive, and the time you want the blending to take. Because you want the clips not to provide any visual information, you should set the weight to 0.

The next few conditionals determine if the player is boosting, ducking, moving normally, or not moving at all. The new piece of information is the inclusion of the nextPlayIdle variable. After each test of movement, nextPlayIdle time is updated with the result of the current time plus the buffer wait time. During the else statement, the current time will be tested against this nextPlayIdle time. If *Widget* hasn't moved at all for the past couple of seconds, nextPlayIdle will not be updated, and eventually the idle animation will play when the current system Time.time surpasses the amount of buffer wait time. This keeps the idle from continuously playing if the player stops moving.

Next you need to play the animations for when *Widget* is jumping or falling down. After this block of code, add the following:

```
else{
    if(Input.GetButtonDown("Jump")){

        animation.CrossFade("Jump");
    }

    if(!playerController.IsGrounded()){

        animation.CrossFade("FallDown", 0.5);
    }
}
```

First the script checked to see if the player is currently pressing jump. Then, if the player is not grounded for any reason, the jump animation will fade to the falling down animation after a period of 0.5 seconds. CrossFade can take one, two, or three arguments, depending on how much control you want. The first you must specify, the animation clip name, but then you can choose to provide the time in seconds you want the crossfade to occur, as well as if you want all other clips to stop playing immediately. Usually, this isn't the case.

Finally, you need to just make a safety check to make sure the player isn't pressing any keys. If the player is doing something onscreen, the idle animation shouldn't ever play. Add this code underneath the else statement:

```
//safety test for idle
if(Input.anyKey){
    nextPlayIdle = Time.time + waitTime;
}
```

The only other thing missing from the Animation Manager is the PlayIdle function and the other small functions to call the unique, context-specific animations. Add the following outside of the Update function:

```
function PlayTaser(){

    animation.CrossFade("Taser", 0.2);
}
```

```
function PlayIdle(){

    animation.CrossFade("Idle", 0.2);
}

function GetHit(){

    animation.CrossFade("GotHit", 0.2);
}

function PlayDie(){

    animation.CrossFade("Die", 0.2);
}
@script AddComponentMenu("Player/Widget'AnimationManager")
```

These other functions, with the exception of Idle, will be used and called once you get combat up and running. The current settings will do for playing any of the clips in a pinch.

Update the controller script on *Widget* and add this script to the prefab. Now when you play the game, *Widget's* imported custom animations will play along with the proper input. Go give him a test spin.

The completed script is also available on the DVD in the Chapter 10 folder.

CREATING ANIMATIONS INSIDE UNITY

Writing a custom class to handle all your animation needs isn't the only option available to you—you can also add new animation clips from within Unity's integrated Animation editor. If you've animated in a different 3D package, the basic concepts and controls won't be drastically unfamiliar for you. If you're new to animation in general, don't worry, the concepts themselves aren't particularly hard to grasp; it's just a lot of new terminology.

The integrated Animation editor is particularly useful for a few applications— adding new animation clips to objects or components created from within

Unity, setting up in-game rendered cutscenes, and adding in events that you want to occur at an exact points of time in a given animation.

Some Basic Concepts

Animations in Unity are controlled by *keys*, which in turn define animation *curves*. A key basically stores a snapshot of a given object's state at a specific time—a GO may be located at point (0,0,0) at time 0 and then have moved to point (1,1,1) at time 5. Each of these two position states would be stored with a key. A curve can then be defined connecting the two or more keys, interpolating a full path of motion for the given object. The smoother the curve, the smoother the resulting animation.

Each part or component of an object can hold its own keys and curves for any given animation clip. For example, in *Widget*'s SlowRoll animation, his wheel child objects are made to turn with some key data. But in the Idle animation, they're not. Any part of a GameObject can be edited in this manner, whether it's a physical piece of geometry, a color value, texture offset, or even an audio cue.

All these keys and curves can be edited directly within Unity's Animation view.

Animation View

To start working with the editor, go to Window▶Animation or press Ctrl+6 to bring up the Animation view, as shown in Figure 10.1. Select an object in the Hierarchy to view its animation data in the Animation view. By selecting *Widget*, you can view his imported clips, with Idle being shown here.

Different available clips for the current GO can be selected from the drop-down menu. A new animation clip can also be created through this window. Any clips created from within Unity can then be edited directly through this view. Right now all of *Widget*'s clips are read only, as they were made and imported from another package.

Without equivocation, it's a complicated screen with a lot going on. The best way though to figure it out is to dive right in—it's far easier to use than it looks.

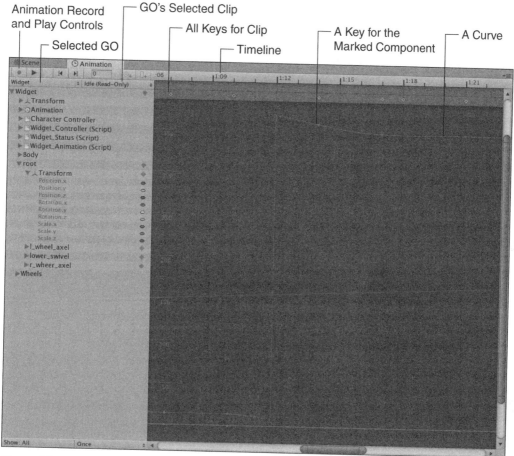

Animation Record
and Play Controls

GO's Selected Clip

Selected GO

All Keys for Clip

Timeline

A Key for the
Marked Component

A Curve

Figure 10.1
The Animation view window.

To facilitate this, you'll make a simple new idle animation clip for *Widget* to play
while he's not doing anything.

SETTING UP A NEW ANIMATION CLIP

Make a new scene for testing and give it some name, like **AnimationTest**. Since
you'll need to have a good view of your test subject, it'll be a lot easier to just
work in a flat, new environment.

Creating the Custom Animation

To create your custom animation, follow these steps:

1. Drop in an instance of the current *Widget* prefab and zoom in on him so he takes up most of the Scene view.

2. Next open the Animation view window and position it so you can still see *Widget* in the Scene view. Select *Widget* in the Hierarchy to populate the Animation view with his data.

3. Start to expand *Widget*'s root component and keep expanding until you reach his head. *Widget* is made up of a hierarchy of smaller component pieces, and you'll need access to these to animate them individually. Your view should now look something like Figure 10.2.

4. To make a new animation clip, select the drop-down menu in the Animation view that currently says Idle (Read-Only) and select the Create New Clip option. Unity will prompt you to name the clip and save it somewhere in the Project folder—save it to the Characters directory and name it something like **Widget_Idle**.

5. Now you're ready to animate. Press the red circle button (it looks like a classic record button) to allow the Animation editor to start recording changes. A red line will appear in the Animation view window signifying your current space in the clip's timeline—by default it will start at the time 0:00. (All times displayed here are in seconds and frames.) The play buttons at the top of the editor will turn red to indicate you're recording.

6. At time 0:00, start by setting a key to save *Widget*'s default stationary stance. Expand the Transform component underneath *Widget*'s lower_ swivel node, select the Rotation.z component, and click the Add Keyframe button, as shown in Figure 10.3. This will save all of *Widget*'s base information. To add keys, you can select all the Position and Rotation components, right-click on the small dash mark to the right of their names, and select Add Key.

7. Now to add some movement. Click and drag on the red line from within the timeline to move it to a new frame position—put it at

roughly 2:00 seconds. You can also type into the small box to the left of the Add Keyframe button an exact frame number if you prefer. Each second has by default 60 frames, so two seconds in would be 120 frames.

8. Expand the Transform component underneath the lower_swivel node. You can now see why good naming conventions are always a plus—trying to do this with poor names would be all but impossible. Also expand the root node of the *Widget* instance in the Hierarchy to gain access to the lower_swivel object. Switch to the rotate gizmo and rotate *Widget*'s lower_swivel object in the Scene view around the z axis slightly. The Animation view will update to display your changes. Unity will automatically add a keyframe for you at the current time. Figure 10.4 shows the current workspace.

9. Now move the red line forward in time to around time 4:00 seconds (240 frames). Rotate *Widget*'s lower_swivel node back the opposite direction, as shown in Figure 10.5. If you zoom in, you can see a nice curve forming. Now if you scrub the red line back and forth you can see *Widget* slowly bobbing. You can also click the small play button next to the record button to have Unity play all the keyed frames in time.

Granted, this isn't the most masterful animation in the world, but it's all your own! Continue to add new keys in this manner and animate an interesting-looking animation for *Widget*'s idle—don't forget that you can access all his other nodes, too. Make him look around, bob his antenna up and down, or whatever; it's up to you. A finished Widget_Idle animation clip is provided in the Chapter 10 folder.

If you find you made a mistake, don't worry. You can always delete a key by selecting it on the curve and pressing the Delete key. You can also right-click and select the Delete Key option from the drop-down menu.

The right-click menu will also give you access to more advanced options like tangent editing. In a nutshell, tangents will change the shape of the curve around a key. The default Auto selection will attempt to keep all your curves smooth

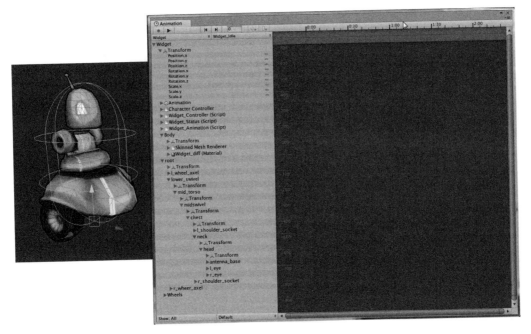

Figure 10.2
Expanding all of *Widget*'s component parts.

and nice, but you can either edit the tangents freely or select one of the premade options. Play around with it and see how it affects *Widget*'s animation.

When you're done, click on the red circle button to stop all recording. Now all that's needed is a few quick final steps, and your new animation will be in the game.

Hooking It Up

First up, you need to explicitly hook up the new clip to *Widget*, or else the script will never be able to find it.

Follow these steps to hook up the new clip:

1. In the Project view, select the *Widget* prefab and expand his Animation component in the Inspector. Expand the Animations array and change the size to 10. Under the last element, select the new animation clip from the drop-down window. Your prefab should now look like Figure 10.6.

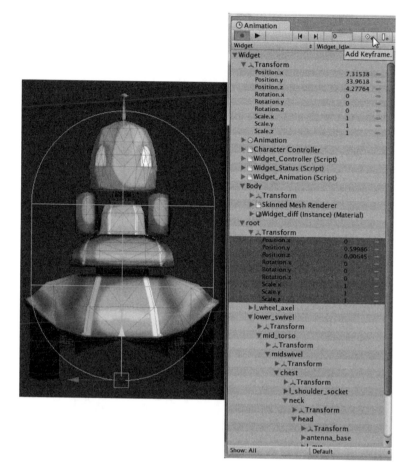

Figure 10.3
Adding a key to *Widget*'s new animation clip.

2. Since you've already done the bulk of the work on the Animation Manager, getting this new clip to play will be pretty painless. Open up the Widget_Animation script to start working.

3. Create a new layer for the Widget_Idle clip at layer number –1. This will give it the lowest priority of the current clips.

```
animation["Widget_Idle"].layer = -1;
```

Then update its WrapMode and set it to PingPong—this will keep it running smoothly from 0:00 to 4:00 then back to 0:00.

```
animation["Widget_Idle"].wrapMode = WrapMode.PingPong;
```

4. In the Update function, add an else statement to tie into the PlayIdle if statement, as shown here:

```
if(Time.time > nextPlayIdle){
    nextPlayIdle= Time.time + waitTime;
    PlayIdle();
    }
  else
    animation.CrossFade("Widget_Idle", 0.2);
```

This will fade in the new idle animation while the player sits around doing nothing.

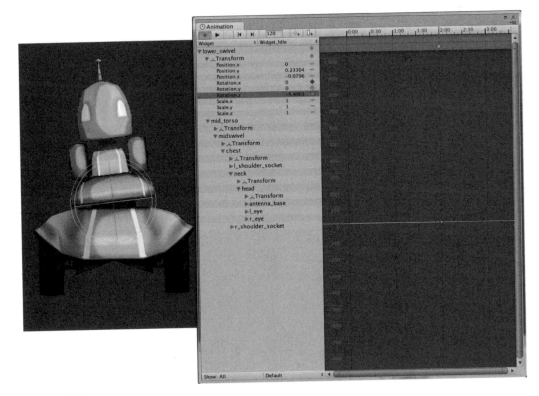

Figure 10.4
Adding a key to *Widget*'s new animation clip.

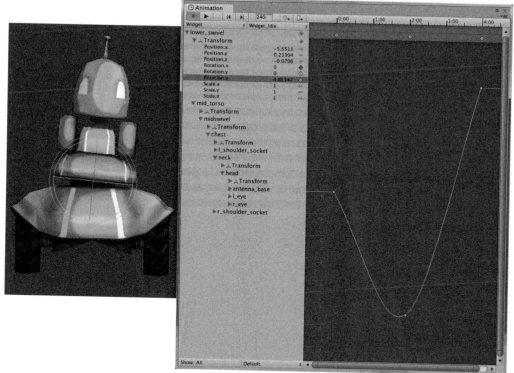

Figure 10.5
Widget's three new keyframes and interpolated curves.

Try the new animation clip by playing the current scene and sit back to watch. Using the Animation editor, you can create small clips like this or complex, multicharacter cutscenes.

ADDING ANIMATION EVENTS

The Animation editor will allow you to add one more useful function—synchronized events to the animation clips. For complex animations that need to correlate with other actions happening onscreen, this is an extremely handy ability to have right at your fingertips.

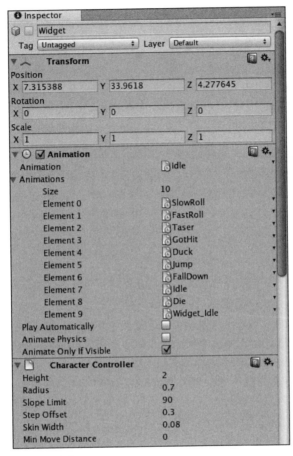

Figure 10.6
The new animation clip loaded into the prefab.

For example, let's say you had a four-legged character that had a complex walk cycle animation clip attached to it. You recently found a nice sound effect that you wanted to play each time the character put his foot down. To do this manually, you'd have to figure out when each foot hit the ground exactly and try to time the sound to match. But what happens if your frame rate varies or slows down for a second? Your effect could be completely mismatched, and it won't look or sound very good.

Using an Animation event ties the event in question directly to the clip's frame, so it's always in sync. For this example, you can simply open up the Animation window, find on the graph where the foot hits the ground, and add your event call to your sound effect. Then, regardless of how fast or slow the animation plays, your sound effect will always be in time.

Unity's Animation events can call any function that takes one or no arguments and works similar to MonoBehaviour's SendMessage. The function argument can be of type float or string or an object reference. Any functions currently attached to the same GameObject as the animation clip that fit this definition can be called.

To illustrate, you'll add a sample event to one of *Widget*'s clips:

1. Open the Animation view and select *Widget* in the Hierarchy. Select the new Widget_Idle clip from the drop-down menu and move the red line to time 2:00.

2. Click on the Add Event button (the one that looks like a small pointed line next to the Add Keyframe button), or right-click on the red line and select Add Event from the menu. When right-clicking on the red line, you must do so in the medium gray bar underneath the timeline. This will open a pop-up box to select your function, as shown in Figure 10.7.

3. For now, select the function AddHealth(float) and type some number into the Parameters box, such as 10. Close the pop-up box.

4. Check to see that the Animation event works by playing the scene. Whenever the event is triggered, 10 health points are added to *Widget*, as indicated by the small print statement in the Console.

If you ever want to edit the event, you can click on the event marker and drag it around the timeline. You can also select it and delete it, much in the same way as the keys. The event's function and parameter can also be changed later by clicking on the marker. Feel free to delete the event after you're satisfied it works and are comfortable with the workflow.

Widget is now fully controllable and animated—the world is his to explore! Next up you need to give him something to actually do out there in the wild world with the introduction of triggers and enemies.

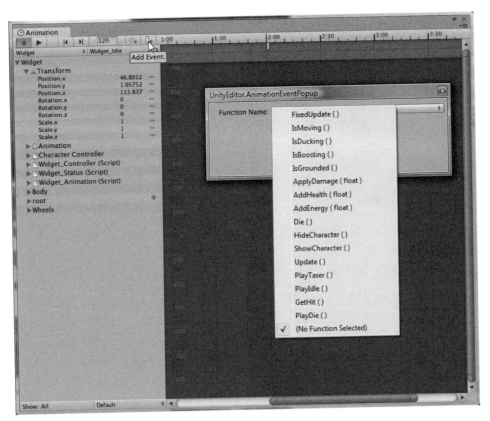

Figure 10.7
Widget's available function to call from the event.

COMPLETED SCRIPTS

These can also be found on the DVD in the Chapter 10 folder but are included here for reference.

Widget_Controller.js Update

```
//Widget_Controller: Handles Widget's movement and player input

//Widget's Movement Variables-----------------------------------
//These can be changed in the Inspector
var rollSpeed = 6.0;
var fastRollSpeed = 2.0;
var jumpSpeed = 8.0;
```

```
var gravity = 20.0;
var rotateSpeed = 4.0;
var duckSpeed = .5;

//private, helper variables------------------------------------
private var moveDirection = Vector3.zero;
private var grounded : boolean = false;
private var moveHorz = 0.0;
private var normalHeight = 2.0;
private var duckHeight = 1.0;
private var rotateDirection = Vector3.zero;

private var isDucking : boolean = false;
private var isBoosting : boolean = false;

var isControllable : boolean = true;

//cache controller so we only have to find it once--------------
var controller : CharacterController ;
controller = GetComponent(CharacterController);
var widgetStatus : Widget_Status;
widgetStatus = GetComponent(Widget_Status);

//Move the controller during the fixed frame updates-----------
function FixedUpdate() {

    //check to make sure the character is controllable and not dead
    if(!isControllable)
        Input.ResetInputAxes();

    else{
        if (grounded) {
            // Since we're touching something solid,
            //like the ground, allow movement
            //Calculate movement directly from Input Axes
            moveDirection = new Vector3(Input.GetAxis
                    ("Horizontal"), 0, Input.GetAxis("Vertical"));
            moveDirection = transform.TransformDirection(moveDirection);
            moveDirection *= rollSpeed;
```

```
//Find rotation based upon axes if need to turn
moveHorz = Input.GetAxis("Horizontal");
if (moveHorz > 0)                       //right turn
    rotateDirection = new Vector3(0, 1, 0);
else if (moveHorz > 0)                  //left turn
    rotateDirection = new Vector3(0, -1, 0);
else                                    //not turning
    rotateDirection = new Vector3 (0, 0, 0);

//Jump Controls
if (Input.GetButton ("Jump")) {
    moveDirection.y = jumpSpeed;
}

//Apply any Boosted Speed
if(Input.GetButton("Boost")){
    if(widgetStatus){
        if(widgetStatus.energy > 0)
        {
            moveDirection *= fastRollSpeed;
            widgetStatus.energy -= widgetStatus.
                widgetBoostUsage *Time.deltaTime;
            isBoosting = true;
        }
    }
}

//Duck the controller
if(Input.GetButton("Duck")){
    controller.height = duckHeight;
    controller.center.y = controller.height/2 + .25;
    moveDirection *= duckSpeed;
    isDucking = true;
}

if(Input.GetButtonUp("Duck")){
    controller.height = normalHeight; //reset for after ducks
    controller.center.y = controller.height/2;
                    //recenter for after ducks
    isDucking = false;
}
```

```
                  if(Input.GetButtonUp("Boost")){
                     isBoosting = false;
                  }

           }

        // Apply gravity to end Jump, enable falling,
        // and make sure he's touching the ground
        moveDirection.y -= gravity * Time.deltaTime;

        // Move and rotate the controller
        var flags = controller.Move(moveDirection * Time.deltaTime);
        controller.transform.Rotate(rotateDirection *
                    Time.deltaTime, rotateSpeed);
        grounded = ((flags & CollisionFlags.CollidedBelow) != 0 );
        }
    }
//----------------------------------------------------------

function IsMoving(){

    return moveDirection.magnitude > 0.5;
}

function IsDucking(){

    return isDucking;
}

function IsBoosting(){

    return isBoosting;
}

function IsGrounded(){

    return grounded;
}

//Make the script easy to find
@script AddComponentMenu("Player/Widget'sController")
```

Widget_Animation.js

```
//Widget_Animation: Animation State Manager for Widget.
//controls layers, blends, and play cues for all imported animations

private var nextPlayIdle = 0.0;
var waitTime = 8.0;

var playerController: Widget_Controller;
playerController = GetComponent(Widget_Controller) ;

//Initialize and set up all imported animations with proper layers--------
function Start(){

//set up layers - high numbers receive priority when blending
    animation["Widget_Idle"].layer = -1;
    animation["Idle"].layer = 0;

//we want to make sure that the rolls are synced
    animation["SlowRoll"].layer = 1;
    animation["FastRoll"].layer = 1;
    animation["Duck"].layer = 1;
    animation.SyncLayer(1);

    animation["Taser"].layer = 3;
    animation["Jump"].layer = 5;

//these should take priority over all others
    animation["FallDown"].layer = 7;
    animation["GotHit"].layer = 8;
    animation["Die"].layer = 10;

    animation["Widget_Idle"].wrapMode = WrapMode.PingPong;
    animation["Duck"].wrapMode = WrapMode.Loop;
    animation["Jump"].wrapMode = WrapMode.ClampForever;
    animation["FallDown"].wrapMode = WrapMode.ClampForever;

//Make sure nothing is playing by accident, then start with a default idle.
    animation.Stop();
```

```
        animation.Play("Idle");


}


//Check for which animation to play------------------------------------
function Update(){

    //on the ground animations
    if(playerController.IsGrounded()){

        animation.Blend("FallDown", 0, 0.2);
        animation.Blend("Jump", 0, 0.2);

        //if boosting
        if (playerController.IsBoosting())
        {
            animation.CrossFade("FastRoll", 0.5);
            nextPlayIdle = Time.time + waitTime;
        }

        else if(playerController.IsDucking()){

            animation.CrossFade("Duck", 0.2);
            nextPlayIdle = Time.time + waitTime;
        }

        // Fade in normal roll
        else if (playerController.IsMoving())
        {
            animation.CrossFade("SlowRoll", 0.5);
            nextPlayIdle = Time.time + waitTime;
        }
        // Fade out walk and run
        else
        {
            animation.Blend("FastRoll", 0.0, 0.3);
            animation.Blend("SlowRoll", 0.0, 0.3);
            animation.Blend("Duck", 0.0, 0.3);
```

```
                if(Time.time > nextPlayIdle){
                    nextPlayIdle= Time.time + waitTime;
                    PlayIdle();
                }
                else
                    animation.CrossFade("Widget_Idle", 0.2);
            }
        }
    //in air animations
    else{
        if(Input.GetButtonDown("Jump")){

            animation.CrossFade("Jump");
        }

        if(!playerController.IsGrounded()){

            animation.CrossFade("FallDown", 0.5);
        }
    }

//test for idle
    if(Input.anyKey){

        nextPlayIdle = Time.time + waitTime;
    }
}

//Other functions-----------------------------------------
function PlayTaser(){

    animation.CrossFade("Taser", 0.2);
}

function PlayIdle(){

    animation.CrossFade("Idle", 0.2);
}
```

```
function GetHit(){

    animation.CrossFade("GotHit", 0.2);
}

function PlayDie(){

    animation.CrossFade("Die", 0.2);
}

@script AddComponentMenu("Player/Widget'AnimationManager")
```

CHAPTER 11

Using Triggers and Creating Environment Interactions

Triggers and other forms of environment interactions form an important part of environment and game design—they help create moving doors, as well as make working pickup items, puzzles, traps, and all sorts of pieces not directly controlled by an enemy AI (artificial intelligence). Setting up a trigger in Unity is as simple as setting up a collision mesh; triggers allow for an infinite number of possible events for your players to experience and explore. Your gameplay doesn't have to revolve around enemies and combative interactions—many successful games have been created solely based upon unique and interesting environment puzzles and interactions. Learning to effectively use and manage triggers will open a whole new host of game design possibilities for you.

Triggers and Collision

In games, a *trigger* is basically anything that can be activated or tripped, which in turn sends some sort of message or starts an event. Triggers are generally invisible areas or volumes that enclose a given space, activating once the player either enters the area or performs a specific action while in the area (like pressing a button). Many activities that involve the player, such as opening something like a door or chest, starting an elevator lift, and picking up a dropped item, all work because of triggers and their volumes.

All game engines define triggers and trigger volumes differently, and Unity is no exception. In Unity, triggers are tied directly to GameObjects—you can't have one without the other. The GameObject's (GO's) collision component (a box, sphere, mesh, and so on) is set to act as a trigger instead of a physics volume in the Inspector, thereby defining the space in which the player can interact. Whenever the player then collides with this GO's collision volume, the trigger can be activated via scripts. The GameObject itself can be invisible (that is, have no mesh renderer) and define a loose area, or it can depict a tangible object the player can see, like a door. Each has its own uses, and you have to set up your own triggers case-by-case; there isn't really any generality to draw from.

SETTING UP A BASIC TRIGGER OBJECT

You've already had a bit of experience setting up collision components for GameObjects, and setting up a trigger volume isn't any more difficult. For your first trigger object, you'll set up a simple pickup item that *Widget* can interact with.

Follow these steps to create a simple pickup item:

1. To get started, import the Pickup_Gear object and the Generic_Pickups texture from the Chapter 11▶Props folder into your game. Review Chapter 6 on importing assets if you need to and ensure that the mesh is scaled correctly in the FBXImporter. Set it up with a new material called generic_pickups and give it a lighted outline Toon shader.

2. Create a prefab of the object and name it Pickup_Gear. Drop this item somewhere near *Widget* in your latest scene file, and ensure that the scale of the item is something big enough for you to comfortably work with. Your scene should look something like Figure 11.1.

3. Give the gear a new Sphere collider by highlighting the prefab in the Project view and going to Component▶Physics▶Sphere Collider. Change the Radius size to something around 0.5 and make sure the sphere is centered at 0 for all three axes.

4. Above the Radius setting in the Sphere Collider component, click the Is Trigger box to set it to True. Voila, instant trigger! The Sphere

collider will now act as a trigger volume instead of a physics one—if you try to run *Widget* into the gear now, he'll roll right through it. All physics collisions from the component are removed when you set the Is Trigger option to True. You can always add a second physics component if you want the object in question to still have basic collision and serve as a trigger. Figure 11.2 shows the finished gear.

With the base item now finished, you need to indicate exactly what it is this pickup is going to do. In the game, *Widget* will be able to pick up gears and screws dropped by fallen enemy robots, and when a certain number have been collected, he can spend them on new upgrades. This gear will form the basis of one of these pickups. For now, you'll work on making it act as a proper pickup item, and you'll learn about having an enemy drop it in Chapter 12.

Basically, you want *Widget* to be able to roll over one of these items on the ground and in effect, pick it up, adding it to his in-game inventory (which you'll set up as well in a bit).

Figure 11.1
The newly imported and instanced gear prefab.

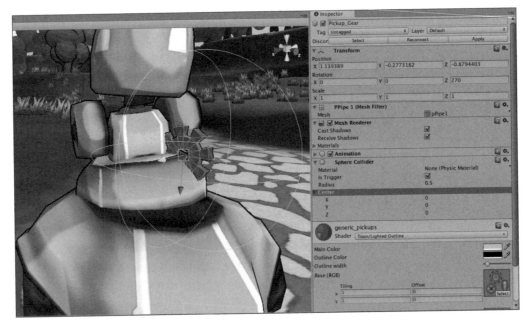

Figure 11.2
The gear trigger, with *Widget* demonstrating the lack of physics collision.

The pickup item will then need to disappear once it's been dutifully catalogued in the inventory. To do this, you'll need to create a script to handle all the pickup functionality.

Make a new JavaScript script and name it **PickupItems**. Place it in the Scripts directory. This script will be a generic one to run all possible pickup items in the game, and not just the gear. Since they all have the basic same functionality, it doesn't really matter to the system what the attached GameObject looks like. Also, feel free to delete the Update function—you'll use a new MonoBehaviour function this time around.

Start off by defining the few variables you'll need:

```
var itemType;
var itemAmount = 1;
private var pickedUp = false;
```

Since the script will be attached to all types of items in due time, you need to keep track of what type of item the particular one in question is, as well as how many there are. You could, for example, have a single GameObject be worth 10 gears and another one be worth only 5. The private variable will track whether the item is currently picked up by the player, in case of any buggy cases whereby the trigger tries to fire off more than once.

Now for the new behavior. Add the next line:

```
function OnTriggerEnter(collider: Collider){  }
```

This is another one of those special Unity functions that you don't have to ever call yourself—it's handled by the engine automatically whenever an object enters the trigger's defined volume area, hence the OnTriggerEnter and collider arguments. OnTriggerEnter will activate *every time* a collidable GameObject enters the trigger's defined collision volume, so you'll need to check to make sure it's *Widget* doing the picking up and not something else. For some games this may be a desirable trait; for this one, not so much.

Add the following to the body of this function:

```
var playerStatus : Widget_Status = collider.GetComponent(Widget_Status);
if(playerStatus == null) return;
```

This code will test to see if the GameObject colliding with the trigger in question has the component Widget_Status attached to it. Since *Widget* is the only one who ever will have this component, you know it's safe to continue. If the GO doesn't have the Widget_Status script attached to it, the function will return, and the pickup will stay where it is.

Next, you need to add the safety check to make sure that the trigger hasn't been called twice by accident and then add the item to *Widget*'s inventory.

```
if(pickedUp) return;
//Everything's good, so put it in Widget's Inventory
/* Add Inventory Code Here! */
pickedUp = true;
```

Well, *Widget*'s inventory doesn't exist quite yet, so you'll just make a placeholder reminder to come back to it later. Now the only thing remaining is to remove the pickup, as it's completed its task of rewarding *Widget* with a cool new item. This is an easy one-line solution:

```
Destroy(gameObject);
```

Destroy is a handy function that all GameObjects possess—it tells Unity to remove the instance of the passed GO from the scene. The keyword gameObject here automatically refers to the GO to which the script is attached. With that, your pickup will work! However, you should add one more safety mechanism just in case something goes wrong when the pickup is added to the scene. It would be incredibly frustrating to the player to have a ton of pickups spawn from a defeated enemy, only to be unusable. Outside of the OnTriggerEnter function, add the following:

```
function Reset ()
{
    if (collider == null)
    {
        gameObject.AddComponent(SphereCollider);
    }
    collider.isTrigger = true;
}
@script AddComponentMenu("Inventory/PickupItems")
```

This will ensure that the trigger always has some form of set trigger volume. The last line of course is the handy shortcut to allow easy attachment of scripts to prefabs.

With that being said, attach this script to the gear prefab and try rolling *Widget* over it in the game. The gear disappears!

Gizmos for Sanity

For something singular like this, it's pretty easy to maneuver the player character over the indicated space and trigger the event in question. However, with more complicated or invisible trigger volumes, it can be incredibly difficult or tiresome to try to get the volume placed just so and the gameplay feeling just right. You could always switch between the Scene and Game views, selecting any finicky triggers one by one to see where their bounding areas lie. As you might think, this is also highly tiresome.

Thankfully, Unity gives you a better way using *gizmos*. Not only the term for the UI elements you use to move and rotate objects in the scene, gizmo is also the name for any small visual element you can place on the screen, usually for debugging or placement aides. Gizmos are created and drawn from their own class (aptly named the Gizmo class) and can be either basic wireframe pictures or custom icons and textures. Some main highlights of the Gizmo class follow:

- **Color**: A class variable that sets the color of the next drawn gizmo. You can either use one of the available color Enums (like Color.Red) or specify an RGB value.

- **DrawWireSphere**: A function that draws a wireframe sphere with a given center location and radius.

- **DrawIcon:** A specified icon is drawn at the given location. If you want to use a custom icon, you need to place the icon file either in the Assets/ Gizmos folder or the Unity/Contents/Resources folder for the engine to be able to find it.

- **DrawGUITexture:** Similar to DrawIcon, you can draw a specified texture spanning the given set of coordinates. As well as for debugging, this particular function can be quite useful for drawing GUI backgrounds that you want to display all the time, like for instance a player HUD.

You can use the OnDrawGizmos() or the OnDrawGizmosSelected function call to place your gizmo code in, depending on what you're after. The former will render all the gizmos every frame, whereas the latter will only render a selected GameObject's gizmos. To set up an example gizmo to view the radius of the gear pickup, add this block of code to the pickup's file:

```
function OnDrawGizmos(){
    Gizmos.color = Color.yellow;
    Gizmos.DrawWireSphere
        ( transform.position, GetComponent(SphereCollider).radius);
}
```

This will draw a yellow wireframe sphere around the gear with the trigger volume's current radius. If you're having trouble viewing a particular item's boundaries, you can always add a similar piece of code to it.

Note

More info on the Color class can be found in Appendix B, "Common Classes," which is on the DVD.

Inventory Management

With the pickup finished and working, you need to create an inventory manager to allow *Widget* to actually store his new-found prize. You'll need some sort of object or array to store the available items in and to keep track of what *Widget* has actually collected, variables to keep track of what each of these items does, and then some helper functions to manage the addition and removal of items.

Make a new JavaScript file in the Scripts directory, name it **Widget_Inventory**, and delete the Update function. To facilitate creating an easy-to-read inventory, you'll make a new enum type called InventoryItem—this will house all the available items in the game and can be easily expanded in the future. Add the following to the top of the file:

```
enum InventoryItem{
    DEBUG_ITEM,
    SCREW,
    NUT,
    BOSS_TRAY,
    BOSS_PLOWBLADE,
    BOSS_WINDBLADE,
    ENERGYPACK,
    REPAIRKIT,
    COUNT_NUM_ITEMS
}
```

DEBUG and COUNT are two special items that aren't actually used in the game. As you might expect, DEBUG is used purely as a placeholder item (in case you need to try out anything and don't want to mess with real items), and COUNT stores the number of the rest of the items in the list, since it will always be placed last in the list. Any new inventory values should be placed between DEBUG and COUNT so that DEBUG is always first (in slot 0) and COUNT is always last. You'll use the value of COUNT to create the inventory array.

Next, create the inventory and a link back to the player's state manager. Also add the variables describing the usage of two of the more common items:

```
var widgetInventory: int[] ;

var playerStatus: Widget_Status;
playerStatus = GetComponent(Widget_Status) ;
```

```
private var repairKitHealAmt = 5.0;
private var energyPackHealAmt = 5.0;
```

The array is of type int, as you'll just be storing the number of each kind of item *Widget* has available. You also need to define the amount of health and energy *Widget* can regain after using the two healing items: the repair kits and energy packs.

With the basic setup out of the way, you need to initialize *Widget*'s inventory so it'll be ready to go at the start of the game.

```
function Start(){

    widgetInventory = new int[InventoryItem.COUNT_NUM_ITEMS];

    for (var item in widgetInventory){
        widgetInventory[item] = 0;
    }

    //Give Widget some starting items
    widgetInventory[InventoryItem.ENERGYPACK] = 1;
    widgetInventory[InventoryItem.REPAIRKIT] = 2;

}
```

This is pretty straightforward. You initialize the inventory to be the same size as the number of available items and then iterate through each available item, setting them all to zero. This kind of for loop is an efficient and easy way to iterate through an array of this type. Using this method, you also don't need to hard-code the exact size of the array using a real number, like 5 or 7. By utilizing the COUNT_NUM_ITEMS variable, the inventory will always be initialized to the proper size, even if you add more items later.

The enum comes into play here and makes it easy to see and update *Widget*'s inventory whenever you need to. No need to remember that energy packs are stored in array index 6—just use the enum's name to reference the item directly.

The only thing remaining now is to provide a few helper functions to give *Widget* the ability to add and remove items from his inventory.

```
function GetItem(item: InventoryItem, amount: int){
    widgetInventory[item] += amount;
}

function UseItem(item: InventoryItem, amount: int){
    if(widgetInventory[item] <= 0) return;
    widgetInventory[item] -= amount;

    switch(item){
        case InventoryItem.ENERGYPACK:
            playerStatus.AddEnergy(energyPackHealAmt);
            break;
        case InventoryItem.REPAIRKIT:
            playerStatus.AddHealth(repairKitHealAmt);
            break;
    }
}
```

The GetItem function is for the pickup items: An item of type InventoryItem is passed to the function, along with how many of it are picked up at once, and the proper amount is added to the inventory. The UseItem does just the opposite, and checks to make sure that *Widget* actually has the item in question in the first place. It then makes a call to the player's state manager if the item used was a healing one, updating *Widget*'s energy or health in the process.

You'll just add two more helper functions that will come in handy later when you need to start checking how many of an item *Widget* currently has.

```
function CompareItemCount(compItem: InventoryItem, compNumber: int){
    return widgetInventory[compItem] >= compNumber;
}
function GetItemCount(compItem: InventoryItem){
    return widgetInventory[compItem];
}
@script AddComponentMenu("Inventory/Widget's Inventory")
```

Attach this new script to the *Widget* prefab.

With *Widget*'s inventory now created (albeit, it's still invisible to the player), you just need to update the PickupItems script to actually add the new item to *Widget*'s inventory.

Open PickupItems.js for editing and make the following changes:

1. Change the var itemType declaration at the top of the file to var itemType : InventoryItem. This will allow you to quickly pick a correct item type for each pickup from within the Inspector.

2. Add these couple of lines to the OnTriggerEnter function, after the if (pickedUp) return statement:

```
var widgetInventory  = collider.GetComponent(Widget_Inventory);
widgetInventory.GetItem(itemType, itemAmount);
```

This will call the new helper function and add the pickup to *Widget's* inventory before it gets destroyed.

3. Update the gear pickup's PickupItems component and change the Item Type field to NUT. This will save the pickup into the correct inventory slot.

Save and try running the game again. If you have *Widget* selected in the Inspector and the Inventory script component expanded, you can watch the inventory update as *Widget* rolls over and collects the item.

Any new pickup item can now be created with an instance of the PickupItems script, and *Widget* will dutifully add all the newly collected finds to his inventory array.

SETTING UP OTHER KINDS OF TRIGGERS

Triggers can also give the players boundaries in the world and repercussions for their gameplay decisions. Being a robot, *Widget* has a natural fear and distrust of water, which will quickly short circuit all his wiring if he were ever to come in contact with it. A trigger placed onto the water plane in the game level could easily handle the effects if such an unfortunate event were to occur. Triggers could then be easily used to craft checkpoints and respawn locations were *Widget* ever to need their use.

Death Triggers

Creating the death trigger is incredibly simple, as you already have most of the work done for you! The water plane already exists in the environment, and you've already written functions to apply damage to *Widget* and kill him if necessary (both in the Widget_Status.js file). Because you've been writing the code to be as generic and reusable as possible, creating these kind of one-off effects isn't too hard or time consuming.

To create a death trigger, follow these steps:

1. With the plane selected, start by adding a Box collider to the water plane by going to Component▶Physics▶Box Collider. If your plane already has a mesh collider attached, you will see a confirmation dialog box asking you to add or replace the collider. Select Add. Click the Is Trigger box on the component in the Inspector to set it to True.

2. Resize the collider so that Size.y = 0.05.

3. Create a new JavaScript file in the Scripts directory and name it **DamageTrigger**. Delete the Update function and add these few lines:

```
var damage: float = 20.0;
var playerStatus : Widget_Status;


function OnTriggerEnter(){
        playerStatus = GameObject.FindWithTag("Player").
                        GetComponent(Widget_Status);
        playerStatus.ApplyDamage(damage);
}
@script AddComponentMenu("Environment Props/DamageTrigger")
```

4. Attach this script to the water plane.

5. Ensure that *Widget*'s tag value is set to Player in the Inspector. This field is located right beneath *Widget*'s object name and right above the first Transform component. Using tags like "Player" can be an effective and fast way to find a specific object in the world.

That's it—short and sweet. The amount of damage can be changed in the Inspector, and this simple script can be attached to any kind of object to make it subtract health from *Widget*. Try rolling *Widget* into the water and watch the sad fate unfold.

Checkpoints—The Anti-Death Trigger

That's really no way for the players to end their journeys, and they should have the opportunity to restart from some earlier point in their adventures. This can easily be achieved through the use of another trigger object. In the game, *Widget* can activate a string of checkpoints to track his journey: If he dies, he can respawn at the last activated one.

These checkpoints will also serve as the mechanism to enter the store later:

1. Start off by importing the new StationRobotRelay.fbx file from the Chapter 11 folder on the DVD. Import his texture (of the same name) and drop both of them in the Props folder. Create a prefab of this new object and name it **Checkpoint**. Make sure the Scale Factor is set to 1.

2. Drop one of these new checkpoint prefabs into the scene somewhere near *Widget*. Your scene should now look something like Figure 11.3.

3. Give the checkpoint prefab a mesh collider (Component▶Physics▶Mesh Collider) and select the robot_station mesh from the drop-down box of the Mesh field.

4. Now add a second capsule collider (click the Add Button on the pop-up that appears) and set this one to be a trigger. Set the Radius to 3, the Height to 2, and the Center.y field to 2. This will place an invisible trigger volume around most of the checkpoint.

Now that the physical trigger object is set up, you need to plan how you want the checkpoints to work.

- You'll need some sort of variable to keep track of which checkpoint is the last one selected by the player.

Figure 11.3
The physical checkpoint added.

While you only have one checkpoint right now, you want the ability to have multiple checkpoints spread out throughout a larger level.

▪ The checkpoint's trigger will need to be able to play some sort of effects when it becomes active or inactive, to give the player some visual feedback.

▪ The checkpoint should also restore the player's health and energy to full whenever he enters the trigger area.

▪ The player's Die function will need to be updated with the pertinent checkpoint information so *Widget* will know where to respawn.

All right, that doesn't sound too bad. To do this, you'll make use of the *static var* for the first time. This will let you keep track of which checkpoint is the current one across *any and all* checkpoints in the level, since it's global.

Create a new JavaScript file and name it **CheckPoint**, placing it in the Scripts directory. Again, feel free to delete the Update function, as you won't be needing it. First off, you should declare the variables you'll need:

```
static var isActivePt : CheckPoint;
var firstPt : CheckPoint;
var playerStatus : Widget_Status;
playerStatus = GameObject.FindWithTag("Player").GetComponent(Widget_Status);
```

The first two variables are defined as type CheckPoint, as you'll be attaching this script to only that kind of prefab object. The first variable will keep track of which checkpoint is the last selected, and the second will be used only for startup initialization. You'll also need the link to the player's state manager to update his health and energy.

Next, initialize the first checkpoint in the level on startup—you want something to be active immediately, or the player's death will be permanent.

```
function Start()
{
    //initialize first point
    isActivePt = firstPt;

    if(isActivePt == this){
        BeActive();
    }
}
```

You're using a new keyword here—*this*. It's a handy way to refer to the GameObject in question. Whenever *Widget* rolls over a checkpoint, it will reference its particular instance of the script, which will use *this checkpoint* as the new active point. BeActive ( ) is a helper function you'll define to add in the visual feedback for the player.

Now you need to set up the actual trigger functionality.

```
function OnTriggerEnter(){
    //first turn off the old respawn point if this is a newly encountered one
    if(isActivePt != this){
        isActivePt.BeInactive();
        //then set the new one
        isActivePt = this;
```

```
        BeActive();
    }
    playerStatus.AddHealth(playerStatus.maxHealth);
    playerStatus.AddEnergy(playerStatus.maxEnergy);
}
```

Again you'll make use of the this keyword functionality. If the currently activated checkpoint isn't "this one," make it so. You'll also need to set the old active one inactive. Lastly, the player's stats are restored to maximum. The two helper functions will be defined now but not fleshed out until later in Chapter 15. Add the following to the bottom of the script:

```
function BeActive(){
//stuff here...
}
function BeInactive(){
//stuff here...
}
@script AddComponentMenu("Environment Props/CheckPt")
```

Hook this script up to the checkpoint prefab. You need to set up the first checkpoint variable now or the script won't function. Select the CheckPoint object in the Hierarchy and drag it onto the First Pt field of the CheckPoint component in the Inspector. Later on you can make whatever checkpoint you want the first point, but for now this will work.

All that's left is to update *Widget*'s status to handle the new checkpoint functionality. Now is also a perfect time to hook up his death animation, as you finally have a reason to use it. Open the Widget_Status.js file and update his Die( ) function to read as follows:

```
function Die(){
    print("dead!");
    playerController.isControllable = false;

    animationState = GetComponent(Widget_Animation);
    animationState.PlayDie();
    yield WaitForSeconds(animation["Die"].length -0.2);

        HideCharacter();
    yield WaitForSeconds(1);
```

```
//restart player at last respawn checkpoint and give max life
if(CheckPoint.isActivePt){
    controller.transform.position
                      = CheckPoint.isActivePt.transform.position;
    controller.transform.position.y += 0.5;
        //so not to get stuck in the platform itself
}
ShowCharacter();
health = maxHealth;
}
```

First, this doubly makes sure that the player loses control of *Widget* the minute his health drops to zero. Next, you find the animation manager and call the PlayDie function to set that clip running. You then ask the Die function to yield as it plays—it wouldn't do any good to keep going with the respawn and not see any of the death animation. *Widget* is hidden briefly (as the script yields yet again) and is then respawned at the last available checkpoint. After *Widget*'s position is moved to that of the checkpoints, he's made visible and controllable again and has his health reset to maximum.

Try the new chain of events by driving *Widget* into the water plane's death trigger and watch as he's happily brought back to life. See Figure 11.4.

This chapter provided a good introduction to using triggers and chaining their effects together to create more complex gameplay experiences. With this knowledge alone, you can create many kinds of fun and meaningful interactions for your players. Play around with combining triggers and coroutines to create new kinds of interaction, such as scripted sequences, removable blockades, moving death traps, and floating health potions.

The only major piece of interaction you still need to create is the enemies—the other robots roaming the world who aren't too keen to share it with *Widget*. Chapter 12 will cover basic AI, spawning, and combat.

COMPLETED SCRIPTS

The newly completed and updated scripts are available on the DVD in the Chapter 11 folder.

Figure 11.4
Widget will be in need of that checkpoint now.

PickupItems.js

```
//PickupItems: handles any items lying around the world that Widget can pick up
var itemType : InventoryItem;
var itemAmount = 1;

private var pickedUp = false;

//When Widget finds an item on the field------------------------------
function OnTriggerEnter(collider: Collider){

    //make sure that this is a player hitting the item and not an enemy
    var playerStatus : Widget_Status = collider.GetComponent(Widget_Status);
    if(playerStatus == null) return;

    //stop it from being picked up twice by accident
    if(pickedUp) return;
```

```
    //If everything's good, put it in Widget's Inventory
    var widgetInventory  = collider.GetComponent(Widget_Inventory);
    widgetInventory.GetItem(itemType, itemAmount);
    pickedUp = true;


    //Get rid of it now that it's in the inventory
    Destroy(gameObject);
}


// Make sure the pickup is set up properly with a collider---------------
function Reset ()
{
    if (collider == null)
    {
        gameObject.AddComponent(SphereCollider);
    }
    collider.isTrigger = true;
}
@script AddComponentMenu("Inventory/PickupItems")
```

Widget_Inventory.js

```
//Widget_Inventory:   All of Widget's collected items are updated here
//Also handles functions for item use and inventory management
//All the items in the game available for the character to find- - - - -
enum InventoryItem{
    DEBUG_ITEM,
    SCREW,
    NUT,
    BOSS_TRAY,
    BOSS_PLOWBLADE,
    BOSS_WINDBLADE,
    ENERGYPACK,
    REPAIRKIT,
    COUNT_NUM_ITEMS
}


//We'll use a statically sized BuiltIn array rather than a
//JavaScript array here.
```

```
var widgetInventory: int[] ;
var playerStatus: Widget_Status;
playerStatus = GetComponent(Widget_Status) ;

//Item Properties------------------------------------------------
private var repairKitHealAmt = 5.0;
private var energyPackHealAmt = 5.0;


//Initialize Widget's starting Inventory-------------------------
function Start(){

    widgetInventory = new int[InventoryItem.COUNT_NUM_ITEMS];

    for (var item in widgetInventory){
        widgetInventory[item] = 0;
    }

    //Give Widget some starting items
    widgetInventory[InventoryItem.ENERGYPACK] = 1;
    widgetInventory[InventoryItem.REPAIRKIT] = 2;
}

//Inventory Management Functions---------------------------------
function GetItem(item: InventoryItem, amount: int){
    widgetInventory[item] += amount;
}


function UseItem(item: InventoryItem, amount: int){

    if(widgetInventory[item] <= 0) return;
    widgetInventory[item] -= amount;

    switch(item){
        case InventoryItem.ENERGYPACK:
            playerStatus.AddEnergy(energyPackHealAmt);
            break;
        case InventoryItem.REPAIRKIT:
            playerStatus.AddHealth(repairKitHealAmt);
```

```
            break;
        }
}

function CompareItemCount(compItem: InventoryItem, compNumber: int){
    return widgetInventory[compItem] >= compNumber;
}

function GetItemCount(compItem: InventoryItem){
    return widgetInventory[compItem];
}
@script AddComponentMenu("Inventory/Widget's Inventory")
```

DamageTrigger.js

```
//DamageTrigger.js: A simple, variable damage trigger that can be
//applied to any kind of object.
//Change the damage amount in the Inspector.

var damage: float = 20.0;
var playerStatus : Widget_Status;

function OnTriggerEnter(){
    print("ow!");
    playerStatus = GameObject.FindWithTag("Player").
                GetComponent(Widget_Status);
    playerStatus.ApplyDamage(damage);
}

@script AddComponentMenu("Environment Props/DamageTrigger")
```

CheckPoint.js

```
//Checkpoint.js: checkpoints in the level - active for the
//last selected one and first for the initial one at startup
//the static declaration makes the isActivePt variable global
//across all instances of this script in the game.

static var isActivePt : CheckPoint;
var firstPt : CheckPoint;
```

```
var playerStatus : Widget_Status;
playerStatus = GameObject.FindWithTag("Player").GetComponent(Widget_Status);

function Start()
{
    //initialize first point
    isActivePt = firstPt;

    if(isActivePt == this){
        BeActive();
    }
}


//When the player encounters a point, this is called when the collision occurs
function OnTriggerEnter(){

    //first turn off the old respawn point if this is a newly encountered one
    if(isActivePt != this){
        isActivePt.BeInactive();

        //then set the new one
        isActivePt = this;
        BeActive();
    }
    playerStatus.AddHealth(playerStatus.maxHealth);
    playerStatus.AddEnergy(playerStatus.maxEnergy);
    print("Player stepped on me");
}
//calls all the FX and audio to make the triggered point "activate" visually
function BeActive(){
//stuff here...
}
//calls all the FX and audio to make any old triggered point
//"inactivate" visually
function BeInactive(){
//stuff here...
}
@script AddComponentMenu("Environment Props/CheckPt")
```

Widget Status

```
//Widget_Status: Handles Widget's state machine.
//Keep track of health, energy, and all the chunky stuff

//vitals-----------------------------------------------------------------
var health: float = 10.0;
var maxHealth: float= 10.0;
var energy: float = 10.0;
var maxEnergy: float = 10.0;
var energyUsageForTransform: float = 3.0;
var widgetBoostUsage :float = 5.0;


//Cache Controllers-------------------------------------------------------
var playerController: Widget_Controller;
playerController = GetComponent(Widget_Controller) ;
var controller : CharacterController;
controller = GetComponent(CharacterController);

//Helper Controller Functions---------------------------------------------
function ApplyDamage(damage: float){

    health -= damage;

    //check health and call Die if need to
    if(health <= 0){
        health = 0; //for GUI
        Die();
    }
}

function AddHealth(boost: float){
    //add health and set to min of (current health+boost) or health max
    health += boost;
    if(health >= maxHealth){
        health = maxHealth;
    }
    print("added health: " + health);
}

function AddEnergy(boost: float){
```

```
    //add energy and set to min of (current energy + boost)
    //or energy maximum
energy += boost;
    if(energy >= maxEnergy){
        energy = maxEnergy;
    }
    print("added energy: " + energy);
}

function Die(){
    print("dead!");
    playerController.isControllable = false;

    animationState = GetComponent(Widget_Animation);
    animationState.PlayDie();
    yield WaitForSeconds(animation["Die"].length -0.2);

        HideCharacter();
    yield WaitForSeconds(1);

    //restart player at last respawn checkpoint and give max life
    if(CheckPoint.isActivePt){
        controller.transform.position =
          CheckPoint.isActivePt.transform.position;
        controller.transform.position.y += 0.5;
                //so not to get stuck in the platform itself
    }
    ShowCharacter();
    health = maxHealth;
}

function HideCharacter(){
    GameObject.Find("Body").GetComponent
                            (SkinnedMeshRenderer).enabled = false;
    GameObject.Find("Wheels").GetComponent
                        (SkinnedMeshRenderer).enabled = false;
    playerController.isControllable = false;
}

function ShowCharacter(){
```

```
        GameObject.Find("Body").GetComponent(SkinnedMeshRenderer).enabled = true;
        GameObject.Find("Wheels").GetComponent(SkinnedMeshRenderer).enabled = true;
        playerController.isControllable = true;
}
@script AddComponentMenu("Player/Widget'sStateManager")
```

CHAPTER 12

BUILDING ADVERSARIES AND AI

Widget's travels would be a lot more interesting if he faced a band of rival robots, seeking to impede his progress through the level. Through the scripting of Artificial Intelligence (or AI), props and lifeless characters can be given commands, routines, and goals, making them appear to be alive, thinking, and functioning. Like many other aspects of game development, writing good AI routines is an art form all unto itself and is a specialized field of study. Although it's pretty easy to give an enemy a list of commands to perform, it's much harder to make the player believe that the enemy is actively thinking and behaving in a manner that's just out to get *him*.

With all that aside, it's still possible to write good, fun AI behaviors even as a beginning game scripter. After you're done with some basics, you can further your knowledge by checking out the references in Appendix D, "Resources and References," found on the DVD, for recommendations on further reading.

ARTIFICIAL INTELLIGENCE: DEFINITELY ARTIFICIAL, NOT MUCH INTELLIGENCE

Although games and game programmers refer to the realm of computer-driven adversaries as AI, the name is really at heart a misnomer, and it's important to recognize that from the very start. Modeling intelligence, or true "thinking" behaviors in a computer, is incredibly difficult and perhaps not a completely solvable problem. Instead, programmers create and script *behaviors* that dictate how the computer will interact and react to stimuli around it. Many different conditions and stimuli can play into a single AI's script, and the numerous behaviors are often prioritized to make it seem as if the computer is actually thinking about how it will respond to its given situation. An amount of randomness can be added into the mix as well to make it seem less "computer like," but in the end the AI is never thinking, it's only reacting. An AI's effectiveness is then only as good as its behaviors and conditions and how adept the programmer was at predicting what kind of situations it would find itself in. When AI programmers say they're "teaching" the AI new tricks and abilities, they're really giving it new conditions and situations to respond to.

One key to writing a good AI is to understand your game mechanics from the inside out. Test and play your game often to see where possible exploits may lie, and look to see what paths or options players tend to pick most often. If you're not the best at playing your game, your AI probably won't be, either.

AIs come in many different shapes, sizes, and flavors—no game necessarily approaches them the same way. Some games may need complex creations, which need to be able to take the role of missing human players. Others may only need to follow a set of nodes around a map and patrol a set path, firing a weapon every couple of seconds. The complexity of your scripts and defined behaviors depends fully upon the nature of your game. Don't try to force something more complex if it doesn't fit, and likewise, don't oversimplify a problem so that players become bored with their opposition.

Some Simple AI Guidelines

Many tips and skills are learned as you go, but there are a few general pointers you should think about on your first foray into AI scripting:

- There is no one-size-fits-all AI script, no easy button, per se. As each AI script is created to respond to given criteria and circumstances, each one needs to be individually made for each occasion. Don't get sidetracked looking for an easy answer. Although there can be tools to make generating AIs faster and easier, there is no "AI" button.

- You need to think about creating meaningful experiences for your players and not just worry about making some numerical quota of encounters. What can a particular AI provide for the character that another couldn't? Will the player take away something important?

- Pure randomness does not always lead to good things. Some randomness is often added to behaviors or numbers to make them seem more realistic to a player, as things in life rarely happen exactly the same every time. However, most players expect and want a particular distribution of randomness, usually something like a *normal* or *Poisson distribution*—these kinds of distributions fit nature more readily than pure randomness does. Notice when you employ the use of randomness in your code and check to sure that you shouldn't be using a distribution of some kind instead. Players learn by recognition of patterns and repetition, and pure randomness is an antithesis to this.

- The AI needs to provide an appropriate challenge level for the players, not play the best game it can. A computer can out-react a player in any given circumstance every time, and care needs to go in to planning exactly "how good" the AI actually is. Players want to feel like they have a chance of beating any AI in your game. Impossible AIs are not fun AIs, and your players will pick this up readily enough. Don't forget that AIs are there to be a fun challenge for the player, not an impossible hurdle. Constant iteration and testing are a must.

- Your goal should be to define a good AI system that makes your players feel clever and awesome about themselves. Don't baby your players by giving them only easy AI adversaries to defeat. Your AIs should ramp up and become more difficult as the players gain more skills and experience in your game. If all the enemies in your game share the same AI patterns, players will quickly pick this up and then stop having fun with your game.

- Be wary of cheating. Sometimes it's easier to just make your AI better by giving it unfair advantages—more health, faster reflexes, better skills or attacks—rather than actually teaching it to behave in a "smarter" manner. Players almost always pick up on this and think of it as cheating; the game plays by different rules than they do. If used in moderation, this can be a good challenge for your players, but if the AI is constantly playing with a different rule set, your players will get frustrated.

With that in mind, you can begin to craft an effective AI. Your goal shouldn't be to make a system that always beats the players, but rather to craft a meaningful and fun experience that ramps up with your players.

A Simple Workflow

Starting off writing your first AI can be a bit daunting, but like with any problem, if you break it into smaller chunks, it'll be easier to approach and solve.

- First off, critically think about what exactly it is you want your AI to do. Be as specific as absolutely possible. "Attack the player" isn't much of a behavior. What does it mean to attack? How will it know to attack? How should it attempt to attack? Will it need to move to the player or see him first? Try to think of all the steps and required conditions that make up your desired behavior.

- Implement your basic outline. If you were detailed enough, your plans from the previous step will form the basic structure of your code.

- Before trying to add more complex behavior or conditions, test your AI. Then test it some more. Trying to spot edge cases and unforeseen circumstances that your AI might find itself in isn't always easy or obvious, and testing is the only way to figure them out. Test early and often.

- After ensuring that your AI is performing as expected, sit back and question whether it's *fun*. While perhaps your AI functions are designed or even behave realistically, it doesn't matter if the end result isn't fun for the players. Get some outside opinions, test some more, and teach away.

- If you need to implement more than one kind of AI script in your game (such as multiple enemies), make sure that they are both discreet and recognizable by the players. Remember, game design is heavily rooted in patterns, and you want your players to be able to learn your rules, not be continually dumbfounded at every turn.

SETTING UP A SIMPLE ENEMY

Widget's first enemy encounter will be a simple robot bunny, native to the hills where *Widget* roams. The AI for this enemy will be fairly straightforward and allow the player to get used to the controls without any real danger of dying. You don't want to scare the players away from the game with presenting a challenge they can't handle from the offset.

Before you get to scripting, however, you need to get the assets set up in Unity and ready to go. Open your saved project and create a new scene. The enemy will be easier to set up and test in his own simple environment, rather than trying to do it all in the main game scene. Follow these steps to do so:

1. Create a new scene in the project and place a basic plane GameObject into the world. Resize it so that it provides ample space to run around on.

2. Import the contents of the Chapter 12▶Characters folder on the DVD and place the pieces in their corresponding folders in the project. Ensure that you keep the root directory the same, so that the links to the prefab are not lost.

3. Change the Scale factor of the E_Bunny object to 1, if it isn't already. (E_Bunny is located under Materials▶Meshes.)

4. Create a new prefab for the bunny character and populate it with this E_Bunny object.

5. Set up the provided material with the Toon shader and assign the provided texture to it. Use the same steps as for setting up the *Widget* character.

6. Add an Animation component to the bunny prefab(Component▶Miscellaneous▶Animation) and change the size of the animation's array in the Inspector to 3. The bunny enemy happens to have three animations she can play, based upon what she is currently up to. Find the provided animation sequences in the Animation Clips folder and populate the elements with these clips. After attaching them to the character, you can play them back in the Animation view.

7. Since the bunny will need to interact and move around the world, she'll also need a Character controller. Add the component from the Component▶Physics menu and change the height and radius of the collider to be 0.65 and the center to (0, 0.52, 0). Your enemy bunny should look like Figure 12.1.

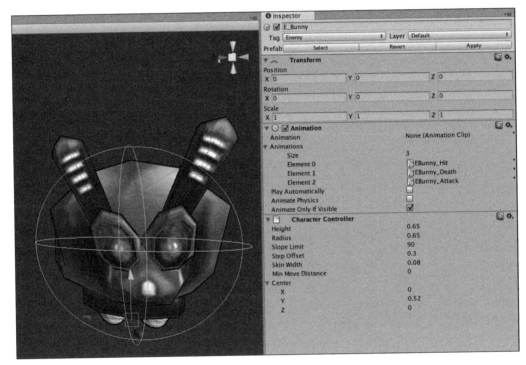

Figure 12.1
The preliminary "Electronic Bunny of Doom."

The AI Controller

Now that your new enemy character is hooked up and ready to go, you'll need to define how you want her to behave. In a single sentence, you want the bunny to wander freely until she spots a player and then turn to hunt him down.

This doesn't lend itself very well to implementation, however, and a more structured approach can yield better results:

1. Slowly and randomly wander a small area.

2. If the character is within some set area bounds, face and head towards him.

3. If you collide with the character, attack. Small pause to allow for a counterattack.

4. Move towards the character again if still within bounds and can see him. If not, try to find him.

5. If the character moves out of bounds, return to wandering.

6. If defeated, drop some random small items and disappear.

From this list, it will be much easier to implement the bunny's behaviors—many of the conditions and criteria for her behaviors are already defined and laid out in a logical order. Much like the *Widget* character, the bunny will also need a Controller class script to dictate how she will behave and move around and a state script to handle her health and state functions. Since you don't need to check for the player's input or actions, playing the proper animations for the bunny is a much more straightforward process and can be handled in the same script as the controller.

Make a new JavaScript file in the Scripts directory, name it **EBunny_ AIController**, and delete the provided Update function. As with *Widget's* controller, you'll need to start off with some variables to define how fast the character can move:

```
var walkSpeed = 3.0;
var rotateSpeed = 30.0;
var attackSpeed = 8.0;
var attackRotateSpeed = 80.0;
```

The bunny will use one base walk and rotate speed for when she's wandering around aimlessly and a faster, more pointed one for when she actually spots the player. Setting these kinds of variables as public will make iteration and testing time much quicker.

Next, you'll need some variables to define how the bunny aimlessly wanders around, as per condition 1, and set the distance for when the bunny can see the player, as per condition 2.

```
var directionTraveltime = 2.0;
var idleTime = 1.5;
var attackDistance = 15.0;
```

The first variable defines how often the bunny will change directions as she wanders. Lastly, you'll need to set up a few last variables for the bunny's attacks:

```
var damage = 1;
var viewAngle = 20.0;
var attackRadius = 2.5;
var attackTurnTime = 1.0;
var attackPosition = new Vector3 (0, 1, 0);
```

These variables define exactly where the attack is generated with respect to the bunny's position, how much of an area the bunny can hit with one attack, and how long it takes the bunny to complete each attack. You'll also set her base damage output here, to make it easy to change later.

The bunny will also need a few private variables to handle the switches between attacking, pausing, and changing direction:

```
private var isAttacking = false;
private var lastAttackTime = 0.0;
private var nextPauseTime = 0.0;
private var distanceToPlayer;
private var timeToNewDirection = 0.0;
```

Lastly, you also need to define a target for the bunny to chase after and cache a reference to the bunny's controller.

```
var target : Transform;
// Cache the controller
private var characterController : CharacterController;
characterController = GetComponent(CharacterController);
```

With this in place, you're ready to start working on the script. Unlike the *Widget* controller, which needs to constantly look for and execute player commands every frame, the bunny doesn't really need this kind of overhead. Instead, this character will be performing a simple action repeatedly (wandering around) until certain criteria are met (finding the player and attacking). These two actions, idling and attacking, encompass all of the bunny's behaviors and will simply switch between each other ad infinitum. Rather than checking to see if the player is within reach of the bunny every frame, you can instead use the power of coroutines to have the bunny switch from one state to the other!

This simplifies the code quite a bit. Now you can set up everything in the Start function and have the two main coroutines, Idle and Attack, handle everything.

Create a Start function and begin to initialize the bunny's basics:

```
function Start ()
{
if (!target)
target = GameObject.FindWithTag("Player").transform;
}
```

As you didn't specify a target earlier in the variable definition, you'll need to set one now. You also need to initialize and set up the animation information, much like for *Widget*. Within the Start function and below the target setup, add the following:

```
animation.wrapMode = WrapMode.Loop;
animation["EBunny_Death"].wrapMode = WrapMode.Once;

animation["EBunny_Attack"].layer = 1;
animation["EBunny_Hit"].layer = 3;
animation["EBunny_Death"].layer = 5;
```

Since the bunny's animations weren't embedded in the FBX file, you need to make sure the Wrap modes are correctly set up for all the available clips and then ensure that they reside in the proper layers for blending.

The bunny's first and default behavior is Idle—wandering aimlessly around the world. Create a new Idle function in the EBunny_AIController file:

```
function Idle ()
{
while (true)
    {
    }
}
```

Rather than call the Idle function every frame with something like Update, you'll instead set it up to run a while loop an infinite number of times until some condition is met. This will make it easier to bounce to the second routine, Attack.

Inside the while loop, create the if statement that controls how often the bunny should change direction:

```
if(Time.time > timeToNewDirection)
{
yield WaitForSeconds(idleTime);

if(Random.value > 0.5)
transform.Rotate(Vector3(0,5,0), rotateSpeed);
else
transform.Rotate(Vector3(0,-5,0),rotateSpeed);
timeToNewDirection = Time.time + directionTraveltime;
}
```

First you check to see if the allotted amount of time wandering in one direction has been reached and, if it has, look for a new direction to move. The bunny also takes this time to wait for a few idle seconds, giving the small illusion that she may be "thinking" about where to go next.

Once the bunny's direction has been set, she needs to start moving forward along that path. Still within the while loop and below the if statement, add the following:

```
var walkForward = transform.TransformDirection(Vector3.forward);
characterController.SimpleMove(walkForward * walkSpeed);
```

These two simple lines grab the bunny's current facing direction, forward, and make her move along that vector at her default walk speed.

If you tried to run this function as it stands now, the bunny would continue to wander for the entire game. You need to create the condition that pops the bunny's controller out of Idle and allows her to continue into the attack. Right below the walk code, add the following:

```
distanceToPlayer   = transform.position - target.position;
if (distanceToPlayer.magnitude < attackDistance)
return;
yield;
```

Every loop iteration, the bunny checks to see how far away she is from the specified target. If this distance is smaller than her attack radius, the Idle function returns and stops executing, allowing the bunny to move into her attack.

Create a new function named Attack and add it below the Idle function in the file.

```
function Attack ()
{
}
```

Since the attacking function will start only once the player is in range, you now only need to check to see whether the bunny can "see" the player. If she can see the player, she should move towards him and attack. If she can't see the player, she should search until she's found her goal.

Start with setting the bunny's Attack state to True and begin playing her animation. Within the Attack function, add the following:

```
isAttacking = true;
animation.Play("EBunny_Attack");
```

Now set up the bunny for the attack by turning her towards the player and moving towards her:

```
var angle  = 0.0;
var time  = 0.0;
var direction : Vector3;
while (angle > viewAngle || time < attackTurnTime)
{
}
```

You'll need to figure out what angle the bunny is actually facing in relation to the player in order to reset the variable *angle*, so create a new function at the bottom of the file and name it FacePlayer. Since you'll also use this function to rotate the bunny, give it two arguments: one for the player's current position and how fast you want the bunny to rotate while attacking.

```
function FacePlayer(targetLocation : Vector3, rotateSpeed
                               : float) : float
{
}
```

First thing up, you need to figure out the relative angle between the player and the bunny. Using simple trigonometry identities, you can find the corresponding angle. Add the following within the FacePlayer function:

```
var relativeLocation = transform.InverseTransformPoint(targetLocation);
var angle = Mathf.Atan2 (relativeLocation.x,
          relativeLocation.z) *  Mathf.Rad2Deg;
```

Now knowing where the player is, you can turn the bunny to face towards him, clamping the speed down by the passed-in speed argument. Allowing the bunny to turn on a dime without clamping would not only be jarring to watch but also difficult to respond to.

```
var maxRotation = rotateSpeed * Time.deltaTime;
var clampedAngle = Mathf.Clamp(angle, -maxRotation, maxRotation);
transform.Rotate(0, clampedAngle, 0);
```

Now that the bunny is being rotated towards the player correctly, all you need to do is return her current angle for the Attack function to use later. Add the following code to the very bottom of the FacePlayer function:

```
return angle;
```

With the helper function completed, you can return to working on the bunny's attack. Back within the while loop, you set up the Attack function:

```
time += Time.deltaTime;
angle = Mathf.Abs(FacePlayer(target.position, attackRotateSpeed));
move = Mathf.Clamp01((90 - angle) / 90);
animation["EBunny_Attack"].weight = animation
        ["EBunny_Attack"].speed = move;
direction = transform.TransformDirection(Vector3.forward *
                                  attackSpeed * move);
characterController.SimpleMove(direction);
yield;
```

Depending on the bunny's angle, you adjust the attack animation's speed and blend weight and then begin to move the bunny towards the player at the increased attack speed. You need to also insert a yield statement, since you'll be running this as a coroutine.

With the bunny moving towards the player now, you need to ensure that you can in fact still see the target—after all, there's nothing saying the player can't move out of the way once he notices the bunny making a beeline straight for him. Create a new while loop beneath the one you just finished:

```
var lostSight = false;
while (!lostSight)
{
}
```

First up, you need to make sure that the player is still within the bunny's eyesight range. Add within the while loop:

```
angle = FacePlayer(target.position, attackRotateSpeed);
if (Mathf.Abs(angle) > viewAngle)
lostSight = true;
if (lostSight)
break;
```

If your player's current relative angle is greater than the bunny's field of vision, the bunny loses sight of the player. If this is the case, you'll have the bunny bounce out of this loop and begin looking again. Now if the bunny hasn't in fact lost sight of the player, you need to check to see if she is within range of the attack. If the player is in fact so unlucky, the bunny attacks:

```
var location = transform.TransformPoint(attackPosition)
                      - target.position;
if(Time.time > lastAttackTime + 1.0 && location.magnitude
                      < attackRadius)
{
// deal damage
target.SendMessage("ApplyDamage", damage);

lastAttackTime = Time.time;
}
```

The SendMessage function calls the specified method, in this case Apply Damage, on the target object every time it is found. If multiple scripts have a function called Apply Damage, each one would be called in turn using damage as its argument. It can be a useful way to trigger multiple scripts on one GameObject—just ensure they share the same function declaration.

Now you'll also check here to make sure that the bunny can actually attack again. You want to give the player a second or so between each of the bunny's attacks, giving him time to move out of the way. Otherwise, the bunny will bite the player every frame he's within range, which can quickly kill the player in an unfun manner.

Conversely, if the player isn't actually within the attack range, you need to break out of the loop and begin looking again. Below these statements (but still within this while loop), add the following:

```
if(location.magnitude > attackRadius)
break;
// Check to make sure our current direction didn't
// collide us with something
if (characterController.velocity.magnitude < attackSpeed * 0.3)
break;
yield;
```

Now is also a good time to check to make sure the bunny's sprint towards the player didn't collide her with something she can't get over, like a big rock. One last thing to add to the Attack function is to reset the bunny's Attack state to False, which would happen if the bunny lost sight and had to start looking again. Outside of the while loop and at the very bottom of the Attack function, reset her state:

```
isAttacking = false;
```

For ease of use, finish the script with the menu command at the bottom:

```
@script AddComponentMenu("Enemies/Bunny'sAIController")
```

Attach this finished controller script to the Bunny prefab. You can now run the test scene by dropping a Bunny prefab object and *Widget* onto the plane and watching as the bunny hunts *Widget* down, as shown in Figure 12.2.

The bunny isn't quite done yet, however. She still needs a state manager.

A Simple State Manager for a Simple Bunny

Unlike *Widget*, the bunny doesn't have many things she'll need to keep track of—pretty much only her health. Create a new JavaScript file in the Scripts directory and name it **EBunny_Status**. Delete the Update function and give the bunny two simple variables:

```
var health: float = 10.0;
private var dead = false;
```

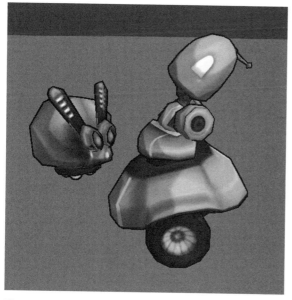

Figure 12.2
Widget meets an untimely end at the paws of the evil bunny.

That's all she'll need for the moment. Like *Widget*, she'll need a function to handle any damage dealt to her and another to deal with her if she dies. Create a new function named ApplyDamage—name it the same as *Widget*'s for a reason. In case you were to have any environment-type damage, like the water, you can send the ApplyDamage message to any robotic target that steps foot into the trap, regardless of whether it's the player or an NPC. Add the following to the file:

```
function ApplyDamage(damage: float){
if (health <= 0)
return;
health -= damage;
animation.Play("EBunny_Hit");

	if(!dead && health <= 0)
    {
```

```
health = 0;
dead = true;
Die();
      }
  }
}
```

Whenever the bunny gets hit, she plays the proper animation. If the bunny's damage takes her health below zero, she dies. Now create her death handler:

```
function Die ()
{
animation.Stop();
animation.Play("EBunny_Death");

Destroy(gameObject.GetComponent(EBunny_AIController));
yield WaitForSeconds(animation["EBunny_Death"].length - 0.5);
Destroy(gameObject);
}
@script AddComponentMenu("Enemies/Bunny'sStateManager")
```

First you stop all attack or hit animations and begin playing the Death one. Then you remove the bunny's AI controller, stopping her from continuing any behaviors, wait the length of the death scene, and then finish the destroying process by removing her entire asset from the scene. Pretty straightforward. Attach the script to the Bunny prefab.

Hooking Up Widget's Attacks

Now that the enemy can move and attack, you need to make *Widget* able to defeat it in battle. *Widget* doesn't currently stand a chance, even against this tiny robot bunny, without some attack moves of his own. *Widget* starts life with a simple laser type attack, called Taser. With it, he can blast any enemy within range, a sphere extending around him for two units on all sides.

Create a new script in the Scripts directory named **Widget_AttackController**, and then add some simple attack handling variables to the top:

```
var attackHitTime = 0.2;
var attackTime = 0.5;
var attackPosition = new Vector3 (0, 1, 0);
```

```
var attackRadius = 2.0;
var damage = 1.0;
```

These describe the basic details of how long it takes him to attack, how often the player can attack, and where on his body the attack originates. He'll only need a few private variables to finish this off:

```
private var busy = false;
private var ourLocation;
private var enemies : GameObject[] ;
```

While the first two are self-explanatory, the enemy's array will hold the information for all objects within his attack range that can be declared as an enemy. *Widget's* attack is known as an *area of effect,* and you need to make sure that any and all enemies caught within its range take damage.

And since you'll be taking input from the players, you also need a cache to *Widget's* controller to make sure any move is valid:

```
var controller : Widget_Controller;
controller = GetComponent(Widget_Controller);
```

Just like with *Widget's* base controller, you first need to determine if the player pressed the Attack button. Recall in Chapter 9 that you set up *Widget's* Attack input button, so calling it now is pretty easy. Within the provided Update function, add the following:

```
if(!busy && Input.GetButtonDown ("Attack") &&
            controller.IsGrounded() && !controller.IsMoving())
{
DidAttack();
busy = true;
}
```

You allow the player to attack again only if *Widget* isn't busy, that is, he's not currently attacking. The player must wait until *Widget* is done with his current attack before attacking again. This loop calls the DidAttack function, which you need to write now. Create a new function named **DidAttack** and add it to the bottom of the file:

```
function DidAttack ()
{
}
```

Figure 12.3
The Tag Manager.

First thing up, you need to provide feedback to the player by starting the Taser animation, letting the player know that his or her attack went through successfully. Inside this function, add the following:

```
animation.CrossFadeQueued("Taser", 0.1, QueueMode.PlayNow);
yield WaitForSeconds(attackHitTime);
```

Now you need to determine which enemies, if any, are within the attack radius. Unity came with a predefined Player tag, but you'll need to make a new tag for all the enemy robots to use.

Select the E_Bunny prefab in the Project view and navigate to its Tag field in the Inspector—this is right up at the top underneath its name. Select Add Tag from the drop-down menu. This takes you to the Tag Manager, shown in Figure 12.3.

Here you can define any number of tags you want to assign to GameObjects in your scene. To do so, change the Tag Size field to any number greater than zero to populate the array with new elements. Double-click on an element to rename it with the tag of your choice, for example, Enemy. Create a new Enemy tag and reselect the E_Bunny prefab from the Project view. Assign this new tag to the prefab.

With your enemy now tagged appropriately, you can easily search for it. Back in *Widget*'s Attack Controller script, continue working in the DidAttack function where you left off.

Add to the function:

```
ourLocation = transform.TransformPoint(attackPosition);
enemies = GameObject.FindGameObjectsWithTag("Enemy");
for (var enemy : GameObject in enemies)
{
var enemyStatus = enemy.GetComponent(EBunny_Status);
if (enemyStatus == null)
    {
continue;
    }

if (Vector3.Distance(enemy.transform.position, ourLocation)
                        < attackRadius)
    {
enemyStatus.ApplyDamage(damage);
    }
}
```

After populating the enemy's array with all the tagged objects in the scene, you search through them item by item to see if any one of the enemies is a bunny. If it is, you check to make sure that it is within range of the attack and then deal it the appropriate amount of damage.

The only thing remaining is to wait for the attack to finish and reset *Widget*'s status to not busy, allowing the players to attack again when ready. Finish off the DidAttack function with the following:

```
yield WaitForSeconds(attackTime - attackHitTime);
busy = false;
```

Add the component string to the bottom of the file and attach this script to *Widget*'s prefab.

```
@script AddComponentMenu("Player/Widget's Attack Controller")
```

Test your hard work in the test scene and battle the nefarious rabbit.

REWARDING THE PLAYER FOR A JOB WELL DONE

Only one thing is now left to do—give the player a reward for his or her victory over the enemy! Recall in Chapter 11 that you wrote a script to allow *Widget* to pick up items and place them in his inventory. Now you need to make enemies spawn and release items into the level upon their defeat, giving *Widget* a tangible reward to roll over and collect.

Reopen the EBunny_Status script file and add some new variables to the top:

```
var numHeldItemsMin = 1;
var numHeldItemsMax = 3;
var pickup1: GameObject;
var pickup2: GameObject;
```

Each bunny enemy can hold a range of items and can hold up to two items at once. These items will be set via the Inspector later.

Go to the Die( ) function and begin working before the last Destroy(Game-Object) line. You basically want the bunny to fall over and finish her death animation, drop the pickups, and then finish disappearing.

At this location in the script, add the following:

```
var itemLocation = gameObject.transform.position;
yield WaitForSeconds(0.5);
var rewardItems = Random.Range(numHeldItemsMin, numHeldItemsMax);
for (var i = 0; i < rewardItems; i++)
{
    var randomItemLocation = itemLocation;
randomItemLocation.x += Random.Range(-2, 2);
    randomItemLocation.y += 1; // Keep it off the ground
randomItemLocation.z += Random.Range(-2, 2);

if (Random.value > 0.5)
    Instantiate(pickup1, randomItemLocation,
            pickup1.transform.rotation);
else
    Instantiate(pickup2, randomItemLocation,
            pickup2.transform.rotation);}
```

First you should save the location of the bunny—you'll use this to assign the drop location of the new items. Then after figuring out how many items you want to give the player, you figure out what each one will be, whether pickup1 or pickup2. Each of these items is then created near the bunny's final resting place. Save the script.

You already have one pickup ready from Chapter 11, the simple gear prefab. Here, you'll add another pickup to give *Widget* some variety:

1. From the Chapter 12 folder on the DVD, import the contents of the Props folder. Assign the Pickup_Screw.fbx object the same material and texture as the gear object.

2. Create a prefab for the Screw using the same settings and information as the gear; refer to the previous chapter if needed.

Armed with two distinct pickups, fill in the variables in the EBunny_Status script component on the Bunny prefab with the Gear and Screw prefabs. Your Inspector view for the Bunny prefab should now look like Figure 12.4.

Test your new script and collect your rewards.

SPAWNING AND OPTIMIZATION

You can add one more bit of functionality to the bunny enemy, while also cutting back on some memory space for better game optimization. Right now, after your players kill the test bunny, she drops her rewards and disappears.

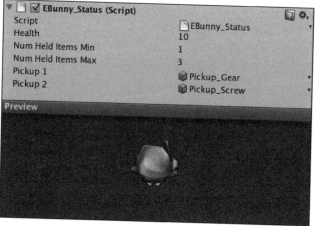

Figure 12.4
The pickups are ready to go.

However, with the addition of a spawn point, you can have new bunnies appear and give *Widget* more adversaries to face. Using this point, you can at the same time remove these same enemies if *Widget* drops out of their radar, saving on unneeded space. There's no need to populate the scene full of enemies and objects if *Widget* can't even see them, so having enemies spawn only when needed can really help cut back on unneeded calls.

Create a new JavaScript file in the Scripts directory and name it **Enemy_ RespawnPoint**. Give it some starting variables to function:

```
var spawnRange = 40.0;
var enemy: GameObject;

private var target : Transform;
private var currentEnemy : GameObject;
private var outsideRange = true;
private var distanceToPlayer;
```

You can now set the exact range of the particular spawn point and set which enemy you want to appear from within the Inspector. You also need to save information on your currently generated enemy, currentEnemy, to allow the point to spawn only one at a time. Otherwise, each frame that *Widget* is caught within the radius, a new enemy will appear.

Initialize the script with a simple Start function, creating a link to the player:

```
function Start ()
{
target = GameObject.FindWithTag("Player").transform;
}
```

Now within the provided Update function, begin checking if the player has crossed the threshold of the spawn's radius of effect:

```
function Update ()
{
distanceToPlayer  = transform.position - target.position;
if (distanceToPlayer.magnitude < spawnRange)
    {
        }
}
```

If the player is in fact within the spawn point's range, you'll create a new enemy if one already doesn't exist. Add the following to the body of the if statement:

```
if (!currentEnemy)
{
currentEnemy = Instantiate(enemy, transform.position, transform.rotation);
}

// the player is now inside the respawn's range
outsideRange = false;
```

As long as the player remains inside the spawn point's range, it will keep one enemy alive to patrol the area.

Create an else case within the Update function to handle when the player does actually begin to move outside the spawn point's area:

```
else
{
if (currentEnemy)
Destroy(currentEnemy);
    }
outsideRange = true;
```

If an instantiated enemy does exist, remove it and reset the state of the spawn point to not create any others. Create the obligatory menu reference at the bottom of the file to find the script easily later on:

```
@script AddComponentMenu("Enemies/Respawn Point")
```

Now you just need to hook it up.

Back in the test file, create a new empty GameObject by navigating to Game Object▶ Create Empty. Rename this object **Spawn Point** and put it somewhere on the plane. Attach the Enemy_Respawn script to the point and assign the Enemy variable using the E_Bunny prefab. Test your scene and play with the spawn range until you get something you like. Try placing more than one spawn point around the level, so you can see how the effect of multiple enemies can change the difficulty.

You can now use your new enemy and enemy spawner in any of your scene files, giving *Widget* some new gameplay options.

In the next few chapters, you'll hook the remaining important bits for game-play—namely the User Interface (UI) and some particle effects—thus making the player's interactions with props and enemies in the world more fun.

COMPLETED SCRIPTS

The newly completed scripts are also available on the DVD in the Chapter 12 folder.

EBunny_AIController.js

```
//EBunny_AIController: Handles both the electronic bunny's AI and animations
//Since we don't need to be checking for the player's input or
//actions, playing the proper animations is much more
//straightforward and can be handled
//in the same script.

//-----------------------------------------------------------------
var walkSpeed = 3.0;
var rotateSpeed = 30.0;
var attackSpeed = 8.0;
var attackRotateSpeed = 80.0;

var directionTraveltime = 2.0;
var idleTime = 1.5;
var attackDistance = 15.0;

var damage = 1;
var attackRadius = 2.5;
var viewAngle = 20.0;
var attackTurnTime = 1.0;
var attackPosition = new Vector3 (0, 1, 0);

//--------------------------------------------------------
private var isAttacking = false;
private var lastAttackTime = 0.0;
private var nextPauseTime = 0.0;
private var distanceToPlayer;
private var timeToNewDirection = 0.0;
```

```
var target : Transform;
// Cache the controller
private var characterController : CharacterController;
characterController = GetComponent(CharacterController);

//----------------------------------------------------
function Start ()
{
if (!target)
target = GameObject.FindWithTag("Player").transform;
//Set up animations---------------------------------
animation.wrapMode = WrapMode.Loop;
animation["EBunny_Death"].wrapMode = WrapMode.Once;
animation["EBunny_Attack"].layer = 1;
animation["EBunny_Hit"].layer = 3;
animation["EBunny_Death"].layer = 5;

yield WaitForSeconds(idleTime);
while (true)
    {
// Idle around and wait for the player
yield Idle();

// Player has been located, prepare for the attack.
yield Attack();
    }
}


function Idle ()
{
// Walk around and pause in random directions
while (true)
    {
// Find a new direction to move
if(Time.time > timeToNewDirection)
        {
yield WaitForSeconds(idleTime);
var RandomDirection = Random.value;
if(Random.value > 0.5)
```

```
transform.Rotate(Vector3(0,5,0), rotateSpeed);
else
transform.Rotate(Vector3(0,-5,0),rotateSpeed);
timeToNewDirection = Time.time + directionTraveltime;
        }

var walkForward = transform.TransformDirection(Vector3.forward);
characterController.SimpleMove(walkForward * walkSpeed);
distanceToPlayer  = transform.position - target.position;
//We found the player! Stop wasting time and go after him
if (distanceToPlayer.magnitude < attackDistance)
return;
    yield;
}
}

function Attack ()
{
isAttacking = true;
animation.Play("EBunny_Attack");

// We need to turn to face the player now that
// the bunny is in range.
var angle  = 0.0;
var time   = 0.0;
var direction : Vector3;
while (angle > viewAngle || time < attackTurnTime)
    {
time += Time.deltaTime;
angle = Mathf.Abs(FacePlayer(target.position, attackRotateSpeed));
move = Mathf.Clamp01((90 - angle) / 90);
// depending on the angle, start moving
        animation["EBunny_Attack"].weight =
                animation["EBunny_Attack"].speed = move;
        direction = transform.TransformDirection(Vector3.forward
                * attackSpeed * move);
characterController.SimpleMove(direction);
 yield;
    }
```

```
// attack if can see player
var lostSight = false;
while (!lostSight)
        {
angle = FacePlayer(target.position, attackRotateSpeed);
// Check to ensure that the target is within the Bunny's eyesight
if (Mathf.Abs(angle) > viewAngle)
lostSight = true;
// If bunny loses site of the player, she jumps out of here.
if (lostSight)
break;
//Check to see if 'bunny is close enough to the
//player to bite 'em.
        var location = transform.TransformPoint
                    (attackPosition) - target.position;
        if(Time.time > lastAttackTime + 1.0 &&
                    location.magnitude < attackRadius)
        {
// deal damage
target.SendMessage("ApplyDamage", damage);
lastAttackTime = Time.time;
        }
if(location.magnitude > attackRadius)
break;
// Check to make sure our current dir didn't
// collide us with something
if (characterController.velocity.magnitude < attackSpeed * 0.3)
break;
// yield for one frame
yield;
    }
isAttacking = false;

}

function FacePlayer(targetLocation : Vector3, rotateSpeed
                                : float) : float
{
// Find the relative place in the world where the player is located
var relativeLocation = transform.InverseTransformPoint(targetLocation);
```

```
        var angle = Mathf.Atan2 (relativeLocation.x,
                    relativeLocation.z) * Mathf.Rad2Deg;

// Clamp it with the max rotation speed so bunny doesn't move too fast
var maxRotation = rotateSpeed * Time.deltaTime;
var clampedAngle = Mathf.Clamp(angle, -maxRotation, maxRotation);
// Rotate
transform.Rotate(0, clampedAngle, 0);
// Return the current angle
return angle;
}


@script AddComponentMenu("Enemies/Bunny'sAIController")
```

EBunny_Status.js

```
//EBunny_Status:    controls the state information of the enemy bunny


//---------------------------------------------------------
var health: float = 10.0;
private var dead = false;

//PickupItems held----------------------------------------
var numHeldItemsMin = 1;
var numHeldItemsMax = 3;
var pickup1: GameObject;
var pickup2: GameObject;

//State Functions--------------------------- - - - - - - - - - - - - - -
function ApplyDamage(damage: float){
if (health <= 0)
return;
health -= damage;
animation.Play("EBunny_Hit");

//check health and call Die if need to
if(!dead && health <= 0)
    {
health = 0; //for GUI
dead = true;
Die();
```

```
        }
}

function Die ()
{
animation.Stop();
animation.Play("EBunny_Death");


Destroy(gameObject.GetComponent(EBunny_AIController));
yield WaitForSeconds(animation["EBunny_Death"].length - 0.5);
//Cache location of dead body for pickups
var itemLocation = gameObject.transform.position;
// drop a random number of reward pickups for the player
yield WaitForSeconds(0.5);
var rewardItems = Random.Range(numHeldItemsMin, numHeldItemsMax);
for (var i = 0; i < rewardItems; i++)
    {
        var randomItemLocation = itemLocation;
        randomItemLocation.x += Random.Range(-2, 2);
        randomItemLocation.y += 1; // Keep it off the ground
        randomItemLocation.z += Random.Range(-2, 2);

        if (Random.value > 0.5)
            Instantiate(pickup1, randomItemLocation,
                        pickup1.transform.rotation);
        else
            Instantiate(pickup2, randomItemLocation,
                        pickup2.transform.rotation);
}

//Remove killed enemy from the scene
Destroy(gameObject);
}
function IsDead() : boolean
{
    return dead;
}

@script AddComponentMenu("Enemies/Bunny'sStateManager")
```

Widget_AttackController.js

```
//Widget_AttackController:   handles the player's attack
//input and deals damage to the targeted enemy

//------------------------------------------------------
var attackHitTime = 0.2;
var attackTime = 0.5;
var attackPosition = new Vector3 (0, 1, 0);
var attackRadius = 2.0;
var damage= 1.0;

//------------------------------------------------------
private var busy = false;
private var ourLocation;
private var enemies : GameObject[] ;

var controller : Widget_Controller;
controller = GetComponent(Widget_Controller);

//Allow the player to attack if he is not busy
//and the Attack button was pressed
function Update ()
{
    if(!busy && Input.GetButtonDown ("Attack") &&
                controller.IsGrounded() && !controller.IsMoving())
    {
DidAttack();
busy = true;
    }
}

function DidAttack ()
{
//Play the animation regardless of whether we hit something or not.
animation.CrossFadeQueued("Taser", 0.1, QueueMode.PlayNow);
yield WaitForSeconds(attackHitTime);
ourLocation = transform.TransformPoint(attackPosition);
enemies = GameObject.FindGameObjectsWithTag("Enemy");
//See if any enemies are within range of the attack.
//This will hit all in range.
```

```
for (var enemy : GameObject in enemies)
    {
var enemyStatus = enemy.GetComponent(EBunny_Status);
if (enemyStatus == null)
        {
continue;
        }

        if (Vector3.Distance(enemy.transform.position,
                             ourLocation) < attackRadius)
        {
enemyStatus.ApplyDamage(damage);
        }
    }
yield WaitForSeconds(attackTime - attackHitTime);
busy = false;
}


@script AddComponentMenu("Player/Widget's Attack Controller")
```

Enemy_RespawnPoint.js

```
//Enemy_RespawnPoint: attach to a GO in the scene to serve
//as a respawn point for enemies. When the player walks into the
//specified area, a new enemy will respawn.

//-----------------------------------------------------------
var spawnRange = 40.0;
var enemy: GameObject;

private var target : Transform;
private var currentEnemy : GameObject;
private var outsideRange = true;
private var distanceToPlayer;

//-----------------------------------------------------------
function Start ()
{
target = GameObject.FindWithTag("Player").transform;
}
```

```
function Update ()
{
distanceToPlayer  = transform.position - target.position;
// check to see if player encounters the respawn point.
if (distanceToPlayer.magnitude < spawnRange)
    {
if (!currentEnemy)
      {
          currentEnemy = Instantiate(enemy,
                         transform.position, transform.rotation);
      }

// the player is now inside the respawn's range
outsideRange = false;
}

// player is moving out of range, so get rid of the
// unnecessary enemy now
else
    {
if (currentEnemy)
Destroy(currentEnemy);
        }
outsideRange = true;
}

@script AddComponentMenu("Enemies/Respawn Point")
```

CHAPTER 13

DESIGNING THE GAME'S GUI (GRAPHICAL USER INTERFACE)

A game's Graphical User Interface (GUI) can be one of the most time-consuming and most-iterated systems in your application. Although it may just look like a simple collection of images and text arranged prettily on the screen, good, usable, attractive, efficient, and friendly GUIs aren't just stumbled upon after one quick sketch or two. Not only does the GUI need to provide the players with all the bits of pertinent information they may need at any time, it also needs to fit within the game's artistic vision, not clutter up the screen, and be easy enough for anyone to use without instruction.

GUIs are the gateway to your game. A bad, hard-to-use GUI will stop players in their tracks and make some stop playing altogether—it doesn't matter how great the gameplay may be, if the GUI sucks, the game sucks. A GUI designed with good usability in mind will often fade away into the background, as the player doesn't need to pay any attention to the interface, just the game itself. A good GUI is an open pathway leading to your gameplay, not a stumbling block the player has to master first.

BASIC INTERFACE THEORY

One of the first things to understand before you start designing your own GUI is how people interact with computers. Sure, you've used hundreds if not thousands of different computer interfaces, but knowing how to use one doesn't necessarily give you the right information on how to start designing one.

Steps of Interaction

Human-computer interaction can be broken into three basic steps:

1. Forming a goal.

2. Executing an action.

3. Evaluating the action.

Before users click on anything in an interface, they first determine what they want to achieve—maybe they want to open a menu screen or use an item. After deciding what it is they want to accomplish, they then have to abstract that goal into something the system can understand and provide. Perhaps the user sees an image on the screen that's labeled Main Menu, providing her with the necessary information to deduce that perhaps this button can help her in achieving her goal. Once an intention using the system is formed, the user executes her action, in this case, clicking the menu command.

Now she needs to evaluate her action and determine if her initial goal is satisfied. This is where timely and descriptive *feedback* in vitally necessary. The user doesn't know, nor can know, how the underlying menu system works or is written. The only way she can glean any information is from the system updating itself and providing her with some sort of feedback for her action. With the button click, this could be a new menu screen opening or a tooltip describing what she did. Without feedback, the user wouldn't ever know if the button she pressed did anything, perhaps was disabled because of some random state, or activated too quickly for her to notice. Feedback is what helps teach the users how to understand your GUI, and through it, your game.

Designing for Your Users

So with this in mind, when you start laying out an interface, your first thoughts should be along the lines of "what do the users need to do?" or "what do the users *think* they need to do?" As the designer, you have a pretty good handle on all the different functions and mechanics that the user could run across, but you need to be able to take a step back and think from a new user's perspective. Consider these main rules:

- **Don't throw all the information at your users at once.** Rather, think of what they would want to know or need only to know.

- **Be consistent.** Users learn by doing, and you want to help that process along as much as possible. Pick a style for buttons, labels, and anything that users will interact with and stick with it. Nothing is more frustrating than seeing a style used for an interactive button on one screen and then finding it used again on another as a static label. Users recognize available functionality as much from visual art cues as from text.

- **Use the standards and paradigms your users are familiar with.** There's no need to reinvent the wheel for some basic principles. For example, most Windows users are comfortable with seeing the Minimize, Maximize, and Close buttons for their applications on the top-right corner of the window. Sure, you could move those buttons wherever you wanted, but you'd only end up confusing and irritating your users for no real gain. If there's a standard interface option that your user base will be aware of, make sure you're not willfully ignoring it.

- **Make feedback quick and meaningful.** Feedback too late is just as bad as no feedback at all. GUIs need to be responsive, optimized, and descriptive. Users learn from the causality chain of "perform action, get response," and if the response is late coming, the users might not always pair it correctly with their previous action.

- **Be clear about the current state of the system.** If the game is paused, make sure there's a pause screen up that obscures the rest of the screen in some way so there's no way to miss it. If the user's character is dead, make sure that it's obvious visually and don't just disable the controls.

- **Be mindful of your users' movements.** It may look nice to ring the screen with lots of different buttons, but be aware of what that means for the users. Especially for faster-paced games, users want to make quick, fast mouse or controller movements, and not have to scroll all the way across the screen and back again to perform a simple action. If there are multiple buttons or controls that users can interact with in a short span of time, try and group them closer together so your screen is easier to navigate.

■ **Above all, test early and test often.** A successful GUI is developed with the game from the very beginning. Trying to slap a GUI onto a mostly finished game will lead to a poor GUI that lacks deep integration with the systems and isn't part of the cohesive whole. Grab a friend who's unfamiliar with your game and watch him (or her) try to play without helping him along. If he can figure out your interface by himself, you're doing something right. If he needs to ask for help or clarification about anything, make a note and address those issues as you develop.

Unity's GUI System

Unlike other event-driven GUI systems you may already be familiar with, Unity's GUI system is based on an Immediate Mode model. Instead of driving the interface with a series of messages, like OnMouseHover or OnClick combined with art objects placed on a screen, a single interface element is drawn and declared in one single step.

```
function OnGUI()
{
    if( GUI.Button( Rect( 10, 10, 320, 80), "Quit Game")) )
    {
        Application.Quit();
    }
}
```

The function OnGUI works similarly to the Update function—it is called at least twice every game frame: once to draw the GUI elements on the screen, and then at least one more time to process any user input. In this example, a new button is drawn at the screen position (10,10) with a width of 320 pixels and a height of 80. The words "Quit Game" are displayed on the button. When the button is clicked, the GUI.Button function returns True, fulfilling the condition of the if statement, which then closes the current game.

Note

Any GUI element you want drawn to the screen *must* be called within the OnGUI function.

All of Unity's GUI controls follow this basic idea of evaluating the return Boolean of any given GUI interaction. The controls themselves are another basic pattern: control type (screen position, control content). The Type declares what kind of control you want (a button, slider, box, and so on), the screen position specifies in pixels where the control is to be displayed, and the content handles the actual visual display of the control.

Unity provides a range of prebuilt basic controls, but you can define your own custom controls using this simple process. You can follow along with the overview of the basic controls by navigating to the Chapter 13 folder on the DVD and opening the Chapter13_Test scene in the GUI Test folder.

Buttons

The first kind of control most people think of when asked about interfaces is the simple button. When users click the button, the button returns True, and some piece of code is executed.

```
if( GUI.Button(Rect(10, 10, 100, 40), "I'm a Button" ))
{
    print("You clicked the button.");
}
```

Regardless of how long the button is held down, the action executes only once, when the user finally releases the button. Besides simple text phrases, buttons can also take images and other complex content forms as arguments, allowing you to create skinned buttons with tooltips and other advanced functionality. Custom buttons like this are covered later in the chapter.

The Rect function defines a rectangular space that the button uses for its display, following the pattern of (left x corner, left y corner, total width, total height). This example button is defined at the space (10,10) and is 100 pixels wide by 40 pixels tall. The Rect function is used for all kinds of GUI controls.

Buttons can also be formatted as RepeatButtons, which will continuously fire as long as the user holds them down. Declaring and using a RepeatButton is done exactly like a normal button:

```
if( GUI.RepeatButton(Rect(10, 60, 200, 40), "I'm a Repeat Button" ))
{
    number = Time.deltaTime + number;
    print("You clicked the button for " + number + " seconds.");
}
```

These kinds of buttons are useful for powerups or anything else that the users need to time.

Sliders

Sliders are another popular form of basic control, and Unity provides you with a basic horizontal and vertical option. The current position of the slider knob is returned from the function as a float, allowing users to click and drag it to a new location.

```
slidervalue = GUI.HorizontalSlider( Rect(10, 110, 200, 40),
            slidervalue, 0.0, 100.0);
slidervalue = GUI.VerticalSlider ( Rect(240, 60 , 200, 60),
            slidervalue, 0.0, 100.0);
print("Slider value: " + slidervalue);
```

By setting the current value of the slider as the return value, the slider becomes interactive. If you didn't save the return value of either slider function, the user wouldn't be able to drag the slider around, making it more of a display than an interaction object.

Labels and Boxes

Besides these basic interactive controls, Unity also defines a set of basic labels and boxes, making it easy to group and manage your different GUI fields.

Labels are your most basic form of display, allowing you to show a line of text or a simple texture anywhere on the screen. Labels have no form of interaction and do not catch mouse clicks.

```
GUI.Label( Rect(10, 150, 200, 40), "I'm a simple label.");
```

To display a label with an image instead of text, simply replace the second argument with a link to a texture instead of providing a string.

A box is similar in nature to a label, but is used instead when you want to provide a bit more visual information for the players. The box is drawn with a default texture background, and the string is applied, much like the label.

```
GUI.Box( Rect(10, 200, 200, 40), "I'm a simple box.");
```

Boxes can also display textures, but are still static and shouldn't be confused with buttons. You can also stack boxes beneath buttons to make a defined button group, complete with a title label.

Text Entry

Sometimes you may want to capture user text input, like storing a custom name for a character. If the text to be entered is relatively short, you can use a one-line TextField for the job. If you think the users will need a bit of space to type (say, for a journal entry), use a TextArea instead.

```
shortText = GUI.TextField( Rect(10, 250, 200, 40), shortText);
longText = GUI.TextArea( Rect(10, 300, 200, 100), longText);
```

TextFields *only* allow one line of text, whereas TextAreas allow the users to enter newline carriage returns. Both text fields support copy and paste functionality. Much like the sliders, you need to return and save the string if you want the control to be interactive.

You can also specify a maximum string length for both kinds of text entries by adding an optional third integer argument to the text function:

```
shortText = GUI.TextField( Rect(10, 400, 200, 40), shortText, 40);
```

Unity will stop the users from entering any new text once the character length has been reached.

Toggle

While looking like a radio button, the Unity Toggle functions like a Boolean checkbox: click once to set it to True, and click again to set to False. The current status of the toggle is returned from the function and should be captured in order to make the control function.

```
toggleState = GUI.Toggle( Rect(10, 400, 200, 40),
            toggleState, "I'm a Toggle/Checkbox");
```

Clicking on either the box or phrase will activate the Toggle.

Toolbars and Selection Grids

Toolbars and selection grids are Unity's answer to the radio button—these compound controls allow users to choose between one of many states but only keep one active at any given time. A toolbar encapsulates a single row of options, whereas a selection grid allows you to create a matrix of options. A toolbar control is created with an array of either string or image variables, with each index of the array corresponding to a new button on the toolbar. The control's function returns the index of the selected button, which must be captured and stored for use.

```
var toolBarState = 0;
var toolBarLabels : String [] = ["Button 1", "Button 2", "Button 3"];
toolBarState = GUI.Toolbar( Rect(10, 450, 300, 40)
                toolBarState, toolBarLabels);
```

Selection grids are defined almost exactly the same, except you also need to specify how many columns you want the controls to span. In this example, only one column is used, creating in effect a vertical toolbar.

```
var selectionState = 1;
var selectionLabels : String[] = ["Button 1", "Button 2",
                    "Button 3", "Button 4", "Button 5"];
selectionState = GUI.SelectionGrid( Rect( Screen.width - 150, 10, 100, 300),
                    selectionState, selectionLabels, 1);
```

Note

While being able to switch between states is a great thing, you'll also probably want to know when a user actually clicks one of these kinds of buttons, or perhaps changes anything else on the GUI. Rather than checking manually every frame, you can make a simple call to the GUI.changed function. GUI.changed will return True anytime the user clicks a button, selects a box, enters text, or changes anything else on the interface.

Windows

The last basic control Unity provides is a bit more complex—a draggable window. These controls float above the other GUI controls and can be clicked to acquire focus. Besides being drawn themselves, windows also need to take a separate function as an argument, declaring what other kinds of controls and goodies should be displayed inside it. An empty window wouldn't be all that interesting.

```
var windowPosition = Rect(Screen.width - 100, Screen.height - 100, 200, 200);

function OnGUI(){
    windowPosition = GUI.Window(0, windowPosition,
                    MyWindowFunction, "My Window");

}
```

```
function MyWindowFunction(windowID : int)
{
    if( GUI.Button(Rect(10, 30, 180, 40), "I'm a Window Button" ))
    {
        print("You clicked the Window button");
    }
    if( GUI.Button(Rect(10, 90, 180, 40), "I'm also a Window Button" ))
    {
        print("You clicked the other Window button");
    }
    GUI.DragWindow (Rect (0,0,1000,1000));
}
```

Each window you create must be given a unique integer ID number, in this case, 0. An initial position is then specified, followed by the function detailing the contents of the window. Like other controls, windows can take a string label or an image to define its look.

The helper function MyWindowFunction defines the basic behavior of the window. In it are two simple buttons and the additional GUI element called DragWindow. Including the GUI.DragWindow function in your windows will allow them to be draggable—if you don't want this functionality, don't include it. The DragWindow function only needs a rectangle to define the space within the window that the user can click to drag. You may only want to make a title bar draggable, or perhaps you don't mind if the user can grab the entire window. If the rectangle you specify is larger than the window itself, it crops itself automatically to the size of the window.

All of these sample control examples are displayed in Figure 13.1 for reference.

With these basic controls under your belt, you're now ready to create your own custom GUI system.

Tip

If you want your GUI elements to show up in the editor without having to press Play, add this command to the button of any of your scripts:

```
@script ExecuteInEditMode()
```

Now the Game view will update live as you edit your GUI, without having to stop and play your scene every time you change something.

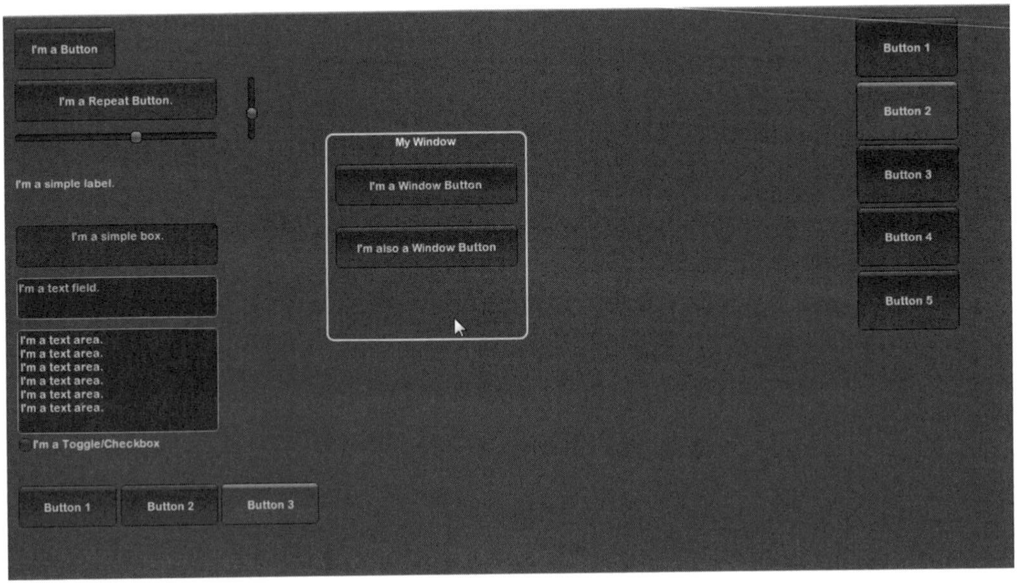

Figure 13.1
The basic Unity controls compared.

A Custom Skin for Widget

The default controls Unity offers come preskinned with a simple blue template, but this won't necessarily work with every game you make. Although you can customize each individual button or toggle as you come across them in your code, this can quickly get tedious and create lots of extra work. Unity provides you with the options of using GUIStyles and GUISkins to help push your workflow along at a speedy pace.

Applying a GUIStyle overrides the appearance of any default control and contains options like displayed texture image, text color, font, or even what highlights to use on a rollover. Defining a single style once and then applying it to multiple controls can save you hours of work. A GUIStyle applies to one type of control at a time, like a button or slider.

GUISkins take customization one step further—a skin is a collection of all the basic, default GUIStyles defined in Unity. Your game can handle more than one GUISkin at once (if you wanted to allow the users to pick their interface wrapper, for example), and you can even add your own custom styles to a GUISkin template. To illustrate, you'll make a new master GUISkin for *Widget*.

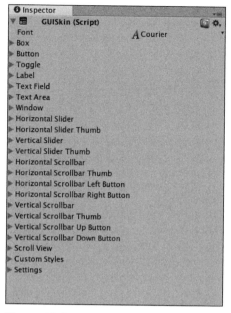

Figure 13.2
A default GUISkin.

Creating the GUISkin

Open your main *Widget* project's latest scene and save it as a new Chapter 13 scene. In the Project view, right-click and select Create▶GUI Skin. Place this new skin in a folder labeled GUI, making it easier to find later. Your new skin will look like Figure 13.2 upon inspection. Rename it something more meaningful, like **Widget_Skin**.

As you can see, the GUISkin lists all the major GUI controls, and then some. Each control listing is its own GUIStyle definition. If you expand any one of the controls, like Button, you can edit and create new default values for all the button's properties, like its hover image, border, font, or normal view. Any value you don't change in the skin reverts to Unity's default.

The Settings tab at the bottom of the list allows you to set some of the basic functionality for text manipulation: whether double-clicking selects a word, the cursor color, and cursor flash speed, to name a few.

The last point of interest in the skin is the Custom Styles tab. If you expand this section, you can enter a new size for the element, allowing you to create new control styles at will. If, for example, you create a new compound control for your game, you can define a default style for it here.

Defining Custom Styles

Defining a custom style is simple and follows the same steps as assigning a texture to a new material. To start, import all the GUI pieces on the DVD, Chapter 13▶GUI, and place these assets into the GUI folder in your project. In it you'll find a collection of buttons, window panels, and backdrops that match the *Widget* art style.

You can now start off by creating a simple, default button for the game:

1. Expand the Button selection on the GUISkin object you just created. Once inside the Button style, expand the Normal, Hover, and Active definitions for the button.

2. Drag (or select from the drop-down menu) the ShortButton_Up image found in the GUI▶Buttons folder into the Normal Background field. This will set all buttons to display this image.

3. Populate the Hover and Active Background fields with the ShortButton_Hover texture. This texture will make it look like the button "glows" when the users click or hover the mouse over it. Set all the text colors for the buttons to a black or dark color by clicking on the colored bar.

4. Farther down the list, change the Alignment setting to MiddleCenter, as you want any text to center along the entire length of the button. Your GUIStyle for the button should now look like Figure 13.3.

Using these simple steps, you can replace and customize any and all of the remaining GUIStyles in the skin.

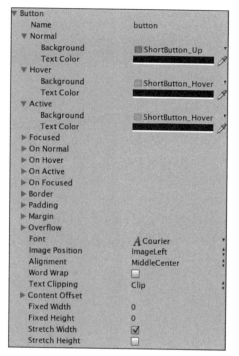

Figure 13.3
The completed GUIStyle.

Importing New Fonts

Besides importing new textures to use as backdrops for the controls, you can also import your own custom fonts. The default font may work well for your project (usually this is something like Courier or Arial), but odds are you're going to want to develop or use a font that defines your game's visual theme.

Unity can import and read any TrueType font. Although you may have hundreds of fonts already installed on your computer, Unity will *not* read these fonts automatically—a new font must be manually imported. Thousands of free fonts are also available for download on the Internet, and you may find something fitting there. Whichever the case, be sure you have the legal right and license to use a font before displaying it in your game.

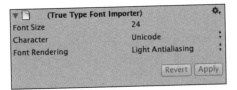

Figure 13.4
Unity's Font Importer.

The *Widget* game makes use of a custom, freeware font, available for download from Marco Rullkötter's site, Designer in Action: (http://www .designerinaction.de/fonts/detail.php?id=206). This is a condensed, futuristic-type font and goes well with the visual atmosphere of *Widget*. Follow these steps:

1. To continue, download the font from the link or copy the included font from the DVD, in the root of the Chapter 13 folder (078MKMC_ .ttf). Or, if you want to use a font already on your computer, locate it on your hard drive.

2. Drag the font onto the Project view to import it. Alternatively, you can copy and paste it directly into the Project folder. Once it's imported, click on it to display the properties in the Inspector, as shown in Figure 13.4.

3. Here you can change the font size, character coding, and how much anti-aliasing (if any) you want to apply to the font. Click on Apply to save any changes. For now, change the font size to 24.

4. Now you can apply this new font to the button style you just custom-ized. Reopen the GUISkin in the Inspector and change the button's font from Courier to the newly imported one.

If you wanted to change the font size of your text later, you'd need to go back in and change the master font file in the Inspector. However, this updates all cases of the font in the game, which may not be what you want. The easiest way to handle multiple font sizes is to create copies of any given font you want in the project, giving each a different default size. You can then easily assign the different font sizes to different GUIStyles, giving you more options. Try this by importing a second copy of the font (give it a different name like **078MKMC_small**) and changing its font size to 16. Assign this new font to the master font style in the GUISkin.

SETTING UP THE HUD

Now that you know how to create basic controls and define their styles in a skin, you're ready to start making the custom HUD (Heads Up Display) for the game.

Looking at the game design, you know you'll need to keep track of a few basic pieces of information for the player and display them when relevant. Primarily, you'll need to show:

- *Widget*'s current health and energy status
- The current health and energy of any enemy *Widget* encounters
- How many energy packs *Widget* has left
- How many health packs *Widget* has left
- How many screws and nuts he's collected on his journey (effectively the world's "cash" commodity)

You'll need to define custom controls for all of these pieces of information, as Unity's basic control options don't quite provide you with everything you'll need. The item displays will need to handle a combined picture of the object and text display of how many *Widget* has in his inventory, and the character displays will need to show both stats in real time plus a picture of the character in question. The inventory buttons can also handle click functionality, allowing the players to quickly use them directly from the main screen.

To start off, you'll make the custom inventory button for the item displays. Create a new JavaScript file in the Scripts directory and name it **GUI_Custom Controls**. All of the new controls will be stored in this directory, making them easier to reference in the future.

Delete the Update function and create a new function, as follows:

```
function InvoHudButton(screenPos: Rect, numAvailable :
            int, itemImage: Texture, itemtooltip: String ) : boolean
{
}
```

This new button, InvoHudButton, takes many of the same kinds of arguments as the normal Unity button but adds a few more for the advanced functionality. You also need to make sure that this function returns a Boolean value (as it is still a button), or else the user wouldn't be able to interact with it. First, you'll make the simple button part using a new GUI concept, called GUIContent.

GUIContent

GUIContent arguments can be used by most of Unity's basic controls and allow you to pass labels, images, and tooltips as one package to any control. The InvoHudButton will use GUIContent to handle the button's image and tooltip.

Inside the InvoHudButton function, add the following:

```
if( GUI.Button(screenPos, GUIContent(itemImage, itemtooltip), "HUD Button") )
{
        return true;
}
```

The first little bit should look familiar. First you call the normal GUI.Button function (placed inside the if conditional to allow interactivity) and give it a Rect screen position. The GUIContent argument then feeds in a display image and tooltip to the button. The last argument, HUD Button, may look like a normal button label, but it isn't—don't get this confused. If you want to pass a label, you need to include it in the GUIContent package. This last piece of information defines what GUIStyle the button should use. Any control can use an optional last argument to define a custom style. For now, finish the button and then go back and define the new HUD button style.

After this conditional, add a new label to display how many units you have of this current item:

```
GUI.Label( Rect(screenPos.xMax - 20, screenPos.yMax - 25, 20, 20 ),
                numAvailable.ToString() );
```

This Rect aligns the label to the bottom right of the whole button, using the larger master Rect as a reference. Lastly, you need to define the space where your tooltips will appear:

```
GUI.Label( Rect( 20, Screen.height - 130, 500, 100), GUI.tooltip);
```

All the InvoHudButton tooltips are now displayed in this one area of the screen.

Having finished the code definition, you need to define the visual style of your new button. Open the Widget_Skin GUISkin object in the Inspector and navigate down to Custom Styles. Increase the size of the object to 1, and name the newly created element **HUD Button**. This will now allow the script to reference this style.

Change the Normal Background field to ItemButtonBackUp and the Hover and Active Background fields to ItemButtonBackDown, both found in the GUI▶Buttons folder. Set the font to the small version of the imported custom font, and change Alignment to MiddleCenter. Change the font colors to white and uncheck Stretch Width. Your new style should now look like Figure 13.5.

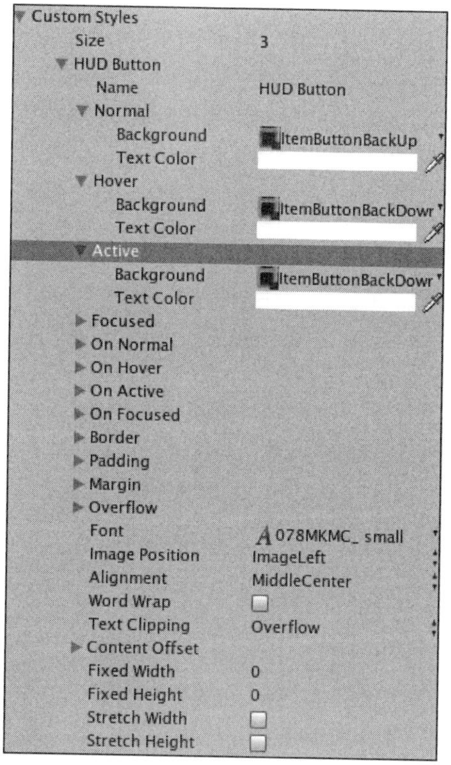

Figure 13.5
The finished custom style.

Now that your custom button's defined, you need to hook it up to the actual game. Follow these steps to do so:

1. Create a new JavaScript file in the Scripts directory and name it **GUI_ HUD**. Delete the Update function.

2. Create a new variable at the top of the script named **customSkin**—this will allow you to tell Unity to use your newly defined GUISkin and not the default one. Also create image variables to hold the special item textures you'll display on the buttons.

```
var customSkin: GUISkin;
var screwImage : Texture2D;
var gearImage : Texture2D;
var repairkitImage : Texture2D;
var energykitImage : Texture2D;
```

3. Next, create a new Awake function so you can cache some of *Widget*'s data up front. The InvoButton needs information stored in *Widget*'s inventory manager, so you'll need to link to it at startup:

```
private var customControls : GUI_CustomControls;
private var playerInvo : Widget_Inventory;

function Awake()
{
        customControls = FindObjectOfType(GUI_CustomControls);
        playerInvo = FindObjectOfType(Widget_Inventory);
}
```

4. With this set up, create the initial OnGUI function and set the GUIS-kin:

```
function OnGUI()
{
    if(customSkin)
        GUI.skin = customSkin;
}
```

5. If a GUISkin is defined in the Inspector for the script to use, all of its defined styles will replace those in the game. Pretty straightforward. Next you just need to write calls to the new custom button. In the OnGUI function, add the following:

```
//Inventory Buttons------------------------
if(customControls.InvoHudButton(Rect(10, Screen.height
        - 100, 93, 95), playerInvo.GetItemCount
        (InventoryItem.ENERGYPACK), energykitImage,
        "Click to use an Energy Pack."))
{
        playerInvo.UseItem(InventoryItem.ENERGYPACK, 1);
}
if(customControls.InvoHudButton(Rect(110, Screen.height
        - 100, 93, 95), playerInvo.GetItemCount
        (InventoryItem.REPAIRKIT), repairkitImage,
        "Click to use a Repair Kit."))
{
        playerInvo.UseItem(InventoryItem.REPAIRKIT, 1);
}
//Non-Usable Inventory Buttons---------------------
customControls.InvoHudButton(Rect(Screen.width - 210,
        Screen.height - 100, 93, 95),
        playerInvo.GetItemCount(InventoryItem.SCREW),
        screwImage, "Number of screws you've collected.");
customControls.InvoHudButton(Rect(Screen.width - 110 ,
        Screen.height - 100, 93, 95), playerInvo.GetItemCount
        (InventoryItem.NUT), gearImage, "Number of gears you've collected.");
```

This may look a little complicated, but just refer back to your InvoHudButton definition. First you define a rectangular space for the button to occupy and then pass it the number of items the player has in her inventory using the GetItemCount function. The overlay image of the item is then passed, followed by the tooltip. For the EnergyPack and RepairKit items, these are housed within an if conditional so the player can click them to use—the appropriate use function is called in each case (remember writing those back a few chapters ago?).

The SCREW and NUT displays don't need to function, so they are simply displayed outside of any if statement.

To see your new buttons in action, attach the GUI_Hud and GUI_CustomControls scripts to the Main Camera object. Populate the Inspector variables for the two scripts as follows:

- Custom Skin: Widget_Skin(GUISkin)
- Screw Image: Item_Overlay_1
- Gear Image: Item_Overlay_2
- RepairKit Image: Item_Overlay_4
- EnergyPack Image: Item_Overlay_3

The Item Overlay images can be found in the GUI▶Buttons folder. Once you're set up, press Play to see your new HUD in action, as shown in Figure 13.6.

Figure 13.6
The new custom buttons in action.

Try clicking on the RepairKit or EnergyPack button to see the number update live.

Note

If you ever have problems with mouse clicking on the buttons, go to Edit▶Project Settings▶Input and verify that mouse clicks aren't being used for any of the axes actions.

Character Displays

Now that the inventory buttons are functioning, you need to add the character displays for *Widget* and whatever enemy he may be facing. *Widget*'s display will need to always be displayed, so the player has tabs on his current health and energy stats. The enemy's status display, however, needs to be adjustable based upon whatever *Widget* is facing. It should appear only when *Widget* is close enough to notice the enemy and update accordingly with any enemy's specific information.

You'll begin with *Widget*'s display, since it's a little more straightforward.

Widget's Character Display

Open the GUI_CustomControls script again, as you'll be adding a new custom control to it. Create a new function called LeftStatusMeter, as follows:

```
function LeftStatusMeter(charImage : Texture, health :
                        float, energy : float, bBarImage : Texture,
                        hBarImage : Texture, eBarImage : Texture)
{
}
```

First up, the control gets a portrait of *Widget*, followed by his current health and energy stats. Next, three more images are loaded: two to handle the current health and energy display, and a third one to provide a nice frame. As you have so many pieces to organize, it's best to use a GUI group to help.

In the function, begin a new group as follows:

```
GUI.BeginGroup( Rect(0,0, 330, 125) );
```

GUI groups are basically large rectangular containers that can hold other kinds of GUI controls, making it easier to move them together en masse. Groups can also nest inside each other, allowing you to create table-like structures of controls. The rectangle defined in the group describes where everything inside the group will be shown on the screen.

Next, you need to create the back framing images of the control. Unity draws the controls onscreen as it comes to them in the code. Images that should be drawn first (and therefore placed in the back) should be listed first.

```
GUI.Label( Rect(40, 10, 272, 90), bBarImage );
```

This line creates a simple Label control using a texture. The rectangle defining this label does not use world coordinates. Instead, this rectangle is defined relative to that of the group.

With the frame in place, you can add the health and energy bars, each of which uses its own nested group.

```
GUI.BeginGroup( Rect(40, 10, 218 * (health/10.0) +35 , 90) );
GUI.Label( Rect(0, 0, 272, 90), hBarImage );
GUI.EndGroup();

GUI.BeginGroup( Rect( 40, 10, 218 * (energy/10.0) +10, 90) );
GUI.Label( Rect(0, 0, 272, 90), eBarImage );
GUI.EndGroup();
```

The rectangle for each subgroup is defined based upon *Widget*'s current health and energy, in effect, creating a moving status bar. The rectangle will clip and update every frame based upon his current vital stats. Full stats will display the bar's full length, whereas decreasing health or energy will shorten the bar.

Lastly, you just need to add another texture displaying *Widget*'s face, notifying the player that these stats belong to *Widget* and not someone else. You can also end the master group for the control:

```
GUI.Label( Rect(0, 0, 330, 125), charImage );
GUI.EndGroup();
```

Switching back to the GUI_HUD script, it's now time to implement it into the scene. Add some more variables to the file to help define the new images and information you'll need:

```
var lbarImage: Texture2D;
var lhbar :Texture2D;
```

```
var lebar : Texture2D;
var widgetImage : Texture2D;

private var playerInfo : Widget_Status;
```

Also add a new line to the Awake function to cache *Widget's* status manager:

```
playerInfo = FindObjectOfType(Widget_Status);
```

Now in the OnGUI function, you can call the new custom display.

```
customControls.LeftStatusMeter(widgetImage,
    playerInfo.health, playerInfo.energy,
    lbarImage, lhbar, lebar);
```

The control grabs *Widget's* current health and energy from the State Manager and populates the control with the proper textures. In the Inspector, assign the textures to GUI_HUD as follows:

- Lbar Image: LeftCornerBarsBack

- Lhbar: LeftCornerHealthBar

- Lebar: LeftCornerEnergyBar

- WidgetImage: WidgetCornerCircle

These images can be located in the GUI▶Panels folder. Play your game to see *Widget's* stats in action. Try using his boost power to see the energy decrease, or add your new enemy from Chapter 12 and allow her to bite *Widget* a few times to test the health decrease. Using the item buttons will now fill *Widget's* health or energy back up, too! See Figure 13.7.

The Enemy's Display Panel

The enemy's display panel follows much of the same format as *Widget's* but will require a little more set up as it needs to be dynamically shown. First up, you need to update your enemy's State Manager to house all the necessary information the display panel will need. Currently the E_Bunny from Chapter 12 has a health stat, but you'll need to add an energy stat and image variable.

Open the EBunny_Status script and add these two variables to the top:

```
var energy: float = 10.0;
var charImage : Texture2D;
```

Figure 13.7
It may be time for an energy pack soon.

Populate the charImage variable with the Enemy_Overlay_1 texture, found in the GUI▶Panels folder. From now on, each enemy *Widget* faces should have a health, energy, and character image variable in order to take advantage of the new display.

You'll also need to add a new accessor function to the enemy's status class, allowing you to grab and reference his image for later:

```
function GetCharImage(): Texture2D
{
    return charImage;
}
```

Next you need to update *Widget's* Attack controller to add some functionality for finding the closest enemy to him. The enemy display will pop up only for the closest enemy, and then only if she's within a certain range.

Open the Widget_AttackController script and add a new function and variables:

```
private var enemies : GameObject[] ;
function GetClosestEnemy() : GameObject
{
}
```

This will allow you to store a list of all current enemies in the scene. In the GetClosestEnemy function, define the enemy list and a few other helper variables:

```
enemies = GameObject.FindGameObjectsWithTag("Enemy");
var distanceToEnemy = Mathf.Infinity;
var wantedEnemy;
```

The Enemy variable is now populated with a list of all the objects in the scene tagged with the phrase Enemy. If you haven't yet, populate the scene with at least one E_Bunny and ensure that it's tagged with Enemy.

Now you can loop through this list of enemies and find which one is the closest to *Widget*. Starting like you did with a default distance equal to infinity (or in reality, a really, really big number) will make it easy to compare and find the closest one. Add to the function:

```
for (var enemy : GameObject in enemies)
    {
        newDistanceToEnemy = Vector3.Distance
            (enemy.transform.position, transform.position);
        if (newDistanceToEnemy < distanceToEnemy)
        {
            distanceToEnemy = newDistanceToEnemy;
            wantedEnemy = enemy;
        }
    }
return wantedEnemy;
```

After looping through all the enemies, you return the closest one. Save and close this file and return to the GUI_CustomControls script.

Writing the custom display control for the enemy panel is basically the same as the one for *Widget*'s, only the direction is reversed. The enemy's panel will be displayed in the top-right corner across from *Widget*'s, taking into account that the bars should move towards the right side of the screen, mirroring *Widget*'s.

Create the new control function:

```
function RightStatusMeter(charImage : Texture,
        health : float, energy : float, bBarImage :
        Texture, hBarImage : Texture, eBarImage :
        Texture, bCircleImage :Texture)
{
    GUI.BeginGroup( Rect(Screen.width - 330,0, 330, 125) );}
```

Next create the bar groups for the enemy's health and energy:

```
GUI.Label( Rect(40, 10, 272, 90), bBarImage );

GUI.BeginGroup( Rect(40 + (218-218*(health/10.0)),
                10, 218*(health/10.0), 90) );
GUI.Label( Rect(0, 0, 272, 90), hBarImage );
GUI.EndGroup();

GUI.BeginGroup( Rect( 40 + (218-218*(energy/10.0)), 10,
                218*(energy/10.0), 90) );
GUI.Label( Rect(0, 0, 272, 90), eBarImage );
GUI.EndGroup();
```

All you have left to do is add a blank circle frame and then an overlay for whichever current enemy *Widget* is facing:

```
GUI.Label( Rect(208, 0, 330, 125), bCircleImage );
GUI.Label( Rect(208, 0, 330, 125), charImage );


GUI.EndGroup();
```

Calling this new control in the GUI_HUD script will require a little bit of extra work as well. You want the display to appear only when there is an enemy in the scene and only when she's close enough to *Widget* to be an immediate threat. Add some variables to the GUI_HUD script to help out with this:

```
var rbarImage: Texture2D;
var rhbar :Texture2D;
var rebar : Texture2D;
var enemyImage : Texture2D;
var circBackImage : Texture2D;
private var playerAttack : Widget_AttackController;
private var closestEnemyStatus ;
private var player;
```

```
var closestEnemy;
var enemyDistance;
```

Then set up the necessary links in the Awake function:

```
playerAttack = FindObjectOfType(Widget_AttackController);
player = GameObject.FindWithTag("Player");
```

Now in the OnGUI function, you need to determine whether the display should be shown, and if so, what to populate it with.

```
closestEnemy = playerAttack.GetClosestEnemy();
if (closestEnemy != null)
{
    enemyDistance = Vector3.Distance
                    (closestEnemy.transform.position,
                    player.transform.position);
    if(enemyDistance < 20.0)
    {
        closestEnemyStatus = closestEnemy.GetComponent(EBunny_Status);
        enemyImage = closestEnemyStatus.GetCharImage();
        customControls.RightStatusMeter(enemyImage,
            closestEnemyStatus.health, closestEnemyStatus.energy,
            rbarImage, rhbar, rebar, circBackImage);
    }
}
```

So first you find the closest enemy to the player. If such an enemy exists, the distance is then computed. If the enemy is deemed to be close enough (under 20 meters in this case), the enemy's status is grabbed, and the new custom control is populated with his information.

In the Inspector, set up the new HUD variables as follows:

- Rbar Image: RightCornerBarsBack
- Rhbar: RightCornerHealthBar
- Rebar: RightCornerEnergyBar
- Circ Back Image: RightCornerCircle

All of these images can also be found in the GUI▶Panels folder. Leave the Enemy Image field blank since it's populated on the fly when you need it. Try your new enemy display and take down that bunny. See Figure 13.8.

Figure 13.8
Battle of the bots has begun.

Resolution

Although you have been docking all your UI images to the sides of the screen, allowing them to be sized somewhat dynamically, early on in your development you should decide what your game's resolution will be. Some games (especially browser-based ones) allow for one specified resolution, whereas others allow the players to pick one of many options.

Widget will officially support only the standalone app's default size of 1024×768, and all the control images have been authored to that exact size. If you want to support different screen resolutions, you should either ensure that your UI is small enough to fit on the lowest resolution or create multiple UI art packs.

The latter option is more time consuming, but it does create a more professional package in the end. Thankfully, with Unity's GUISkins, it's also not that hard to implement. Basically, you need to create a new GUISkin for each supported resolution, populating the styles with the correct version of each control's image. Then upon startup when the players select their resolution preference, you simply load the GUISkin variable with the correct option.

Now would also be a good time to change your game's test resolution to the supported 1024 × 768 setting (found on the Game tab in the top-left corner) to best view the UI images at their proper resolution.

A Sample Pop-up Screen

The HUD is coming along nicely now, but what if you wanted to add some dynamic pop-ups to the scene, based upon what the player was doing? You can try this by adding a storefront functionality to the CheckPoint prefab object you've already made. While standing on the checkpoint platform, *Widget* can receive a notification that he can begin shopping at the robot's latest, greatest, and classiest boutique if he so wishes. By clicking a button that appears, the player can open and close the store at will.

First you need to make a new script to handle the actual store display. Make a new JavaScript file in the Scripts directory and name it **GUI_WaypointStore**. Add some basic variables to handle the GUI images and player information:

```
var storeBG : Texture2D;
var customSkin: GUISkin;

private var playerInventory : Widget_Inventory;
private var openStore = false;
```

You'll need to link to the player's inventory and also keep track of whether the storefront is currently open or closed. Delete the Update function and add a new Awake function, linking the inventory to the script:

```
function Awake(){
    playerInventory = FindObjectOfType(Widget_Inventory);
    if (!playerInventory)
        Debug.Log("No link to player's inventory.");

}
```

Now you just need to determine when to display the store window. Create a new OnGUI function and link the custom skin to it:

```
function OnGUI()
{
    if(customSkin)
        GUI.skin = customSkin;
}
```

Inside the OnGUI function, add an if statement that displays the store images only if openStore = true:

```
if(openStore)
{
    GUI.Box(Rect(0,0,Screen.width, Screen.height), " ");
    GUI.Label(Rect(Screen.width/2 - storeBG.width/2,
            Screen.height/2- storeBG.height/2, storeBG.width,
            storeBG.height ), storeBG);

    if(GUI.Button(Rect(Screen.width/2 -126 , Screen.height
            - 100 , 252, 113), "Close  Store")){
        StoreFrontToggle();
    }
}
```

The label handles the actual store display, and the button appears to toggle the store on and off. The box creates a dark backdrop across the entire screen, dimming the rest of the game while the player is in the store.

All that's left to do is to create the StoreFrontToggle helper function and add an accessor function for the status of the store:

```
function StoreFrontToggle()
{
    if(openStore == false)
        openStore = true;
    else openStore = false;
}

function GetStoreStatus(){
    return openStore;
}
```

Open the GUISkin in the Inspector so you can set up the default box. Open the box style and assign the DarkenScreen image to the Normal Background field, found in the GUI▸Backdrops folder. This small, tileable image places a light gray overlay across the entire field of the Box control. Ensure also that the DarkenScreen image was imported with DXT5 compression, to preserve the alpha channel. Otherwise the image will appear opaque black.

Assign the Store BG variable from the GUI_WaypointStore script the Inventory Screen_bg file (found in the GUI▸Panels folder). Populate the Custom Skin variable with the Widget_Skin (GUISkin) object. Attach this script to the CheckPoint prefab.

The last little step to get the store operational is to create the WaypointBehavior script. Create a new JavaScript file and name it **WaypointBehavior**—this will handle the actual GUI implementation of the robot checkpoints. This could be incorporated into the original CheckPoint script, but I prefer to keep it separate, in case one of the two systems needs a drastic change.

Delete the provided Update function and add this to the file:

```
var customSkin: GUISkin;
private var isTriggered  = false;
```

Next you need to set up two simple triggers to determine if *Widget* has entered the waypoint, and not some random enemy. Add these two new functions to the script:

```
function OnTriggerEnter(collider: Collider){

    //make sure that this is a player hitting the platform and not an enemy
    var playerStatus : Widget_Status = collider.GetComponent(Widget_Status);
    if(playerStatus == null) return;

    isTriggered = true;

}


function OnTriggerExit(collider: Collider){

    //make sure that this is a player leaving the platform and not an enemy
    var playerStatus : Widget_Status = collider.GetComponent(Widget_Status);
```

```
        if(playerStatus == null) return;

        isTriggered = false;

}
```

Now you only need to hook up the GUI bits to make the store operational. Continuing in the script, add to the bottom a new function:

```
function OnGUI()
{
    if(customSkin)
        GUI.skin = customSkin;
}
```

Since you've already got a variable in place tracking whether the player is triggering the waypoint, hooking up the store button trigger is easy. Add to the OnGUI function:

```
if(isTriggered)
{
    var store = this.GetComponent(GUI_WaypointStore);

    //Display open button only if store is currently closed
    if( !store.GetStoreStatus() )
    {
        if(GUI.Button(Rect(Screen.width/2 -126 ,
            Screen.height - 100 , 252, 113), "Open  Store"))
        {
            store.StoreFrontToggle();
        }
    }
}
```

If the player is currently standing on the checkpoint, and the store isn't already opened, an Open Store button will appear on the screen, allowing the player to bring up the pop-up at will. Save the script and attach it to your CheckPoint prefab, populating the CustomSkin variable with your *Widget* GUI Skin. Figure 13.9 shows the empty storefront in all its glory.

From here, you can populate the storefront with any kind of button or list you want. Perhaps a nice window or two would make it easy to use the same basic functionality while easily switching stock between different stores.

Figure 13.9
Open for business.

ADDING FULL-SCREEN MENUS

One other kind of UI option available is a full-screen menu, useful for such things as pause screens and main menus. Although these can be created inline in the current scene, some full-screen menus function better as their own unique scene files. To try this out, you'll make a main menu screen for the *Widget* game and allow the player to click a button to start.

Save your current scene and create a new empty one, naming it **Chapter13_ MainMenu**. The only object you need in here is the Main Camera; delete anything else. With the camera selected, change the background color in the Inspector to a dark black color. The default blue is a little much for the main menu. Now if you preview your scene, you're met with a nice blank canvas, perfect for putting main interface elements on.

Create a new JavaScript file in the Scripts folder and name it **GUI_MainMenu**. Delete the Update function, as normal. For the main menu, you'll need to link to your custom skin and then provide a link to a title and background image. Create some new variables at the top of the file:

```
var customSkin: GUISkin;
var mainMenuBG : Texture2D;
var mainTitle : Texture2D;
```

You should also create one more variable, a Boolean, to track whether the game is currently loading. Otherwise, the player may think the game is just hanging if he clicks on the load game button and nothing happens.

```
private var isLoading : boolean;
```

In a new OnGUI function, make a link to the custom skin:

```
function OnGUI()
{
    if(customSkin)
        GUI.skin = customSkin;
}
```

Now create another dark box to hide the screen (just in case) and a label to display the splash image and title.

```
GUI.Box(Rect( 0, 0, Screen.width, Screen.height), " ");
GUI.Label(Rect( 0, 30, Screen.width, Screen.height), mainMenuBG);
GUI.Label(Rect(Screen.width - 500, 50, mainTitle.width,
               mainTitle.height), mainTitle);
```

All that's left to add is the two buttons: one to load the game and one to quit out of the application. Because these buttons are going to be a whole lot bigger, you'll also need to define a new button style in the custom skin.

Follow these steps to create a new button style:

1. In the Widget_Skin object, create a new custom style by increasing the size count, and name it **Long Button**.

2. Expand the Normal, Hover, and Active fields, setting Normal Background with the LongButton_Up file and the Hover and Active

> Background fields with LongButton_Hover. Both of these textures can be found in the GUI▶Buttons folder.
>
> 3. Change the Alignment to MiddleCenter and place the larger of your two font files in the Font field.

Back in the GUI_MainMenu file, create the two buttons in the OnGUI function:

```
if(GUI.Button( Rect(Screen.width - 380, Screen.height - 280,
            320, 80), "Start Game", "Long Button") )
{
    isLoading = true;
    Application.LoadLevel("Chapter_13");
}

if(GUI.Button( Rect(Screen.width - 380, Screen.height - 180,
            320, 80), "Quit Game", "Long Button") )
{
    Application.Quit();
}
```

The Application class is a special class used to access and control runtime data, like whether to quit the game or load a specific scene. It will be covered in greater detail in Chapter 18, but for now you'll use these two simple functions.

The last thing you should add to the menu is a small text popup letting the players know the game is loading. In the OnGUI function, add the following:

```
if (isLoading)
{
    GUI.Label( Rect(Screen.width/2 - 50, Screen.height - 40,
            100, 50), "Now Loading");
}
```

Once the player clicks the Loading button, this conditional will begin to fire, and a Now Loading tag will display at the bottom of the screen. To make it easier for testing, add the customary script tags at the bottom of the file:

```
@script ExecuteInEditMode()
@script AddComponentMenu("GUI/MainMenu")
```

Note

Beyond starting up the Loading string, these buttons will not function as expected yet, yielding an assert in the Debug Console. Before you can load different levels in the application, they need to be set up in the build. This is covered in full in Chapter 18.

To see your main menu in action, attach it to the Main Camera already populating the scene and set up the texture variables as follows:

- Main Menu BG: MainMenu_SplashScreen
- Main Title: WidgetTitle

These two new textures can be found in the GUI▸panels and GUI▸backdrops folders. The finished main menu with the loading tag active is displayed in Figure 13.10.

Figure 13.10
Now loading, or will be shortly.

You're now ready to make custom interfaces of your own. By combining small and simple controls, it's possible to create complex UI pieces capable of displaying any kind of information you could want.

In its current state, the *Widget* game is mostly playable from a system's point of view and is only lacking in expanded content and polish. Moving forward, you'll look at how to add those last little bits of extra shine, such as lighting, particle effects, and sound.

COMPLETED AND UPDATED SCRIPTS

The newly completed and updated scripts are also available on the DVD in the Chapter 13 folder.

GUI_CustomControls.js

```
//GUI_CustomControls:   Contains the custom compound control
//classes for use elsewhere in the GUI_CustomControls


//Item HUD Button-----------------------------------------
//Displays the button, correct overlay item picture, and the
// number of the item currently in Widget's Invo.
function InvoHudButton(screenPos: Rect, numAvailable :
        int, itemImage: Texture, itemtooltip: String ) : boolean
{
    if( GUI.Button(screenPos, GUIContent(itemImage,
                  itemtooltip), "HUD Button") )
        return true;
    GUI.Label( Rect(screenPos.xMax - 20, screenPos.yMax - 25,
              20, 20 ), numAvailable.ToString() );

    //display area for tooltips
    GUI.Label( Rect( 20, Screen.height - 130, 500, 100), GUI.tooltip);
}
//Left Hand Health----------------------------------------
function LeftStatusMeter(charImage : Texture, health :
                        float, energy : float, bBarImage : Texture,
                        hBarImage : Texture, eBarImage : Texture)
{
    GUI.BeginGroup( Rect(0,0, 330, 125) );
```

```
    //Place Back Bars
    GUI.Label( Rect(40, 10, 272, 90), bBarImage );

    //Place Front Bars
    GUI.BeginGroup( Rect(40, 10, 218 * (health/10.0) +35 , 90) );
    GUI.Label( Rect(0, 0, 272, 90), hBarImage );
    GUI.EndGroup();

    GUI.BeginGroup( Rect( 40, 10, 218 * (energy/10.0) +10, 90) );
    GUI.Label( Rect(0, 0, 272, 90), eBarImage );
    GUI.EndGroup();

    //Place Head Circle
    GUI.Label( Rect(0, 0, 330, 125), charImage );

    GUI.EndGroup();


}
//Right Hand Health----------------------------------
function RightStatusMeter(charImage : Texture, health :
                          float, energy : float, bBarImage :
                          Texture, hBarImage : Texture, eBarImage :
                          Texture, bCircleImage :Texture)
{
    GUI.BeginGroup( Rect(Screen.width - 330,0, 330, 125) );

    //Place Back Bars
    GUI.Label( Rect(40, 10, 272, 90), bBarImage );

    //Place Front Bars
    GUI.BeginGroup( Rect(40 + (218-218*(health/10.0)),
                    10, 218*(health/10.0), 90) );
    GUI.Label( Rect(0, 0, 272, 90), hBarImage );
    GUI.EndGroup();

    GUI.BeginGroup( Rect( 40 + (218-218*(energy/10.0)), 10,
                    218*(energy/10.0), 90) );
    GUI.Label( Rect(0, 0, 272, 90), eBarImage );
    GUI.EndGroup();
```

```
        //Place Back Circle
        GUI.Label( Rect(208, 0, 330, 125), bCircleImage );

        //Place Head Circle
        GUI.Label( Rect(208, 0, 330, 125), charImage );

        GUI.EndGroup();
    }
    @script AddComponentMenu("GUI/CustomControls")
```

GUI_HUD.js

```
//GUI_HUD: displays the pertinent information for Widget,
//his items, and any current enemy
//Set up Textures--------------------------------------
//For larger games, this should be done programmatically
var customSkin: GUISkin;

var screwImage : Texture2D;
var gearImage : Texture2D;
var repairkitImage : Texture2D;
var energykitImage : Texture2D;

//Left Vital Tex
var lbarImage: Texture2D;
var lhbar :Texture2D;
var lebar : Texture2D;
var widgetImage : Texture2D;

//Right Vital Tex
var rbarImage: Texture2D;
var rhbar :Texture2D;
var rebar : Texture2D;
var enemyImage : Texture2D;
var circBackImage : Texture2D;


//----------------------------------------------------
private var customControls : GUI_CustomControls;
private var playerInfo : Widget_Status;
private var playerInvo : Widget_Inventory;
private var playerAttack : Widget_AttackController;
```

```
private var closestEnemyStatus ;
private var player;

var closestEnemy;
var enemyDistance;

//Initialize Player info-------------------------------------
function Awake()
{
    playerInfo = FindObjectOfType(Widget_Status);
    customControls = FindObjectOfType(GUI_CustomControls);
    playerInvo = FindObjectOfType(Widget_Inventory);
    playerAttack = FindObjectOfType(Widget_AttackController);
    player = GameObject.FindWithTag("Player");
}

//Display----------------------------------------------------
function OnGUI()
{
    if(customSkin)
        GUI.skin = customSkin;

    //Widget's Vitals
    customControls.LeftStatusMeter(widgetImage,
                        playerInfo.health, playerInfo.energy,
                        lbarImage, lhbar, lebar);

    //Inventory Buttons-----------------------------------------
    if(customControls.InvoHudButton(Rect(10, Screen.height - 100,
                        93, 95), playerInvo.GetItemCount
                        (InventoryItem.ENERGYPACK),
                         energykitImage,
                        "Click to use an Energy Pack."))
    {
        playerInvo.UseItem(InventoryItem.ENERGYPACK, 1);
    }
    if(customControls.InvoHudButton(Rect(110, Screen.height - 100,
                        93, 95), playerInvo.GetItemCount
                        (InventoryItem.REPAIRKIT),
```

```
                                          repairkitImage,
                                          "Click to use a Repair Kit."))
        {
            playerInvo.UseItem(InventoryItem.REPAIRKIT, 1);
        }
        //Non-Usable Inventory Buttons----------------------------------
        customControls.InvoHudButton(Rect(Screen.width - 210,
                                Screen.height - 100, 93, 95),
                                playerInvo.GetItemCount(InventoryItem.SCREW),
                                screwImage, "Number of screws you've
                                collected.");
        customControls.InvoHudButton(Rect(Screen.width - 110 , Screen.height - 100,
                                93, 95), playerInvo.
                                GetItemCount(InventoryItem.NUT), gearImage,
                                "Number of gears you've collected.");


        //Enemy Vitals
        closestEnemy = playerAttack.GetClosestEnemy();
        if (closestEnemy != null)
        {
            enemyDistance = Vector3.Distance(closestEnemy.
                            transform.position, player.transform.position);
            if(enemyDistance < 20.0)
            {
                closestEnemyStatus = closestEnemy.GetComponent(EBunny_Status);
                enemyImage = closestEnemyStatus.GetCharImage();
                customControls.RightStatusMeter(enemyImage, closestEnemyStatus.
                            health, closestEnemyStatus.energy, rbarImage,
                            rhbar, rebar, circBackImage);
            }
        }
    }
}
@script ExecuteInEditMode()
@script AddComponentMenu("GUI/HUD")
```

Widget_Attack_Controller.js

```
//Widget_AttackController:   handles the player's attack input
//and deals damage to the targeted enemy

//------------------------------------------------------------
var attackHitTime = 0.2;
var attackTime = 0.5;
var attackPosition = new Vector3 (0, 1, 0);
var attackRadius = 2.0;
var damage= 1.0;

//------------------------------------------------------------
private var busy = false;
private var ourLocation;
private var enemies : GameObject[] ;

var controller : Widget_Controller;
controller = GetComponent(Widget_Controller);

//Allow the player to attack if he is not busy and the
//Attack button was pressed
function Update ()
{
    if(!busy && Input.GetButtonDown ("Attack") && controller.IsGrounded()
            && !controller.IsMoving())
    {
        DidAttack();
        busy = true;
    }
}

function DidAttack ()
{
    //Play the animation regardless of whether we hit something or not.
    animation.CrossFadeQueued("Taser", 0.1, QueueMode.PlayNow);
    yield WaitForSeconds(attackHitTime);

    ourLocation = transform.TransformPoint(attackPosition);
    enemies = GameObject.FindGameObjectsWithTag("Enemy");
    //See if any enemies are within range of the attack.
```

```
    //This will hit all in range.
    for (var enemy : GameObject in enemies)
    {
        var enemyStatus = enemy.GetComponent(EBunny_Status);
        if (enemyStatus == null)
        {
            continue;
        }

        if (Vector3.Distance(enemy.transform.position,
            ourLocation) < attackRadius)
        {
            enemyStatus.ApplyDamage(damage);
        }
    }
    yield WaitForSeconds(attackTime - attackHitTime);
    busy = false;
}


function GetClosestEnemy() : GameObject
{
    enemies = GameObject.FindGameObjectsWithTag("Enemy");
    var distanceToEnemy = Mathf.Infinity;
    var wantedEnemy;

    for (var enemy : GameObject in enemies)
        {
            newDistanceToEnemy = Vector3.Distance(enemy.transform.
                                  position, transform.position);
            if (newDistanceToEnemy < distanceToEnemy)
            {
                distanceToEnemy = newDistanceToEnemy;
                wantedEnemy = enemy;
            }
        }
    return wantedEnemy;
}


@script AddComponentMenu("Player/Widget's Attack Controller")
```

EBunny_Status.js

```
//EBunny_Status:   controls the state information of the enemy bunny


//---------------------------------------------------------
var health: float = 10.0;
var energy: float = 10.0;
private var dead = false;

var charImage : Texture2D;

//PickupItems held----------------------------------------
var numHeldItemsMin = 1;
var numHeldItemsMax = 3;
var pickup1: GameObject;
var pickup2: GameObject;

//State Functions-----------------------------------------
function ApplyDamage(damage: float){

    if (health <= 0)
        return;

    health -= damage;

    animation.Play("EBunny_Hit");

    //check health and call Die if need to
    if(!dead && health <= 0)
    {
        health = 0; //for GUI
        dead = true;
        Die();
    }
}

function Die ()
{
    animation.Stop();
    animation.Play("EBunny_Death");
```

```
        Destroy(gameObject.GetComponent(EBunny_AIController));
        yield WaitForSeconds(animation["EBunny_Death"].length - 0.5);

        //Cache location of dead body for pickups
        var itemLocation = gameObject.transform.position;

        // drop a random number of reward pickups for the player
        yield WaitForSeconds(0.5);

        var rewardItems = Random.Range(numHeldItemsMin, numHeldItemsMax) + 1;

    for (var i = 0; i < rewardItems; i++)
        {

            var randomItemLocation = itemLocation;
            randomItemLocation.x += Random.Range(-2, 2);
            randomItemLocation.y += 1; // Keep it off the ground
            randomItemLocation.z += Random.Range(-2, 2);

            if (Random.value > 0.5)
                Instantiate(pickup1, randomItemLocation,
                            pickup1.transform.rotation);
            else
                Instantiate(pickup2, randomItemLocation,
                            pickup2.transform.rotation);
    }

        //Remove killed enemy from the scene
        Destroy(gameObject);
}

function IsDead() : boolean
{
    return dead;
}
function GetCharImage(): Texture2D
{
    return charImage;
}


@script AddComponentMenu("Enemies/Bunny'sStateManager")
```

GUI_WaypointStore.js

```
//GUI_WaypointStore : handles the interface for the store transactions
//shows the available items for purchase, allows the player
//to sell his own inventory and buy transforms

var storeBG : Texture2D;
var customSkin: GUISkin;

private var playerInventory : Widget_Inventory;
private var openStore = false;


//-------------------------------------------------------------
function Awake(){
    playerInventory = FindObjectOfType(Widget_Inventory);
    if (!playerInventory)
        Debug.Log("No link to player's inventory.");

}


//enable and disable script as needed----------------------
function OnGUI(){
    if(customSkin)
        GUI.skin = customSkin;

    if(openStore){
        GUI.Box(Rect(0,0,Screen.width, Screen.height), " ");
        GUI.Label(Rect(Screen.width/2 - storeBG.width/2,
                Screen.height/2- storeBG.height/2, storeBG.width,
                storeBG.height ), storeBG);

        if(GUI.Button(Rect(Screen.width/2 -126 , Screen.height - 100 ,
                        252, 113), "Close   Store")){
            StoreFrontToggle();
        }
    }
}

function StoreFrontToggle(){
```

```
        if(openStore == false)
            openStore = true;
        else openStore = false;
    }


function GetStoreStatus(){
    return openStore;
}
@script AddComponentMenu("GUI/Store")
```

WaypointBehavior.js

```
//WaypointBehavior:   Handles the scripts on all the waypoints
// Gives the player the option of
//opening the store or not.
var customSkin: GUISkin;
private var isTriggered   = false;

function OnTriggerEnter(collider: Collider){

    //make sure that this is a player hitting the platform and not an enemy
    var playerStatus : Widget_Status = collider.GetComponent(Widget_Status);
    if(playerStatus == null) return;

    isTriggered = true;

    playerStatus.energy = playerStatus.maxEnergy;
    playerStatus.health = playerStatus.maxHealth;

}

function OnTriggerExit(collider: Collider){

    //make sure that this is a player leaving the platform and not an enemy
    var playerStatus : Widget_Status = collider.GetComponent(Widget_Status);
    if(playerStatus == null) return;

    isTriggered = false;
}

function OnGUI(){
```

```
    if(customSkin)
        GUI.skin = customSkin;

    if(isTriggered)
    {
        var store = this.GetComponent(GUI_WaypointStore);

        //Only display open button if store is currently closed
        if( !store.GetStoreStatus() )
        {
            if(GUI.Button(Rect(Screen.width/2 -126 ,
                        Screen.height - 100 , 252, 113), "Open  Store")){
                store.StoreFrontToggle();
            }
        }
    }
}
@script AddComponentMenu("GUI/WaypointGUI")
```

GUI_MainMenu.js

```
//GUI_MainMenu:  adds the backdrop and main navigation buttons to the scene.
//This scene will be the first thing the app loads and
//will allow the player to pick a level to load or quit.

var customSkin: GUISkin;
var mainMenuBG : Texture2D;
var mainTitle : Texture2D;
private var isLoading : boolean;

//Main Menu-------------------------------------------------------
function OnGUI()
{
    if(customSkin)
        GUI.skin = customSkin;

    //BG Images
    GUI.Box(Rect( 0, 0, Screen.width, Screen.height), " ");
    GUI.Label(Rect( 0, 30, Screen.width, Screen.height), mainMenuBG);
```

```
    //Title and Buttons
    GUI.Label(Rect(Screen.width - 500, 50, mainTitle.width,
            mainTitle.height), mainTitle);

    if(GUI.Button(Rect(Screen.width - 380, Screen.height - 280,
                320, 80), "Start Game", "Long Button") )
    {
        isLoading = true;
        Application.LoadLevel("Chapter_13");
    }

    if(GUI.Button( Rect(Screen.width - 380, Screen.height - 180,
                320, 80), "Quit Game", "Long Button") )
    {
        Application.Quit();
    }

    //If game is currently loading, display a notification to the user
    if (isLoading)
    {
        GUI.Label( Rect(Screen.width/2 - 50, Screen.height - 40, 100, 50),
                    "Now Loading");
    }
}
@script ExecuteInEditMode()
@script AddComponentMenu("GUI/MainMenu")
```

PART IV

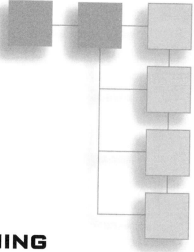

POLISH AND THE FINISHING TOUCHES

All the remains now for your game is to add some artistic and audio refinements. Although technically playable at this stage, some important feedback systems and ambience are still missing. Chapters 14 and 16 will take a look at boosting the world's atmosphere with the addition of environment lights and sound effects, and Chapter 15 will help provide some extra feedback for the player's attacks and movements by employing particle systems.

CHAPTER 14

CREATING LIGHTING AND SHADOWS

Although it's easy to add some quick working lighting to any given scene, lights are one of the most important parts to get right when trying to set a mood. A small change in the temperature of a light can make a scene seem inviting and open or dark and sinister. Lights can also be used in a more gameplay-oriented facility. Lights and shadows can be used to guide a player down particular paths, illuminate an important object, or draw attention to an often-overlooked detail. Lights can make your textures look dull and flat or bring out all the little details in your world and make it come to life.

TYPES OF LIGHTS

Unity comes packaged with three kinds of lights, each simulating a common source of light in the real world—directional, point, and spotlight.

- *Directional lights* function similar to the sun; they simulate a large, distant light source that points in one direction. Everything in the scene is illuminated from this light in the same manner, and any shadows cast would follow the same path. A combination of directional lights can quickly illuminate an entire scene, but they can also blow some details out or light some areas that you wanted to remain hidden.

- *Point lights* function like a common light bulb—they emit light from a central point outwards in a sphere. The light can either taper off naturally or be made to stop on a hard line.

The size of the sphere of influence can change, and only the objects within the point light's radius will be affected by the light.

▪ *Spotlights* function exactly like their namesake. Light is emitted from a defined point outwards in one direction, taking the shape of a cone. The light also can taper off naturally, and the angle of the spot's cone can be changed.

Although this may not seem like a great number of different possibilities to play with, once you begin to mix different kinds of lights (and their shadow effects) together, just about any lighting effect is possible. Figure 14.1 demonstrates some of the possibilities available with just the simple lights.

Figure 14.1
Different base lighting effects.

To add a light to a scene, from the main menu go to GameObject▶Create Other and select the desired light from the list. Open Unity and add any light to a scene. Click on it to view its properties in the Inspector.

Light Properties

Light properties dictate the size, intensity, color (or temperature), and angle of a light. Properties can also change any cast shadows or add special effects like halos or lens flares. All lights have the same basic list of properties, as shown in Figure 14.2.

- **Type:** This property changes what kind of light is being emitted. You can select from the drop-down menu the three different lights available.

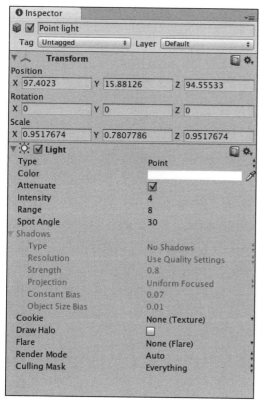

Figure 14.2
Light properties.

Doing so will not overwrite any other properties you have set, so it can be a quick way to test different options if you're unsure of what kind of light to use.

- **Color:** Changes the emitted color of the light. This can be extremely useful for setting a particular mood or achieving a special effect.

- **Attenuate:** Makes the light taper off naturally to its given range value. This value does not change the light emitted from a directional light.

- **Intensity:** Determines how "bright" the light is.

- **Range:** For point lights and spotlights, this dictates how far away the light is emitted from the central point. This also has no effect on the directional light.

- **Spot Angle:** For the spotlight only, this changes the activated angle of the emitted light. A smaller number will create a clean, pointed cone of light, while a larger one will illuminate a larger area.

- **Shadows:** Shadows are only available in Unity Pro and will be dimmed out (as shown in Figure 14.2) in the free version of the software. If you do have access to shadows, these options will describe how any object affected by this light casts a shadow.

- **Type:** Choose Hard or Soft from the drop-down menu, describing the kind of line the shadow casts onto other objects. Soft shadows often look more realistic but are more expensive to draw.

- **Resolution:** The detail level of the shadow cast. High will have smoother, more accurate lines, whereas the lowest option may look more blobby but will be faster to render.

- **Strength:** How "dark" the shadow is. Smaller numbers (closer to 0) will cast a more transparent and light shadow, whereas numbers closer to 1 will be very dark and opaque.

- **Projection:** For directional lights only, this describes how the shadows should be cast.

- **Constant Bias and Object Size:** Neither of these options is available for point lights. These options apply the bias in world units as well as any bias applied for the casting object's size.

- **Cookie:** Cookies are textures assigned to lights to create the illusion of more complex lighting rigs or to apply special effects (more on these later in the chapter). Directional and spotlights use a 2D texture, whereas point lights need a cube map.

- **Draw Halo:** Checking this box will render a hazy halo effect equal to the light's range. This can be useful for mood or effect lighting.

- **Flare:** Assigns a lens flare effect to the light. Choose the desired flare type from the drop-down list—some are included with the Standard Assets package.

- **Render Mode:** Choose how the light will render on any objects it illuminates: vertex, pixels, or auto.

- **Culling Mask:** Used for optimization and effects, you can set which layers the light can affect. New layers can be created in the Layers drop-down menu and then selected from here.

Drop a few random objects into your scene and play around with some of the basic settings on your test light to get a feel for how the properties affect the light.

Note

> While placement in the world is vital to the proper functioning of the spot and point light, the directional light, because of its nature, can be placed *anywhere* and still emit the same kind of light. All that matters positionally for the directional light is its current rotation, unless you're attaching a flare to it.

Basics of Lighting

Creating a light rig for a game is very similar to the processes used by movie and stage lighting technicians—all three are trying to simulate natural or mood lighting conditions in an artificial setting. Most scenes, even simple ones, are lit with a combination of different lights working in tandem, which together help to mimic the quality of natural lights and bounce effects seen in the real world.

A Simple Three-Point Lighting Rig

Many basic scenes start with a three-point lighting rig solution—these are especially useful when the scene's camera is fixed and you have complete control over how the user will view the scene. As suggested by the name, the rig uses three basic lights for the composition. Any default lighting should be removed prior to setting up the first light or it could throw off the entire final result.

- **Key Light:** The key light is the scene's main light and should be added first. This light mimics the strongest light source available in the scene, whether that's the sun, a large overhead lamp, or a giant bonfire. Spot-lights and directional lights work well as key lights. Make sure you like the effects of your key light first before placing your others.

- **Fill Light:** The fill light (or lights in some cases) helps create the illusion of light bouncing around the scene and helps to fill in and soften some of the darker shadows cast by the key light. Secondary light sources, like candles or small lamps, should be implemented with fill lights. Point lights make excellent fill lights, but you can use low-intensity directional and spotlights to great effect. Keep the intensity low for all fill lights at first, and build up to create the effect you want.

- **Back Light:** Back (or rim) lights help define important objects and "pop" them out from the scenery. Placed directly behind the subject and opposite the camera, they create a nice, bright line outline around the given subject.

Try setting up a sample scene in Unity using a three-point rig. Experiment with moving the relative positions of the lights, like moving the key light higher or lower to the subject than the fill light. Light rigs like this can either lay independently in a scene or be attached to moving objects, like a character. A sample diagram of a three-point rig is shown in Figure 14.3.

Remember, this is just a simple lighting rig example and isn't a one-catch-all solution for every scene you may create. Start with a practical look at which objects in your scene would be casting light first, determine the mood you want to achieve, and work from there.

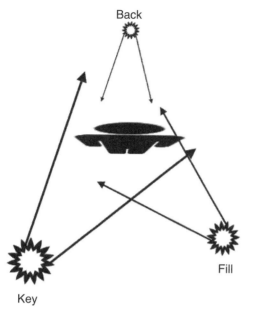

Figure 14.3
An overhead schematic of a three-point rig.

Lighting for Different Functions

Besides the obvious of lighting a scene so the players know where they are going, lighting can serve multiple purposes simultaneously in any given level. When placing a light in a scene, try to identify what purpose (or purposes) it's currently serving.

On the most basic level, lights are used for simple illumination. If your level isn't lit, the players won't be able to see where they are going or what they are doing. Providing enough light for the players to adequately judge their surroundings should be one of the first parts tackled when lighting a new scene.

Lights can also be used as gameplay devices or help direct or attract players to a particular point or object. Players tend to follow lit paths rather than explore only dark corners, and placing a subtle string of lights around your level can help guide the players without resorting to more obvious means. Lights can also be used to illuminate levels, triggers, or other important objects that the players should focus on.

Mood is one of the biggest visual factors that lights can influence. One scene can have multiple different moods associated with it, based solely on lighting alone. A wash of red tinted lights can make a scene seem more sinister, whereas blues and greens are more calming and tranquil. Also, play with the contrast of strong lights and dark shadows when trying to make more intense scenes.

For an outdoor scene, lights play an important role in determining the time of day. While this sounds painfully obvious, the color of the light is almost more important than the intensity when setting the scene. Blue lights are effective for simulating moonlight and night skies, oranges and reds are used for dawn and dusk, and *very* pale green lights are perfect for noon-day skies.

Lights can also be controlled via scripts and can be shut on or off or have their properties changed on the fly. The possibilities for achieving the look you want are just about endless.

Lighting the World

Currently, the *Widget* scene has only one directional light in it, placed in Chapter 6. This light works well as a base key light for the scene, but it can use a few tweaks.

The scene could also use some more ambient and mood lighting. Let's do that now:

1. Open your latest scene in Unity and save a new copy of it, naming it **Chapter 14**. Click on your directional light in the Hierarchy to bring up its properties in the Inspector.

2. The light probably hasn't been changed from any of its default values, so begin by setting its color to a pale green (R=253, G=255, B=218 works well). The effect on the terrain is subtle, but it helps.

3. Next import the Props folder from Chapter 14 on the DVD and place the objects and textures into their respective folders. Make sure the Scale Factors on the meshes are at 1, and assign basic outline Toon shaders to the materials. This package includes a cottage, some wooden

structures, and two light props to use. Make prefabs of the new objects if you plan on using and changing any aspects of them in the future.

4. Find a nice open spot in your scene and drop the cottage there. Place a few fences and lights, and span the river with the included bridge piece. A sample placement is shown in Figure 14.4.

5. Now that you've got some light-emitting props down, you can set up some mood lighting. Find one of your lamps and create a new point light around it; choose GameObject▶Create Other▶ Point Light. Set this lamp up with an appealing color and intensity for the light.

6. Duplicate this light and leave it sitting on top of each other. This light will serve as a halo for the lamp, so check the Draw Halo box and turn the intensity down until you like the effect. Also play with the range and color. You can apply this double light/halo light effect to other lamps in the scene if you want.

7. Find the checkpoint object you've placed previously in the scene and add some lights to it as well. You want to draw the player's attention to the checkpoint, and lights are an easy way to do this. Figures 14.5 and 14.6 show the finished cottage and checkpoint robot.

Continue adding lights around the scene as you want. Try adding some subtle light cues along the path to direct the players along it.

Tip

If you notice strange lines or clipping from lights on the ground, this usually means your terrain resolution is too low.

CREATING SHADOWS

Even without the Pro version of Unity, you can still add the effects of shadows on your terrain and objects. Primarily, you can use a combination of terrain painting, lightmaps, and projectors to give the effect of objects casting shadows.

Figure 14.4
A pastoral setting.

Figure 14.5
The lit cottage and fencing.

Figure 14.6
Lights and halos adorning the checkpoint robot.

Lightmaps

Chapter 5 briefly mentioned lightmaps and how they can be useful for painting shadows on terrain. Now you'll actually create the illusion of cast shadows on the terrain by painting up a custom lightmap.

To create a shadow with a lightmap, follow these steps:

1. Grab the LightmapExport.cs file from the Chapter 14▶Scripts folder on the DVD if you didn't import this in Chapter 5.

2. In your own project Assets folder, create an Editor folder and drop the copied script file into it. This Editor folder is special in that it allows custom scripts to be run directly from within the editor. Failure to place the script in the properly named folder will result in it not working.

3. Once you do this, a new menu option will appear between Terrain and Window: CUSTOM. If you look in here, the custom script called Duplicate Texture is now available. This is exactly what you need to export your lightmap for edits.

4. In the Project view, find your terrain asset (probably called New Terrain unless you changed it earlier). Expand its hierarchy to see its Lightmap texture. Select this texture and then run the Duplicate Texture option from the menu.

5. Your new texture file LightmapDuplicate will be placed into the root of your Assets folder. It may not show up in the Project view until you manually refresh (press Ctrl+R to do so).

Now take this file into your graphics editor of choice and paint onto it—make your adjustments on new layers to save yourself headaches later. GIMP is a free graphics editor (read more about GIMP in Appendix D, on the DVD) if you need to install one.

To best know where to place your edits, take a screenshot of your current level from a top-down view, and import that as well into your graphics editor. You can then apply this as a layer or mask and know exactly where to edit. Figure 14.7 shows an example of this.

After painting, you just need to assign your new lightmap to the terrain:

1. Click on your new Lightmap file in the Project view to bring up its properties. In the Inspector, change its Texture Format setting to RGB 24-bit. Your lightmap *will not* work if you forget to do this.

2. Click on your base terrain asset in the Project view (not the Hierarchy view).

3. Its Inspector view will only show one option: Lightmap. Drag your new Lightmap texture file onto this slot (or select it from the drop-down menu) to apply.

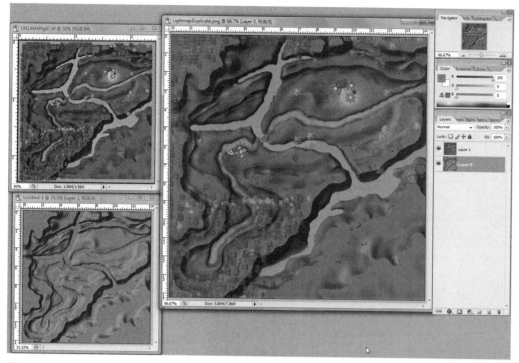

Figure 14.7
Aligning layers in Photoshop to paint shadows.

Take a spin around your level and verify that the shadows you painted look the way you want them to. If you saved your edits on separate layers in your Lightmap file, you can continuously tweak and edit even as you add new content to your scene.

Projector-Made Shadows

Another method for applying shadows is by use of *projectors*. A Unity projector acts just like one in real life—it projects a given material or image onto a surface. This can be used to project pictures and patterns onto objects in the scene (like bullet holes or foot steps) or, when used with a dark material, to project blobby shadows underneath characters and objects.

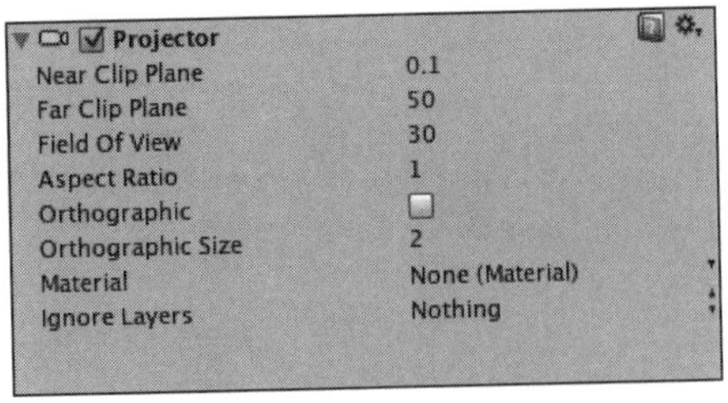

Figure 14.8
A sample Projector object.

To create a simple projector object, make an empty GameObject and then add a Project component by selecting Component▶Rendering▶Projector. A sample projector is shown in Figure 14.8.

Many of a projector's properties are similar to those of a camera or light source:

- **Near Clip Plane:** Any object that is closer than the distance specified will not be projected upon.

- **Far Clip Plane:** Any object that is farther away than the distance specified will not be projected upon.

- **Field of View:** The degrees of the projector's field of view. If the projector is orthographic, this value is not used.

- **Aspect Ratio:** The aspect ratio, the projector, allowing you to create other rectangular shapes besides squares.

- **Orthographic:** Check this box if you want to disable perspective for the projector.

- **Orthographic Size:** If the projector is orthographic, this dictates how big an area it covers.

- **Material:** The material and texture to be projected onto any object the projector encounters.

- **Ignore Layers:** Select layers in the drop-down menu to disable the projector's effects. This is useful to disable a character, so his own projector doesn't place him in shadow.

The Standard Assets package comes with a Blob-Shadow projector premade, so all you need to do is hook it up:

1. Find the blob shadow projector in the Standard Assets folder by navigating to Standard Assets▶Blob-Shadow▶blob shadow projector.

2. Make an instance of this prefab in the scene and then parent it to a *Widget* object. Allow this to break the link to the parent *Widget* prefab.

3. Maneuver the projector so that it points down directly over *Widget*. A position value of (0,5,0) and rotation of (90,0,0) works well. *Widget* should now be cast in darkness, as shown in Figure 14.9.

4. Now you need to set up a new layer so the projector can ignore the *Widget* mesh, while still projecting the blobby shadow onto the ground. From the Layers drop-down box in the top-right corner, select Edit Layers.

5. Click on the empty space to the right of User Layer 8 (the first editable layer) when the mouse cursor changes to the text editing cursor. Enter a new name for this layer, such as **Player**.

6. Select the *Widget* prefab and change the Layer option (directly under the name in the Inspector) to **Player**. Also change this field on the *Widget* model in the scene. Select Apply to All Children when prompted by the pop-up.

7. Now return to the blob shadow projector. From the Ignore Layers property field, select the new Player layer from the drop-down menu. Voila, *Widget* is now casting a shadow! Update the links to the *Widget* prefab with this new shadow version, shown in Figure 14.10.

Add more projectors to the enemies or to any other object you want in the scene. Projectors can also be placed over all the trees to simulate dappled foliage, rather than painting individual lightmaps.

Projectors can also be used to create the effect of moving clouds, when tied to an appropriate script. The material can be slowly animated, making it look like rolling clouds are crossing the landscape. Even without dynamically cast

Figure 14.9
The early shadow projector.

shadows, many kinds of shadow effects are possible by combining clever projector usage and texture painting.

OTHER LIGHT EFFECTS

There are a few last effects you can add to your lights to add a final layer of polish to your game. These should be used sparingly and only when appropriate, so that they don't appear cheesy or overused to your players.

Lens Flares

Unity supports the classic lens flare and comes prepackaged with a few flare options. Flares are built from a Flare component and a specially laid out texture, which can be attached to any GameObject in the scene—not just lights. The flare works by reading in the texture file, splitting it into a set number of component images, and then stringing these images out upon a line. The line is calculated by comparing the position of the Flare object to the center of the screen.

Figure 14.10
Widget's final shadow.

To make a basic Lens Flare effect, create an empty GameObject in the scene and then attach the Lens Flare component by selecting Component▶Rendering▶Lens Flare. Rename your GameObject to something like **Lens Flare** and view its properties in the Inspector.

- **Flare:** Select the kind of flare effect you want from the drop-down menu. Standard Assets comes prepackaged with a Sun, 50mm Zoom camera, and Small Flare effect. Try each of these to see the different effects.

- **Color:** This tints the flare's texture.

- **Brightness:** Change the overall brightness of the flare effect.

- **Directional:** Check this box to make the flare appear far away in the distance. It will attach itself to the positive end of the Z axis.

If you decide to attach your flare to a GameObject and not through a light component, be careful about where you place the object. Flares should always be tied to a light source in some way, and players will easily become distracted by misplaced flare effects.

Cookies

Cookies are another form of lighting effect, useful for creating the illusion of light being obstructed in some way. Cookies are like gobos in stage lighting—you basically place a black and white texture mask over the light in question, which then acts to obstruct the light according to its pattern. Full white areas will allow the light to pass through unobstructed, and fully black areas will not emit any light at all. Cookies can be used to create illusions ranging from light passing through barred windows to dappling between tree leaves.

Unity comes with two cookies in the Standard Assets folder, but it's simple to create and import your own:

1. To start, find a black and white image or make one in the graphics editor of your choice. Make sure that the edges of the image are all black; otherwise, it'll look like light is "leaking" out the sides of the image. A sample cookie image is included on the Chapter 14 DVD as well.

2. Import the image into the Assets folder and set the Wrap mode to Clamp.

3. Select Build Alpha from Grayscale and Border Mipmaps from the import settings list.

4. Change the Texture Format to Alpha 8 and click Apply to save all your import changes.

5. Make a new spotlight (GameObject▶Create Other▶Spot Light) and position it so that you can see the cone of light easily in the scene.

6. Duplicate this light and move it so that the two lights sit side by side. With one light selected, assign the new cookie texture to the Cookie property in the light's Inspector view. Figure 14.11 shows the simple spot and the spot with the cookie applied.

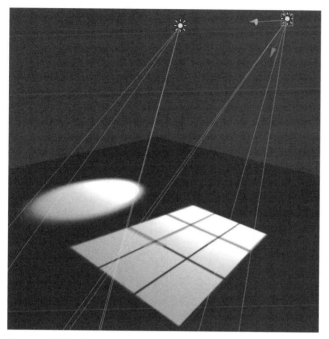

Figure 14.11
A window-esque cookie's effect on a spotlight.

2D texture cookies can be applied to either directional or spotlights, and point lights can take a cube map texture as a cookie as well. A simple and quickly authored black and white image can lend the illusion that you have complicated geometry in your scene, saving both time and rendering power.

Lights are a fast and relatively cheap way to add depth, personality, and interest to your scenes. A few mood and interest lights can be all that differentiates a fun and interesting game from a boring and lifeless level.

CHAPTER 15

USING PARTICLE SYSTEMS

Particles are another way you can add life and polish to your game levels. They can provide feedback to players based on their actions, can be a useful method to grab the player's attention, or can simply help illustrate a pretty area of the scene with special effects. Particle systems can be hooked up and controlled like any other object in Unity and can be easily started and stopped from within scripts. Although they are computationally expensive when overused, particles can add a pleasing amount of movement and interest to an otherwise static scene.

PARTICLES: FROM SMOKE TO STARDUST

In 3D graphics (and games), particles are a way to render certain kinds of effects and materials that aren't simple or efficient to model in a traditional way—things like smoke, stars, sparks, fire, and dust clouds. Particles are generally represented by 2D planes, known as *billboards* or *sprites*, which are then discharged from an object called an *emitter*. The combination of rendered particles and emitter is what makes up a basic particle system.

To render complex objects like a flickering torch or plume of smoke, an emitter is first attached to the object in question. The emitter can be a basic shape, like a sphere, or use a detailed mesh to create special effects. The sprites are discharged along the surface of the emitter (usually at the vertices) at a set rate and velocity and drawn layered on top of each other to create the illusion of substance. Animations and forces are also applied to the sprites to achieve different effects.

Figure 15.1
A simple particle system.

Figure 15.2
The same particles as in Figure 15.1, but with different forces.

Sometimes, the textures the sprites use are tiled with different images, allowing for even more complex effects with minimal work. Figure 15.1 shows a sample explosion effect that was created using only a single-texture sprite.

Depending on the forces and animations applied, the same particle emitter can take on wildly different effects, as illustrated in Figure 15.2.

Getting the exact effect you want can sometimes be a lengthy process of trial and error, but the end result is worth it.

Setting Up a Simple System

Creating a new particle system is as easy as making a new GameObject. Open a new scene in Unity and navigate to GameObject▶Create Other▶Particle System. This places a new, ready-to-go particle system in the scene. If you select it in the Hierarchy and focus on it in the scene, it will begin animating with the default selections. Figure 15.3 shows the basic particle system in action.

The default system uses an ellipsoid particle emitter (in simple terms, a sphere) and comes prepopulated with a particle animator and renderer. To customize

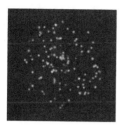

Figure 15.3
A default particle system.

the system to fit any of your needs, from dust cloud to bonfire, you just need to tweak the three components.

Particle Emitter

Unity's particle emitters come in two types—ellipsoid and mesh. Ellipsoids are good for most basic particle systems, as they can emit from all directions at once in any kind of spherical shape. Mesh emitters are more particular (and can be more expensive to render) and allow special shapes to take the form of the emitter, perfect for elements like blazing swords or ghostly forms. The default particle system always uses the ellipsoid.

Figure 15.4 illustrates the various properties that an ellipsoid emitter uses to discharge the particle sprites.

The emitter randomizes the particles rendered, changing the size, visible duration, and velocity of each sprite based upon the set properties in the component.

- **Emit:** Toggle to enable the system to emit particles. This affects both the Scene view and particles in game.
- **Min Size:** The minimum size of the sprite emitted.
- **Max Size:** The maximum size of the sprite emitted. If you want your sprites to be of a uniform size, set the Min and Max Size fields to the same number.
- **Min Energy:** The minimum amount of time (in seconds) that the sprite exists in the scene.

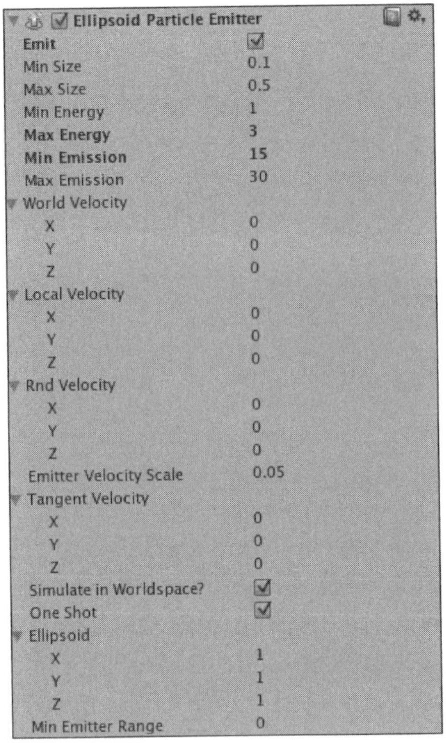

Figure 15.4
The emitter component.

- **Max Energy:** The maximum amount of time that a sprite can exist. For static durations, set the Min and Max Energy to the same value.

- **Min Emission:** The minimum number of sprites that the emitter discharges per second.

- **Max Emission:** The maximum number of sprites that the emitter can discharge per second. For a constant effect, set the Min and Max Emission values to be equal.

- **World Velocity:** The starting speed of the particles along each of the X, Y, and Z axes, relative to the world space. Setting the Y axis in particular can make the particles look like they're rising into the air or falling to the ground. The X and Z axes are good for simulating particles moving in the wind.

- **Local Velocity:** The starting speed of the particles along each of the X, Y, and Z axes, relative to the system's own local space (position and orientation).

- **Rnd Velocity:** A random amount of speed to add to the individual X, Y, and Z axes.

- **Emitter Velocity Scale:** The amount of the emitter's own speed that the individual particles inherit. If the particle emitter isn't moving, this has no effect. Set this field to 1 to have the particles match the speed of the emitter, set to 2 to double, 3 to triple, and so on.

- **Tangent Velocity:** The starting speed of the particles along the emitter's surface.

- **Simulate in Worldspace:** Check this box to make the emitted particles independent of a moving emitter. When checked, if the emitter moves, the particles won't move with it. If left unchecked, the particles will follow the emitter around in a stream for their set duration.

- **One Shot:** Toggles whether the system should release all its particles at once or in one long continuous stream.

- **Ellipsoid:** Rescale the ellipsoid emitter's shape along the X, Y, or Z axis.

- **Min Emitter Range:** Specifies where in the sphere the particles can start emitting. If set to the radius of the ellipsoid, the particles will appear to emit from only its surface. If set to 0, the particles will emit from any space within the ellipsoid.

Try changing some of these basic properties around to see how the basic particle system changes. In particular, the different velocity fields may not seem that different until you start to fiddle with each individually.

Particle Animator

The second component of the basic particle system is the animator—driving exactly how each individual sprite looks and behaves as it moves around the scene. The animator (shown in Figure 15.5) controls the forces, rotations, and different color tints that can be applied to any sprite.

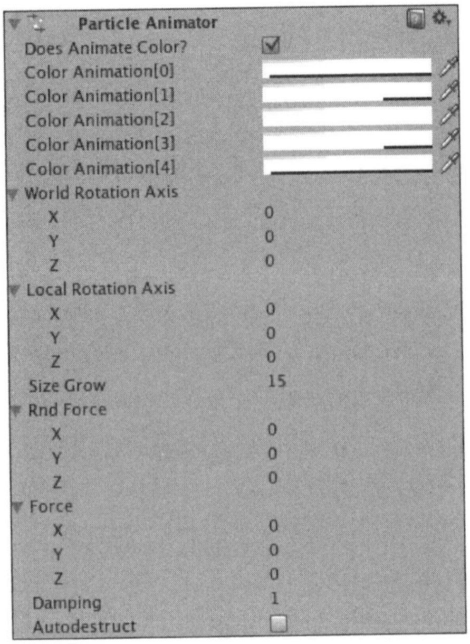

Figure 15.5
The particle animator.

- **Does Animate Color?:** Check this box to enable the Color Animation fields below.

- **Color Animation[0]–[4]:** The five alpha and color tint stages that each sprite will go through during its lifespan.

- **World Rotation Axis:** The amount of rotation to apply to the sprite along the X, Y, or Z axis, relative to the world space.

- **Local Rotation Axis:** The amount of rotation to apply to the sprite along the X, Y, or Z axis, relative to the emitter's orientation.

- **Size Grow:** How many times the sprite should grow in size, especially useful for when forces spread the particles out. This looks particularly nice with an alpha animation making the particles fade out as they become larger.

- **Rnd Force:** A random amount of force being applied to the particle *every frame*, relative to the world space.

- **Force:** The amount of force being applied to the particle *every frame*, relative to the world space.

- **Damping:** How much the particle's speed changes from frame to frame. Setting this field to 1 will allow damping to have no effect, setting it to any number less than 1 will begin to slow the particles down, and setting it to any number greater than 1 will speed the particles up.

- **Autodestruct:** Check this box to destroy any GameObject that the particles are attached to. When the last particle disappears from the emitter, the GameObject is destroyed.

By default, the color animator is set to also animate the alphas of each sprite, making it appear as if each sprite fades in and out of existence. These alphas can be tweaked individually to suit your needs, or the entire system can be turned off if you want your particles to "pop" in and out of existence. The color tints, which multiply the sprite's texture, are by default set to white, but you can achieve quick, fun effects by changing these to any bright color. This can be particularly useful for spell-like effects.

Particle Renderer and Materials

While the emitter and animator control the system as a whole, the particle renderer component sets up the basic look of each individual sprite in the system (see Figure 15.6). This is where the particular material and textures for the sprites are hooked up.

- **Cast Shadows:** Sets whether the sprites cast any shadows as they pass over geometry in the scene.

- **Receive Shadows:** Sets whether shadows can be cast onto the individual sprites from other sources in the scene.

- **Materials:** A list of materials to apply to the sprites over their lifetime.

- **Camera Velocity Scale:** The amount of distortion to apply to the particles based upon any camera movement. By default this is set to 0.

- **Stretch Particles:** Determines by what method the particles are rendered, defaulted to Billboard. Billboard renderers the particles plainly facing the camera, Sorted Billboard does the same but sorts by depth as well (good for blending textures), Stretched distorts the particles and faces them along the vector they're moving, Vertical Billboard renders the particles along the X-Z axes, and Horizontal Billboard renders the particles along the X-Y axes.

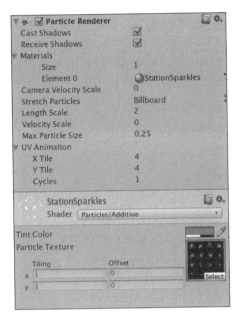

Figure 15.6
The particle renderer component.

- **Length Scale:** If Stretched is selected above, this sets how much to stretch and distort each sprite.

- **Velocity Scale:** If Stretched is selected above, this dictates the rate at which the particles are distorted, based upon their speed.

- **UV Animation:** Sets how the material's texture is animated. As shown in Figure 15.6, the texture applied to this particle material has 16 unique tiles, four across and four down. By setting the X and Y Tile properties of this field to 4 and 4, Unity knows to split the texture up and animate the sprites using these individual tiles, kind of like a flipbook. The Cycles field determines how many times during the sprite's lifespan the sequence of tiles is repeated.

- **Max Particle Size:** Sets the maximum size the particles will reach, if they grow in size over time.

Using tiled textures for sprites is another quick and easy way to introduce more complexity and depth to particle systems without significantly increasing the overhead in any way. Your tiled textures don't need to be square—you could for example have a texture that tiles four frames across one row.

Making Custom Tiled Textures in Photoshop

Photoshop (and other graphics editors) makes it easy to create custom tiled texture sheets (or *atlases*) for use in particle systems. First, decide how many tiles you want, how large each will be, and how you plan on laying them out. For example, say you want eight tiles to animate through, each 64 × 64 pixels. If arranged in a 4 × 2 grid, your file needs to be 256 × 128. You could also arrange them in a straight line, for a file size of 512 × 64. Create a new file using the correct dimensions.

Navigate to View▶Show▶Grid, or press Ctrl+', displaying a regular grid across your work surface. To set the grid up so that each square corresponds to one tile, go to Edit▶ Preferences▶Guides, Grid, and Slices. Under the Grid section, change the Gridline Every field to 64 (for this example), and set the drop-down box to pixels. Change the subdivisions to 1 unless you want extra gridlines within each tile. Press OK to save your changes. See Figure 15.7.

Now when you paint your new particle textures, just ensure that each tile stays neatly within each grid line, and save the file in a format that preserves the alpha channel of your particles.

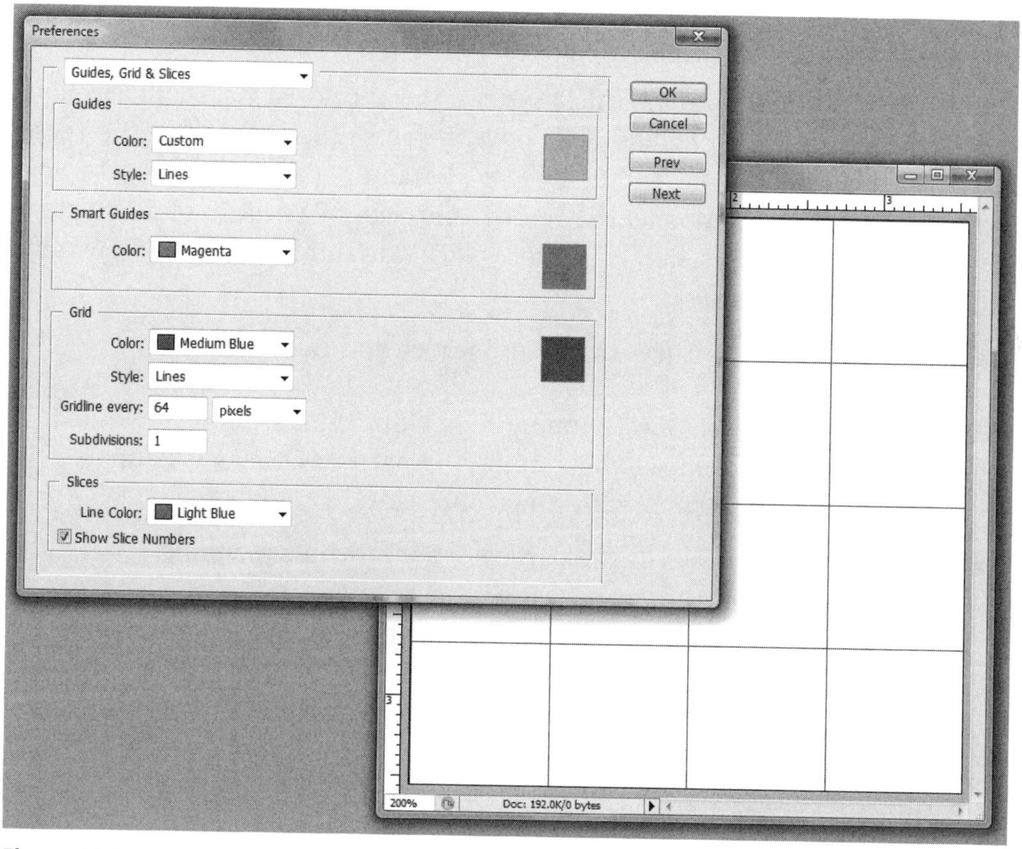

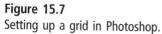

Figure 15.7
Setting up a grid in Photoshop.

Although you can theoretically use any kind of material for your particle system, Unity prepackages a few particle-specific shaders that interact well with the emitters. Most of these shaders blend the different sprites nicer than a normal Diffuse would and are conveniently grouped under their own category— Particles.

ADVANCED PARTICLE COMPONENTS

These simple particle systems are good for most jobs you'll run across, but Unity also offers a few advanced components and features that can greatly expand your particle repertoire.

World Particle Collider

An optional component to a particle system, the World Particle collider allows the individual sprites to collide and move around other objects in the scene, instead of just flying right through them. To add a particle collider to your system, navigate to Component▶Particles and select World Particle Collider. Now any sprite created from this emitter will collide and bounce off of any other collider it touches in the scene.

The particle collider has a few simple properties you can tweak.

- **Bounce Factor:** Like the Damping field from the Particle Animator component, this field sets how much the particle either picks up or loses speed as it collides with other objects.

- **Collision Energy Loss:** If the particle collides with something, determines how many seconds (if any) should be subtracted from its total life expectancy. If this causes the duration to fall below 0, the particle is destroyed.

- **Collides With:** Select the layers that the particle can interact with from the drop-down menu. Smart layer selection can save a lot of unnecessary computing power.

- **Send Collision Message:** Check this box to have each particle send out a message whenever it collides with something, which you can catch via scripting.

- **Min Kill Velocity:** The minimum amount of speed a particle can have before being destroyed.

This component can drastically reduce your frame rate if overused or abused and should only be applied to systems that definitely need it.

Trail Renderer

A trail renderer is used to draw a motion trail behind any object, great for anything that moves at a quick speed (like a bullet or comet). Although not a particle system in itself, the renderer uses the same shaders as other kinds of particles. Trails take the place of other kinds of visual renderers on an object (like a mesh renderer), so they should be placed into their own empty Game-Object. This object can then be attached to whatever other mesh you want to give the trail effect to. See Figure 15.8.

To create a trail, first make an empty GameObject and then attach a Trail Renderer component to it by navigating to Component▶Particles▶Trail Renderer. Many of the properties for this component are similar to the particle renderer (see Figure 15.9). The particular differences are listed here:

- **Time:** Length of the displayed trail, in seconds.
- **Start Width:** Width of the trail at the object's current position.

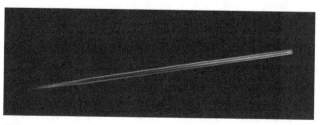

Figure 15.8
A sample trail.

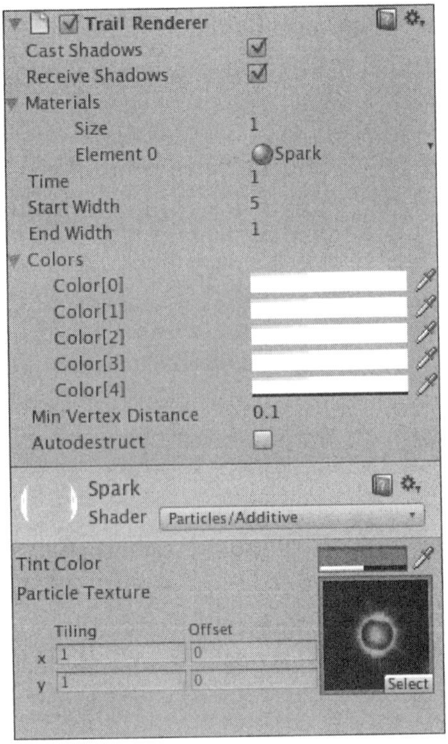

Figure 15.9
The Trail Renderer component.

- **End Width:** Width of the trail at its end.

- **Min Vertex Distance:** How far apart each new vertex of the trail is placed. Larger numbers will render faster but produce trails that are more jagged in appearance.

The material used should use a particle shader, Additive being an often-used one. The texture applied to the material shouldn't be tiled and works best when comprised of square dimensions (like 128×128).

Create a basic trail renderer and drag it around the Scene view to watch it in action.

Line Renderer

Similar to the trail renderer, a line renderer draws a path between specified points using a particle shader. The line renderer, unlike its name suggests, does not draw a thin, one dimensional line, but rather draws a billboarded image specified in the material.

Like the trail renderer, the line renderer should also be used on an object without a renderer already in place, like an empty GameObject. To add a Line Renderer component to a GameObject, select Component▶Miscellaneous▶Line Renderer. The only differences between this component and the trail are the point positions and color parameters. See Figure 15.10.

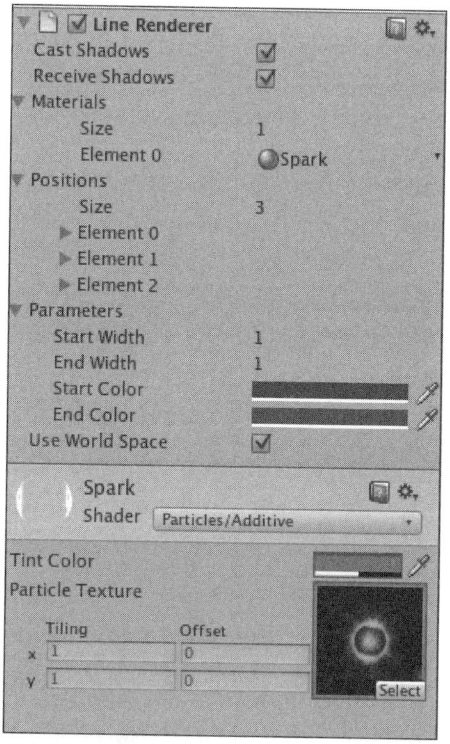

Figure 15.10
The Line Renderer component.

- **Positions:** The number of points that the line uses, determined by the Size field. Each element in the field specifies a new point in X,Y,Z coordinates. For a straight line, use two points. For a complex spiral, increase the Size number.

- **Parameters:** Like the trail, the start and end widths of the line can be independently set. Unlike the other particle systems, the line does not animate over time, which is why only start and end colors are needed.

The same kind of square textured particle shader should be used for the line renderer as used for a trail. Line renderers, while not an animating system, are good for static effects like laser traps or force field boundaries.

PARTICLES FOR WIDGET

Some aspects of the *Widget* game can definitely make use of particle systems, like *Widget* taser attack, which at the moment consists of only a simple animation.

Open your latest Unity scene file and save a new copy of it, naming it **Chapter15**. From the DVD, import the contents of the Chapter 15▶Textures folder into the *Widget* project, placing them in the Particles directory of the Assets folder. Make sure that all the particle textures are imported with an alpha-ready compression, like DXT5. Otherwise, they won't show up as expected in the shader.

Pickup Items

The first simple particle system you can make is an attention-grabber for the various pickup items around the scene. Currently, the objects can be a little hard to spot from a distance, and a simple sparkle effect can help the players see the objects as *Widget* rolls along.

For this simple sparkle effect, you'll create a simple ellipsoid particle system:

1. Create a new particle system by navigating to GameObject▶Create Other▶Particle System and naming it something more descriptive like **Attention Sparkles**.

2. Next create a new material to use with the system. Make a new material in the Particles folder and assign it the Particles▶Additive Shader. Locate the newly imported attention_sparkle_PART texture and assign it to the material.

3. Assign this new sparkle material to the particle system's renderer component, and change the UV animation fields to X = 4 and Y = 2. Because the image is tiled with eight frames, you need to make sure to set the UV field correctly.

4. Now begin tweaking the particle system. To start, set the following properties as follows:

Ellipsoid Particle Emitter:

Min Size = 0.1
Max Size = 0.3
Min Energy = 0.5
Max Energy = 5
Min Emission = 5
Max Emission = 10
Local Velocity.Y = 1
Rnd Velocity.Y = 0.3
Ellipsoid.X and Ellipsoid.Z = 0.5

Particle Animator:

Size Grow = 1.5

Particle Renderer:

Cast Shadows and Receive Shadows = disable
UV Animation.X = 4
UV Animation.Y = 2

This will produce a slowly animating sparkle effect that rises into the sky before fading from view, as shown in Figure 15.11. Make a prefab of this finished effect.

Figure 15.11
A sparkle effect.

Now you need to assign the new effect to your prefabs. Create an instance of the gear and pickup prefabs in the scene (if they do not exist already) and parent the newly created sparkle effect to the pickups, allowing this to break the old prefab connections. Move the sparkle effect so that it rests nicely on top of the pickup items. Reconnect these new object groups to the old prefab by dragging the group from the Hierarchy to the prefab in the Project view.

All that's left is to run the effect from the pickup script you wrote earlier, as you want to make sure that it starts and stops emitting at the proper times. Open the PickupItems.js script and create a new variable for the emitter at the top of the file:

```
var sparkleEmitter : ParticleEmitter;
```

In the OnTriggerEnter function, after where you set the pickedUp variable equal to True, add a new line to turn off the emitter when the player grabs the item:

```
sparkleEmitter.emit = false;
```

Now scroll down the file to the Reset function. Add the following to the bottom of this function:

```
sparkleEmitter.emit = true;
```

This ensures that the emitter will start playing when the pickup object is instantiated. Back in the pickups prefab, assign your new particle systems to this variable in the Inspector. Save your work and test your new pickups; they should be much more shiny and easier to spot now. Any one of the particle's property fields, like emit, can be changed via scripting, allowing you complete and precise control over every aspect of your system.

Checkpoint Activation

The checkpoint object could also use a particle effect to notify the player which checkpoint is currently active—right now they all look the same. Instead of using a spherical-shaped emitter, you'll create a cylindrical emitter that fits the base of the checkpoint, using a mesh emitter.

To create a cylindrical emitter, follow these steps:

1. Start by creating a new simple cylinder object, by going to Game Object▶Create Other▶Cylinder. You'll use this mesh as a starting point for the new system. Rescale the cylinder to X=4, Y=0, and Z=4.

2. Delete both the Mesh Renderer and Capsule Collider components from the cylinder—neither of these is needed for the particle system. This leaves you with just the mesh filter. Now add the particle components from the Component▶Particles menu: Mesh Particle Emitter, Particle Animator, and Particle Renderer. The base setup for a mesh emitter is now complete.

3. Now create a new material to use with the mesh particle system and name it **Station Sparkles**. Find the newly imported texture file station_spark_PART.tif and assign it to the material. For this material, also use a Particle▶Additive Shader.

4. Assign this new material to the particle renderer and set up the rest of the properties as follows:

Mesh Particle Emitter:

Emit = Disabled (you can keep this enabled while tweaking, but be sure to turn it off when you're done)

Min Size = 0.2
Max Size = 0.6
Min Energy = 3
Max Energy = 5
Min Emission = 60
Max Emission = 60
Local Velocity.Y = 0.2

Particle Renderer:

Cast Shadows and Receive Shadows = Disabled

UV Animation.X = 4
UV Animation.Y = 4

Change any other properties to achieve the look you want.

5. Create a prefab of this new effect, parent it to one of the CheckPoint objects in the scene (break the old connections), and then reparent this new checkpoint object to the old CheckPoint prefab to update it with the sparkle effect. Align the sparkle effect so that it sits nicely on the platform, as shown in Figure 15.12.

As with the pickups, you'll also need to update a script in order to make the particles function as wanted.

Open the CheckPoint.js script and add a new variable at the top of the file for your sparkle emitter:

```
var activeEmitter : ParticleEmitter;
```

Figure 15.12
An activated checkpoint.

You'll set this to activate only when the player sets a new checkpoint as his current respawn point. Scroll down to the BeActive function and add:

```
activeEmitter.emit = true;
```

This will start the emitter when the player triggers the checkpoint by rolling over. Now you just need to turn it off when the player sets a new point as active. In the BeInactive function, add:

```
activeEmitter.emit = false;
```

That's it. Assign the particle system to the activeEmitter variable in the Inspector. Save your script and test your new systems by putting at least two checkpoint objects down in the scene and rolling between the two. The particle systems will turn on and off depending on whichever one *Widget* sets as last active.

Widget's Attack

Widget's taser attack is up next for a particle treatment. Applying a one-shot effect whenever the player presses the Attack key will provide a bit more much-needed feedback.

To create a particle system for *Widget*'s attack, follow these steps:

1. Create a new ellipsoid particle system and name it **electricity**.

2. Now create a new material to use with the particle system. Find the newly imported texture file electricity_PART.tif and assign it to the material. For this material, use a Particle▶Additive Shader.

3. Assign this new material to the particle renderer and set up the rest of the properties as follows:

   Ellipsoid Particle Emitter:

   Emit = Disabled (you can keep this enabled while tweaking, but be sure to turn it off when you're done)
   Min Size = 0.1
   Max Size = 0.5
   Min Energy = 1
   Max Energy = 2
   Min Emission = 50
   Max Emission = 50
   Rnd Velocity X,Y, and Z = 1
   One Shot = enabled

   Particle Animator:
   Local Rotation Axis X,Y and Z = 1
   Rnd Force X,Y,Z = 2

   Particle Renderer:
   Cast Shadows and Receive Shadows = Disabled
   UV Animation.X = 4
   UV Animation.Y = 1

Change any other properties to achieve the look you want.

4. Create a prefab of this new effect, parent it to *Widget* (break the old connections), and then reparent this new checkpoint object to the old *Widget* prefab to update it with the effect link. Align the effect so that it sits neatly around *Widget*.

Now you just need to attach the emitter to *Widget*'s attack. Open the Widget_AttackContoller.js file and add a new variable for the emitter:

```
var attackEmitter : ParticleEmitter;
```

You need to create a new function to handle the particles, instead of just turning the emitter on and off. Create a new function at the bottom of the file:

```
function PlayParticles()
{
}
```

Within this function, you'll start and stop the emitter directly, but also give it some time to play the effects. Add the following to the middle of the function body:

```
attackEmitter.emit = true;
yield WaitForSeconds(attackEmitter.minEnergy );
attackEmitter.emit = false;
```

The function will now wait for the minimum amount of time for the emitter to play before shutting off again. In the DidAttack function above this, add a call to this function beneath the line yield WaitForSeconds(attackHitTime):

```
PlayParticles();
```

Now whenever the player successfully attacks, the one-shot system will trigger. Connect the electricity particle system to the attackEmitter variable in the Inspector and test it. See Figure 15.13.

Figure 15.13
Widget attacks!

Enemy Explosion

Making an explosion for a dying enemy is a little more complicated—you'll need to use two particle systems in tandem to get the right effect: one for the explosion and one for the resulting smoke.

> Try creating this pair of particle systems on your own, using the hints that follow. If you get stuck, you can always review the Final Project files on the DVD to see how the sample explosion system is set up.
>
> 1. Make a one-shot particle system for the explosion. Use the spark_PART.tif texture file and make sure that the particles grow in size to simulate the spreading explosion. Try to get the timing of the emitter right so that the particles look like their being emitted with great force over the course of just one second.
>
> 2. Create a smoke effect particle system using the smoke_PART.tif file and a Particles▸Multiply shader. Remember to make the smoke rise upwards, and have the effect last about five seconds long. Play with some of the random force or rotation values to try to get a more "billowy" look.
>
> 3. Make a new prefab with these two systems and name it **Explosion**. Attach this object to the E_Bunny prefab.

Open the EBunny_Status.js file and make two new variables for your particle effects:

```
var explosion : ParticleEmitter;
var smoke : ParticleEmitter;
```

Assign these variables in the Inspector with your new explosion and smoke effects. Remember to align the particles correctly on the Bunny prefab or you'll never see it in action.

Now create a new function to handle the effects at the bottom of the file:

```
function PlayEffects()
{

}
```

Like with *Widget*, you'll need to control exactly when each emitter turns on and off. Add the following to the body of this function:

```
explosion.emit = true;
smoke.emit = true;
yield WaitForSeconds(.5);
GameObject.Find("root").GetComponent(SkinnedMeshRenderer).enabled = false;
yield WaitForSeconds(.5);
explosion.emit = false;
yield WaitForSeconds(3.5);
smoke.emit = false;
```

First up, you need to start both emitters playing. After waiting for a brief pause, you then turn off the bunny's mesh renderer, making her invisible. This way her body won't poke through any piece of the resulting explosion. After waiting a bit more, you turn off the fire part of the explosion, wait a bit longer, and then finish off by completing the smoke emitter. Scroll up to the EBunny's Die( ) function and insert a call to the Play Effects function here:

```
[...]
Destroy(gameObject.GetComponent(EBunny_AIController));
yield WaitForSeconds(animation["EBunny_Death"].length - 5);

//Play effects goes here
PlayEffects();

//Cache location of dead body for pickups
var itemLocation = gameObject.transform.position;
[...]
```

Try testing your newly improved exploding bunny, as shown in Figure 15.14!

Create and add more particle effects as you see fit. Possible areas to explore include some simple water splashes around the bridge and a trail renderer for *Widget* when he uses his boost skill.

As you can see, particles are a relatively quick and easy way to add some punch and pizzazz to your game, while also sometimes making it easier to play. Only one last kind of effect is left to add to *Widget* now—audio.

Figure 15.14
Gone in a flash.

Updated Scripts

The newly completed and updated scripts are also available on the DVD in the Chapter 15 folder.

PickupItems.js

```
//PickupItems: handles any items lying around the world that Widget can pick up

var itemType : InventoryItem;
var itemAmount = 1;
var sparkleEmitter : ParticleEmitter;

private var pickedUp = false;

//When Widget finds an item on the field------------------------------
function OnTriggerEnter(collider: Collider){

    //make sure that this is a player hitting the item and not an enemy
    var playerStatus : Widget_Status = collider.GetComponent(Widget_Status);
    if(playerStatus == null) return;

    //stop it from being picked up twice by accident
    if(pickedUp) return;
```

```
    //If everything's good, put it in Widget's Inventory
    var widgetInventory  = collider.GetComponent(Widget_Inventory);
    widgetInventory.GetItem(itemType, itemAmount);
    pickedUp = true;

    //stop any FX when picking it up
    sparkleEmitter.emit = false;

    //Get rid of it now that it's in the inventory
    Destroy(gameObject);
}


// Make sure the pickup is set up properly with a collider---------------
function Reset ()
{
    if (collider == null)
    {
        gameObject.AddComponent(SphereCollider);
    }
    collider.isTrigger = true;

    sparkleEmitter.emit = true;
}
@script AddComponentMenu("Inventory/PickupItems")
```

CheckPoint.js

```
//Checkpoint.js: checkpoints in the level - active for
//the last selected one and first for the initial one at startup
//the static declaration makes the isActivePt variable global
//across all instances of this script in the game.

static var isActivePt : CheckPoint;
var firstPt : CheckPoint;
var activeEmitter : ParticleEmitter;

var playerStatus : Widget_Status;
playerStatus = GameObject.FindWithTag("Player").
                GetComponent(Widget_Status);
```

```
function Start()
{
     //initialize first point
isActivePt = firstPt;

     if(isActivePt == this){
          BeActive();
     }
}

//When the player encounters a point, this is called
//when the collision occurs
function OnTriggerEnter(){

     //first turn off the old respawn point if this is a
     //newly encountered one
     if(isActivePt != this){
          isActivePt.BeInactive();

          //then set the new one
          isActivePt = this;
          BeActive();
     }
     playerStatus.AddHealth(playerStatus.maxHealth);
     playerStatus.AddEnergy(playerStatus.maxEnergy);
     //print("Player stepped on me");
}

//calls all the FX and audio to make the triggered point
//"activate" visually
function BeActive()
{
activeEmitter.emit = true;
}

//calls all the FX and audio to make any old triggered point
//"inactivate" visually
function BeInactive()
```

```
{
activeEmitter.emit = false;
}
@script AddComponentMenu("Environment Props/CheckPt")
```

Widget_AttackController.js

```
//Widget_AttackController:   handles the player's attack
//input and deals damage to the targeted enemy
var attackHitTime = 0.2;
var attackTime = 0.5;
var attackPosition = new Vector3 (0, 1, 0);
var attackRadius = 2.0;
var damage= 1.0;

var attackEmitter : ParticleEmitter;

//---------------------------------------------------
private var busy = false;
private var ourLocation;
private var enemies : GameObject[] ;

var controller : Widget_Controller;
controller = GetComponent(Widget_Controller);

//Allow the player to attack if he is not busy and
//the Attack button was pressed
function Update ()
{
    if(!busy && Input.GetButtonDown ("Attack") &&
                controller.IsGrounded() && !controller.IsMoving())
    {
        DidAttack();
        busy = true;
    }
}

function DidAttack ()
{
    //Play the animation regardless of whether we hit something.
    animation.CrossFadeQueued("Taser", 0.1, QueueMode.PlayNow);
    yield WaitForSeconds(attackHitTime);
```

```
        //Play effects
        PlayParticles();

        ourLocation = transform.TransformPoint(attackPosition);
        enemies = GameObject.FindGameObjectsWithTag("Enemy");
        //See if any enemies are within range of the attack.
        //This will hit all in range.
        for (var enemy : GameObject in enemies)
        {
            var enemyStatus = enemy.GetComponent(EBunny_Status);
            if (enemyStatus == null)
            {
                continue;
            }

            if (Vector3.Distance(enemy.transform.position,
                        ourLocation) < attackRadius)
            {
                //apply damage for hitting
                enemyStatus.ApplyDamage(damage);
            }
        }
        yield WaitForSeconds(attackTime - attackHitTime);
        busy = false;
}

function GetClosestEnemy() : GameObject
{
        enemies = GameObject.FindGameObjectsWithTag("Enemy");
        var distanceToEnemy = Mathf.Infinity;
        var wantedEnemy;

        for (var enemy : GameObject in enemies)
            {
                newDistanceToEnemy = Vector3.Distance
                    (enemy.transform.position, transform.position);
                if (newDistanceToEnemy < distanceToEnemy)
                {
                    distanceToEnemy = newDistanceToEnemy;
                    wantedEnemy = enemy;
```

```
            }
        }
    return wantedEnemy;
}

function PlayParticles()
{
    attackEmitter.emit = true;
    yield WaitForSeconds(attackEmitter.minEnergy );
    attackEmitter.emit = false;
}

@script AddComponentMenu("Player/Widget's Attack Controller")
```

EBunny_Status

```
//EBunny_Status: controls the state information of the enemy bunny

var health: float = 10.0;
var energy: float = 10.0;
private var dead = false;

var charImage : Texture2D;
var explosion : ParticleEmitter;
var smoke : ParticleEmitter;

//PickupItems held-------------------------------------
var numHeldItemsMin = 1;
var numHeldItemsMax = 3;
var pickup1: GameObject;
var pickup2: GameObject;

//State Functions--------------------------------------
function ApplyDamage(damage: float){
    if (health <= 0)
        return;

    health -= damage;

    animation.Play("EBunny_Hit");
```

```
    //check health and call Die if need to
    if(!dead && health <= 0)
    {
        health = 0; //for GUI
        dead = true;
        Die();
    }
}
function Die ()
{
    animation.Stop();
    animation.Play("EBunny_Death");

    Destroy(gameObject.GetComponent(EBunny_AIController));
    yield WaitForSeconds(animation["EBunny_Death"].length - 0.5);

    //Play effects
    PlayEffects();

    //Cache location of dead body for pickups
    var itemLocation = gameObject.transform.position;

    // drop a random number of reward pickups for the player
    yield WaitForSeconds(5);
    var rewardItems = Random.Range(numHeldItemsMin, numHeldItemsMax) + 1;

    for (var i = 0; i < rewardItems; i++)
    {
        var randomItemLocation = itemLocation;
        randomItemLocation.x += Random.Range(-2, 2);
        randomItemLocation.y += 1; // Keep it off the ground
        randomItemLocation.z += Random.Range(-2, 2);

        if (Random.value > 0.5)
            Instantiate(pickup1, randomItemLocation,
                        pickup1.transform.rotation);
        else
            Instantiate(pickup2, randomItemLocation,
                        pickup2.transform.rotation);
    }
```

```
}

    //Remove killed enemy from the scene
    Destroy(gameObject);
}
function IsDead() : boolean
{
    return dead;
}
function GetCharImage(): Texture2D
{
    return charImage;
}
function PlayEffects()
{
    explosion.emit = true;
    smoke.emit = true;
    yield WaitForSeconds(.5);
    GameObject.Find("root").GetComponent(SkinnedMeshRenderer).enabled = false;
    yield WaitForSeconds(.5);
    explosion.emit = false;
    yield WaitForSeconds(3.5);
    smoke.emit = false;
}
@script AddComponentMenu("Enemies/Bunny'sStateManager")
```

CHAPTER 16

ADDING AUDIO AND MUSIC

Sound effects and music can be overlooked and sidelined during much of a game's development—the important stuff is in the gameplay, right? Besides being one of the most effective ways of setting a mood for a level, sounds also provide much needed feedback and information, from weapon firings to interface clicks. Sounds need to provide meaningful information and fit the game world; finding just the right sound for a footstep or button click can be an arduous task. While training, trial and error and perseverance are the only ways to find just the right sound; Unity at least makes it easy to put sound into your game once you're ready.

FEEDBACK AND AMBIENCE

One of the more recognizable aspects of game audio is the background music track. Most games play some sort of music during level exploration, battles, or menu selection. By switching out the background music, the mood of the scene can then easily (and relatively cheaply) be changed. Demure, sad scene? Plop in a solo piano or violin. Need to increase the player's adrenaline? Write or find a song with heavy, percussive beats and short quippy lines. If you're fairly new to audio, analyze some of your favorite games and movies. Identify the scenes you think are the most successful in mood and tone, and study what the audio designer did. Although you may need a fair amount of training and experience to write music, you just need to train your ear to be good at selecting it.

Although most games make heavy use of MIDI and sampled sounds, more and more titles are starting to use live recordings from individual instruments or complete orchestras. The live instruments for the most part sound better in every way, but there is a slight increase in memory overhead and monetary expense when going this way. For the solo developer or hobbyist, MIDI transcriptions and mixes are still the best way to go. For information on free MIDI libraries, transcription, and mixing software packages, see Appendix D, "Resources and References," found on the DVD. There are a lot of resources for audio out on the Internet, and you may even be able to work out a deal with a composer or sound designer who wants to show his work in games and interactive media.

Caution

When scouring the Internet for background music pieces, make absolutely sure you have the legal rights to use the work in your game. If the copyright and fair use agreement are vague, contact the artist. Most semi-professional and amateur musicians love to have their songs featured to new potential audiences, and many will allow you to do so free if proper credit is given.

Audio cues and sound effects are also highly important to get right when making a game. Play one of your favorite games for five minutes and just note how many different sounds are employed at any given moment. Footsteps on the ground need individual sounds (often of more than one variety for different materials), buttons need clicks, ambient objects like birds and water need noises, collisions need explosions, and the list goes on. While a given game may need 20 or so background musical pieces, the same game may require well over 1,000 unique sounds and effects to correctly portray the audio of the levels. There are tricks you can employ, like pitch bending and remixing, to reuse a single sound multiple times, but in general, be prepared to devote a large amount of time to finding and hooking up sound effects.

For the *Widget* game, a small selection of sound effects and background music is provided for your use. These recordings were made on a Yamaha CVP401 and mixed in Adobe Audition and are free for you to use for your own projects. You can find the music and sound effect files in the DVD under the Chapters▶ Chapter 16 folder.

SETTING UP A SIMPLE AUDIO CLIP

Any audio file is imported into Unity as an audio clip, which supports the following formats: .aif, .wav, .mp3, and .ogg. By default, Unity does not compress your files, but you may change this through the Inspector.

To start, locate the Chapter 16 folder on the DVD and import the contents of the Audio folder into your project, placing it into the Audio folder there. You should have BG Tracks (background music) and Sound FX (shorter effect clips). You don't need to import the Source folder into your project.

Select any one of the imported audio files while in the Project view to see its import information in the Inspector. Figure 16.1 shows the BG track.

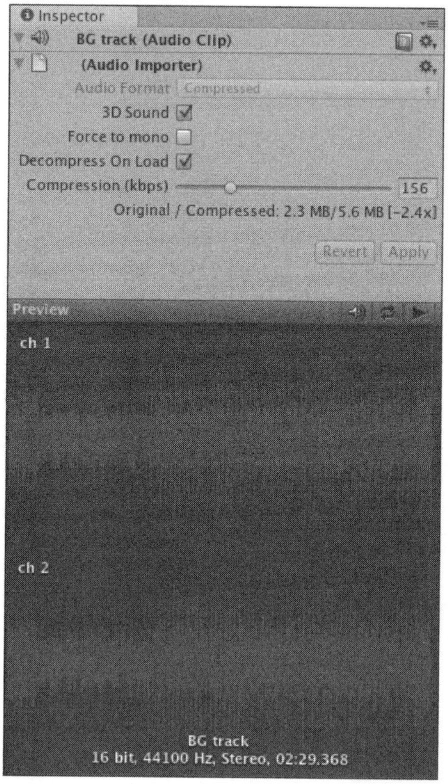

Figure 16.1
An imported audio clip.

- **Audio Format:** Selects whether to import the file as compressed or native. Native files are larger but have better sound quality. For shorter files, this is okay, but any lengthier piece of music should be compressed. MP3 format files are automatically set as compressed.

- **3D Sound:** Plays this sound in 3D space. Both mono and stereo sounds can be played in 3D.

- **Force to Mono:** Plays a stereo sound as mono.

- **Decompress on Load:** Loads the audio clip into working memory once the scene is loaded. By default this is checked, as you may experience a performance hit if sounds are decompressed in real time.

- **Compression:** The amount of compression Unity should apply to the clip. If your game file is a little on the large size, try increasing the compression ratio of your audio files. In general, you should look to compress your files until you start to get some audible deterioration.

A graph of the waveform is also displayed in the Inspector, and you can preview the sound by clicking the black arrow button at the top-right of the Preview pane.

In general, audio in Unity is played by various audio sources, which are picked up by the Audio Listener. You can think of the Listener as a giant microphone that picks up any audio around it. Since Unity does play sound in 3D, sounds placed farther away in the scene will be quieter than those closest to the Listener. Each scene can only have one Audio Listener active at any time.

By default, the Main Camera is populated with the Audio Listener component. Depending on your game, this may be the perfect spot for it. If you're making a first-person type game, you'll probably want the Listener attached to your player object, so 3D sounds correctly positioned. Since the Main Camera follows *Widget* around, it's an acceptable place to keep the Listener. If you want to move the Listener, simply select the GameObject you want to attach it to and navigate to Component▶Audio▶Audio Listener. This component has no properties to set.

Audio sources are used to simulate anything in your world that could emit sound, including ambient bird calls, running water, falling rocks, and so on. The source controls all the major properties of sound playback, like pitch, volume, and rolloff, and can play any audio clip you have imported into the game.

Ambient Sound Effects

Open your last save of the *Widget* game or open the Chapter 16 Scene file on the DVD. Import the audio clips as described earlier if you haven't yet. You'll give *Widget* a little bit of ambient noise before moving on to more singular sounds.

To add ambient noise, follow these steps:

1. Navigate to the place in your level where you placed the bridge over the river. Create an empty GameObject and place it near the surface of the water. Rename it **Water Sound**.

2. Add an Audio Source component to the GameObject by navigating to Component▸Audio▸Audio Source. This will also create a little speaker icon at the GameObject's location, making it easier to place. An example of the source is shown in Figure 16.2.

3. Now you need to actually give the source something to play. Either drag and drop the newly imported water.mp3 clip into the audio clip field or select it from the drop-down menu. Change the volume to something around 0.5 and check the Loop box to have the sound run continuously. You can leave the other selections as they are.

4. Test the sound in the game by rolling *Widget* towards the water. The sound should get louder as *Widget* approaches the bridge and fade out the farther he gets away.

All ambient sound effects can be set up in this way. You can also try parenting these audio sources to moving GameObjects, to simulate moving sounds like birds.

Controlling Sounds Through Scripts

Calling sounds with scripts isn't much harder than setting up an audio source, and it does give you a lot more finesse in how you use them.

Figure 16.2
The water audio source.

To start, you'll add a hit sound and death sound for *Widget*, which will give the players some better feedback on their health.

First, you need to set up the *Widget* prefab to play sounds. Select the prefab in the Project view and add an Audio Source component (choose Component▶Audio▶Audio Source). Don't worry about setting up any of the Source properties, as you'll do that on the script side. Any GameObject you want to play sounds must have an Audio Source component, even if it is completely script driven.

Open the Widget_Status.js script and add some new variables to the top of the file. You'll need to make an AudioClip variable for each of the two sounds:

```
//Sound Effects---------------------
var hitSound: AudioClip;
var deathSound: AudioClip;
```

As you've already written functions in this script to handle both damage done to *Widget* and his eventual death, adding in the audio functionality is simple. Locate the ApplyDamage function in this file and add a new if statement to handle the sound. Place the if statement after the health-=damage line:

```
health -= damage;
if(hitSound)
{
}
```

Now that you've verified that a clip exists and that *Widget* did in fact get damaged, you just need to play the sound. Inside the if statement, add the following:

```
audio.clip = hitSound;
audio.Play();
```

audio is a special key word Unity uses to reference the clip stored in the Audio Source component of a GameObject. Here, you're telling Unity which sound to populate the source with, and then to play it. The death sound will be set up similarly. Locate the Die function in the script and add to the top of the function:

```
if(deathSound)
{
    audio.clip = deathSound;
    audio.Play();
}
```

Unity will now fill the audio source with a new clip, the death sound, and then play it whenever *Widget* loses all his hit points. By calling audio clips from scripts, you can easily store and play more than one file per source.

Back in the editor, populate the hitSound field on the *Widget* prefab with the crash.mp3 sound, and place the taser.mp3 clip into the deathSound field. Test your game by running into one of the EBunny enemies or by rolling into the water.

A few other sound effects have also been provided for you. Try hooking up similar sounds to the *Widget* Attack controller (a sound to play when *Widget* uses his attack) and for the EBunny's own attacks and death. Figure 16.3 shows the *Widget* prefab with these two sounds and a third attack sound attached to the Attack controller.

The AudioSource class also has other useful functions that you may find beneficial when setting up more complex clips. You can programmatically change the pitch and volume, stop or pause the given clip, or determine whether a given audio clip is playing. Check Appendix B, "Common Classes," on the DVD, for more information on this class.

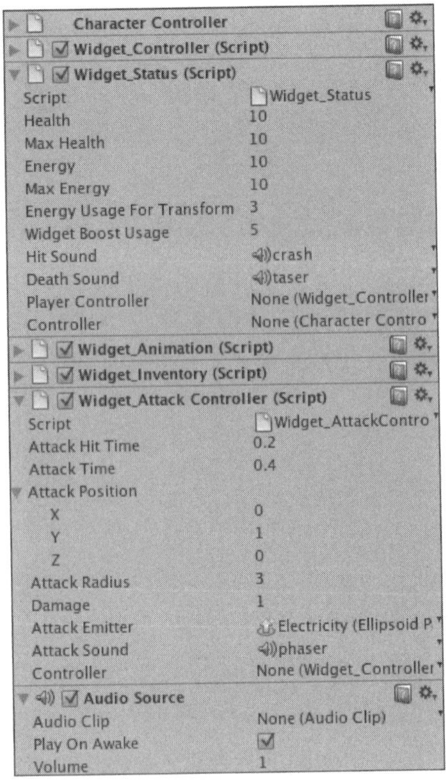

Figure 16.3
The finished *Widget* prefab.

Adding Background Music

All that's left now is to set up some background music for the menu and main game level. For both of these, you'll set up a new Audio Source object and attach it to the Main Camera in each scene. You specifically don't want these clips to be located or played in 3D space, as they should be heard regardless of where the player currently is.

Let's start off with the level music:

1. Create a new empty GameObject and rename it **BGMusic**. Parent this new object to the Main Camera in the scene. Give this new object an Audio Source component. You could of course attach an audio source

directly to the camera, but as this houses the Listener, it's better to keep the two separate. Reset the position of the BGMusic object to (0,0,0).

2. Locate the BG track file in the Audio folder and populate the BGMusic audio source with it. Check the Loop box and set the volume to about 0.5. You can also uncheck the 3D Sound field on the track's Import properties. Because you're only using this as simple, static music, this functionality isn't needed.

3. Test your game with the new background music in place. Specifically try to fire all the sound effects you placed to ensure that the different volumes are set correctly. You may want to lower the background music volume to suit your personal taste.

4. The main menu scene is handled much the same. Save your work in the Chapter16 scene file, and then open the scene file where you saved your main menu screen from Chapter 13.

5. Follow the same steps to attach a new Audio Source GameObject to the Main Camera. Populate the audio source with the BG track and reset the loop and volume fields.

Congratulations! You now know all the basics for making your own games in Unity, from concept to scripts to sound. Take this time now to open the Final Project Files on the DVD and import any additional pieces you want. Many more art and GUI pieces have been provided on the DVD for you to expand your game, or you can go and make your own assets to use. Make new levels, expand the current one, and just have fun with it.

The last two chapters go over some basic optimization and debugging techniques in Unity, as well as how to package up your game as either a standalone app or as a web game.

UPDATED SCRIPTS

These can also be found on the DVD in the Chapter 16 folder, but are included here for reference.

```
//Widget_Status: Handles Widget's state machine.
//Keep track of health, energy and all the chunky stuff

//vitals--------------------------------
var health: float = 10.0;
var maxHealth: float= 10.0;
var energy: float = 10.0;
var maxEnergy: float = 10.0;
var energyUsageForTransform: float = 3.0;
var widgetBoostUsage :float = 5.0;

//Sound Effects--------------------------
var hitSound: AudioClip;
var deathSound: AudioClip;

//Cache Controllers--------------------
var playerController: Widget_Controller;
playerController = GetComponent(Widget_Controller) ;
var controller : CharacterController;
controller = GetComponent(CharacterController);

//Helper Controller Functions-----------
function ApplyDamage(damage: float){

    health -= damage;

    //play hit sound if it exists
    if(hitSound)
    {
        audio.clip = hitSound;
        audio.Play();
    }
    //check health and call Die if need to
    if(health <= 0){
        health = 0; //for GUI
        Die();
    }

}
```

```
function AddHealth(boost: float){
   //add health and set to min of (current health+boost) or health max
   health += boost;
   if(health >= maxHealth){
      health = maxHealth;
   }
   print("added health: " + health);
}

function AddEnergy(boost: float){
   //add energy and set to nim of (current en + boost) or en max
   energy += boost;
   if(energy >= maxEnergy){
      energy = maxEnergy;
   }
   print("added energy: " + energy);
}

function Die(){
   //play death sound if it exists
   if(deathSound)
   {
      audio.clip = deathSound;
      audio.Play();
   }
   print("dead!");
   playerController.isControllable = false;

   animationState = GetComponent(Widget_Animation);
   animationState.PlayDie();
   yield WaitForSeconds(animation["Die"].length -0.2);
   HideCharacter();

   yield WaitForSeconds(1);

   //restart player at last respawn check point and give max life
   if(CheckPoint.isActivePt){
      controller.transform.position=CheckPoint.isActivePt.transform.position;
      controller.transform.position.y += 0.5;
            //so not to get stuck in the platform itself
```

```
    }
    ShowCharacter();
    health = maxHealth;
}

function HideCharacter(){
    GameObject.Find("Body").GetComponent(SkinnedMeshRenderer).enabled = false;
    GameObject.Find("Wheels").GetComponent(SkinnedMeshRenderer).enabled = false;
    playerController.isControllable = false;


}

function ShowCharacter(){
    GameObject.Find("Body").GetComponent(SkinnedMeshRenderer).enabled = true;
    GameObject.Find("Wheels").GetComponent(SkinnedMeshRenderer).enabled = true;
    playerController.isControllable = true;


}

@script AddComponentMenu("Player/Widget'sStateManager")
```

PART V

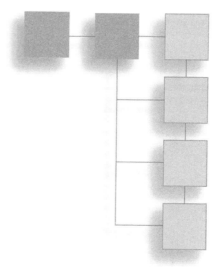

PUBLISHING AND DISTRIBUTING BUILDS

At this point, your game is fully playable and functioning, but probably shouldn't be shown to others quite yet. First, it could benefit from a quick debugging and optimization pass, ensuring that no little errors linger to trip up the players and that everything runs as smoothly as possible. After this there's only one final thing left to do—build and save your game as a stand-alone application, so that any and all can enjoy it without being tethered to a computer.

CHAPTER 17

BASIC UNITY DEBUGGING AND OPTIMIZATION

Anyone who's written any kind of software knows about the importance of debugging and code optimization. Bugs and errors always creep in (often in completely unexpected and hard-to-test areas), and code can run slower and slower as more stuff gets thrown in. Most games are pretty complicated pieces of software, and many months are devoted at the end of the project to bug finding, fixing, and optimization.

Beyond code, the artwork in a game also needs to be compressed and optimized, both to speed up performance and to reduce final file size. You may have the best-looking game ever, but if it doesn't fit on your platform's distributable, no one is going to see it. The new editions of Unity now include many tools and utilities to help developers in their quest against buggy code and bloated artwork.

DEBUGGING IN UNITY

With Unity's code-and-test as you go methodology, it's usually pretty hard to introduce blatant errors into your game: Upon clicking the Play button, any simple error will quickly be spotted in the Console. However, as your game becomes more complex, hidden and infrequent bugs may start to creep into your work, and tracking these down can become a lengthy and time-consuming process. Good tools and coding practices can help, but there's no quick fix or magic solution for easy debugging.

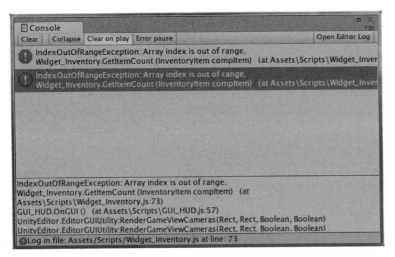

Figure 17.1
A sample error in the Console window.

The Console

You've already done a bit of basic debugging through your work in the Console window. Non-fatal errors that the game runs into are printed here, marked by a red octagonal symbol, and warning messages are displayed with a yellow symbol, one of which is shown in Figure 17.1.

The Console tries to narrow down the work of finding the source of the bug for you, listing the script and line number of where the error occurred. Unity will also provide you with a small description of what actually went wrong, as in this case, an index for an array is out of range. Although this won't always be the original source of the error, it can help in starting to track it down.

If you're using a third-party coding environment (like Visual Studio), you'll have access to all the debugging tools you're accustomed to, like dump files and breakpoints. However, if you are using the scripting environment that came with Unity, the Console debugger is going to be your main tool. Ample use of print statements and output strings to a log file are some of the only ways to track down errors in UniSciTE. It's not the prettiest or easiest way of finding bugs, but in general the Console does a good job at locating errors and giving them meaningful labels.

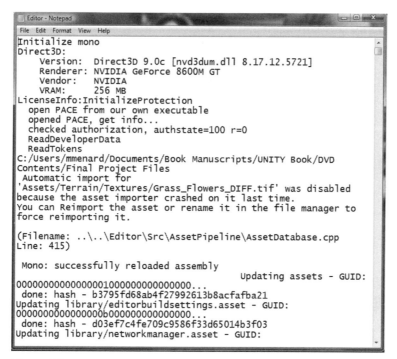

Figure 17.2
The startup information from playing the game in the editor.

The Log Files

Your game's log files can also provide needed information on what was exactly going on when the bug or crash occurred. Log files are stored in two locations on your computer, based on whether the file was created from within the editor or from a standalone game application or web player. Figure 17.2 shows a sample log file created from within the editor.

Errors shown on the Console will be printed into the logs each time they occur, with information on the location and type of error found. The editor log file is easily accessed from within Unity on the Console window. Open the Console and then click the Open Editor Log button in the upper-right corner of the Console. If you want to see log files generated from a built game, you'll need to manually find them on your computer.

For Mac users, all the logs are stored in one place:

~ /Library/Logs/Unity/

If you're using a Windows machine, the editor and game logs are stored in two different locations.

Windows XP:

- C:\Documents and Settings\Local Settings\temp\UnityWebPlayer\log
- C:\Documents and Settings*UserName*\Local Settings\Application Data \Unity\Editor

Vista/Windows 7:

- C:\Users\AppData\Local\Temp\Low\UnityWebPlayer\log
- C:\Users*UserName*\AppData\Local\Unity\Editor

Note

On Windows machines, the Local Settings folder is hidden by default, so you'll need to enable viewing permissions first. In XP, navigate to Tools▶ Folder Options and click on the View tab. Under the Advanced Settings section, click on Show Hidden Files and Folders to enable it. In Vista and Windows 7, the Folder Options menu can be accessed from Organize▶ Folder and Search Options.

The Editor.log file is updated and rewritten each time you play the game in the editor, but Unity does automatically store the previous log file for you in the same location, naming it Editor-prev.log. If you want to save and examine more previous logs, you'll need to save them manually.

Some of these log files can become large and unwieldy, and it can be hard to spot where things worked differently or changed from one version to the next. A neat way to deal with this problem is have the computer do the work for you—many text editors are equipped with a utility to detect and highlight line changes, making your job a whole lot faster. Notepad++ is an example of a down-loadable free text editor capable of highlighting changes, a link to which is included in Appendix D, "Resources and References," found on the DVD.

OPTIMIZATION

While debugging utilities in Unity may be a little on the light side, the editor does come packed full with a multitude of different tools and emulators to help with optimization and cleanup. Many of these are fairly new and have been introduced as the engine has grown and developed over the years. With the notable exception of the Profiler, all the optimization tools are available in both Unity Free and Pro.

The Profiler

Available only to users with a Pro license, the Profiler instruments your code, letting you know exactly how the game utilizes your computer's resources and the time it takes to render, animate, or run through code. By default, the Profiler doesn't cause a noticeable delay or lag in your game and has a rather small overhead. If you turn on Deep Profiling, all of your code is instrumented and recorded, and this does create a very large and noticeable memory overhead. For some complex games, Deep Profiling may actually not be an option—it is definitely possible to crash Unity and make the editor run out of memory using this approach.

The main Profiler window can be accessed from Window▶Profiler or by pressing Ctrl+7. If instead you'd like to just profile specific areas of your game (like a single function), you can use the BeginSample and EndSample function calls found within the Profiler class to do so.

For those with the Pro version, the Profiler provides a nice peek into how your game runs and functions from frame to frame, but it isn't the only option available to you for optimization. For everyone else with the Free license, there are still many things you can do to make your game run faster, smarter, and smaller. See Figure 17.3.

Basic Code Optimization

One of the first areas you can look to optimize is your scripts. Although it may appear at first glance that your code is clean and fast, there are a few tricks you can employ to make it run even better in Unity. A few milliseconds may not sound like much, but you'll see a noticeable jump in framerate if you can even shave one millisecond off of each function call.

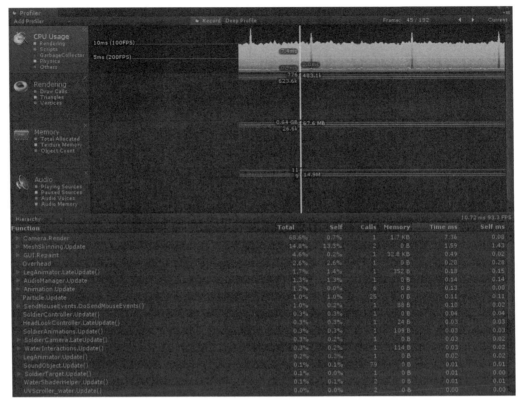

Figure 17.3
The Profiler view for a sample game, *Boot Camp.*

Static Typing

If you've been using JavaScript for your code, go back over it and ensure that you've statically typed all your variables. While dynamically typed variables may be easier and faster for you to write, they are incredibly slow to run, as Unity has to infer the type every time it uses the variable. This can add up ridiculously quickly.

Sometimes it's simple to see where you've dynamically typed a variable, but it's still easy to miss a few while wading in thousands of lines of code. Luckily, you can quickly test for any dynamically typed variables by putting #pragma strict at the top of every script file. This one line will force Unity to disable dynamic typing. When the engine then encounters a variable that isn't statically typed, it will report an error in the Console.

Cache Lookups to Components

As you've done in many of the scripts, caching a link to a GameObject or component can make your game run much faster. Normally, each time a function like GetComponent is used, Unity has to search through all the objects and components until it finds the one you requested. If you know you'll need a particular object multiple times, create a variable that links to it directly.

```
Function Awake() {
    var controller : CharacterController ;
    controller = GetComponent(CharacterController);
}
```

The variable controller can now be used to reference the component directly, instead of having to search for it. Of course you won't need (or want) to do this every time you use GetComponent, but if you know you'll be manipulating objects every frame, it's definitely worth creating a cache.

Cull Based on Player Location

The best way to make your code faster is to never call it in the first place. If the player can't see something on the screen, then odds are it doesn't need to be running. You can use techniques to check the distance to the player or use the provided functions OnBecameVisible and OnBecameInvisible to do the work for you. These two functions check to see whether the given object is in the field of the camera and can be quickly and easily used to start up and shut down unnecessary commands and actions. Triggers can also be handy ways to tell if a player is close enough for something to start running. If the player enters a given field of influence, start the script running. When he leaves, shut it down.

So even without the Profiler, there still are a lot of tweaks you can do on your own to make your scripts run faster and more efficiently.

Emulation

Unity offers two emulation utilities to test how your game would run on different hardware: Graphics Emulation and Network Emulation. Both are accessed from the Edit menu of the editor.

Graphics Emulation limits the capabilities of your graphics card, disabling features as the list goes down. Figure 17.4 shows Graphics Emulation at work.

Figure 17.4
No emulation, DX7 emulation, and Dinosaur.

If you're writing custom shaders or use lots of flashy effects, emulation can provide a quick look into how your game would likely perform on hardware of that nature. This is not a replacement for standard compatibility testing, but it does provide a quick approximation of some of the errors you could expect to see.

If your game is destined for the web player, you can also emulate what kind of Internet connection your player could be using. Network emulation attempts to parody the different kinds of connections (broadband, DSL, dial-up, and so on) by delaying packet information and inflating the ping. For dial-up connections, the developers at Unity even went a step further by introducing dropped packets and variance, creating a truly nasty connection.

Rendering Statistics Page

Besides the emulation test, there are other aspects of graphics optimization you can pursue to make your game run smoother. On the Game View window, click the Stats button in the upper-right corner. This brings up a Statistics page for your game, displaying information like the number of draw calls and framerate. As you play your game, the window will update with current information, allowing you to quickly identify problem areas in your levels. Figure 17.5 shows the statistics for the *Widget* game.

Figure 17.5
Widget's basic stats.

From this, you can see at a quick glance that the FPS (frames per second) is pretty good, but the game is using a fair number of animations and a large number of draw calls. With this information in hand, targeted optimization can begin. A breakdown of the different readouts follows:

- **FPS information:** How much time it takes to render and process one frame in milliseconds, and the derived framerate in seconds.

- **Draw calls:** How many total objects are rendered in the scene. Some objects may be counted more than once, as some kinds of lighting will result in multiple draw calls for a single object.

- **Tris and Verts:** The number of triangles and vertices drawn.

- **Used textures:** The total number textures drawn that frame, and how much memory is used.

- **Render textures:** The total number and size of render textures drawn that frame.

- **Screen:** The current screen resolution and memory used.

- **VRAM usage:** An approximation of how much video memory your game is using. Your total available memory is displayed afterwards.

- **VBO total:** The number of unique meshes that were uploaded to the graphics card, and the memory used.

- **VB uploads:** The amount of vertex data updated this frame.

- **IB uploads:** The amount of triangle data updated this frame.

- **Visible skinned meshes:** How many skinned meshes are currently being rendered.

- **Animations:** How many animations are actively playing.

- **Network:** The number of players connected, if any.

With this information always at your fingertips, you can quickly update any art and see immediate feedback on what the changes provide.

Reducing File Size

One of the first ways to optimize your graphics is to critically look at the size of your assets. Textures and audio are two of the main culprits for large game installs, and they should be the first place you look to compress or shorten.

Since Unity processes all your art assets when you import, it's quick and easy to compress or limit your texture sizes used. In most development environments, you would need to go back to your original art, resize it manually, and then reimport it back into the engine. In Unity, you can set the Max Texture Size in the Inspector for each texture used in your game, as well as change the compression format. Reduce the rendered texture size and increase the compression for all your textures until you just begin to see some deterioration in the visuals. As these tweaks do not permanently change anything in your original art files, you can always go back and change the levels again at your convenience.

Ensure that all your audio clips are also compressed and do not contain any unnecessary silence or lead time. If a sound needs to be played multiple times, loop it in the engine and not in the actual file itself. Be cognizant of how your audio clips are stored, especially if you're developing for the web player.

If you're still having memory issues, look into compressing your imported meshes and animation clips. Compressing meshes will make your game take up less disk space, while compressing animations saves both runtime memory and disk space. Compressing animations too much, however, can lead to jumpy behavior, so always use small tweaks at first.

Finally, Unity only builds your game with the assets you actually used in your levels. If you have a few assets sitting in your Project folder that you never used, it's okay, they can stay there. Unity removes any unused assets from the project list during the game build, so you don't need to worry about stray pieces of art making your game bigger than it should be.

Other Ways to Optimize Graphics

Compression and reducing file size is a great way to save memory space for your game's disk footprint, but you'll also need to look into optimizing the graphics while the game is running. The Rendering Statistics window can help pinpoint particular areas in need of more attention and work.

If you notice a drop in framerate in an area in your level, check to see how far it goes. Does the drop only occur when a particular object is onscreen? When a certain particle effect is playing? Try to narrow down the cause of your bad performance before you start randomly changing different things.

One cause of bad performance to check for is lighting. Pixel lights look great and can really set the mood of a scene, but they're much more intensive to render than a vertex light. If the light isn't that important, or the objects lit are far away from the player, change the lighting to Force Vertex to start.

Baking in simple light data (like with the terrain lightmaps) is another great way to save perf while not compromising visual quality. If your objects never move and are always illuminated from the same, non-moving source, consider baking the light data into your textures directly. Maya and other 3D graphics packages can make great-looking light bakes quickly and easily.

If you're using generated shadows in your game (not fake ones like the projector blob), check to see if they're the cause of a possible performance hit. You don't need to cut your shadows out completely, but make sure the quality settings are as low as they can go. Also, look at using hard shadows rather than soft ones. For important objects, like a main character, you can still use a nicer shadow quality, but you can save on performance by using cheaper shadows for less-important things.

Finally, if you have multiple meshes using the same material and shader, you can consider combining them into one mesh. It's always faster for Unity to render one object versus many, even if they all share the same texture and have the same number of polygons. This usually isn't something you can easily do engine side, but if you need to make drastic performance tweaks, every little bit helps.

With optimization and debugging complete, it's now time to bundle up your game and prepare to show it to the world!

CHAPTER 18

CREATING THE FINAL BUILD

Now that all the hard work is finished, you need to be able to show the world your creation. The basic Unity license allows you to deploy your game as either a standalone app (Windows and Mac) or as a web player. With the standalone app, you can also customize your loading screen, complete with a custom banner, icons, and menus to allow the users to change both graphic and input options.

PREPPING FOR THE BUILD

Before you set the build options and select the scenes you want to include in the final game, you need to make sure that all the basic player options are set to your satisfaction. Depending on the size of your game, building can take anywhere from a few seconds to hours, so it's usually worthwhile to check that all your basic settings are correct up front, rather than have to rebuild a whole project because one text field was wrong.

Setting Up the Player

The basic information for your final game is stored in the Player Settings Manager, accessed from Edit▶Project Settings▶Player. Open this menu to view the various properties in the Inspector, as shown in Figure 18.1.

- **Company Name:** Enter the name of your company or studio. This name will be used by the game install to house the Preferences file.

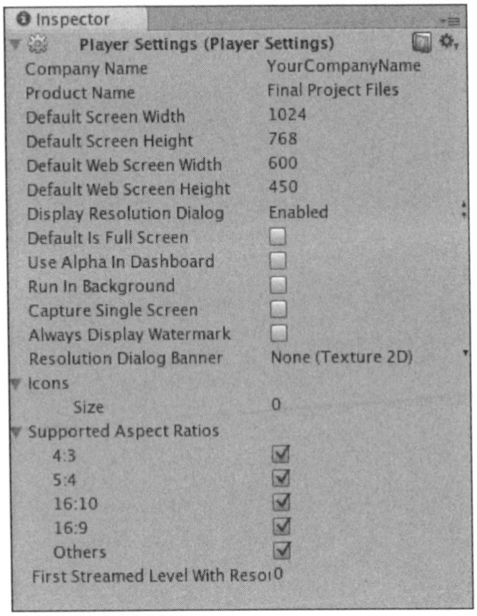

Figure 18.1
The Player Settings Manager.

- **Product Name:** The name of your game! This name will appear in the menu bar and in the Install folder.

- **Default Screen Width:** The default width of the game screen for a standalone app.

- **Default Screen Height:** The default height of the game screen for a standalone app.

- **Default Web Screen Width:** The default width of the game screen for a web app.

- **Default Web Screen Height:** The default height of the game screen for a web app.

- **Display Resolution Dialog Box:** This will display a launch window when the player starts up your game. Here the player can change some basic graphic and input options.

- **Default Is Full Screen:** Starts the game in full screen mode by default.

- **Use Alpha in Dashboard:** If you want your Mac icon to use an alpha channel when being displayed in the OSX dashboard, enable this feature.

- **Run in Background:** Check this if you want your game to continuing running, even if the window loses focus.

- **Capture Single Screen:** For use with the standalone app. If the player has a second monitor set up, checking this will make a full screen game only use one monitor.

- **Always Display Watermark:** Check to always display the Unity logo in the lower-right corner.

- **Resolution Dialog Banner:** Sets the banner image you want your launch window to use.

- **Icons:** Assign the icons for the standalone app to use. Usually, you'll want to include multiple icon files to account for the different possible sizes, specifically 32×32, 48×48, and 128×128.

- **Supported Aspect Ratios:** Check the boxes for which screen ratios you want enabled. The users can then select which one they want from the launch window.

- **First Streamed Level with Resources:** For use with the web player. If you're specifically creating a streamed web player game, you need to specify the index of the first level that has access to all your game assets.

There's no time like the present, so fill out your name and game name and set the properties to whatever you'd like. Sample icons and a banner image are provided in the Chapter 18 folder on the DVD. A sample setup for a standalone app of *Widget* is shown in Figure 18.2.

Finally, the Application Class

Now you just need to make sure that the main menu is ready to go. Back in Chapter 13, you set up the basic script to load your game from the Play button. Open the GUI_MainMenu.js script and ensure that the Application.LoadLevel function is loading the correct scene file. Change the name of the scene file to match whichever level you want the application to start with. For example, my main menu will load the Chapter_18 scene file, as it is my most recent version.

The Application class houses all the important functions that load your various game levels, as well as the basic commands for starting and quitting the game.

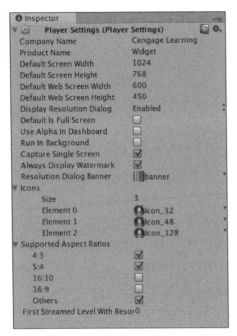

Figure 18.2
The *Widget* game settings.

The class also contains quite a few useful methods for looking up important information on the current state of your application: Is it loading a level, what version of Unity is it using, or is it running in the editor? Some of the more notable members are described here:

- **levelCount**: This read-only variable returns the total number of levels contained in your game. This is particularly useful if you want to load a random level.

- **isEditor**: The variable returns whether the game is running in the editor. You may find later you only want some things to function while in the editor or have the game disable large features for testing quickly and easily.

- **runInBackground**: You can set whether the game should continue to run if it loses focus.

- **unityVersion**: The version of Unity being used to play the game.

- **Quit:** Call this function to quit the application (like you did in the Main Menu script). This is ignored if the game is a web app.
- **LoadLevel:** Load the specified level.

Once you've updated or verified your Main Menu script, it's time to actually make a build.

Build Settings

To create a build of your game, you need to first specify what levels you want Unity to include. Unity will not just create a mass build of all your project files and instead requires you to pick and choose exactly what scenes are to be included. From your scene selection, it will then only include the needed assets into the build package—unused assets will not be included or take up any unnecessary space.

To start your build process, navigate to File▶Build Settings or press Ctrl+Shift+B. In this dialog box, you add the scene files you'd like to include and decide which kind of application Unity should make. An empty Build Settings box is displayed in Figure 18.3.

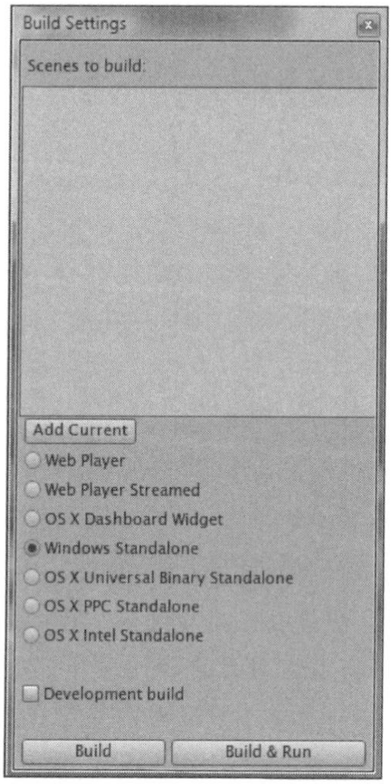

Figure 18.3
The empty Build Settings window.

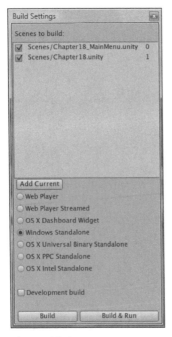

Figure 18.4
Two scenes loaded.

To start populating your build, open your Main Menu scene file, and then click the Add Current button in Build Settings. This will tell Unity you want to include this file in your final game. Next open your main game level and click the Add Current button again. Your settings should now look similar to Figure 18.4.

You'll notice that Unity assigns an index number to each scene file as you add it in, starting at 0, and renumbers them based on each scene's position in the list. If you uncheck a box next to a scene file, it won't be loaded in the Build. You can also rearrange the scenes in the list by clicking and dragging, an easy fix if you happen to load them out of order. Just remember that whichever scene file is assigned the index value of 0 will always start up your game. Make sure it's the main menu in this case.

Note

Now that your scene files have associated index values in the Build menu, you may find it easier from now on to reference the index number with Application.LoadLevel calls. Instead of having to type a name or change it later, just use the index to load whichever level you want, such as Application.LoadLevel(1).

The Build Settings information is saved with your project file, and you don't need to redo each time you want to make a new build. For now, set the game to create as a standalone app, either Windows standalone or an OSX dashboard widget (depending on your own computer). Click the Build Button to create your game. Unity will prompt you for a filename and save path at this time. You can click Build & Run if you want Unity to also launch the game when it's finished.

Once Unity finishes building, it will kindly open the folder where you saved your game. Double-click on it to run your finished game! Go enjoy the fruits of your labor, you've earned it. See Figure 18.5.

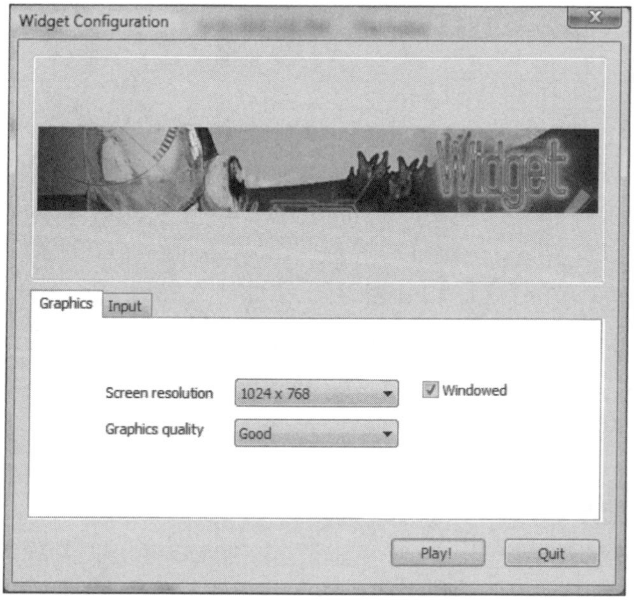

Figure 18.5
The *Widget* launch window.

OTHER BUILD FEATURES

Once you've made your first game or two, you may want to add some new features for dedicated players or package your asset files for use in another project.

New Assets and DLC

Perhaps you were hasty in one of your builds, or maybe you want to offer DLC (downloadable content) to your players. Either way, you don't need to create a new build of your game—you can instead have the player load separate asset packs on load.

Asset Bundles

If you have a Unity Pro license, you can use an asset bundle to handle your new additions. There is no limit on the number of different bundles you can associate with a game, and the creation of one is rather simple.

From within a script, call the function BuildPipeline.BuildAssetBundle(). The argument is an array containing a list of all the additional objects you want to include. Once this is made, you can later load this bundle by calling AssetBundle.Load().

Resource Folders

If you have the free version of Unity, you can still create add-ons for your game with resource folders. To do this, simply create a new folder in your Project view and name it **Resources**. If you want to load an object inside this, simply call Resources.Load().

You may also find asset bundles and resource folders an easy way to load assets at runtime, which can be incredibly useful for a web player game. The app itself is pretty tiny and loads quickly, and then you can stream in only the assets you need, only when you need them.

Packing Up Assets for Later

You can also create asset packages from within your Project view, making it easy to share your assets with another user or save them for later use on a different project.

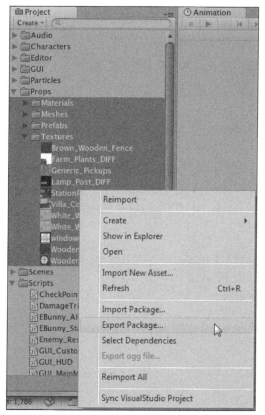

Figure 18.6
Exporting a package.

To create a package, simply highlight all the items in the Project view you want to include. Then right-click and select Export Package, as shown in Figure 18.6.

This will bring up a dialog box where you can select the individual files you want to include and also decide whether you want to include any dependencies (nice if you don't know what the other project already has). Click the Export button and choose a destination for the saved file. Depending on the number and size of the assets selected, this process can take a while.

Once you have a package ready to go, you can import it into any project you want by right-clicking in the Project view and selecting Import Package.

The End of the Road?

You've now made your first Unity game from start to finish, but it doesn't end here. There are many more advanced features not covered in this book and many changes and tweaks you can make to the *Widget* game alone.

Appendix D, "Resources and References," lists some books and websites for extended reading. Appendix C, "Going Forward," discusses some areas of the *Widget* game that you might like to try to improve. Both appendixes are found on the DVD. *Widget* has some intentional flaws and underdeveloped areas, specifically so you can try your new skills in an unguided manner. If you're not ready to start your own project from scratch, it's a good place to continue working on your own.

Unity is an exciting engine that has started to really gain some ground as a competitive option for the hobbyist, student, and professional developer. However, it isn't an engine that makes games. People do. You do. You've now got enough knowledge and know-how; go out and make games.

INDEX

Symbols

% (modulus) operator, 172
+ (plus sign), 171
++ (increment) operator, 172
-- (decrement) operator, 172
== (equality comparison) operator, 173

A

accessing water prefabs, 95–96
actions, feedback, 310, 311
activating checkpoints, 397–399
Add Grass Texture options box, 83
adding
    ambient noise, 417
    animation events, 239–242
    audio, 413–424
    background music, 420–421
    detail meshes, 85, 86
    distance fog, 93–95
    full-screen menus, 341–345
    grass, 82–87, 84
    helper functions, 260
    keys, 237
    lighting, 363
    plants, 133
    skyboxes, 93–95
    trees, 79
    water, 95–96, 134–136
Add Terrain Texture dialog box, 75, 76
advanced viewing options, 28–29
AI (Artificial Intelligence), 277–280
    attacks, 292–295
    controllers, 282–290
    enemies, creating, 281–292
    guidelines, 278–280
    optimizing, 297–300
    scripting, 300–308
    spawning, 297–300
    state managers, 290–292
    victories, 295–297
    workflows, 280
All Negative Button setting, 199
All Positive Button setting, 199
alpha channels, 77
ambient lighting, 369, 413–414
    sound effects, 417
AND operator, 174
angles, anisotropic filtering, 100
animation
    clips, 233–239
    configuring, 221–249
    creating, 231–233
    customizing, 234–235
    events, adding, 239–242
    importing, 116
    naming, 145
    PCs (player characters), 224–231
    renaming, 146
    testing, 147
Animation API, 222–225
Animation class, 222–224
Animation Compression setting, 144
Animation Generation setting, 144
Animation Manager, formatting, 227–231
Animation view, 39–40, 232–233
Animation Wrap Mode setting, 144

animators, particle systems,
    385–387
Aniso Level setting, 100
APIs (application programming
    interfaces), 222–225
Application class, 441–443
ApplyDamage function, 291
applying
    GUISkins, 319–320
    HUD (Heads Up Display),
        323–337
    parented objects, 20
    particle systems, 381–411
    terrain, 106
area of effect, 293
arguments, 181
arrays, 164–166
assembling
    game assets, 62
    status controllers, 208–213
Asset folders, managing, 98
assets
    bundles, 446
    enemies, 281
    files, moving, 17
    First Person Controller, 78
    games, assembling, 62
    optimizing, 137–140
    packages, 446–447
Asset Server, 40
Assets folder, 16
Assets menu, 22
assigning
    materials, 127–132
    shaders, 127–132
Attack Controller script, 294
Attack coroutine, 285
attacks
    AI (Artificial Intelligence), 292–295
    Widget, 399–401
Attenuate property, 365
audio
    adding, 413–424
    clip settings, 415–421
    feedback, 413–414
    scripting, 421–424
Audio Format, 416
AudioSource class, 419
autocompletion functionality,
    157–159
Awake() function, 190

axes
    Input Manager, 197
    intersections, 26
    naming conventions, 201–202
Axis setting, 199

B

background music, adding, 420–421
Back Light, 367
Bake Animation setting, 144
Barthwaite, Brenda, 3
Base Diffuse Color (Base RGB), 125
Base Terrain settings, 87–88
basic design theory, 47–51
BeginSample function, 431
behaviors, AI (Artificial Intelligence), 277
BeInactive function, 399
billboard treatments, 78
Blender, 115
Blend function, 224
Boo, scripting in, 157
Booleans, 163
Border Mip Maps setting, 102
boxes, GUIs, 314
brainstorming, 51–53
browsing bookstores, 52–53
brushes
    height, painting with, 68–74
    selecting, 71, 72
Bryce, 67
Build Alpha from Grayscale setting, 101
building
    environments, 97–98
    final builds, 439–448
    settings, 443–445
Build Settings window, 443
bump maps, 103, 124
Bump property, 123
bundles, assets, 446
buttons
    customizing, 326–327
    GUIs, 313–314
    styles, creating, 342–343

C

C#, 158
    scripting in, 157
caches
    character controllers, 190
    lookups, 433

Calculate Normals setting, 118
cameras
    configuring, 203–207
    events, 190
    First Person Controller asset, 78
    Main Camera, 341–345
    navigating, 24–28
Capsule Collider component, 150
case sensitivity, 160
C/Cþþ/Objective-C Plugins Support, 43
Center, 25
ChangeGameState function, 182
channels, alpha, 77
characters
    creating, 141–151
    displays, 329–336
    importing, 142–151
    PCs (player characters), 141–142
    third-person controllers, 186–197
    updating, 212–213
cheating, 279
CheckPoint.js, 271–272, 405–407
checkpoints, 263–267
    activating, 397–399
Cheetah3D 2.6, 115
child objects, 19
Cinema 4D 8.5, 115
classes
    Animation, 222–224
    Application, 441–443
    AudioSource, 419
    Input, 200–201
    MonoBehavior, 189–191
clips, 147, 223. See also animation
    animation, configuring, 233–239
    audio settings, 415–421
code
    optimization, 431–433
    Profiler, 431
    testing, 427–430
collisions
    detection, 189
    trees, generating, 82
    triggers, 251–252
Color property, 365
colors
    gizmos, 257
    particle animators, 385
    terrain, editing, 77
common variable types, 161
comparisons, scripting, 173–175

Component menu, 22
components
    animation, 148. See also animation
    cache lookups, 433
    Capsule Collider, 150
    expanding, 236
    particle systems, 389–394
    Terrain, 70
    types, 168–169
    Wave Script component, 37
compression, 416. See also importing
    DXT5, 111
    meshes, 437
    support, 103–104
concatenation, 172
conditional operators, 178
conditionals, scripting, 175–178
configuring
    animation, 221–249
        clips, 233–239
        PCs (player characters), 224–231
    audio clips, 415–421
    cameras, 203–207
    characters, 141–151
    HUD (Heads Up Display), 323–337
    importing, 99–103
    Input Manager, 197–203
    lighting, 362–380
    materials, 119–136
    particle systems, 382–389
    players, 439–441
    shaders, 119–136
    shadows, 362–380
    status controllers, 208–213
    USB-powered game controllers, 202–203
    Widget, 149–150
connections, Internet, 21
consistency of interfaces, 311
Console window, 428–429
Constant Bias property, 365
Context menu, 21
Control Bar
    Game View, 38
    Scene view, 28
controllers
    AI (Artificial Intelligence), 282–290
    characters, updating, 212–213
    status, configuring, 208–213
    third-person, 186–197
    updating, 225–226
    variables, 188–189

controlling sounds through scripts, 417–420

controls, play, 23

conventions, naming, 184

for axes, 201–202

converting arrays, 166

Cookie property, 365

cookies, 378–380

coordinates, 32

core ideas, finding, 51–55

core statements, 48, 50

coroutines, 210–212

Attack, 285

Idle, 285

Correct Gamma setting, 102

COUNT, 258

COUNT_NUM_ITEMS variable, 259

creating. *See* formatting

CrossFade function, 224

CrossFadeQueued function, 224

cube maps, 126

Culling Mask property, 366

curves, defining, 232

customizing

animation, 234–235

assets, importing, 99

cameras, 203–207

characters, 141–151

editors, 40–41

full-screen menus, 341–345

HUD (Heads Up Display), 323–337

particle systems, 381–411

resolution, 336–337

skins for *Widget,* 318–323

skyboxes, 132–134

styles, 320–321, 325

terrain, 67–90

tiled textures in Photoshop, 389

cutting paths, 112

cylindrical emitters, 397–398

D

DamageTrigger.js, 271

Dead setting, 199

death triggers, 262–263

DEBUG, 258

debugging, 427–430

Console window, 428–429

games, 37

declaring variables, 169–171

Decompress on Load, 416

decrement (--) operator, 172

default keys, modifying, 32

default terrain, 66

defining

animation curves, 232

custom styles, 320–321

game ideas, 49

deleting

mass deleting trees, 81

trees, 79

descriptive feedback, 310

Descriptive Name setting, 198

design

basic design theory, 47–51

core ideas, finding, 51–55

environments, building, 97–98

GUIs, 309–357

lighting, 89–93

planning, 55–60

shadows, 89–93

skyboxes, 94

terrain, 63. *See also* terrain

Design Documents, 109

Destroy() function, 256

detail

maps, 127

meshes, 82–87

object settings, 88–89

detecting collisions, 189

dialog boxes

Add Terrain Texture, 75, 76

Snap Settings, 139

DidAttack function, 293

Die() function, 296

diffuse, 109

Diffuse property, 123

directional lights, 361

dirt textures, 111. *See also* textures

Disney, 7

displays. *See also* viewing

characters, 329–336

full-screen menus, 341–345

popup screens, 337–341

distance fog, adding, 93–95

distribution, 279

DLC (downloadable content), 446

documents, simple level design, 56–60

DrawGUITexture, 257

Draw Halo property, 366

DrawIcon, 257
Draw Modes, 28
DrawWireSphere function, 257
DVDs, installing, 12
DXT5 compression, 111

E

EBunny_AIController.js, 300–304
EBunny_Status.js, 304–305, 352–353, 409–411
editing
    animation, adding events, 239–242
    files, 17
    Input Manager, 198–199
    terrain, 77, 139–140
    trees, 78
Edit menu, 22
editors
    customizing, 40–41
    scripting, selecting, 157–159
effects
    area of, 293
    lighting, 377–380
    sound, 414. *See also* sound
    sparkle, 394–396
Electronic Arts (EA), 7
emitters
    cylindrical, 397–398
    particle systems, 383–385
emulation, 433–435
EndSample function, 431
enemies
    character displays, 331–336
    creating, 281–292
    explosions, 401–404
Enemy_RespawnPoint.js, 307–308
engines, terrain, 64–66
entering text, GUIs (graphical user interfaces), 315
enums, 167–168
environments
    building, 97–98
    scripting, 157
equality comparison (==) operator, 173
erasing trees, 79. *See also* deleting
errors, debugging, 428
events
    animation, adding, 239–242
    cameras, 190
    mouse, 189
expanding components, 236

explosions, enemies, 401–404
exporting
    lightmaps, 109
    packages, 447
External Version Control Support, 43

F

Fadeout setting, 103
feature sets, 49
feedback, 310, 311, 413–414
File menu, 22
files. *See also* folders
    assets, moving, 17
    editing, 17
    importing, 116
    log, 429–430
    multiple animation, 145
    renaming, 18
    size, reducing, 437
    support, 103–104
Fill Light, 367
filtering, anisotropic, 100
Filter Mode setting, 101
final builds, 439–448
finding core ideas, 51–55
First Person Controller asset, 78
FixedUpdate() function, 190, 191–197
Flare property, 366
Flatten Heightmap tool, 70
floating point numbers, 162
Flythrough mode, 25
fog, adding, 93–95
folders
    Asset, 16, 98
    Local Settings, 430
    nested, 99
    renaming, 18
    resources, 446
fonts, importing, 321–323
Force to mono, 416
for loops, 178–179
formatting
    animation, 231–233
    Animation Manager, 227–231
    audio clips, 415–421
    button styles, 342–343
    characters, 141–151
    checkpoints, 263–267
    death triggers, 262–263
    enemies, 281–292

formatting (*continued*)
file support, 103–104
full-screen menus, 341–345
GUISkins, 319–320
HUD (Heads Up Display), 323–337
lighting, 362–380
lightmaps, 372–374
native texture formats, 101–102
packages, 447
particle systems, 382–389
players, 439–441
popup screens, 337–341
resolution, 336–337
shadows, 362–380
skyboxes, 94
terrain, 87–89
triggers, 252–261
FPS (Frames Per Second), 39, 436
free writing, 51–52
full-screen menus, adding, 341–345
Full Screen Mode, 25
Full-Screen Post-Processing Effects, 43
functions
Animation class, 224
ApplyDamage, 291
Awake(), 190
BeginSample, 431
BeInactive, 399
Blend, 224
CrossFade, 224
CrossFadeQueued, 224
Destroy(), 256
DidAttack, 293
Die(), 296
DrawWireSphere, 257
EndSample, 431
FixedUpdate(), 190, 191–197
GetComponent(), 191
GetItem, 260
GUI.DragWindow, 317
Input class, 200–201
InvoHudButton, 324
isPlaying, 224
LastUpdate(), 190
LookAtMe, 207
Mass Place Trees, 81
MonoBehavior, 254
OnGUI, 343
OnTriggerEnter(), 256, 397
Play, 224
PlayQueued, 224

Quit, 443
scripting, 180–184
SendMessage(), 289
Start(), 190, 285
SyncLayer, 224
Update(), 190, 238, 298
fundamentals of scripting, 159–171

G

GameObject menu, 22
GameObjects (GO), 42
collisions, 252
games
assets, assembling, 62
basic design theory, 47–51
debugging, 37
planning, 55–60
researching other, 53–54
settings, 442
testing, 36
Game view, 33–39
Control Bar, 38
gear triggers, 254
Generate Bump Map setting, 103
Generate Colliders setting, 118
Generate Cubemap setting, 102
Generate Mip Maps setting, 102
generating tree collisions, 82
GetComponent() function, 191
GetItem function, 260
GIMP, 67
gizmos, 26, 256–257
Transform Gizmo Toggles, 33
global coordinates, 32
global variables, 170, 171
graphics, optimizing, 437–438
grass, 77, 82–87. *See also* **terrain**
adding, 84
textures, 112
Gravity setting, 199
grayscale images, 67. *See also* **heightmaps**
greyboxing, 97
grids, GUIs (graphical user interfaces), 315–316
grouping objects, 138–139
GUIContent, 324–329
GUI_CustomControls.js, 345–347
guidelines, AI (Artificial Intelligence), 278–280
GUI.DragWindow function, 317
GUI_HUD.js, 347–349
GUI_MainMenu.js, 356–357

GUIs (graphical user interfaces). *See also* **interfaces**
boxes, 314
buttons, 313–314
custom skins for *Widget,* 318–323
design, 309–357
full-screen menus, adding, 341–345
HUD (Heads Up Display), formatting, 323–337
labels, 314
navigating, 312–318
popup screens, 337–341
scripting, 345–357
selection grids, 315–316
sliders, 314
testing, 312
text entries, 315
theories, 309–312
toggles, 315
toolbars, 315–316
windows, 316–318
GUISkins, 319–320
GUI_WaypointStore.js, 354–355

H

height
brushes, painting with, 68–74
terrain, 65
heightmaps, 67–68
importing, 67, 69
viewing, 107
help, 21
helper functions, adding, 260
Help menu, 22
Hierarchy view, 18–19
hills, 77. *See also* **terrain**
Horizontal Axes, 200
HUD (Heads Up Display), formatting, 323–337

I

ideas, 50. *See also* **design**
finding core, 51–55
Idle coroutine, 285
if-else **statements, 176**
if **statements, 175**
illumination maps, 125–126
images, square, 126
importing
animation, 116
audio clips, 415

characters, 142–151
configuring, 99–103
cookies, 378–379
files, 116
fonts, 321–323
heightmaps, 67, 69
meshes, 114–119
nonstatic meshes, 142–151
textures, 78, 99–114
increment (++) operator, 172
index numbers, assigning, 444
Input class, 200–201
Input Manager, configuring, 197–203
Inspector, 20–22, 32
installation instructions, 10–13
instances, 19
integers, 161
Intensity property, 365
interaction, steps of interface, 310
interactivity, 153
interfaces
Animation API, 222–225
design, 309–357
navigating, 15–41
testing, 312
theories, 309–312
Internet connections, 21
interpolation, 205
intersections, axes, 26
inventory management, 258–261
Invert setting, 199
InvoHudButton function, 324
isEditor function, 442
isometric views, 28
isPlaying function, 223, 224
Is Readable setting, 102
items, pickup, 394–397

J

JavaScript, 158, 159
Joy Num setting, 199

K

Key Light, 367
keys, 232
adding, 237
modifying, 32
keywords, static, 170

L

labels, GUIs (graphical user interfaces), 314
LastUpdate() function, 190
layers drop-down, 23
layout drop-down, 23
layouts, customizing editors, 40–41
length, terrain, 65
lens flares, 377–378
levelCount, 442
licenses, 43–44
lighting
    adding, 363
    creating, 362–380
    design, 89–93
    effects, 377–380
    overview of, 366–369
    properties, 364–366
    scenes, 369–372
    types of lights, 362–363
Lightmap Family shaders, 122
lightmaps, 90
    exporting, 109
    shadows, 372–374
Lightware 8.0, 115
lines, renderers, 393–394
linking objects, 19
loading scenes, 444
Loading string, 344
local coordinates, 32
Local Settings folder, 430
log files, 429–430
logical comparison operators, 174
LookAtMe function, 207
lookups, caches, 433
loops
    for, 178–179
    scripting, 178–180
    while, 179–180, 286
Low-Level Rendering Access, 44

M

Mac, Unitron, 157
Main Camera, adding full-screen menus, 341–345
Main Color property, 132
managing
    Animation Manager, 227–231
    Asset folders, 98
    Input Manager, configuring, 197–203
    inventory management, 258–261
    Player Settings Manager, 440
    state managers, 290–292
    Tag Manager, 294
manipulating objects, 29–32
maps, 97
    bump, 103, 124
    cubes, 126
    detail, 127
    heightmaps, 107. *See also* heightmaps
    illumination, 125–126
    lightmaps, 90, 109, 372–374
    mip maps, 102
    specular, 125–126
    splat, 75
    starting, 104–106
Mass Place Trees function, 81
mass selecting, 138–139
matching items, 52
Material object, 128
materials
    assigning, 127–132
    configuring, 119–136
    particle systems, 387–389
    skyboxes, customizing, 132–134
Materials Generation setting, 118–119
Max Texture Size setting, 101
Maya, 114
mechanics, 48
member variables, 169
    Animation class, 223–224
menus
    Assets, 22
    Component, 22
    Context, 21
    Edit, 22
    File, 22
    full-screen, adding, 341–345
    GameObject, 22
    Help, 22
    Quick Creation, 17
    Terrain, 22
    Window, 22
Mesh Compression setting, 116–118
meshes
    compression, 437
    detail, 82–87
    importing, 114–119
    nonstatic, importing, 142–151
    triangulation, 143

MIDI (Musical Instrument Digital Interface), 414. *See also* audio
Min Move Distance property, 188
Mip Map Filtering setting, 103
mip maps, 102
mockups, 97
modifying
    default keys, 32
    objects, 29–32
    parent objects, 20
    trees, 80
    values, 37
    variables, 37
Modo, 115
modulus (%) operator, 172
MonoBehavior class, 189–191, 254
MonoDevelop, 158
mood lighting, 369
mouse events, 189
moving
    asset files, 17
    multiple objects, 32–33
    third-person controllers, 186–197
multiple animation files, 145
multiple objects, moving, 32–33
multiple terrain, 67
music. *See also* audio
    adding, 413–424
    background, 420–421

N

Name setting, 198
naming
    animation, 145
    axes, 201–202
    conventions, 184
    files, 18
    spawn points, 299
native texture formats, 101–102
navigating
    Animation API, 222–225
    cameras, 24–28
    GUIs, 312–318
    interfaces, 15–41
Negative Button setting, 198
Negative Descriptive Name setting, 198
nested folders, 99
noise, adding ambient, 417
Non Power of 2 Sizes settings, 101–102
nonstatic meshes, importing, 142–151

normal distribution, 279
Normal Family shaders, 121
notebooks, consulting, 53
NOT operator, 174
null values, 166
numbers, variables, 161–163

O

objects
    2D, 26
    child, 19
    grouping, 138–139
    manipulating, 29–32
    Material, 128
    moving, 32–33
    parenting, 19, 20
    Plane, 26
    Primitives, 32
    Sphere, 36
    unparented, 20
Object Size property, 365
OnGUI function, 343
OnTriggerEnter() function, 256, 397
Opacity setting, 71
Open Log Editor button, 429
open world games, 49
operators
    conditional, 178
    logical comparison, 174
    scripting, 171–173
optimizing, 431–438
    AI (Artificial Intelligence), 297–300
    assets, 137–140
optional installs, 12–13
orientation, views, 27
OR operator, 174
outlining designs, 55–56

P

packages
    assets, 446–447
    exporting, 447
    Standard Assets, 83
    Toon Shader, 130
painting
    height with brushes, 68–74
    terrain, 110–111
    textures, 74–78
    trees, 78–82
Paint Terrain Texture component toolbox, 76

palm trees, 78. *See also* trees
paper prototyping, 54–55
paradigms, interfaces, 311
Parallax Bump property, 123
parenting objects, 19, 20, 32–33
particle systems, 381–411
    animators, 385–387
    attacks, 399–401
    components, 389–394
    emitters, 383–385
    formatting, 382–389
    materials, 387–389
    overview of, 381–382
    pickup items, 394–397
    renderers, 387–389
    scripting, 404–411
    Widget, 394–404
paths, cutting, 112
PCs (player characters), 141–142
    configuring animation,
        224–231
Perspective (3D) view, 26, 28
Photoshop, 67
    tiling textures, 389
pickup items, 252–253
    particle systems, 394–397
PickupItems.js, 261, 268–269,
    404–405
pipelines, 44
pivot points, 33
Pivot Toggle, 33
pixels, lighting, 90
placing trees, 78–82
Plane object, 26
planning
    design, 55–60
    final builds, 439–445
    greyboxing, 97
    scripting, 185–186
plants, adding, 133
play controls, 23
players, formatting, 439–441
Player Settings Manager, 440
Play function, 224
PlayQueued function, 224
plus sign (+), 171
point lights, 361–362
Poisson distribution, 279
Popfly Game Creator (Microsoft), 3
popup screens, 337–341
Positive Button setting, 198

prefabs, 137–138
    animation, loading, 240
    water, accessing, 95–96
preparing final builds, 439–445
Primitives object, 32
print() function, 182
print statements, 428
private variables, 170
Profiler, 40, 44, 431
programming, debugging, 427–430
Projection property, 365
projector-made shadows, 374–377
Project view, 16–18
properties
    lighting, 364–366
    terrain, 71
    Transform component, 30
prototyping paper, 54–55

Q

Quick Creation menu, 17
Quit function, 443

R

random searches, 52
Range property, 365
Reader Mode property, 366
Realtime Shadows, 44
reducing file sizes, 437
Reflective Family shaders, 122
renaming
    animation, 146
    files, 18
    spawn points, 299
renderers
    lines, 393–394
    particle systems, 387–389
    trail, 391–393
rendering Statistics pages, 435–436
Rendering Statistics window, 437
Render Modes drop-down, 28
researching other games, 53–54
resolution, 336–337
    terrain, 65
Resolution property, 365
resources
    folders, 446
returning values, 182
return statements, 182

right-clicking Project view, 18
Rotate tool, 31
rotating
    interpolation, 205
    particle animators, 385
runInBackground, 442

S

Scale Factor setting, 116
Scale tool, 31
scenes
    lighting, 363, 368, 369–372. *See also* lighting
    loading, 444
Scene view, 23–33
scope, variables, 183–184
screens, popup, 337–341
Script Access to Asset Pipeline, 44
scripting, 155–184
    AI (Artificial Intelligence), 300–308
    Attack Controller, 294
    audio, 421–424
    comparisons, 173–175
    conditionals, 175–178
    editors, selecting, 157–159
    enemies, 281
    functions, 180–184
    fundamentals of, 159–171
    GUIs, 345–357
    loops, 178–180
    naming conventions, 184
    operators, 171–173
    overview of, 155–157
    particle systems, 404–411
    planning, 185–186
    sounds, controlling, 417–420
    third-person controllers, 186–197
    triggers, 267–275
    variables, 160–171
    Widget_Animation.js, 246–249
    Widget_Camera.js, 218–220
    Widget_Controller.js, 213–216
    Widget_Controller.js Update, 242–245
    Widget_Status.js, 216–218
scrubbing values, 30
Search bar, 17
selecting
    brushes, 71, 72
    mass, 138–139
    scripting editors, 157–159
selection grids, GUIs, 315–316

Self-Illuminated family shaders, 122
SendMessage() function, 289
Sensitivity setting, 199
servers, Asset Servers, 40
settings
    All Negative Button, 198, 199
    All Positive Button, 199
    Animation Compression, 144
    Animation Generation, 144
    Animation Wrap Mode, 144
    Aniso Level, 100
    audio clips, 415–421
    Axis, 199
    Bake Animation, 144
    Border Mip Maps, 102
    Build Alpha from Grayscale, 101
    building, 443–445
    Calculate Normals, 118
    cameras, 203–207
    Correct Gamma, 102
    Dead, 199
    Descriptive Name, 198
    enemies, 281–29
    Fadeout, 103
    Filter Mode, 101
    games, 442
    Generate Bump Map, 103
    Generate Colliders, 118
    Generate Cubemap, 102
    Generate Mip Maps, 102
    Gravity, 199
    HUD (Heads Up Display), 323–337
    importing, 99–103
    Input Manager, 198–199
    Invert, 199
    Is Readable, 102
    Joy Num, 199
    Local Settings folder, 430
    Materials Generation, 118–119
    Max Texture Size, 101
    Mesh Compression, 116–118
    Mip Map Filtering, 103
    Name, 198
    Negative Button, 198
    Negative Descriptive Name, 198
    Non Power of 2 Sizes, 101–102
    Player Settings Manager, 440
    Positive Button, 198
    Scale Factor, 116
    Sensitivity, 199
    Smoothing Angle, 118

settings (*continued*)
  Snap, 199
  spawn points, 298
  Split Animations, 144
  Split Tangents, 118
  Swap UVs, 118
  Tangent Space Generation, 118
  terrain, 87–89
  Texture Format, 101
  triggers, 261–267
  Type, 199
  Wrap Mode, 101
shaders
  assigning, 127–132
  configuring, 119–136
  toon, 148
  Unity-provided shaders, 121–123
shadows
  design, 89–93
  formatting, 362–380
  lightmaps, 372–374
  projector-made, 374–377
  Realtime Shadows, 44
Shadows property, 365
simple level design documents, 56–60
simple pickup items, 252–253
Size setting, 71
sizing
  files, reducing, 437
  terrain, 65
skins
  GUISkins, 319–320
  Widget, customizing, 318–323
Skin Width property, 188
skyboxes
  adding, 93–95
  customizing, 132–134
sliders, 314
Slope Limit property, 187–188
Smooth Height tool, 73
Smoothing Angle setting, 118
Snap setting, 199
Snap Settings dialog box, 139
sound, 414. *See also* audio
sounds, scripting, 417–420
sparkle effects, 394–396
spawning, 297–300
specular maps, 125–126
Specular property, 123
Sphere object, 36

splat maps, 75
Split Animations setting, 144
Split Tangents setting, 118
Spot Angle property, 365
spotlights, 362
square images, 126
Standard Assets package, 83
standards for interfaces, 311
Start function, 190, 285
starting maps, 104–106
state
  machines, 151
  managers, AI (Artificial Intelligence),
    290–292
statements
  core, 48, 50
  if, 175
  if-else, 176
  print, 428
  return, 182
  switch, 177–178
static keyword, 170
static meshes, 114. *See also* meshes
static typing, 432
Statistics pages, rendering, 435–436
status controllers, configuring, 208–213
steep angles, anisotropic filtering, 100
steep terrain, troubleshooting, 87
Step Offset property, 188
steps of interface interaction, 310
Strength property, 365
strings
  concatenating, 172
  Loading, 344
  variables, 163
styles
  buttons, creating, 342–343
  customizing, 320–321, 325
SubEthaEdit, 158
support for file formats,
  103–104
Swap UVs setting, 118
switch statements, 177–178
SyncLayer function, 224
systems, 48

T

Tag Manager, 294
Tangent Space Generation setting, 118

Tanner, Jonathon, 6
Tempas, Sarah, 6
templates, terrain, 75
Terragen, 67
terrain, 63
    customizing, 67–90
    editing, 77, 139–140
    engines, 64–66
    formatting, 87–89
    heightmaps, 67–68
    lighting, 91
    painting, 110–111
    sizing, 65
    templates, 75
    textures, 92
        importing, 104–115
        painting, 74–78
    troubleshooting, 87
    water, adding, 95–96
Terrain component, 70
Terrain menu, 22
testing
    animation, 147
    code, 427–430
    games, 36
    GUIs (graphical user interfaces), 312
text
    entries, 315
    fonts, importing, 321–323
Texture Format setting, 101
textures
    grass, 83, 112
    importing, 78, 99–114
    native texture formats, 101–102
    painting, 74–78
    terrain, 92
    tiling, 389
theories
    basic design, 47–51
    GUIs, 309–312
third-person controllers, 186–197
3D
    heightmaps, 67
    Sound, 416
    Studio Max, 115
    terrain, 64. *See also* terrain
three-point lighting rigs,
    366–367
tiling textures, 389
tint, particle animators, 385

toggles
    GUIs (graphical user interfaces), 315
    Pivot Toggle, 33
    Transform Gizmo Toggles, 33
Toolbar, 22–23
toolbars, GUIs, 315–316
tools
    debugging, 428–429
    Flatten Heightmap, 70
    Rotate, 31
    Scale, 31
    Smooth Height, 73
    Transform, 23
    Translate, 30
Toon Shader package, 130
toon shaders, 148
Track, 25
trail renderer, 391–393
Transform Component property, 30
Transform Gizmo Toggles, 23, 33
Transform tools, 23
Translate tool, 30
Transparent Cutout Family shaders, 122
Transparent Family shaders, 122
trees
    collisions, generating, 82
    placing, 78–82
    settings, 88–89
triangulating meshes, 143
triggers
    checkpoints, 263–267
    collisions, 251–252
    death, 262–263
    formatting, 252–261
    gear, 254
    scripting, 267–275
    settings, 261–267
troubleshooting, 21
    steep terrain, 87
Tumble, 24, 25
2D objects, 26
Type property, 364, 365
types
    common variable, 161
    components, 168–169
    enums, 167–168
    of lights, 362–363
    of triggers, 261–267
Type setting, 199
typing, static, 432

U

Ubisoft, 7
Unified Theory of Game Development and
    Design, 8
UniSciTE, 157, 158
Unitron, 157
Unity
    basic concepts, 42–43
    installing, 10–11
    licenses, 43–44
    overview of, 15–45
    Unity-provided shaders, 121–123
UnityDevelop, 158
unityVersion, 442
unparented objects, 20
Update() function, 190, 238, 298
updating
    character controllers, 212–213
    controllers, 225–226
    inventory, 259
USB-powered game controllers, configuring,
    202–203
users, designing for, 310–312

V

values
    modifying, 37
    null, 166
    returning, 182
    scrubbing, 30
variables, 160–171
    controllers, 188–189
    COUNT_NUM_ITEMS, 259
    declaring, 169–171
    members, Animation class, 223–224
    modifying, 37
    numbers, 161–163
    scope, 183–184
Vertical Axes, 200
vertices, lighting, 90
victories, AI (Artificial Intelligence),
    295–297
video games, 47. See also games
viewing
    anisotropic filtering, 100
    full-screen menus, 341–345
    heightmaps, 107
    popup screens, 337–341
    resolution, 336–337

views
    Animation, 39–40, 232–233
    Game, 33–39
    Hierarchy, 18–19
    Inspector, 20–22, 32
    isometric, 28
    orientation, 27
    Perspective (3D), 26, 28
    Project, 16–18
    Scene, 23–33
    zooming, 23
virtual cubes, 126
Visual Studio C#, 158

W

water
    adding, 95–96, 134–136
    audio sources, 418
Wave Script component, 37
WaypointBehavior.js, 355–356
while loops, 179–180, 286
Widget
    attacks, 292–295, 399–401
    cameras, 203–207
    characters, 142–151, 329–331
    configuring, 149–150
    launch window, 445
    lighting, 369–372
    particle systems, 394–404
    settings, 442
    skins, customizing, 318–323
    terrain, importing textures, 104–115
    textures, importing, 99–114
    third-person controllers, 186–197
Widget_Animation.js, 246–249
Widget_AttackController.js, 306–307,
    407–409
Widget_Attack_Controller.js,
    350–351
Widget_Camera.js, 218–220
Widget_Controller.js, 213–216
Widget_Controller.js Update, 242–245
Widget_Inventory.js, 269–271
Widget_Status.js, 216–218, 273–275
width, terrain, 65
Window menu, 22
windows
    Build Settings, 443
    Console, 428–429

GUIs, 316–318
Rendering Statistics, 437
wind settings, 89
**workflows, AI (Artificial
    Intelligence), 280**
World Particle collider, 389–391
wrapMode, 223

Wrap Mode setting, 101
writing AI (Artificial Intelligence), 278

Z
Zoom, 25
zooming views, 23